The daughte   n in 1903 in
Liddesdale, i.   r her educa-

                                                CTION

                                                he.
Scottish   adults and for children, where
her range was wide: from Saint Columba through Queen
Margaret to James IV and James VI. She was happily married to
John Llewelyn Rhys, who was also a writer; he was killed during the Second World War and she founded the literary prize,
for writers under thirty, that bears his name. Jane Oliver died
in 1970.

THE
BLUE HEAVEN
BENDS OVER ALL

·

A NOVEL
of the LIFE *of*
SIR WALTER SCOTT

·

by

JANE OLIVER

THE
BLACKSTAFF PRESS
BELFAST

Jane Oliver would have wished to thank Mrs Maxwell-Scott of Abbotsford, Dr James C. Corson and Miss Marion Lochhead for their help over this book. There are others whom she would also have thanked but since she alone knew all the names, it is hoped that those concerned will accept this general acknowledgement.

First published in hardback in 1971 by
William Collins Sons and Company Limited, Glasgow
This Blackstaff Press edition is a photolithographic facsimile of the first
edition printed by William Collins Sons and Company Limited, Glasgow

First published in paperback in 1992 by
The Blackstaff Press Limited
3 Galway Park, Dundonald, Belfast BT16 0AN, Northern Ireland
with the assistance of
The Arts Council of Northern Ireland

Printed by The Guernsey Press Company Limited

British Library Cataloguing in Publication Data
Blue Heaven Bends Over All: Novel of the
Life of Sir Walter Scott. – New ed
I. Title
823.914 [F]
ISBN 0-85640-450-0

Contents

"But the blue heaven bends over all . . ."

SIR WALTER SCOTT
Journal, 17th March, 1831

Part One

THE SAP RISES

THE door of the farmhouse kitchen stood open to the rolling, heat-hazed perspective of the Scottish Border hills, beyond the cobbled yard across which a few fowls diligently strutted, pecking here and there. On the threshold of a dim, cool barn a tortoiseshell cat purred languorously, and swifts swooped whickering, high above the eaves. On the summit of the sandy knowe which gave its name to the cluster of buildings below stood the dark, gaunt ruin of Smailholm Tower, looking out across undulating moorland to the chain of hills dominated by the harsh bulk of Cheviot, which had not long shed its last, lingering scarf of snow.

It was midsummer 1775, and thunderously still. From the hillsides came the bleating of half-grown lambs, the deeper motherly reassurance of the ewes, while the remote notes of a curlew's call seemed to tumble from heaven like a cascade of jewels. Once in a way, a little breeze, hot as the air from an oven, stirred the line of clothes hung out in the little green and long since dry. The farm dogs lay as if dead, tongues lolling, in a patch of shade.

But within the stone-flagged, stone-walled farmhouse kitchen it was blissfully cool. The old farmer, Robert Scott, whose active days were done, sat in his usual place by the smoored peat fire; his hands, gnarled as the roots of a thorn bush, were closely clenched on the arms of his chair, as if ready to rise at any moment. But his white head nodded in a doze. Opposite him, his wife was busy at her spinning-wheel, her white cap, with its freshly goffered edging and ribbons neatly tied below her bony chin, tidily constraining hair that still showed darker strands in the ringlets which bobbed beside her ears in the fashion of an earlier day. Their daughter Janet, middle-aged, but cheerfully unembittered by spinsterhood, sat, with a great basket of household mending, by the little window that looked out on Cheviot, singing to herself as she sewed.

Suddenly, the old man's head jerked back, his blue eyes, pale with age, now wide with anxiety. "Mother, where's the bairn?"

His wife's busy fingers paused. Her cracked voice soothed him, as so often of late years. "Why, ye ken fine where he is. Oot-bye with the ewe-milkers as usual."

"He's been awa' since dawn. It's time he was hame," said the old man obstinately.

"Why, Father?" Janet asked, looking up from her mending. "He's happier up yonder among the sheep and lambs than any other bit, puir lame bairn. He loves the creatures. And it's early yet."

"This weather's no' canny, I'm telling ye." The old man clasped and unclasped his fingers on the arms of his chair. "There's a storm coming," he said. "The bairn should be indoors."

His wife set her wheel spinning again. "A storm? With the sky as blue as forget-me-nots? A likely thing."

"Look out westward, woman. That's where the weather comes frae."

"He's never wrong, Mother," Janet said. She leant forward to try and get a glimpse of the western sky, pursed her lips, and rose. "I'll go across the yard and see if anybody's caught sight of the ewe-milkers. Mebbe they're on their way back."

The old couple could hear her stoutly-shod feet cross the cobbles of the yard, her clear voice calling. Then all was quiet again, quiet enough for the distant rumble of thunder to sound dramatic as a trumpet-call.

"What did I tell ye?" The old man's voice was triumphant, his next words anxious. "Where's the bairn?"

"Janet's gone to find out," his wife reminded him.

The thunder rumbled again, much nearer now, borne on a sudden gust of wind that made the yard door slam and the windows rattle. The sunlight sickened luridly. Inside the dim kitchen it seemed almost dark. The old man began to drum on the arms of his chair. In seventy years he had seen too much of Border weather to mistake the signs of a swiftly moving summer storm, the urgency of the need to get all vulnerable creatures into shelter. And there he was, helpless as an old log, scarcely able to get to his feet without a helping arm.

"Where's Janet got to now?" he demanded peevishly.

"I'm here, Father," Janet said quietly. She shut the door behind her against the dust that the wind had set whirling about the yard. "I had to get old Sandy Ormiston, and send him off up the hill."

"What's come of the ewe-milkers, then?"

"They're back, hiding their faces in the barn because of the thunder, the silly lassies. They came running down at the first clap, leaving Wattie up there among the sheep. The sky's black as night over yonder, and they forgot all about him – "

"Mercy on us, he'll catch his death," the old woman said. "Now sit where you are, Father," she added, as the old man began to struggle out of his chair, a sudden blaze of lightning illuminating the craggy resolution of his face. "Janet's sent Sandy after him, and it's no' that far. He'll have the wee lad hame in no time. Just take the bellows, and blow up the fire while Janet and I seek out some dry clothes. I can hear the rain starting. He'll be soaked to the skin."

Out on the hillside the terrified lambs had run to find their mothers, and the douce old ewes, who had seen many storms before, had led them to shelter among the rocks and gorse bushes. Old Sandy Ormiston, clambering up the path towards the summit, saw the huddling herd and knew just where to go. Somewhere among them, he guessed, the child who could scarcely stand would be cowering, scared as the ewe-milkers who had forgotten him. He was horrified by the thought of the poor lame bairn, not yet four years old, more helpless in his terror than one of the bleating lambs. As he went, he shouted against the thunder-claps, with all the breath the climb had left him.

"I'm coming, Wattie. Never – fear, lad. I'll sune hae ye – hame!"

The towering thunder-clouds seemed almost to rest on the hilltops, mocking the summer noon with a Wagnerian sense of doom. Scrolls and zigzags of lightning tore across the lurid sky, crash upon crash of thunder shook the ground under his feet. Rain began to pelt down like rods of steel; then, as the flock scattered, Sandy saw the child he had come to save.

Young Walter was sitting in the lee of a rock, clapping his hands and shouting with laughter in the midst of a huddle of ewes and lambs. Without breath left even to swear, Sandy stood there, incredulous. The child's wet face was turned towards the battling sky. His voice could be heard between thunder-claps, wild with excitement. "Oh, bonny, bonny!" he was crying. "More!"

"Gude save us a'!" said the old cow baillie hoarsely, as he stumbled forward. "Wattie, my bairn, are ye no' feared?"

It was obvious that young Walter was nothing of the sort. He waved his arms exuberantly at the sight of his good friend. "Sandy, look! Yon bonny lights!" Then he rolled round, clutched the rock, and hauled himself triumphantly to his feet. For a moment or two he stood there, teetering, while the old man, checked in mid-stride, held his breath. Then, as a jagged fork of lightning sizzled overhead, he let go to clap his hands, his weakened right leg gave way, and he fell headlong.

"Mercy on us. He'll do himsel' a mischief," muttered old Ormiston, hurrying forward. But by the time he reached the child, Walter was already on hands and knees, beaming up at his rescuer. "I did it. I stood. Can walk now." He crawled vigorously back to the rock through the sheeting rain. Round him the ewes moved uneasily, muzzling their complaining lambs. The warm, tarry smell of their soaked fleece was harsh and strong as Sandy Ormiston waded among them to reach the child now doggedly hauling himself to his feet again. At the touch of the old man's hand on his shoulder he turned his head and grinned.

"I can. I can. Watch me!"

"Wattie, my man, ye've dune real well. But that's enough for now. I've come to seek ye. Ye're to come hame."

Walter's face puckered, but he did not cry. He shook soaked strands of hair out of his eyes and the jut of his chin was defiant.

"I'll no' come!"

Sandy Ormiston knew him too well to insist. Hands on hips, he surveyed the child. "Wattie," he said gravely, "your grandfather's fretting sair for ye. It's no gude for an auld man. Nor for your granny. And your auntie's upset forby. Be a good bairn, and set their minds at rest."

Walter blinked up at the tumult overhead, screwing his eyes up against the pelting rain. His mouth set dourly, as he fought against surrender. Then he sighed deeply, and his whole face was changed by a slow, sweet smile.

"All right. I'll come."

"There's my gude lad." Sandy stooped towards him, holding out his arms. But Walter shook his head.

"Give me a ride, then. On your shoulders. I'll no' be carried like a bundle."

Sandy Ormiston chuckled as he knelt so that the child could put his arms round his neck while he tucked the thin shanks under his arms and heaved himself laboriously to his feet. "Now then, how'll that suit ye?"

"Fine. Look, look! More lights!"

"Aye, mebbe. I'll be right glad to get indoors," said Sandy Ormiston. "Doon the hill we go. Keep still, lad. Ye're mair trouble than a bull-calf."

Walter giggled, as Sandy trudged on.

"Mercy, there's water right across the yard. Here we are now. Duck your heid, Wattie, or ye'll crack it on the top of the doorway."

Aunt Janet ran to lift Walter down, and his grandmother hurried forward with dry clothes.

"Tuts, the bairn might as weel have been through the river! I'll sit him on my knee, Janet, while you get yon wet things off him. Here's a dry shirt and breeks."

Obediently Walter held up his arms for Aunt Janet to strip off his shirt. From within the folds his excited voice came blurrily.

"It was bonny, Grandpa. Big black clouds and lights coming out. Great jags . . ."

His grandfather chuckled as he laid down the bellows. "Wattie, my bairn, there'll be no holding ye now. Time's past for ye to be carried here and there on auld folks' backs. Ye need a pony of your ain."

"Mercy on us, whatever next?" said his grandmother, now vigorously towelling Walter's wet hair. "A pony for a wee bairn that's scarcely four years auld? Have ye forgotten his lame leg that we've had sic a work aboot?"

"His lame leg's all the mair reason for him to have a beast wi' four gude-ganging legs to carry him," said the old man decisively. "Would ye like a pony, Walter?"

Walter, half eclipsed by the floss of fair hair that stood out in all directions as it dried, nodded vigorously. "Aye, Grandpa."

"What d'ye say, Sandy? Could ye learn him to ride a douce wee shelty as time goes on?"

"I could that," said Sandy Ormiston cheerfully.

"Then we'll have to see whit we can find. There was a wee beast I kinda liked the look on last time I was in Melrose. I'll get your Uncle Thomas to see to it the next time he comes. I doot – " He sighed. "I doot I'm no likely to take to the hills again, but she'll carry you out-by by the side of Sandy Ormiston like a grown laddie, instead of round his neck like a millstone."

"A moss trooper!" Walter shouted suddenly. "I'll be a moss trooper. Like Aunt Janet's stories. No, like a soldier. I'm going to be a soldier when I'm a man."

His words fell into a sudden pool of silence, unexpected as a ditch on a dark night. Walter looked round the tongue-tied circle, eyes widening as their thought engulfed him in the possibility that he might never walk like other folk all his life long. He rejected it incredulously. "A soldier," he repeated, looking from one grown-up to another.

"Oh, Wattie, Wattie . . ." Janet said unsteadily. "You'll be a right warrior always, lame leg and all."

From the fireside the old man noisily cleared his throat. "Ye'll keep me in mind o' that pony, Sandy, now?"

"I will that."

"I want his uncle to see to it the very next time he comes."

"And now away wi' ye, Sandy, and get out of those wet clothes," said Janet, "or we'll have your rheumatism that bad you'll never be fit to hoist him on to its back."

"How soon will Uncle Thomas come?" Walter demanded, from the sheepskin in front of the fireside.

"As soon as he can, my bairn," said the old man reassuringly. "Aye . . . as sune as ever he . . . can. Eh, but I'm glad . . . yon thunder's awa' . . . Such weather's no' canny . . . no canny at a' . . ."

He dozed off, exhausted by anxiety and too sharply contrasting relief. His head fell forward on to his chest, his hands relaxed their grasp on the arms of his chair and slid nervelessly on to his knees. Aunt Janet returned to her mending. The soft whirr of the spinning-wheel, the slash of the rain on the cobblestones, blended with the old man's stertorous breathing into a soporific rhythm which young Walter found hard to resist.

Walter fought against sleep as he lay full length on the sheepskin rug, propping himself on his elbows, chin on fists. Had Grandfather really meant what he said about the pony? To ride a pony would be so splendid that he scarcely dared believe it could ever happen. And when would Uncle Thomas come? If he didn't come soon . . . he must come soon . . . With his last waking thoughts Walter tried to reach Uncle Thomas and beg him to come to Sandy Knowe.

Uncle Thomas, as a matter of fact, came to Sandy Knowe regularly now that his father's health was failing, to give what help the old man would accept with the problems of running the farm. But on his next visit the prospect of the pony, which had scarcely been out of Walter's mind since his grandfather mentioned it, was sadly eclipsed. For the old man's tenuous hold on life, frayed apart like the last strands of a staunch cable by small frettings which would once never have troubled him, gave way at last. One morning he failed to wake, and the pleasant sequence of the summer days at Sandy Knowe was darkened by all the panoply of death, which turned Walter's sunlit world into a wilderness.

The blinds in the parlour were drawn, quantities of food pre-pared, and as the family assembled even his pleasure in the arrival of his parents was quenched by the sight of his mother's black gloves. The service, taken in the parlour by the minister, was a weird experience for the child who sat on Aunt Janet's knee in the background, awed and yet fascinated by the strangeness of his first encounter with death.

His parents did not remain long at Sandy Knowe after the funeral, for his father's legal work required his presence at Parliament House where the autumn session of the Law Courts had begun. But after the men had come back from the churchyard, his mother left them to their business talk and came to sit beside Grandmother and Aunt Janet in the parlour with Walter at her feet, a short, dumpy figure in unbecoming black, her plain face redeemed by the warmth of her interest in every aspect of life on the little Border farm.

"Ye've worked wonders for the bairn," she told the sad old lady who sat on the far side of the prim, Sunday-best room, pleasantly redolent of the beeswax and turpentine with which the good, plain furniture was carefully polished, the family Bible in the place of honour on the central table. "He's as brown as a berry. He must have been out of doors all day long."

"Aye, so he has," Grandmother agreed tonelessly.

"And standing on his feet, he tells me."

"I walked three steps yesterday," Walter said. "Sandy had haud o' me, though," he added honourably.

"Eh, but that's grand, Wattie, my lamb," said his mother warmly, smiling down at his eager face. Then she turned back to the old lady. "I can never thank you enough. I'll admit it was hard to let the wee lad leave home, but the country life's been the making of him. I can see that now."

The decision to send Walter to spend at least part of his childhood with her husband's parents had been taken on the advice of her own father, Dr John Rutherford, the eminent Professor of Physic at Edinburgh University, after every known treatment had been tried, without the slightest effect, on the paralysis which had stricken the sturdy baby at eighteen months. It had been a hard choice for his mother. Seven of her children had already died, in infancy or childhood, while the family lived in antiquated, insanitary quarters at College Wynd, and Walter's illness had made her fear that even their move to a newer and more spacious house in George's Square might not prevent another tragedy. So, though her remaining boys, Robert and John, Thomas and baby Daniel, seemed to thrive in the big new house and garden, and poor, feckless Anne ailed nothing in particular, she had let Walter go to his grandparents to see what country air would do. Now, however, old Dr Rutherford had had another idea. "My father, that's a medical professor in Edinburgh, was wondering if the waters at Bath might help that leg of his. But it's an awful long way to send such a wee bairn, I'm thinking."

"Give us just a while longer with him here," begged Aunt Janet. "Then I'll take him to Bath if needs must."

"His grandfather was talking of a pony," the old lady said remotely, as if recalling words heard in a dream.

Walter gave a long sigh of relief. He had hoped so much that they wouldn't forget.

"Just a wee shelty," said Aunt Janet, smiling at his incredulous face. Walter turned anxiously to his mother, who always understood everything. If she were to say that he couldn't possibly have a pony till he could walk properly it would have been more than he could bear.

"Would ye like a pony, Walter?" his mother asked, twinkling down at him in the conspiratorial way he knew so well.

Walter nodded, speechless with anxiety.

"Sandy Ormiston's devoted to the bairn," said Aunt Janet. "He'll see no harm comes to him while he's leading the beast about. And it'll make a change for Wattie from riding on Sandy's shoulders."

"And high time too," said Walter's mother practically. "He's too big a burden for an old man's back. I'll not say no, my lamb," she told him comfortingly. "But I'll have to have a word with your father."

Walter sighed, for he already had an inkling that his austere and much respected father thought that doing without things did people good. But Mr Scott, thankful for anything which stressed his ailing child's chances of normality, made no objection, and Walter looked confidently for the pony's arrival, as if by magic, the instant parental consent had been given.

But when the days followed each other uneventfully, he did not pester the grown-ups with complaints, for he was already a philosophic child, to whom the dream of riding into the hills on his own pony instead of on Sandy Ormiston's shoulders, was almost as vivid as the physical reality of the men on horseback who came and went about the farm to do business with his grandmother. And so, when Uncle Thomas rode into the cobbled yard one afternoon with a broad grin on his face, and called for his nephew, Walter could not believe that his long-cherished dream had been reinforced by the reality of a ponderous farm-wagon, drawn by a broad-beamed, hairy-fetlocked carthorse, with a net over the back. But Uncle Thomas whipped him up from the kitchen floor, on which he had been rolling with the patient old sheepdog, whispered something to his grandmother and Aunt Janet, and bore him out into the sunny yard, shouting for Sandy Ormiston.

Then Walter was dumped on the mounting-block, while Uncle Thomas and Sandy Ormiston helped the carter to take the net off the Shetland mare who was so tiny that the two men together could lift her down. Then Uncle Thomas led her across the yard and put the end of her halter into Walter's outstretched hands.

"Her name's Marion."

"Marion . . ." Walter said softly. "Marion . . ."

The whole household had assembled now. Word had gone round to bring the maidservants from kitchen and dairy, farm-workers from barn to byre. And in the midst of them Walter sat on the mounting-block, smiling incredulously at the stout little pony, not much bigger than a St Bernard dog, with a dark mane that almost hid her bright eyes and a tail that touched the cobbles.

"Shall I lift ye on to her back?" asked Uncle Thomas.

Walter nodded, utterly deprived of words.

"Where's her saddle and bridle?" asked Uncle Thomas.

"Here, sir," the old carter said, grinning at the miniature equipment which Uncle Thomas had had specially made.

But it was no laughing matter for Walter. He was lifted back to the mounting-block, and his first lesson in horse management began. "Best begin as ye mean to go on, lad," said Uncle Thomas, as he handed Sandy the bridle. "Watch what he does. You'll be doing it yourself before long. See him putting the reins over her back . . . one hand on the poll and the bit in the other . . . watch how nicely and gently he wheedles the bit into her mouth. Jab her teeth and she'll be headshy for life. Now, here's the saddle. See how he settles it on her back. Slam it down and she'll buck . . ."

It was a long time before Uncle Thomas and Sandy were satisfied that every strap and buckle had been accurately adjusted. But at last Walter was lifted on to the saddle, the stirrups shortened, the reins put into his hands while Sandy held the halter. Uncle Thomas patted the front of the saddle. "Take a grip of this if you start slipping," he said. "You should grip with your knees, but we'll have to see what that right leg of yours can do. Bairns mostly ride by balance, anyway," he added.

Throughout his life Walter was to ride more by balance than anything else. But with his weight taken by the saddle and his feet in the stirrups, he felt a new, exciting confidence. Balanced on the little pony's back, his leg could not double up under him. He could go anywhere, do anything. He flapped the reins and leant forward to try and see Marion's face. Sandy Ormiston just caught him as he slithered off the saddle, laughing with delight as Sandy heaved him up again. In the background Grandmother shrieked and Aunt Janet covered her face with her hands.

"Keep your weight in the middle of the saddle. Now, we'll just walk her forward," said Uncle Thomas.

So began Walter's liberation. For a long time they did no more than walk about the farm, then Sandy Ormiston led Marion up into the hills when he went out after the cattle. Walter learned to trot round the fields, with Sandy pounding beside him. In a few months he was demanding to be let off the leading-rein. From time to time he fell off. But Marion seemed to prefer his company, for she always waited meekly for someone to hoist him back into the saddle. She was without malice, unlike many of her kind, and Walter had learned to walk, after a fashion, by the time he was six, by supporting himself against her. She was his constant companion, following him into the house, accepting bits of bread at meals, while Grandmother shook her head and murmured: "Dear only knows what your grandfather would have said."

The improvement in his health delighted the entire household, for he had always been everybody's darling. He talked without ceasing now to anybody who would listen. But he would listen himself for hours in the evenings to his grandmother's Bible stories or the ballads Aunt Janet recited while she was busy with the mending-basket. And by the time he was seven he was able to repeat them back to her, word for word, lying on his back on the sheepskin rug, his hands clasped behind his head.

But Aunt Janet was anxious about the future. For after his last visit to see his grandson, Dr John Rutherford's verdict had been disquieting. He had chuckled at the sight of Walter cantering up the hillside on his pony, been much impressed by the steady improvement in his general health and delighted by the boy's high spirits and obvious intelligence. But he could see no improvement whatever in the condition of the wasted muscles of his right leg, though the exercise on horseback had considerably strengthened those which were unaffected, and he had returned to Edinburgh to investigate the possibility of sending him for a course of the medicinal waters at Bath.

Bath! He might almost as well have said Timbuktu, Janet thought ruefully, for all the idea anybody at Sandy Knowe had of how to get there, or to arrange their affairs when they did. But her offer to go with Wattie had been gratefully accepted, and her brother, the seafaring Uncle Robert for whom young Robert in Edinburgh was named, happened to be on leave when plans were being discussed, and nonchalantly arranged their journey, by sea to London and from London to Bath by stage coach. He obtained lodgings, saw them settled, and showed them the sights. He also took them to the theatre, for the first time in their lives. The play was *As You Like It*, at which Walter shouted with delight. With that enchanted evening his lifelong passion for Shakespeare began.

But the famous waters, Aunt Janet eventually decided, weren't doing his lame leg a bit of good. Walter was learning to read at a dame school, going to the theatre whenever a Shakespeare play was on, and watching the strange goings-on of the society folk at the Pump House with incredulous fascination. But she felt compelled to tell his family in Edinburgh that they were wasting their money.

So Walter returned to the house in George's Square, surprised by the noisy crowd of strangers who were his brothers, and the meekness of his mouse-like only sister, Anne. There was to be no more nonsense, his father decided, after the further experiment of sea-bathing at Portobello had proved a failure. Lame or not, Walter must settle down at home and start his education.

Chapter 2

As the floorboards creaked outside his door, the shock-headed small boy, spread-eagled disconsolately across the rumpled bed, was instantly alert. The window curtains, drawn to exclude the lingering summer twilight, stirred slightly, betraying the soundless opening of the door. He propped himself on his elbows, watching. An impish smile touched the corners of his mouth, widened into eager welcome at the sight of the stocky maternal figure in the doorway, candle in hand.

"Wattie, my lamb, are you never sleeping yet?"

"No, Mother. Are the others away to bed?"

"Long since." His mother shook her head at him. "And asleep, as you should be."

"Is Father coming up?"

"Not yet. He's working late on some papers for the Court tomorrow."

"Then you can tell me a story," he said triumphantly.

His mother set the candle down on the table beside the bed, then ran her fingers through the strands of fair hair plastered across the boy's high forehead.

"Does your head ache?"

"No, not now. But I can't sleep without a story."

His mother stooped to straighten the wildly disordered bed-clothes, put an arm round his shoulders while she shook up the pillows, then turned to draw forward a wooden chair. "What sort of a story shall it be, my man? It's ower late for bogles, mind."

She sat down beside the bed, a short, rather stout figure, very straight, her hands folded in her lap, her back as always unsupported by the back of the chair, her plain face redeemed by the humour and gentleness of her smile.

"Tell me a true story, then. Something that happened to you. Here in Edinburgh."

"I can mind nothing very special, Wattie, that doesn't happen to most folk." Then she chuckled. "There was one time, though, when I set out to investigate what didn't concern me and got more than I expected."

Walter sat up eagerly, chin on knees, his hands clasped round his ankles. "Go on, go on. Was it in this house?"

His mother shook her head at him. "Not a word will I tell, while you sit there glowering. Lie back on your bed like a good bairn. That's better," she added, as Walter flung himself back on his pillows. "Well, this was a while ago now – "

"Was I born?"

"No. It was before you were born. It was one winter when your father kept seeing a stranger in his study, once every so often, late at night. He came by sedan chair, and went the same way. Your father admitted him and saw him out himself. The servants had orders not to answer the doorbell."

"That was awful queer . . ."

"So I thought," his mother agreed, smiling at the memory. "But your father's not one to ask about a thing he doesn't wish to mention. So after a while I thought I'd find out for myself. Surely it was thirsty work for the pair of them, conferring there late into the night, with never a word of refreshment. Your father, worthy man, would never dream of offering his visitor a glass of toddy, but he's ever been one for a cup of tea last thing. After the servants were away to bed, then, what did I do but set my best china cups on a tray, and take a pot of tea into the study when I judged it was about the stranger's time to leave."

"Was he a warlock?" said Walter fearfully.

"Nothing of the sort. Just a nippit, elderly body that never even took off his overcoat though he was sitting by your father's bonny fire. He took the tea, though, and thanked me. But your father never said a word while he drank his. And after he'd seen his visitor out, into the chair that was waiting, he came back looking properly vexed. Never a word he said, but he picked up the cup that the stranger had left by his chair, threw up the window and flung the cup out into the street."

"Whatever did he do that for?"

"That's just what I asked him. But he just shut the window and dusted his hands together. Then he marched across the room with his head held high, like a man that's struck a right blow for a cause dear to his heart. 'Whatever I may see fit to do in the course of business,' he said, 'no lip of me or mine shall touch a cup used by Murray of Broughton.' It was him, ye mind, that turned King's Evidence against Prince Charlie to save his skin after Culloden. Aweel, he's dead now, puir body, and gone to his account. But I was sore vexed for my best china."

"What became of the saucer?" Walter demanded eagerly.

"I put it back in the press."

"Mother, can I have it?"

"Bless the bairn, what for?"

"It's – it's part of history now. Please can I have it?"

"You're a real wee magpie, lad. What else have you got in that old box of yours?"

"Not an awful lot yet," Walter admitted. "But Grandfather gave me a great key from Smailholm Tower – can ye not see them slam the door and turn it against the riders from across the Border – " He was sitting up in bed now, pointing across the shadowy room – "Look where the moonlight glints yonder on their spears – "

"Tuts, no need to fash yourself, now ye've turned the key on them," said his mother composedly. "Shoot the bolts, now, and shutter the window. Smailholm's stood many a siege. I'll see ye have the saucer in the morning."

"You promise?"

"Aye. Now go off to sleep like a wise bairn, and morning'll come the sooner."

"Mebbe so," Walter agreed with a sigh. He flung himself back on his pillows, screwing his eyes tight shut as if to exclude the dark shape of the Border keep about which he had so often scrambled, mounting guard on the rocky knoll with long-dead Borderers

against reivers from the far side of Cheviot. "Mebbe . . . so . . ."
He drifted at last into a dream.

But his mother sat for a long time, watching the boy whose mind
was already as stuffed with songs and stories of the past as his old
wooden kist was crammed with bits of old iron and all those ballad
sheets and chapbooks from the Luckenbooths that he was already
collecting. Sometimes she was afraid for him, with his lame leg and
his dogged refusal to accept its limitations, his sweet temper and
occasional rages, his canny ways for which the big boys teased him
so sorely. She'd need to speak to Robert again. He was worse than
John, and old enough to know better than to kick and punch the
younger boys just because he didn't know what to do with himself.
He'd always been set on a seafaring life, like his uncles. Perhaps his
father would come round to the idea in the end. It might be best for
them all. She couldn't see him accepting the drudgery of the law,
nor would John, with his heart set on being a soldier. Maybe it was
all for the best that Wattie's lame leg would keep him from following either of them, for his father would be sorely disjaskit if none of
his sons turned to the law. There was young Tom, of course:
sweet, biddable, but scatterbrain. And Daniel, her youngest, who
just smiled at the world and expected it to smile back.

It was as well also that Walter's lame leg kept him from being an
actor. At the very mention of it, his father would just about have
turned him out of doors. The Church would scarcely do, either.
Wattie was the one she always had to poke awake at least twice
during the sermon in Greyfriars Kirk. So that only left the law.

She sighed. What would he make of the drudgery of the dusty,
book-walled room in which her husband's apprentices sat from
morning till night, with rounded shoulders and legs twisted about
their high stools as they copied page after folio page with chilly,
ink-stained fingers and monotonously complaining quills? To make
a legal apprentice of Wattie, with his head stuffed full of ballads and
battles and wonderful adventures, would be like chaining an eagle
to a post. But the lad must earn his living in the Scotland of 1780,
and for the life of her she couldn't see how his passion for the life
of other days could help him to do that.

Ah, well, there was time enough yet, with Wattie not long started at the High School, and only going to be ten in August. She smiled down at the snub-featured, sleeping face with the fair hair straying across the high, domed forehead, then reached for her candle, rose and went quietly out of the room.

The household at 25 George's Square was always early astir, with the elder boys to be roused, fed and seen off to school, and Mr Walter Scott, Writer to the Signet, not long behind them on his way to the Parliament House. So there was not much conversation round the breakfast table once grace had been said. Spoons clashed as the older children energetically supped their porridge, while Mr Scott paused to glance from time to time over his spectacles at the formidable gold watch on the table before him, and his wife busied herself with the little ones, pouring more milk into Thomas's bowl, tying Daniel's table napkin more firmly at the back of his neck, trying to persuade pale Anne to take another spoonful. Between whiles, she cut generous slices of barley bannock and made sure that Wattie had enough butter.

"For what we have received, may the Lord make us truly thankful," said Mr Scott decisively, almost before the last bite had been swallowed. "Time you were off, boys."

Chairs were slammed back, mouths hastily wiped, bonnets and satchels snatched from the hall. Then Robert and John were off, pelting down the front steps and across the cobbled square, while Walter limped philosophically after them, swinging his stick and pretending it was a broadsword. Young Robert Dundas, his classmate from the far side of the Square, was not in sight. He hummed a snatch from a ballad as he stumped off alone.

The High School, to which Walter was making his way without marked enthusiasm, was one of the city's most ancient educational establishments, founded in the time of James IV, and required by Parliament to provide facilities for the eldest sons of barons and freeholders of substance to become "perfect in Latin", starting instruction at six or nine years old. The original school had been quite a small, crow-stepped building, with two pepperpot turrets and a spire, which eventually became inadequate to the increasing number of pupils. So, two years before Walter was enrolled as a pupil, it had been rebuilt, on a much grander scale, with a great hall for prayers, and a library at each end of it, on the ground floor, and large enough classrooms above to accommodate the four classes of anything up to a hundred boys each. The four lower classes were taught by under-masters, the top class by the Rector, the scholarly, imaginative Dr Adam himself. Normally, Walter would have been entered in the lowest class – nicknamed the Gytes – but when Mr Scott had taken his son for a preliminary interview, the Rector, listening courteously to the various reasons why his son might be found somewhat backward in his studies, had decided other-wise.

He was aware, from many years' experience of the young, that the lame boy with the oddly domed head and thoughtful, downcast eyes, was a character likely to prove amenable to reason, but stubborn enough to resist force till his body broke. And the master in charge of the Gytes that year had the name of being a brutal disciplinarian. So Walter found himself entered in the second class, where he would be among the youngest, and expected to work harder for the privilege.

So far, Walter had kept out of trouble, and since he usually went to school with Robert Dundas, who was punctual and law-abiding, he had less temptation to linger by the way. But when, as now, he was alone, the early morning sights of the city inevitably distracted him. At the end of Crichton Street he paused to watch the London coach thunder past, gaudy behind its shining horses, sparks flying from the cobbles as they cantered across the open space where the Cross Causeway met the Potterrow and turned into the road for Carlisle with a flourish from the guard's long horn.

His own way led along the Potterrow, between tall tenements, a thoroughfare noisy with the clamour of street vendors hauling high-piled barrows, water-sellers bowed beneath their heavy leather containers, sweet or strident-voiced fisher lassies from Leith, their wicker creels glinting with silver fish, country carts laden with squawking fowls, sedan chairmen shouting for fares, strings of pack ponies trotting along between panniers of coal, housewives hurrying to market with plaids thrown over hair curlers, apprentices strolling on their masters' errands.

Walter, who loved such a hubbub, stopped to stare, and was only brought back to his own affairs by the distant clanging of the High School bell. A horde of boys raced past him, satchels banging wildly on their backs. But for him it was hopeless. The bell stopped as he passed the Royal Infirmary, and the uneven beat of his footsteps sounded hideously loud as he crossed the empty schoolyard and the echoing, stone-flagged hall, to climb the new stone staircase and open the door of the huge bare room where over seventy boys were crowded in rows at knife-hacked desks. All heads turned in hopeful curiosity as the master reached for his tawse at the sound of the opening door.

"You're late, boy," said Mr Luke Fraser. "Oh, it's you, Scott. Er – hurrumph . . ." He laid the tawse down. "Mebbe it takes you a bit longer to get here than the other lads."

But Walter's chin went up. "No, sir. I stopped ower-lang to watch the London coach go by."

Mr Fraser's craggy brows met in a tremendous frown as he turned on the crowd of boys who were now whispering, giggling, and standing up to see what was going on.

"Silence!" he thundered, "or I'll tawse the lot of ye. Go and sit down, Scott. Turn your back on the London coach another time."

"Aye, sir," Walter said, as he turned to push his way to his accustomed place, midway down the class of boys mostly older and bigger than himself, fists clenched and elbows thrusting aside those who blocked his way. He would much have preferred to be beaten, as any other boy would have been. For the master the incident had ended. But Walter knew very well that he would have to face the consequences later, in the Yards.

"Back to your verrrbs, lads," shouted Mr Fraser. "First conjugation. *Amo* . . ."

"*Amo, amas, amat*," droned the class ironically. "*Amamus* . . ."

Walter's lips moved as he mouthed the Latin with all the others, but his mind was busy working out his best line of defence against the ordeal ahead. How best to make the fight different, so that his game leg wouldn't count? When he was at Sandy Knowe, riding Marion, he'd been able to forget his leg altogether. If he had Marion here now . . .

The morning wore on. The class finished the repetition of Latin verbs, went on to nouns, began to shuffle and yawn. Mr Fraser scrawled a sentence on the blackboard. The dux of the class stood up to translate. At last the clanging of the bell liberated them. Almost before Mr Fraser had spoken the words of dismissal they were thundering out of the classroom, along the passage, out into the arid sunshine of the dusty Yards.

About a dozen boys were waiting for Walter, with a crowd of others in the background to see the fun. A big boy, hands on hips, watched him limp doggedly towards his tormentors, then demanded ironically:

"And what did ye make of the London coach, my man?"

"Were the horses driven to your liking?" said the boy beside him.

"Did ye not think the paint was a wee bit shabby?"

"Yah, teacher's pet," gibed a stout, sullen boy, some inches taller than Walter, swaggering up to him with his thumbs in the armholes of his waistcoat, chewing a straw in imitation of one of his father's grooms.

"Gee-up, gee-up . . ." chanted a giggling chorus.

"Tarantera, tarantera . . ." someone carolled, in imitation of the guard's horn. The circle began to close in, mocking.

But Walter's attention was all for the big boy chewing a straw who had mocked him directly. He limped up to him, fists clenched, chin up, and eyes blazing.

"Take that back, Geordie. Or else – "

"Or else what, my wee gamecock?" Geordie grinned.

"I'll fight ye."

The crowd roared with laughter.

"I will so," Walter shouted above the din.

The big boy shrugged, half turned away. "What's the use to argy-bargy with a cripple?"

"Mebbe my leg's no' right, but there's no reason for not fighting equal," said Walter fiercely. "I'd best you on horseback."

Geordie grinned. "That's easy said, when there's nae horses here."

"Benches will do instead," said Walter. "If ye sit across one and I sit across another . . ."

"Yon's a braw thought," said one of the bigger boys unexpectedly. "Seek out a couple from the classroom. We'll strap them on with our belts and see who lasts longest."

Half a dozen boys rushed indoors, several others unbuckled their belts, the senior boys in the class amused themselves by taking charge of the proceedings. Those at each end of the benches lifted them off the ground and shuffled forward at an irregular trot, bringing the champions within range of each other as if they had been mounted knights.

Walter's opponent, jolted unmercifully by the boys who swung his bench about, was obliged, every now and then, to drop his hands and grab the wood for fear of overturning. But Walter was laughing with excitement as his bench lurched to and fro, and sat it as gaily as though it had been his pony. When he was near enough, careless of the blows he received, he punched at his opponent's astonished face. Blood flowed from the bigger boy's nose, an eye closed from a shrewd blow, and his mouth gaped wide as he yelled for mercy, as much from the delighted boys who were trying to make his bench plunge and rear like a medieval charger, as from his opponent.

The crowd had grown now, as boys from other classes ran across the Yards to see what was going on. The combatants were surrounded by a roaring, delighted audience, incredulous and grinning, since young Walter was obviously getting the better of the strange contest.

"Never would I have believed the bit bairn had that much spunk," said the dux of the school.

The clanging of the bell brought the combat to an abrupt conclusion. Those holding the benches dumped them abruptly, while the owners of the belts hastened to claim them, setting the combatants free. The big boy ran off, blubbering and mopping at his face with a large and filthy handkerchief. But Walter sat where he was, blinking and weary as the heroic combat dwindled to an escapade for which he would no doubt be beaten if the ushers caught him. He swung his good leg over the bench and started to hobble after the others. But his legs seemed to fold under him and he would have fallen if Robert Dundas and two other boys had not caught him and heaved him on to his feet.

"Haud up, now. We'll give ye a lift."

Together they hauled him across the Yards and into the hall, pushing him through the classroom doorway just as Mr Fraser turned the corner. Walter scrambled to his place on hands and knees, yanked along by helping hands, cheered by the grins and back-slappings that greeted him as he passed. He was weary, aching, but jubilant. He could sense both amusement and respect in the glances of the boys about him. He was no longer to be despised as a cripple. He had laid down the conditions for combat. He had fought his first battle. And he had held his own.

It was the beginning of an era. His device for counterbalancing his lameness had caught the fancy of his classmates. His fury in attack had earned their respect. And his brother Robert, elated because their father had at last agreed to let him join the Navy, announced his intention of coaching Walter in the principles of defence. He pointed out that Walter would not always be able to lay down his own conditions. He would have to be prepared to fight on his feet, somehow or other, and the best way to strengthen his wasted leg, Robert said, was to use it.

"Mebbe ye'll hirple all your days," he said gloomily, surveying Walter with an expert eye. "But there's no reason why ye shouldn't learn to use your fists." He pinched Walter's arm muscles critically. "Ye'll need to do an awful lot of climbing to strengthen these. Start on yon old apple tree in the garden. We'll soon have you on the Castle rock."

The prospect fired Walter's imagination. He set about climbing every tree in the garden of 25 George's Square, extended his operations to every tree within miles, then graduated to more perilous feats of rock-climbing. By the time he was twelve, he was negotiating the Kittle Nine Stanes, a really tricky traverse, high on the Castle rock, and strictly forbidden by the military authorities, with the most athletic boys in his class.

But he also walked for hours in the long summer evenings, accepting a stick because Robert had said it was as much a weapon as a support. And as he walked, he amused himself by making up fearful and wonderful tales which delighted his friend John Irving, who was a thoughtful boy, and took his turn in inventing equally lurid stories as they rested under Salisbury Crags or on the summit of Arthur's Seat.

Both boys were tremendous readers, seldom without books in their pockets. But the tales they invented were weirder and wilder than anything they could buy for a few pence from the booths in the High Street. John felt his spine tingle with almost superstitious uneasiness as he sat opposite Walter in the ruined cottage, high on Salisbury Crags, trying to kindle a fire on the forlorn hearth, and listening to his companion's soft, unfaltering voice.

> " 'Round about the cauldron go;
> In the poison'd entrails throw.
> Toad that under cold stone
> Days and nights has thirty-one
> Swelter'd venom sleeping got
> Boil thou first i' th' charmed pot . . .' "

He glanced over his shoulder into the dusk. When Walter was in one of his fey moods, he could make a body feel the powers of darkness at his elbow. John wished the fire would burn. Then at least he would be able to see his companion's face and be sure it was only young Wattie Scott and not a visitant from the other world he could make so uncomfortably real.

"It's you now, John," said Walter in his usual voice. "You say:

> 'Double, double toil and trouble;
> Fire burn, and cauldron bubble . . .' "

John mumbled obediently, then stopped to blow at the sulky, smouldering sticks as Walter went gleefully on.

" 'Fillet of a fenny snake,
   In the cauldron boil and bake;
   Eye of newt, and toe of frog,
   Wool of bat, and tongue of dog – '

I wouldn't put that in, though," he said abruptly. "It gars me grue to think of an old witch cutting out a poor dog's tongue. Puff away, man. The flame's coming. Here's the cauldron I found. I can stir it wi' a stick."

"What's in it?" John asked fearfully. But Walter just smiled to himself in the dimness and began to declaim again:

" 'Scale of dragon, tooth of wolf,
   Witch's mummy, maw and gulf
   Of the ravin'd salt-sea shark,
   Root of hemlock digg'd i' th' dark,
   Liver of blaspheming Jew,
   Gall of goat, and slips of yew
   Sliver'd in the moon's eclipse,
   Nose of Turk, and Tartar's lips,
   Finger of birth-strangled babe
   Ditch-deliver'd by a drab –
   Make the gruel thick and slab . . .' "

"Here's the flame at last," said John Irving thankfully. Now he could be sure it was only Wattie after all.

"Ye never made all yon poetry up?"

Walter laughed. "No. Shakespeare did."

"However long did it take ye to learn it?"

"Nae time at all," said Water casually. "I can mind a thing when I've just read it the once."

"Ye canna'!" said John Irving unbelievingly.

"I can so," Walter said calmly.

"It's no' fair," John exploded.

"Mebbe it's odds and evens," Walter said wistfully. "I'd like fine to go for a soldier . . ."

It was not long before Walter got the opportunity for action.

Except when they united against mutual enemies such as the Town Guard, the boys of George's Square kept up a lively feud with those of less select but equally militant areas such as the Cross Causeway and the Potterrow. Every now and then hostilities blew up into full-scale street fights, known as "bickers", of which sober citizens like Mr Walter Scott thoroughly disapproved.

Mr Scott, at fifty-one a man of precise and regular habits, habitually returned from Parliament House at the end of his day's work, placed his silver-headed cane in the hallstand, hung his well-worn black hat on one of the pegs above it, and let himself into his study, closing the door behind him with a small decisive sound that told the time of day as accurately as if a clock had struck.

So, one autumn evening, when, instead of these familiar sounds, his wife heard Mr Scott's footsteps mounting the stairs, his short, dry cough outside her drawing-room door, her busy knitting needles ceased to clash round the good warm sock she was making for Robert, now a midshipman in the Royal Navy and shortly expected home on leave. Sitting quite still, she braced herself against emergency as her husband came in, looking overheated and vexed.

"I've this very minute seen Walter – "

"He's not ill?" At once alert, Mrs Scott prepared to battle with whatever new calamity had overtaken the child who would always be just a little dearer to her than all the rest.

"He is not," said Mr Scott, taking a turn up and down the pleasant, over-furnished room. "But I have this very minute seen him hirpling across the Square in the midst of a dozen lads, waving his stick and bawling as loud as a town crier, when he should be studying his books."

With a sigh of relief, Mrs Scott took up her knitting again. "And thankful I am to hear it," she said cheerfully.

Mr Scott laid his hat and stick on a small table, endangering various china objects, and sat heavily down in an armchair. "Thankful? How can you say sic a thing? Mr Fraser gave me a very poor report of his industry when I met him in Parliament Close last week."

Mrs Scott smiled to herself as she began to turn the heel of Robert's sock. "Aye, thankful's the word I used and the word I meant. When I remember what he was like when he came home first, sic an elderly wee lad with his learning and his English accent that sent his brothers into fits of laughter! He'd lie on the floor with some great book in front of him, not to be persuaded to play with the boys in the Square. I didn't realise, said he, how ignorant they were. Mercy on us, he seemed like never to be long for this world."

"You should see him now," said Mr Scott, still unsmiling. "His hair's all on end and his coat half off his back, wrestling with another lad like a wild thing."

"That's more bairnlike," said Mrs Scott approvingly. "He'll work hard enough when the time comes, husband. Let him learn to play like other lads now he's got the chance. He's not the bairn to thole being done up like a poke of lavender."

"It's nae kindness to the bairn to let him run wild," said Mr Scott severely.

Mrs Scott, counting stitches, sighed. "Let him be for a wee while, to play himself after all the set-back he's had. He'll have time enough to study. Mercy on us, he's only a bairn. Give him time to get up his strength."

Mr Scott considered her plea judicially. "Aweel, there may be something in what you say, wife," he admitted at last. "I'll away to my work." He gathered up his hat and umbrella, turned his back on the open window through which the yells of the boys playing in the Square rang clearly, and went sedately downstairs, leaving his wife to smile to herself as she listened, resisting the temptation to put down the sock and go to the window just to make sure that Wattie was not getting the worst of it out there.

The bickers between rival gangs of boys who fell upon each other at street corners were only half-serious in the general way, though the boys of the George's Square gang, of which Walter had become an accepted member, had to fight off rougher lads from the Cross Causeway, the Potterrow, or Bristo Street, who used sticks as well as fists, and were deadly accurate with rotten apples or potatoes, snowballs in season, or even stones that could cut open a boy's scalp if he were unwary enough to go out looking for trouble bareheaded. It was no sport for weaklings, and strongly disapproved of by the irascible, elderly Highlanders who made up the Town Guard, and were the sworn enemies of boys from all the adjacent districts, who sank their differences to man the Cowgate Port during the Christmas holidays and defy the veterans with showers of snowballs, till threats of reinforcements from the Castle sent them racing for home.

On this particular evening, the George's Square lads were having a rowdy conference over their vendetta with the Cross Causeway gang, whose leader, nicknamed Greenbreeks, had a real turn for organizing his ragged forces, and had contrived on more than one occasion to waylay and put the George's Square boys to flight. Everybody talked at once, and it was some time before anybody's suggestions could be heard. But at last Walter's proposal dominated the clamour.

"We'll need to lead them into an ambush," he said, for perhaps the sixth time.

The idea caught their fancy, with its military flavour.

"An ambush. That'll sort them . . ."

"It's time yon Cross Causeway loons had a lesson . . ."

"Yon Greenbreeks . . ."

"Aye, an ambush . . ."

"What sort of an ambush, Wattie?"

They were all listening now. Walter assembled his ideas rapidly. He had remembered something his Uncle Thomas had said about the tactics of the American colonists when he brought news of their rebellion to Sandy Knowe. It was easy to translate them into terms of George's Square and the Cross Causeway.

"We'll need reinforcements, though," he said, thinking aloud. "There's my brother Robert. He's coming home on leave. And there's some fine strong stable-lads that work for George's Square folk – "

"There's the garden boys as well – "

"My brother's at the College – "

"We'll tell them it's an affair of honour," Walter said. "We're outnumbered, by the loons from out yonder. If they'll assemble just by the alley-way yonder we'll take on the Cross Causeway lads at the far end, fight them for a wee while, then turn and run – or hirple – " he added, with a quick grin, "doon the alley with the Cross Causeway lads at our heels. When they rush out at the far end they'll find every man and boy from George's Square that's fit to bear arms waiting for them. They'll no' take us on for a wee while after the beating they'll get."

"Wattie, my man, ye're a wonder!"

"How soon can we do it?"

"We'll need a week," Walter said.

The plan caught the fancy of those in George's Square whose help the boys sought to enlist. Elder brothers were amused, but helpful. Within a week the reinforcements were mustered, the time and place of the ambush confirmed, recruits armed with cudgels, and the assault force of George's Square boys briefed on their tactics. Walter had decided, with great regret, that his place was with the ambushing forces, since he could not hope to maintain the headlong flight down the alley which would lure the rival gang into the reckless pursuit which was essential. So he remained with the motley company who waited on either side of the alley, while the George's Square boys left the square by another way and prepared to encounter their enemies at the end of the Cross Causeway, as dusk came down on a crisp October evening.

The boys of the Cross Causeway were not hard to find, for the George's Square challengers were making as much noise as possible to attract attention to their challenge. Whistles and cat-calls echoed as they rushed out of the shadows, infuriating sedate coachmen as they raced across the London Road almost under the horses' feet, to fall on the noisy crowd shouting insults at them from the cover of the wall surrounding the Chapel of Ease.

According to plan, the George's Square boys fought them furiously among rough grass and forgotten tombstones for long enough to draw every member of the rival gang to the conflict. Then they wavered under a hail of missiles, began to run, turned again, then vaulted the back wall and let the Cross Causeway boys almost come up to them.

"Finish them of!" yelled Greenbreeks. "Doon on your knees, ye scum, or we'll hae the hide off ye!"

The George's Square boys turned and fled, at top speed this time, with Greenbreeks and his tattered army at their heels. The pounding of footsteps, the yells of the triumphant pursuers, echoed down the alley, drowning the incautious sounds of cracking branches as those in ambush made ready to emerge. As the breathless allies burst headlong into the Square they fell on their triumphant pursuers from all sides.

The surprise was complete. The boys from the Cross Causeway were belaboured with cudgels, seized by the scruff of the neck, shaken like rats and punched in the ribs by the older boys, who were thoroughly enjoying themselves, while behind them the decoying forces paused to get breath before plunging into the battle again.

The noise was tremendous. All round the Square, windows were flung up and outraged citizens shouted protests, threatened the combatants with dire penalties, called for the City Guard. But the battle went on, for the Cross Causeway boys were good fighters, even against such odds as they had never expected, and Greenbreeks himself rallied them with his piercing, gap-toothed whistles; flailing, butting, kicking at everyone he could see in the gathering twilight, furious as he realised the trap into which he and his followers had been led.

The conflict reeled all round the Square, invaded the central gardens as boys vaulted the railings, crashed among the bushes, grabbed each other by the hair and banged heads on the ground. Walter limped to and fro, yelling with excitement, staggering as he swung his stick like a flail and brought it down on anyone within reach. It was all a wild scrimmage of hard hitting without much harm done, till the boy with the cutlass found himself face to face with Greenbreeks, raised his unaccustomed weapon as if it had only been a cudgel, and brought it down with all his strength on the opposing leader's head.

Greenbreeks went down like a felled tree and lay quite still, spread-eagled dreadfully on the cobbles, as the boy with the cutlass, stricken with horror, let it drop limply to fall beside him with a clang. His shrill yell as he turned and ran pierced through the hubbub. Those nearest glanced over their shoulders, relaxed their throttling grip on opponents, lowered their flailing cudgels, came to peer at the figure on the ground.

"Mercy on us, he's deid!" somebody said hoarsely.

A sort of shudder ran through the gathering crowd as they came to stand round, panting. Then, one by one, they disappeared, the whisper and shuffle of their hurrying feet the only sound in the dim Square as the boys stood round in dismay. Then, from the distance, came a heavy, rhythmic sound.

"Here comes the Guard!"

"We'd better no' be found here," said a young law student.

"But mebbe he's no' deid," Walter protested. "There's nae blood."

Robert kicked at the cutlass. "I doubt the lad who used this didna ken the harm it could do. Come away, Wattie. If it's murder they'll see someone swings for it."

By the time the veterans of the City Guard tramped into the Square it was deserted. Only the litter of stones and cudgels, scraps of torn clothing and discarded caps remained. And the unmoving figure of the boy on the ground.

But from scores of windows, outraged citizens watched the lanterns swinging here and there as the men of the Guard inspected the whole area, then came together to stoop over Greenbreeks, muttering angrily together. After what seemed a very long time, they picked him up between them and moved laboriously away.

From area steps, at attic windows, those concerned in the light-hearted ambush which had turned out so badly, watched and whispered. Others hastily washed the blood from their faces and brushed down their clothes before facing parents or employers.

"Where'll they take him?" Walter asked Robert anxiously.

"To the Infirmary, I'd think."

"That means he's no' deid, then?"

"Deid or alive, the doctors'll want a look at him."

Downstairs in his study, Mr Scott was assuring neighbours that he would see that the affair came to the notice of the authorities, that it was indeed time that such rowdyism was put a stop to, agreeing that this time the boys of the district had gone too far. He himself would take the matter up in the morning, they might rest assured of that. But as he showed the indignant gentlemen out, and waited, watch in hand in the doorway of his study, for his disorganised household to assemble for supper, followed by the customary family prayers, he was speculating uneasily where Walter was, and what part he had had in the outrageous affair.

At last the flustered maidservants hurried in the meal, and the family belatedly appeared, Mrs Scott from the drawing-room with her arm round the scared and sobbing Anne, Thomas and Daniel tumbling downstairs in a state of hastily suppressed excitement, Robert following them more slowly with Walter limping behind.

When they were in their places, Mr Scott cleared his throat to declaim grace, then looked round the apprehensive company, without making any movement towards the carving knife and fork beside him.

"You must all have heard, if not seen, something of the recent disgraceful behaviour in the Square. I will say only that when the on-goings of wild lads reach sic a pitch as they have done this nicht, some such fell deed as the death of this puir lad is the inevitable outcome. I pray only that no member of my household or any of our friends in the Square has it on his conscience. Naebody can shield him. The law must take its course."

In a profound silence, he began to carve the meat before him, while Mrs Scott, ready as always to redress the balance, began to talk to the little ones about the happier events of their day with a determination which did something to reassure them sufficiently to eat their supper. Robert, responding, carried off the situation with something of his habitual nonchalance, but Walter sat silent throughout the meal, choking down the food he could scarcely swallow, incoherently blaming himself for a tragedy he could never have foreseen, in which he himself had played no part.

"It was my idea . . . I killed him . . . they'll hang me for it . . ."

His dramatic imagination pictured his body rotting on the gibbet, his eyes pecked out by crows, his clothes flapping loosely round his shrivelled limbs, his purple tongue protruding like that of the murderer hanged in chains which was luridly depicted on the cover of one of the melodramatic chapbooks he and John Irving had discovered in the High Street booths. The prospect haunted him till he went to bed, coloured the nightmares from which he woke screaming, resisted even his mother's soothing presence, went with him to school next morning. It was not till the Rector, making one of his rare visitations, descended on Mr Fraser's classroom in a rage which Walter would not have believed possible for that gentle scholar, that he learned that Greenbreeks was not dead after all.

The relief was so overwhelming that he scarcely heard a word of the Rector's thunderous denunciation of any High School boys who had been involved in the affair, the categorical condemnation of all street warfare, and the threat of immediate expulsion for any boy in the school who was discovered taking part in it again. As for the present offender, the city authorities were taking the matter up, and when his name was known, the Rector would personally administer a flogging in the presence of the whole school.

Out in the Yards, those who had been involved in the previous evening's affray drifted uneasily together to discuss the situation. The boy with the cutlass, on the verge of hysterical confession, was roughly advised to "haud his wheesht", and contributions levied on all present for a gift of "smart money" to be made to Greenbreeks on his return home.

The bickers went on, though with greater caution to avoid further collision with the authorities. In his fourth year Walter entered the Rector's class. Dr Adam was a man of genius who loved and spoke the Latin language as if it had been his own.

In a class of nearly a hundred boys, individual instruction was obviously impossible, but Dr Adam's vivid awareness of the beauty of the Latin prose and verse they studied together, the ease with which he spoke it casually as if it was his native tongue, the warmth of his praise for their fumbling efforts at translation, and the humour and gentleness of his scholarly personality, made membership of his class a new and inspiring experience to which Walter responded eagerly.

He floundered, inevitably, like a puppy flung into deep water, over the reading of Caesar and Livy and Sallust, uneasily aware that if he had been more diligent over the droning repetitions of the Latin rudiments on which Mr Fraser had insisted, he would have been in a better position to grasp the subtler points in the verse of Virgil and Horace which delighted Dr Adam. But at last he recognised the adventure of reaching out towards the thought of the long-dead poets of genius who wrote of familiar experiences in a language which had for years seemed incomprehensible. His imagination, once caught, began to bring the unwieldy structure to life. The Rector, always delighted to find a pupil who showed signs of sharing his own passionate appreciation of beauty in prose and verse, was quick to praise his efforts, building up his confidence by a word here and there, till Walter was able to use the gifts he scarcely realised he possessed.

Dr Adam was well aware of the dangers of monotony, and varied the reading of the classics by selecting passages which those interested might try their hand at translating into verse. This was not a compulsory task, but a suggestion thrown out by the wily Rector for those most likely to profit by it, which gave it, as intended, an additional appeal. Walter's response did not go unnoticed.

"Many boys in this class," said Dr Adam one morning, "may understand the Latin texts better than Gualterus Scott. But he is behind few of them in his understanding and enjoyment of the author's meaning." The Rector paused, ruffling through the sheaf of papers in his hand. "These lines here . . . On a Thunderstorm . . . I like them. And you seem to like thunder, eh? Don't hide your head under your pillow from the lightning, boy?"

"No, sir," Walter managed to mumble, aware of many turning heads and surprised faces.

"Some of you might care to try your hand at something different. Write me a poem on a lesser subject. Something homelier. Write one – let me think – write on the setting sun. Meanwhile, I shall keep these verses, Scott. Now, let us continue with our reading of Horace."

Walter returned home that evening feeling tall as a steeple, and hurried in search of his mother, whose delight in his success never failed him. Such things as verse-making did not impress his father, nor the tutor whom he had installed at George's Square to supplement Walter's education. It would soon be time for Walter to leave the High School for the University, and ever since Mr Scott's attention had been forcibly drawn to Walter's fondness for street-fighting in his spare time, he had determined that it should be better occupied.

James Mitchell was a student of Divinity, with sufficient qualifications to coach Walter after school hours in writing, arithmetic and French. He was a likeable young man, in spite of a set of convictions which opposed Walter's at almost every point. Mitchell was a Roundhead, Walter a Cavalier. Walter was for Montrose, Mitchell for Argyll. But both were enthusiasts, mature in their respect for opposing views.

It was a time of discovery, excitement, intoxication with ideas for Walter. He revered the Rector, argued with James Mitchell, using his sparse pocket money to buy candles so that his mother, that thrifty housewife, should not guess how many hours he spent over his books when he should have been asleep, while Thomas, who shared his bed, turned to the wall and snored. So Walter read far into the night from a vast, unregulated choice of books, alternating Shakespeare's plays with his own beloved Border ballads, with *Pilgrim's Progress*, *Paradise Lost*, Ramsay's *Tea-table Miscellany*, *The Arabian Nights*, and many more, till his eyes closed and the book fell from his hands. A few hours later, his mother would reluctantly waken him out of the deep sleep of exhaustion, in the deadly cold of dawn, to blunder into his clothes, to eat, and stumble off to school. So, early in the morning, and into the small hours of the night, his dwindling candle burned.

Chapter 3

DURING the spring of 1783, Aunt Janet came to visit her relations in George's Square, and Walter, coming home from school with Thomas and Daniel one bleak March evening, found her sitting with his mother in the drawing-room, cosily gossiping over the teacups before a pleasant fire.

As Walter dropped his satchel on the threshold and limped eagerly forward, Aunt Janet ran to meet him, arms outstretched. She hugged him in her usual strenuous way, her plain, kind face illumined with delight as she afterwards held him at arm's length, her head a little on one side as she looked him up and down.

"Eh, Wattie, my man, how you've grown!" she said inevitably. "I've wearied this long time for a sight of my wee lad, and look what a great tall fellow I've found instead. And this'll be Thomas? My, you're a fine strong bairn. And Daniel? At school already? When I saw this wee lad last," she said over her shoulder to his mother, "he was in his cot. But Wattie's my own boy, and you other laddies will just have to thole it. Fine time we had together, did we no'?"

"Off ye go then, bairns, to your tea. Wattie, you'd best bide a while with your auntie," said Mrs Scott.

So Walter came to sit at his mother's feet, smiling up at Aunt Janet. "How's Marion?"

"Marion's fine," said Aunt Janet. "Mind, she's an old lady now, like myself – "

Walter grinned unbelievingly. The people he loved he also endowed, throughout his life, with perpetual youth.

" – but Sandy Ormiston found a fine home for her when we gave up the farm after your granny died. He goes and sees her once in a wee while, though he wouldn't retire himself, as your Uncle Thomas wanted. So he's still out after the cattle – "

Walter wanted to know, not only about the members of the household, but every horse, cow and dog he had known at Sandy Knowe, till at last Aunt Janet put her hands over her ears.

"Mercy on us, Wattie, I'm fair deaved. Dear only knows what became of the cat and her kitlings that lived at the back of the barn, but depend upon it, they'll have found a good home. And now perhaps ye'd like to know what became of your old auntie, when the day of flitting came round."

"Oh, yes, please, Auntie. I was just going to ask."

Aunt Janet laughed gaily, shaking a finger at him. "You old fraud, you were nothing of the sort. You'd rather know what came of the old tup that butted you over backwards, or the cock that used to crow on the top of the midden till your granny was ready to wring his neck. Anyway, thanks to your father, I'm in this bonny wee house in Kelso, and it's time ye came to see it . . ."

She rattled on cheerfully till Mrs Scott remembered that Walter had never had his tea, and sent him off to get it with the younger children in the big untidy schoolroom on the floor above. But once he had reluctantly gone, Aunt Janet turned to Mrs Scott in dismay.

"Mercy on us, but the bairn's just wearing himself out! Aye, he's grown, grown like a tree, but he's white as a dishcloot and thin as skim milk. What's he been doing with himself?"

Mrs Scott sighed. "I'm not happy about the bairn, Janet, and that's a fact, but I said nothing till ye'd seen him yourself, for a new eye sees more than those that look on him every day. I wish you'd have a word with his father. He's that determined that Wattie must get his education that he never thinks he may be driving him too hard. And Wattie's never one to complain."

"I know that well," said Aunt Janet with a worried frown. "But it gave me a fair turn when he walked in, and that's the truth."

"It's not just the school work," said Mrs Scott. "Nor the wild climbing and fighting he does, just to show he can best the lot of them, lame leg or no. But once he's back home he scarcely takes his nose out of a book while he can keep his eyes open."

"I thought you said he idled, whiles, at school, though," Janet said hopefully.

"Not now he's in the Rector's class. Dr Adam's quite taken up with him, seemingly, and Wattie's been doing translations into verse that I'd like ye to see."

"I'd like to see them fine. But I'd like to see more colour on Wattie's cheeks and more flesh on his bones besides."

"Wattie's father saÿs I'm far ower anxious about the bairns, and Wattie in particular. Now he's getting his education, I'd best let him be."

Janet tightened her lips into a purposeful line. "Just wait till I've had a word with his father."

Once his attention had been forcibly drawn to the fact that his son was overworking, Walter's father consented at once to take medical advice. The great Dr John Rutherford had died four years ago, but his son, Dr Daniel, was requested to express his opinion, and bring any other doctors he advised, to confirm it. The result of the conclave was a verdict that Walter had outgrown his strength and overtaxed his brains. He had admitted to headaches, and his red-rimmed eyes showed obvious signs of overstrain. Dr Daniel swung his stethoscope and tweaked Walter by the ear.

"Nothing wrong with you, my lad, that a month or two in the fresh air won't cure. Good food, plenty of sleep, out of doors all day long."

"Send him back to Kelso with me," Aunt Janet suggested to her brother that evening.

"I'd be sorry to think," said Walter's father, "that he'd not be keeping up his Latin."

"We've a real good school," Janet protested. "The dominie has a fine reputation as a Latin scholar."

So it was decided, and Walter, greatly elated to be off adventuring with Aunt Janet again, set out with her on the coach, which left the yard of the White Hart Inn at nine o'clock of a fine spring morning, bound for the Border country, behind the team of spanking horses which Walter had so often wistfully admired on his way to school. Perched high on the outside of the coach, he shouted with delight as the undulating note of the guard's horn soared above the clatter of the horses' hooves and the rumble of wheels on the cobbles. Street vendors hauled their barrows to safety, pedestrians scurried, dogs shot out of every alley barking furiously, heads popped out of high windows, groups of house-wives waved an amused response to Walter's excited gesticulations. He lost his bonnet within a mile, and his shock of hair streamed out behind him in the snell air.

Mr Scott had decided that when he returned to Edinburgh Walter should go on to the University, and meanwhile his Latin must be kept up. Aunt Janet, however, managed to put off his attendance at Kelso Grammar School for a few days, sending a pleasant little note to the dominie to explain that it would take her nephew a little while to get over the fatigue of the journey.

Walter's fatigue was not, actually, very evident as he swung himself from branch to branch of the great plane tree which was immediately his chosen refuge, or splashed exuberantly in and out of the Tweed, guddling for trout under the instruction of the local lads. It was his first encounter with the Border river which was to be one of the dearest things in his life. But after he had returned to dinner, drenched and filthy, so often that he had no dry clothes to wear, Aunt Janet decided that the legend of her nephew's fatigue could be maintained no longer. Next morning she escorted Walter reluctantly to the Grammar School.

It seemed an almost ludicrously small place after the vast bleakness of the High School. But the same hubbub greeted him, the same smell of ink and exercise books, blackboard chalk and boys. The dominie himself was an almost incredible figure of a man, between six and seven feet tall, stooping and shambling, with fiercely frowning eyebrows and an unexpectedly guileless smile. He pre-sented Walter to his senior class as one of the students of Edinburgh's High School who had done them the honour of coming to Kelso to keep up his studies before entering the University, and Walter took his place with some embarrassment among the boys at the head of the little school. As the door closed behind the dominie, the plump, brown-haired boy beside Walter turned to him with a quizzical stare.

"What's your name?"

"Walter Scott. What's yours?"

"Jamie Ballantyne. Where d'ye live?"

"Edinburgh."

"Mercy on us, it's a lang walk ye hae to Kelso School," said James Ballantyne unbelievingly.

"I'm biding with my auntie in Kelso."

"Whit does your father dae?"

"He's a Writer to the Signet, if you ken what that means."

"I do not. Mine keeps a shop."

An interested group had converged on the two boys, and a slight, wiry youngster thrust himself forward, his thin face lit with mischief. "Hey, will ye do me a favour?"

"That depends," said Walter warily.

"It's awful simple. The dominie never answers questions frae us wee yins. But he'd tak' notice o' you. Ask him – " He clapped a hand over his mouth to stifle the fizzing giggles.

"Ask him what?"

"Ask him his opinion o' the prophet Jonah," said little Johnny Ballantyne impishly.

But his elder brother turned round on him indignantly. "Haud your wheesht, Johnny. The lad's just this verra day come to Kelso School. It's no' him that should get the tawse."

"What for would I get the tawse for speiring about Jonah?" Walter asked in surprise.

As heavy steps sounded in the corridor outside, James Ballantyne said: "Because his name's Whale. He'll beat any boy that dares to mention fish or waterspouts, I promise ye."

When the mid-morning break came, young Johnny Ballantyne was loudly disappointed. But his elder brother cuffed him into silence, and the morning ended without disturbance. As the term went on, Walter came to respect Lancelot Whale for his patience and scholarship, endured without protest the extra coaching in Latin which his father had demanded, and struck up a friendship with James Ballantyne, who also had ambitions of going to Edinburgh University and unexpectedly shared his own passion for the weird and wonderful in prose or verse.

Walter was obliged to give more attention to his Latin than he had expected, for the fantastic Mr Whale was a considerable scholar, and determined to justify the confidence shown in him by carrying on the Rector's work. But there were times when his attention was inevitably taken up with the younger boys who, led by the mercurial Johnny Ballantyne, were apt to produce an uproar if left too long to memorise lists of nouns and verbs. Then Walter would look up from the translation with which the older boys at the back of the classroom were struggling, and whisper to the boy at the other end of the bench: "Slink along beside me, Jamie, and I'll tell ye a story." It was an invitation James Ballantyne could never resist.

Out of school hours, the stories which filled Walter's mind coloured the games the boys played with new splendour. The Tweed ran with blood as the armies of the Scots in armour drove their enemies back across its shallows. A tree-trunk which some winter's gale had blown down, half in and half out of the water, became the man-of-war commanded by Sir Andrew Barton which terrorised all English merchants till King Henry's over-whelming force, led by James Ballantyne, mortally wounded their leader.

" '*Fight on, my men,*' *says Sir Andrew Barton*," Walter declaimed, beaten to his knees on the broad tree-trunk,

> " '*I am hurt, but I am not slain;*
> *I'll lay me down and bleed awhile,*
> *And then I'll rise and fight again . . .*'
> " '*Fight on, my men!*' *says Sir Andrew Barton,*
> '*These English dogs they bite so lowe;*
> *Fight on for Scotland and Saint Andrew*
> *While that you hear my whistle blow!*' "

A dozen hands reached up and caught him round the ankles. The branch he grasped to save himself broke in his hands, and with a sousing splash and a roar of delight from his attackers, Walter disappeared into a deep pool, from which he emerged spluttering but unconcerned. So Aunt Janet had more clothes to dry, for he returned home so obviously drenched that she refused to serve the supper while he dripped like an otter all over the carpets.

Walter discovered Bishop Percy's *Reliques of Ancient English Poetry* in a dusty corner of a Kelso bookshop that summer, and spent hours reading it, stretched at full length in the shade of a great plane tree in the cottage garden, chin propped on fists, till the persecution of the midges drove him unwillingly indoors.

When autumn came, Walter returned to Edinburgh, brown and disreputable, having put on weight and grown out of all his clothes, so that he had to be measured for new ones before presenting himself at the University. There he found himself allocated to the class presided over by Mr John Hill, Professor of Humanity, with many of his former High School classmates, to continue his Latin studies. He was also expected, in his first session at the University, to attend Mr Dalzell's classes in Greek, which was a compulsory subject for graduation in which the University had claimed the monopoly of instruction for over a hundred years, resenting all suggestions that boys should learn at least the rudiments while they were still at school.

Dr Adam, who considered this embargo absurd, had been teaching Greek to his senior class at the High School during their final terms for quite some time, in defiance of protests from University authorities, but Walter's absence in Kelso had prevented him from beginning Greek with his contemporaries, and so he found himself relegated to the bottom of Professor Dalzell's class with those who, like himself, did not even know the alphabet, while his friends were already tackling the incomprehensibilities of grammar and translation.

Here was a different sort of challenge. It was even harder, Walter found, to be called a dunce than a cripple. His injured pride took refuge in defiance. He would refuse to learn the language at all.

The gentle Dalzell's genuine love and understanding of his subject, his vivid lectures on the classical background, and his acute awareness of the beauty locked away in the mysterious symbols which Walter had decided to despise, communicated itself to the majority of his students, while Walter yawned ostentatiously and scribbled ribald verses instead of copying out the Greek alphabet like the other beginners. Professor Dalzell was patient, till Walter spent the time allocated to writing an essay on the work of Homer in composing a flippant rigmarole to justify his own imagined preference for Ariosto. This was too much. The Professor strode to the back of the room and brandished Walter's essay in his sulky face.

"This is either impudence or idiocy. How dare you present me with such an argument, and use such irrelevant quotations to support it? Where you came by such stuff I cannot imagine. At least you seem to have read more than novels from the circulating library. But your arguments are trumpery, your contention so fantastic that I suspect you of trying to make a fool of me."

"Oh, no, sir," said Walter, surprised.

"Then you are the more fool yourself. A dunce you are and a dunce you will remain so long as you maintain this attitude. My time is too valuable to waste over whigmaleeries like you."

He slapped Walter's essay, now decorated with a splutter of question marks and ferocious marginal comments, in red ink, down on the desk before him, and turned back to the grinning assembly of more willing Greek scholars.

The incident hardened Walter's attitude, since to show interest now would be to admit defeat. He remained, obstinate and aloof, at the bottom of the class, ignored by Professor Dalzell and mildly teased by his companions, who warily stopped short, however, of provoking him to violence. "Wattie Scott's an awfu' yin, mind, once he gets his birse up," John Irving whispered to his neighbour. "Aye, d'ye mind yon bickers wi' the Cross Causeway loons?" agreed Robert Dundas.

One evening, when Walter was re-arranging his books in the little basement room which was now considered his den, his mother opened the door to announce a visitor. "Here's one of your mates from the College come to see you, Wattie. My, that's an awful poor fire you've got."

"Come away in, Archibald," said Walter in surprise. "Wait till I put some coal on the fire. I forgot about it." He limped about the little room, lifting a pile of books from one of the few chairs to offer it, sending another pile cascading to the floor from the corner of the table as he went to stoke the fire, turning down the wick of the oil lamp which had flared at the opening of the door. He was polite but puzzled at Archibald's arrival, for he was one of Professor Dalzell's most brilliant scholars, with whom Walter could expect to have little in common.

"Ye'll wonder what brings me here, no doubt," said Archibald as he tried to sit down without upsetting other piles of books which teetered here and there.

"Aye, I did," Walter agreed, sitting down himself on the edge of the table.

"Ye've got a wonderful lot of scholarship here," the older boy said in some admiration. "It was about scholarship I came, too." He paused, looking appreciatively about him. "Wattie, what in all the world makes you act so daft as to make out ye'll never learn Greek?"

"No more I will," said Walter obstinately.

"Man, ye'll regret it."

"I will not," said Walter with extra emphasis intended to hide the fact that he was already regretting his uncompromising attitude just a little.

"Do ye like to be called the Greek Blockhead?"

"They could call me a worse name."

"But there's no need," said Archibald earnestly. "I was in Dr Adam's class wi' ye at the High School for long enough to ken ye're no blockhead when ye've a mind to be otherwise. Man, Greek's a great language. There's things in Greek that – that beat all else – "

"Mebbe. But there's enough to be going on with written in our own tongue," said Walter, with an airy gesture round the piles of books. "What's the work of yon long-deid Greeks alongside what I've got here?"

"If ye'd just try to learn the language, ye'd find out," said Archibald. "Man, I ken fine it's no' easy to start with the tyros when the lads from your own High School class are far aheid. But

I'll gie ye a hand. I'll come here in the evenings. I'll have ye at the heid o' the class afore I've done."

Walter shook his head, surveying the anxious, uncouth Archibald with an air of youthful arrogance.

"I consider the language not worth the effort," he said loftily.

"Ye dinna ken what ye're talking about," said Archibald, as indignant now as Dalzell.

"Then it's not worth wasting your time with," Walter retorted. "I ken fine it's an awful kind offer, and I'm obliged to you for taking so much trouble with a blockhead – "

"But ye need never be a blockhead," Archibald insisted, "if ye'd just put your mind to learning the rudiments. Folk would soon stop making a mock of ye."

"If I don't start, they'll never get the chance at all," said Walter doggedly.

"And that's your last word?"

"Aye. No, it's not." Walter grinned suddenly, holding out a coal-streaked hand. "Thank ye, Archibald, for it was real kind to seek me out."

Archibald went away looking so downcast that Mrs Scott, who met them as Walter showed his visitor out, waited till he had shut the door behind him to ask what in the world had been going on. Walter shrugged his shoulders, looked down at his feet, shifted from a black square to a red one. "Nothing much, Mother. Archibald's grand at Greek. He wants to make me study more."

Mrs Scott looked her tall son up and down. "Aren't you studying, Walter?"

Walter shook his head.

"Why not, lad?"

Walter looked at her helplessly, ashamed to admit that he would rather not compete than fail to excel. But his mother, whose insight perpetually astonished him, smiled.

"Ye have to let other folks best ye, whiles," she said quietly.

His quick, rebellious temper flared, and he brought his heavy stick down on the tiles with almost enough violence to split them. "Mother! Ye ken fine I never will."

She looked at him sorrowfully. He was so habitually uncomplaining that when the pent-up resentment of an active, adventure-loving boy shackled for life with a lame leg, for once broke out, it was with a violence that brought him, as now, to the verge of tears. She took him by the arm.

"Come away, Wattie, my lamb," she said. "I've got a history of ancient remedies belonging to your grandfather that I came across the other day when I was redding up his papers. I was saving it for when you had the time to take a look through it."

"Grandfather? I never knew he bothered about history." Walter's attention was immediately caught.

"Oh, aye, but he did. And I'd like fine to ken what ye make of it."

They set off together, the broken rhythm of his uneven progress contrasting with his mother's deliberate, even tread as they crossed the hall.

Chapter 4

IMPATIENT as Walter was to lay his hands on his grandfather's ancient volumes, he understood and shared the respect for books which had made his mother wrap them so carefully in linen and lock the drawer of family relics from which she produced them.

"Have a care of them, now," she commanded, as he held out his hands for them. "Dear knows we'll not see their like again. Set them down on yon table and draw up a chair." Walter, opening the first volume, with its weird woodcuts and sinister remedies, was immediately absorbed, and his mother permitted herself a small smile of satisfaction as she turned back to the pretty walnut escritoire, and sat down to re-arrange the contents of the drawer from which the books had come.

As she folded and replaced the linen wrappings, she came on a small packet tied with a white ribbon, but unlabelled, contrary to her meticulous habit. To check its contents, she undid it, finding, as she had half expected, six carefully disposed locks of hair, each one named and dated, and each contributing to her strongly controlled anxiety for the health of her already stricken son. The recurring names were like echoes of those her living children now bore. There had been another Anne, the eldest, born more than twenty years ago, another John, another Walter, two other Roberts. And Anne's name was borne by the frail little girl whose life now seemed to flicker like a guttering candle; Robert and John seemed well enough, and the little ones, cheerful Thomas and wayward, idle Daniel, never ailed much. But Walter, that loving, strong-willed child, had already been strangely stricken, and sometimes he looked so overstrained and peaky still that the old fear clutched at her again.

Her fears were justified. For Walter's second-year courses in Greek Logic, were interrupted by another spell of undefined ill-health which meant more time off at Kelso that summer. Mr Scott's anxiety for his son expressed itself in an irritable preoccupation with the progress of his education, and he was determined when Walter returned in the autumn, apparently recovered and in his usual high spirits, to ensure that he fully understood the need for additional diligence during his third year at the University. As he rose from supper one evening, therefore, Walter's father issued one of the summonses to his study which all his sons knew well. Sympathetic glances followed Walter as he left the dining-room, and Mrs Scott hustled the younger children about their business when they showed signs of wishing to linger in the hall.

Mr Scott did not mean to be cross with Walter. But his standards of behaviour and achievement were so uncompromising that it was often difficult for his family to distinguish between displeasure and anxiety when summoned to his presence, and surveyed from the far side of a table covered with precisely-ranged piles of legal papers, a magnificent brass inkstand, flanked by jars containing, respectively, cut and uncut quills.

"Sit down, my boy. It's time we had a word about your studies. Aye, it's unfortunate ye've missed so much already. I hope ye're minded to set about catching up now. You are to continue with Logic and Metaphysics with Mr Bruce. That's well enough. But you've aye been deficient in mathematics. We must remedy that. I have arranged for you to be tutored by Dr MacFait. He holds his classes in Merlin's Wynd."

Walter sighed. The study of mathematics made no appeal, and he had plans for attending classes of his own choice, in Italian and History. But this seemed no moment to mention them. He also wanted to learn to draw and paint, in order to keep his own record of the hills and rivers, ruined castles and pleasant homesteads of the Border country. Such extra-mural classes would obviously have to be paid for out of his small savings.

"This seems to provide a sufficient curriculum. But ye'll have to work hard, mind, if you're going to keep up after all ye've missed with yon travels to Kelso."

"Oh, aye. I'll work," said Walter cheerfully.

And he returned to the University determined to do justice to the curriculum chosen by his father, and yet, somehow or other, to find time for the less obviously advantageous subjects of his own choice. At first, his exacting programme went well enough. He satisfied the professors in Logic, Metaphysics and Moral Philosophy, responded with delight to Fraser Tytler's lectures on History, and unofficially acquired a surprising amount of Italian in a short time, with enough French and Spanish to find his way through *Gil Blas* and *Don Quixote*.

Even without the sketching classes which both he and John Irving attended with an almost ludicrous lack of success, Walter's third year at the University was stuffed to bursting with official and unofficial occupation. He was making new friends all the time, without forgetting his former companions of the Yards. John Irving was still a constant companion on his country walks, and their private world of romantic story-telling had been enriched by their Italian studies. But they kept their engrossing hobby discreetly to themselves, knowing very well what uproarious teasing they would have had to endure from worldlier and wittier friends.

But the story-telling was no mere childish hobby for Walter. Spencer, Tasso and Ariosto had swept him into a new world of vivid imagining and passionate adoration, and he did not despise the less distinguished romances to be found in Mr Sibbald's Circulating library in Parliament Close. He habitually returned home unobtrusively with such booty, guessing that his father would condemn it out of hand as unprofitable trash. But one evening, careless in his haste, he was unlucky enough to miscalculate his entrance and let slip a cascade of contemporary romances at the feet of his father, who was just crossing the hall.

"Tch, tch, my boy," said Mr Scott testily, "it's time ye learned to take better care of your text-books."

Walter crouched on the tiles, sweeping the volumes together in an effort to prevent a closer inspection, blurting out the news which he hoped would provide a distraction.

"Father, I saw Robert Burns – he was in the library – almost as near as you're standing now – "

Mr Scott surveyed his son over the steel rims of his glasses. "Robert Burns? And who may he be?"

"Father!" Walter was almost speechless. "He's our greatest poet! Here, here in Edinburgh!"

Mr Scott produced a handkerchief with a flourish, as the dust from the scattered volumes made him sneeze. "A poet, indeed. I've nae use for sic whigmaleeries. Gather up yon books, boy, and sit down to your work."

"Yes, Father," said Walter flatly. He felt suddenly very weary as he went down the stone stairs to his own room. He was listless all evening, ate little at supper and slept badly, tossing about till good-natured Thomas protested.

"What ails ye, Wattie?" he mumbled sleepily, grabbing at the tumbled bedclothes. "Can ye no' sleep?"

"No' yet. But I soon will," said Walter, with a sigh.

They both slept at last, but next morning, to their unbelieving consternation, Walter wakened in a pool of blood. Thomas ran shouting to his mother, who was long since dressed, sitting by her bedroom window with her Bible, and Mrs Scott, after a single glance, sent one terrified maidservant running for the doctor, and another in search of her husband, while she knelt by the bedside, with Walter's head cradled in her arms, her lips moving in a desperate, yet disciplined stream of prayer.

Walter himself felt strangely far away. His forehead was clammy as his mother laid her cheek on it. His breathing was a series of shallow sighs, and he was only aware of the comfort of his mother's presence. Then at last he opened his eyes.

"Eh, Wattie, my lamb," she said softly, "heaven be praised for that."

Walter looked vaguely from his mother's face to his father's rigid figure on the other side of the bed. He tried to speak and found he could only whisper. "Whatever's . . . happened?"

"Don't try to talk, my lamb. You've been taken ill, and the doctor's on the way."

"It's to be hoped," said his father, precise even in emergency, "yon daft girl gave your message correctly." He pulled out his heavy gold watch. "She's been gone half an hour." He looked anxiously at his son's bloodless face. "Is there nothing we can give the boy?"

Walter felt rather than saw his mother shake her head, and his defiant spirit instinctively rose to combat their fears for him. A faint smile just curled the corners of his long upper lip. "Dinna fret," he reassured them, as he would have reassured his comrades sharing some desperate venture in the Yards, "mair were lost at Sheriffmuir."

The old saying was almost inaudible, but it brought tears to his father's eyes. "I'll away and see if the doctor's no' coming yet," said Mr Scott abruptly as he turned away.

His uncle the doctor's arrival was only a blur to Walter. So was the emergency bleeding and blistering and other treatment which followed. Walter's circulation and body temperature were reduced by taking most of his blankets away and throwing the window wide on the chilly air of an early spring morning in Edinburgh. But he now felt too remote to care. Dr Daniel Rutherford's grave face was featureless as a pinkish balloon as he elaborated the comfortless régime which he considered the only chance of saving Walter's life.

"I'm thirsty," Walter whispered.

"Gie him a couple of sips of cauld water. Nae mair," said Dr Daniel, "for the time being." He began to pack up his medical gear. "I'll away now," he told Walter's parents, "but I'll be back shortly, with a colleague I'd like to have a look at the laddie. Keep him where he is. And dinna shut yon window," he commanded.

So began the long, desperate struggle for Walter's life which his uncle at first undertook with very little hope of success. The doctors returned, conferred, withdrew to consult, summoned Walter's parents to inform them that Walter was suffering from the bursting of a blood vessel in the lower bowel, and unless the haemorrhage could be arrested he would undoubtedly die. Everything possible must be done to reduce the flow of blood and give the damaged vessel the chance to heal. The patient should only be allowed to drink a few sips of cold water, and kept on a starvation diet consisting mainly of vegetables. On no account was he to be allowed to move, even to talk, for the present.

"The poor lamb, the last's going to be the sorest deprivation," said Mrs Scott sadly.

"No doubt," said Dr Daniel.

"But we must count on your co-operation," said Dr Daniel's cadaverous-looking companion. "The laddie must not be left, ma'am, by night or day, till we see which way things are going."

"I'll not leave him, Doctor," Mrs Scott said quietly. She settled herself, bolt-upright as usual, on a hard chair beside Walter, who lay inert and exhausted from loss of blood, under the one thin blanket they had left him, the lower end of the bed raised on piles of legal tomes from his father's study. Beside the wide-flung window the curtains billowed into the room.

Thomas and Daniel were fed and sent off to school, Anne drifted in and out, glad to be sent on errands, bringing extra shawls for her mother's shoulders, her knitting, her mending basket, a glass of cold water. The servants came for orders about meals. The doctors came and went. Between visitors, Mrs Scott sat quite still with her blue-cold hands folded in her lap, looking out of the window, past the bare tree-tops in the Meadows towards the mist-hung Pentlands. Words she had always loved drifted in and out of her mind throughout the first, unbelievably long day. "I will lift up mine eyes unto the hills, from whence cometh my help. My help cometh from the Lord . . ."

Every now and then, it seemed, the clock at the corner of the stairs chimed another hour. But she had no idea whether the intervals between the chimes were long or short. Sometimes the gap apparently stretched for years. She heard her husband go off, later than usual, to Parliament Close. And then, unexpectedly, she felt rather than saw Walter's eyes open. She turned towards him, took the hand he raised uncertainly between both of her own, was astonished by his crooked grin.

"How cold your hands . . . are," he whispered. "You . . . need mittens for . . . the Arctic . . ."

"That's a fine idea, Wattie. I'll send Anne to fetch them when she comes back."

"Tell me . . ." he began, looking about him in bewilderment, "what's been happening . . ."

"There's not much to tell. It's what the doctors wanted. And they don't want you to talk. So you'll have to save up all your questions for later. I'll read to you, if you like, though."

"Say something from the ballads instead."

"The Battle of Otterburn?"

"Aye."

"You'll have to lie still, though."

"Still's deid," Walter promised.

As the grey light of the afternoon began to fade, Mrs Scott put Walter's hand gently back on the blanket, cleared her throat, and began the ballad they both loved.

> *"It fell about the Lammas tide*
> *When husbands win their hay . . .*
> *The doughty Douglas bound him to ride*
> *In England to take a prey . . ."*

Walter's eyes closed again, but a smile just curled up the corners of his mouth as he listened to the familiar tale of the gallant conflict between Douglas and Percy, set against the bright background of shining armour and flying banners, with the white clouds piled in the blue sky above the Border hills.

Mrs Scott's fingers closed over his pulse, thready and almost imperceptible. His shallow breathing was still steady, the smile had gone, and his mouth was resolute, his fist clenched as he followed the words, happy as he shared the adventure of the Border knights. She went on.

> *"My wound is deep; I am fayn to sleep, . . ."*

The door opened softly, to admit a servant bearing candles, followed by her husband, whose return she had for once not heard.

"Well, I must say," Mr Scott remarked dryly, "you've chosen an odd way of entertaining the laddie in the circumstances. How is he?"

"Just the same, as is only to be expected. And the ballad was of his own choosing, my dear."

He turned up the collar of his overcoat and rubbed his hands together. "Ye must be fair perished, wife. Have ye been here all the day long?"

"Aye," said Mrs Scott placidly. "And I'll be here all night too, and take no harm, once I've got the mittens Walter said I needed."

"Are you expecting the doctors back?"

"Daniel said he'd look in last thing. Have a word with Walter now. He's looking at you all the time."

Mr Scott brought a chair to the other side of the bed, sat down and cleared his throat uncomfortably. He found illness an embarrassment, almost an affront. Like many people whose own health gives them little trouble, he had difficulty in comprehending the sufferings of others. But he could see for himself that his son's loss of blood had brought him very near to death.

"Ye were aye a fechter, Wattie my man," he said at last.

Walter smiled remotely. "Aye, Father. I'll fecht," he whispered. Then he let his eyelids fall over his tired eyes. He felt dizzy when he tried to look at anybody. There was a queer dirling in his ears. His mother's voice, repeating the words of the ballad, seemed to echo about him. "My wound is deep, I fayn would sleep . . ."

"Send the lassie for Dr Daniel," said Mrs Scott urgently.

But Walter did not die that night. Nor the next day. Nor the next. As his father had reminded him, he had always been a fighter. And so, though it was in a strange battle, without weapons, or horses, or armour, he fought on. It was bitterly cold. His mother, his Rutherford kinswomen, who took turn and turn about with her at his bedside, seemed to come and go like creatures in a dream. He was aware of nothing but the urgency of his father's words. He must fight on.

Time seemed without significance during the first weeks of his illness. Day alternated with night, the occasional thin sunshine with the draught-beset flicker of candles; the doctors came and went, blistering and bleeding, reducing in the only way they knew the strain on the weakened blood vessel, in the desperate hope that it would heal before their patient died of weakness. He was never alone: only aware of the coming and going of many friendly shadows. His maternal aunts, Mrs Russell of Ashiestiel and her younger sister, Miss Christian, relieved his mother in the constant watch. Aunt Janet came up from Kelso, his brothers, Robert and John, came whenever they were on leave, John Irving came daily, with armfuls of books which he read aloud till he was hoarse, Thomas looked in anxiously after school.

His mother had never doubted that Walter would live, even when things looked worst, and recognised the first signs of returning life with joy. "Mother," Walter whispered one April morning, "I'm awful hungry. Will they no' let me have a bit more to eat than gruel?"

She stooped to kiss him. "Aye, my lamb, I'm sure they will."

He was allowed more, but much less than he wanted. A dish of vegetables was a poor substitute for the roast beef or grilled steaks which haunted his dreams. But gradually the world began to seem solid again, and as he was allowed to talk a little, even to make the cautious exertion of moving chessmen about, John Irving was able to take the edge off the monotony of his days. Walter wanted to look out of the window to watch people coming and going across the Meadows, so John also rigged up a combination of mirrors, which delighted the invalid, as he could even see soldiers from the Castle drilling on the greens. And as Walter was now allowed to read, John ransacked the circulating library for subjects likely to interest him.

But convalescence brought its own problems. The course of the illness had been arrested, almost miraculously in his Uncle Daniel's opinion. But he still insisted that Walter should go very slowly indeed. Walter had, actually, no alternative, for after many weeks in bed he was so weak that he almost wept with impatience, and became the victim of bouts of depression which seemed to plunge him into the uttermost pit of despair. In his worst moods nothing could keep him from a completely uncharacteristic fear of the future. What was to become of him if he was doomed to be an invalid for ever? One evening, his father came in to find him sitting on the edge of his bed with his head in his hands.

Mr Scott, who had the greatest aversion from emotional scenes, cleared his throat to attract attention, and went to look out of the window till Walter had composed himself. "A very fine prospect you have, my boy, now that the green is coming on the trees. You seem to have books on every chair, and I should like to sit down for a chat."

Walter was at once on his feet, limping about to clear a chair and set it for his father by the open window so that he could enjoy the prospect he had praised. Then, exasperatingly exhausted by the effort, he sagged down on the bed again. "Shall I ever be good for anything again?" he said wearily.

Mr Scott looked at his son over the rims of his glasses. "That's a daft-like question," he retorted severely. "And at the verra time I've got plans made out for ye, too."

"Plans?" said Walter bleakly.

"Aye. You are of an age now to get started with your life work. And that's the Law."

"What do I know of the Law?"

"Naething yet," said his father dryly. "But I warrant ye learn something in five years, or I'd best retire from business. Come on, lad. I need an apprentice. You need the work. You'll be paid for doing it. Mebbe it won't seem like a fortune," he admitted dryly. "Threepence a page is the apprentice rate for copying documents. You'll spend many long hours earning it. But a Writer's Apprentice does more than sit at his desk. If he can sit a horse and find his way about he may travel the length and breadth of Scotland on his master's business before the five years have gone by."

As Walter's head went up and his eyes showed the first signs of interest, his father, watching him over his glasses, pursued his advantage. His smile had unexpected warmth. "I believe in ye, lad. Whit mair need ye seek, when there's work I can give?"

The dark mood dissolved like a sea fret in sunshine. "I'll be glad of the chance, Father," he said.

Mr Scott nodded satisfaction. "That's right, lad. We'll soon have you at work. But you'd best have a wee while in the country first. Ye've been long enough in the old wives' care. It's time ye had a man's company. D'ye mind your Uncle Robert?"

"Aye. He took me to my first theatre, yon time I was in Bath."

"Er-hrrmph." Mr Scott, who disapproved of all theatrical entertainments, cleared his throat. "There's no theatres in Kelso that I'm aware of. Your uncle's bought himself a bonny property there, not far from your Aunt Janet, now he's given up seafaring. He'd be willing to have you with him, I believe."

"Would he? I'd like that fine."

So, in due course, Walter went to spend the summer with his Uncle Robert, at Rosebank, on the edge of the Tweed. In a lifetime of seafaring, Uncle Robert had seen enough of hardship and danger to know when a man or a boy was in need of understanding rather than naval discipline. His bachelor household was comfortable, his kind old housekeeper devoted, Aunt Janet only a short walk away.

And Uncle Robert's mellow, tolerant personality gave Walter confidence. He still limped, but had now reconciled himself to the use of the stout stick which made long walks possible, and as his strength came back, Uncle Robert could offer instruction in all the manly sports appropriate in a Borderer. He learned to handle a boat, to play and land a salmon, to sit horses which could carry him farther and faster than his first favourite. Once again, the healing charm of the Border country was doing its work, and when the strange internal lesion finally healed, Walter began to gain new strength and stamina which were to stand him in good stead throughout an arduous life.

It was otherwise with Robert, Walter's much feared, yet greatly admired elder brother, with his swashbuckling ways and passion for the sea. He had served under the great Admiral Rodney, and seen several engagements, but had no patience with the prospects of a peace-time Navy and, after the Peace of Versailles, had sought remoter adventures with the East India Company. Now a letter had come from Edinburgh which Uncle Robert gravely read aloud.

For Robert, who had always seemed so much fuller of life than anybody else, had died of a fever contracted in the alien climate, and been buried at sea, on his way home. "I – I canna believe it," Walter said, struggling with sudden tears.

"No more can I, lad," said Uncle Robert. For the boy who had been named after him had always seemed to set the changes and chances of mortal life at defiance, while his younger brother had been the sort of bairn you might expect the wind to blow away. But now Robert was dead, and Walter stood beside him, broad-shouldered and deep-chested, with healthy colour in his cheeks and a new brightness in his eyes. He folded his sister-in-law's letter carefully and put it in his pocket.

"God rest him, poor lad," Robert's uncle said soberly. "Now, Walter, we'll saddle up the horses and ride across the hill to yon old kirk ye were asking about. We'll come to no good moping here."

So they rode over to the ruin that Walter had wanted to see. And in the evening, as usual, he brought the notes he had hastily scrawled of all he had seen that day, for his uncle's inspection, after an enormous supper, when candles had been lit and they were settled in front of the log fire. For Uncle Robert was not only a man of action. He shared his nephew's love of good stories and valiant ballads, and as he sat smoking the cheroot he had got a fancy for in foreign parts, his comments on Walter's scribblings were very much to the point. But that night Uncle Robert's acuteness took his nephew unawares.

"Where did ye meet her, Wattie?"

Crimson and startled, Walter stammered: "W-who?"

Uncle Robert chuckled. "The lassie ye wrote these verses for. Why should ye not? They're the best ye've read me yet. What's her name?"

But Walter ducked his head and grinned. He had slid from his chair to the hearthrug, to sit there, clasping his knees, his eye on the play of the flames about the logs.

"If it's the Queen of Elfland ye've been seeing, lad," said Uncle Robert, who never sought to force a confidence, "she's the very company we need for versifying. Read me yon poem again."

"I'm real glad ye liked it, Uncle," said Walter, much relieved.

But that night, upstairs in his little room under the eaves, with his window flung wide so that he could hear the sound of the river Tweed hurrying over the shallows at the far end of the garden, he settled himself at a table in front of it and took out his papers again. The night was so still that the flame of his candle scarcely wavered as he dipped his quill and began to write. But this time it was not a poem.

"Dear Jessie," he scribbled experimentally,

"I hope you will pardon my thus addressing you, after so short an acquaintance, but in truth I cannot commence writing to you in any other way. I do regard you as my dear Jessie, and if you will only allow me that favour be assured you shall have no cause to regret having done so." He paused, chewed the end of his quill, re-read what he had written with an anxious frown. Presently he wrote on.

"Your gentleness, your goodness, your kindness, have filled me with the sweetest feelings I have ever known . . . I have scribbled the enclosed lines . . ."

He rummaged through a sheaf of haphazardly covered pages, frowning anxiously over various attempts, eventually selecting the simplest.

> *"Lassie, can you love me weel?*
> *Ask your heart and answer true.*
> *Doth that gentle bosom feel*
> *Love for one who loveth you?"*

"They at least have one recommendation – " he wrote decisively, "the sentiments they contain are as sincere as any that ever influenced a human bosom. If you are not offended with my boldness I hope to see you tomorrow morning. Sweet dreams attend you! Allow me to write myself," he concluded, in the form most approved by the romantic authors he admired, "Your obedient admirer,

Walter Scott."

He folded, addressed, and sealed the letter, blew out his candle and picked up his stick. Leaning out of the window, he dropped it carefully into a flower-bed below, then bestrode the window-sill, grasped the nearest branch of the ancient apple-tree trained against the house, and clambered as boldly down into the moonwashed stillness of the summer night as he had ever clambered across the Kittle Nine Stanes on the Castle rock.

For Jessie had warned him with real terror of her parents' strictness. They would be scandalised by their chance acquaintance, and would certainly beat her if they discovered it. So he must neither visit her nor write to her. The door would be shut in his face. Letters would be opened and read. But she did admit, a trifle archly, that there was a hollow tree outside their garden which would make a possible posting box.

"Dearest Jessie," he wrote a few days later,

"I am glad that you have told me you like poetry, and you may be well assured I am not less so at your liking my poor efforts in that way. However since this is the case I can afford you as much as you can find time to read, for, for a long time past I have been spoiling a vast quantity of good paper with my attempts at the poetical . . . I have addressed the moon – that most be-rhimed of planets – so often I am ashamed to look her in the face. I have made odes to nightingales so numerous that they might suffice for all that ever were hatched . . . I have enclosed my attempt at a ballad . . ."

That night the bundle he stuffed into the usual cranny was a bulky one. The need for secrecy was exciting, and he was careful to reassure her. "I have burnt whatever notes I have received from you though very unwillingly, and I did so from the fear that they might be discovered by some curious person, and the course of our true love made to run less smooth even than it does at present."

The dream world shared with Jessie slid like his shadow beside the robust everyday world in which he rode, fished and shot with his Uncle Robert, visited his Aunt Janet, wrote dutifully to his parents in Edinburgh. Walter had long ceased to think of the state of his health. It had not occurred to him that its restoration must carry the penalty of exile. Very sadly, as autumnal frosts sent the first vivid leaves spinning down, he wrote for the last time:

"Dearest Jessie,
    "To my exceeding regret I am obliged to start for Edinburgh tomorrow. With how extreme a reluctance I tear myself away from your delicious presence it would be in vain attempting to tell. As you will not allow me to write from there for fear of a discovery I know not how I shall get over the time that must elapse before I can again possess the dear sweet happiness of your society . . ."

Next morning Walter climbed sombrely to an outside seat on the Edinburgh coach, his feet on his portmanteau and his chin cupped in his hands. The sadness of the morning echoed the ache which seemed to clench his heart like the fingers of Giant Despair. She had forbidden him to write to her, denied him even that slender thread of consolation, tenuous as the spiders' threads that spanned the gorse bushes that loomed through the mist on either side of the road. In spite of his determination to descend to the uttermost depths, Walter was surprised by one small spark of consolation. She might forbid letters, but she could not stop him writing poems. Surely she would be delighted by the arrival of a handsome collection, bound in leather, of course, containing all the love poems he would shortly write and dedicated – "To Jessie"? No, "To my Unknown Love" would be better. Walter smiled for the first time that day, raised his head, and dashed the mist-soaked hair out of his eyes.

As the coach rumbled to a halt outside the White Hart Inn, Walter heaved himself and his portmanteau down, made his farewells to the friendly guard, and limped through the small crowd of old ladies anxious about their luggage, wives looking for their husbands and men shouting for caddies or sedan chairs. He wanted to be alone with his bitter-sweet memories just a little longer before facing his family.

So he turned out of the Grassmarket and began to climb the

crooked, sinister ascent of the West Bow, where the old, crazily
irregular houses seemed to lean towards each other across the
narrow street, noisy with the rumble of hand-barrows, the shouts
of street vendors, the clang of smiths' hammers from basement
workshops and the undertone of heavily shod feet as the citizens of
Edinburgh went about their business. None spared time for a glance
at the dawdling lad who paused every now and then to set down
his portmanteau and stare up at the storied house-fronts, about
which legend and history hung thick as cobwebs, with ancient
coats-of-arms half hidden by lines of tattered clothes hung out to
dry: the iron cross of the Knights of the Temple let into the stone-
work of the timber-fronted Mahogany Land, outside which
Walter paused to decipher a half-obliterated inscription – "He yt
tholis overcommis".

"He that endures shall overcome," he said aloud, to the surprise
of a passing fisher lass from Leith. It was a motto after his own
heart. But he lingered longest outside the strange and dreaded
tenement known as Major Weir's Land, past which a dank and
dismal close led to a court in which the wizard, Major Weir, and
his crazed sister Grizel were believed to have associated with the
devil and a horde of evil spirits. The tall house stood empty, for
nobody had ever dared to live there since the Major and his sister
died at the stake. Walter shivered as he stood in the entrance to the
dreadful place. The flap of a tattered curtain at a broken window
gave the illusion of a beckoning arm, and he was glad to emerge at
last into the broader thoroughfare where the Lawnmarket met
Castle Hill at the head of the Bow, with the Castle towering
beyond.

Without any conscious purpose, Walter turned towards it,
smiling at the memory of many successful adventures on its rock,
newly aware of the contrast between the ancient street from which
he had emerged and the revolutionary work going on across the
valley below. As a High School boy, the narrow wynds, the
cobbled closes and the stinking marsh that had once been the city's
northern defence, when the Nor' Loch had lapped the foot of the
Castle rock, had been his playground. His home in George's

Square had been part of the city's plans for development of which he had often heard his father speak. But his own fancy had always been for the old and crooked houses of the past, even though the narrow wynds stank and the steeply cobbled slopes tried his lame leg.

Now, for the first time, he was aware of the change in the city which was his home. As he approached the Castle, the countryside spread out below him as far as the mist-hung Forth, and the contrast with the fabled West Bow was as dramatic as his own growth towards manhood. At a mounting-block by the outer gate he paused to rest, looking down with incredulity to the uncompleted work below.

The marsh which was all that remained of the Nor' Loch had been conveniently spanned in Walter's schooldays by a casual causeway known as "Geordie Boyd's Mud Brig", consisting of stepping-stones, tree-trunks and wheelbarrow loads of rubbish, assembled by an enterprising citizen of Gosford's Close in the Old Town. In recent years, it seemed, other people had taken advantage of such access, which offered those with eggs, poultry or vegetables for sale to the city folk in the tall tenements of the High Street a quicker crossing than the fine North Bridge farther down the valley. So Geordie's short cut had taken so many thrifty folks' fancy that the earthen mound had grown into a sort of thoroughfare, across which Walter was amused to see men going with carts and horses, some tipping further rubbish over its sides to widen it, others leading loads of farm produce or driving herds of sheep and cattle.

Even more dramatic were the changes in the countryside beyond the Mound. In the distance, where sound foundations had at last been laid for its five arches, the North Bridge now linked the old city officially with the new, spanning the unsavoury area of the Shambles in the valley below. Directly across the marsh the air was hazed with bonfires where trees and hedges had been grubbed up to make way for the raw new roads. Elegant buildings were already rising here and there along the north side of the Lang Dykes, the country road which had for centuries run parallel to the Nor' Loch and had recently been renamed Prince's Street. Undulating green fields had been invaded by the new roads which drove on from St Andrew's Square towards yet unbuilt Charlotte Square at the other end, devouring farmland, overwhelming homesteads, heralded by the reek of scores of fires which drifted towards the Old Town on the snell wind from the Forth.

The scene of turmoil, change and destruction exactly suited Walter's mood, which found an echo in the ravaged countryside through which the forces of established authority so relentlessly drove. He was in no mood to appreciate the potential beauty and grandeur of the architect's vision. At fifteen, with his own life eclipsed in misery, he could only see the sorrow of a countryside despoiled. So it was only with a supreme effort that he summoned the resolution to turn towards George's Square and the bondage which awaited him.

But like many things most dreaded, the new phase of his life was not without its compensations. His mother's delight at the sight of him, sunburned and sturdier than she had dared to hope, thawed the icy surface of his misery so that he was able to smile at Tom's excitement at his return, kiss a little colour into Anne's pale face, forgive young Daniel's pertness for once, and listen with respectful attention to his father's plans for his immediate future. As they sat down to dinner, his mother raised her bowed head after grace to exclaim with innocent pleasure:

"Eh, Wattie, my lamb, ye might never have been away!"

Walter smiled at her, but he still felt as if he were moving through a dream, in which his family were kindly shadows, and the only reality the honey-coloured Border hills, the shimmer of autumn sunlight on the broken waters of Tweed, the tender warmth in Jessie's eyes. If his mother noticed, she gave no sign, his father was cheerfully preoccupied in outlining Walter's new duties as a Writer's Apprentice, and the children chiefly interested in their own affairs.

At breakfast next morning, his father lost no time in reminding Walter of his new status. When the meal was over and grace said, he detained the younger boys, who were about to scramble for their satchels, and produced an official-looking document from his breast pocket.

"It – er – seems appropriate that ye should all hear of the undertaking mutually assumed by your brother Walter and myself," he informed his family, pausing to make sure of their attention with a sharp glance round the room over the rims of his spectacles. Then he cleared his throat and proceeded to read aloud in the dry tones of an advocate addressing a Court of Law.

"The following entry in the Minute Books of the Society of Writers to the Signet will be of interest to all present. 'Edinburgh, 15th May, 1786. Compeared Walter Scott and presented indenture dated 31st March last, entered into between him and Walter Scott, his son, for five years from date thereof, under mutual penalty of £40 sterling.' "

He lowered the paper and smiled thinly at his son. "Well, my boy, ye've got a man's job now, and the sooner we get started the better. Away and get your hat. Ye'll be at your desk from now on by the time the Tron kirk clock chaps nine."

"Aye, Father." Walter squared his shoulders and thrust out his chest with an air of mature resolution which made the younger children stare and his mother sigh. Then he rose, made a polite little bow to his father at the head of the table, and limped off in search of his hat and stick.

So began the first of many monotonous days at his high desk in the apprentices' room at his father's office in Parliament Square. But he took a certain pride in his appointment, for his father's confidence in him had come at a time when he needed it most. There were, he found, compensations to offset the monotony of his labours. His fellow apprentices were friendly lads, who enjoyed a joke when the testy old clerk in charge of them was occupied elsewhere, the open fire made the bare room seem snug when the autumnal gales blew the rain in sheets against the windowpanes, and he earned his first money at the rate of 3d per folio sheet, which made diligence worth while when he could buy himself the books he coveted from the proceeds of copying legal documents.

In the evenings and on Sundays, between church services, he

sought out his High School friends again. John Irving and Adam Ferguson were also Writers' Apprentices, but as they served other masters, they only met when working hours were over. Still, they could walk farther now, for Walter's health was established at last. He was taller than his father, with strong arms, a great breadth of chest, and delighted in strenuous exercise, whether on foot or horseback, which made him ready to walk for twenty or thirty miles and ride a horse all day long whenever he got the chance.

As his days filled, with long hours at his desk and evenings with his friends, the balance of his life began, inexorably, to shift. Now his surroundings in Edinburgh were clear-cut, the memories of his idyllic summer in Kelso became shadowy. The poems he had planned remained unwritten. No letters came. Against his will, the memory of Jessie's face blurred, his protestations of undying love died, like a child's wildflower posy, by the wayside.

His father was pleased with his progress, amused by his determination to earn every penny he could, though he sometimes shook his head when Walter appeared with another armful of books from Sibbald's Circulating Library. At the back of his hero-worshipping mind, Walter was always hoping for another glimpse of Robert Burns, whose poetry he admired as much as anyone in Edinburgh at a time when Burns was at the height of his fame. And he did see the poet just once more, when Adam Ferguson took him to a literary gathering given by his father, the eminent University professor, and Walter was overwhelmed with shyness and delight when he was able to provide Burns with the name of the author of an obscure poem which he alone had read.

As Walter established himself as a reliable apprentice, his father began to give him small commissions which took him to the Highlands collecting debts or enforcing the execution of an eviction order against defaulting tenants, impressively escorted by a sergeant and six armed men. Walter, who talked to everybody he encountered, and forgot nothing he learned, hoarded all the first-hand reminiscences of the Stewart Risings from a veteran of both the Fifteen and the Forty-five. For he was beginning, subconsciously, to store his remarkable memory, not only with the masterpieces of other men, but with every sort of quirk and facet of character, every detail of beauty seen or drama described.

After Walter had completed two years of his apprenticeship, his father decided that it was time to consider his future more closely. He was committed, now, to the legal profession, but he was still free to choose between its several branches.

"Mind ye," said Mr Scott, as he and Walter walked homeward one pleasant summer evening, by way of the Cowgate and Candlemakers' Row, "there's nothing that would please me better than to have ye with me in the firm. But there's Tom to be thought on."

"Aye, Father," Walter agreed. "There is indeed." He spoke warmly, for goodhearted, haphazard Tom was his favourite brother, and his future an anxiety to them all.

"He's a good lad, and well-intentioned, but he's no' got your gift of the gab. He'd be clean useless in Court. I could never recommend him to read for the Bar. But I've greater hopes for you, Wattie. Have ye considered reading for the Bar?"

Walter looked at him in astonishment. Ambition had not yet quickened in him. He asked little more than the pittance which enabled him to buy books and pay his score in tavern or eating-house on equal terms with his friends. His well-worn dark coat and useful corduroy breeches were carefully mended by his thrifty mother and he never gave their lack of elegance a thought.

"Me read for the Bar?" he said blankly. Had he ever assessed his future chances, he would have dismissed the highest branch of the legal profession as hopelessly beyond his reach.

"Aye, just so," said his father briskly. "I've given careful consideration to the proposeetion, and I believe ye could do us all credit if ye had the diligence to study for your examinations. I may say that Dr Adam is of the same opinion."

"Is he so?" said Walter, innocently astonished.

"Mind you," his father went on, pausing to shake an admonitory finger at his son, to the amusement of passers-by, "ye'll need to give up yon transcribing that ye've been making a fortune from, and study Civil and Scots Law at the University."

Walter pondered. To submit to his father's decision must mean the end of his easy-going life. But with Tom to be trained for a partnership in the family firm, his apprenticeship must lead only to a dead end, or to similar drudgery among strangers. If his father believed him capable of qualifying for the Bar, he must not disappoint him. "I'd like that fine," he said at last. But he returned to the warren of ancient buildings which made up Edinburgh University, with very mixed feelings.

His father had been at pains to make it clear, before term began, that after three years' study Walter must be prepared to pass his final Trials in Civil and Scots Law before assuming the advocate's gown, adding somewhat tartly that if Walter maintained the attitude of a scapegrace apprentice it would take him all his time to do it. The challenge was just what Walter needed. He was no longer an ailing boy, but a robust and energetic young man, warm-hearted, quick-tempered, utterly unaware of his prodigious gifts which were as yet unfocused by any driving purpose.

Some sort of purpose, however, had been evoked, and Walter re-entered the University with the determination to show his father that he deserved to be taken more seriously than an idling apprentice. And he found the members of Dugald Stewart's class in Moral Philosophy at least as stimulating as their great Professor.

Now he was working daily with old friends such as John Irving and Adam Ferguson, and making many new ones among the students, particularly Irving's kinsman, William Clerk, whose argumentative wit delighted him as much as Adam Ferguson's gaiety; though perhaps Walter's most significant encounter at that time was with the young man who was most temperamentally unlike him, yet on whose judgment and integrity he was throughout his life most to rely, the frail, unathletic William Erskine. They formed a group of brilliant and ambitious young men, whose discussions ranged from the relative merits of the Clubs they joined to the future of the fast-changing world of which they were newly aware.

For the successful revolt of the American colonies and the defiant establishment of the United States of America had touched off a much bloodier rebellion against authority in France, where writers such as Rousseau and Voltaire had for many years been rousing the intellectuals by their diatribes against corruption and incompetence in Church and State which thrived on the ignorance and poverty of the people. The climax came in the spring of that very year, 1789, and its effects were soon lapping the shores of the kingdom across the Channel.

In July, the men of Paris stormed the fortress prison of the Bastille, and in October, as the University's autumn term began, the women of Paris were marching to Versailles to bring the royal family as virtual prisoners to the Tuileries.

Across the Channel the reaction was mixed. The young and romantic followed the lead of poets like Wordsworth and Coleridge in acclaiming the new dawn of freedom and joy. Most of the progressive Whigs approved, though the Prime Minister, Pitt, deferred judgment and said that he watched it as a spectator, and the great statesman, Burke, was against it from the first "in its act, its consequences, and most of all in its example". Fox, on the other hand, gave his lead to the Whigs by describing the fall of the Bastille in no uncertain terms. "How much the greatest event that has happened in the world, and how much the best!"

In University quadrangles, north and south of the Border, the subject could be guaranteed to produce prolonged and violent argument. In Edinburgh it added extra pungency to the students' particular grievance, the long-drawn-out delay in implementing the plans for much-needed University buildings which had been drawn up nearly thirty years before, deferred on account of the American war, and not yet put into effect.

But now, at last, something was to be done. The ceremony for the laying of the foundation stone of the new University was to take place on the 16th of November. All classes were cancelled, the processional route from Parliament House lined with men of the 35th Regiment and the veterans of the City Guard, whose presence caused considerable mirth to former High School boys in the great crowd of jubilant students jostling for vantage points among the already partly demolished buildings nearby.

"Look yonder, Wattie," shouted Adam Ferguson above the

hubbub. "There's the auld gomeril that tried to drag me frae the Potterrow Port by the seat of my breeks yon time when we captured it wi' snowballs."

"Mercy on us, I thought he was in his grave lang syne," Walter shouted back from the ridge of the half-stripped roof to which he had scrambled in spite of a cascade of dislodged tiles. "View Hulloo ... oo ... oo!" he yelled, as the banners appeared in the distance, borne by splendidly dressed officials before the illustrious and reverend procession of the Lord Provost and Magistrates in their robes and chains of office, the Principal and Senate of the University in their gowns, preceded by the University's silver mace, the representatives of all the Masonic lodges, the city's ministers in Geneva gowns and bands and all available noblemen and gentlefolk, while the townsfolk, dressed in their best, crowded the streets or hung out of their windows. Even the students, as instructed, wore sprigs of laurel in their hats.

"So Birnam Wood has come to Dunsinane once more," said Walter from his vantage point. "We'll no' be long now."

In this expectation he was disappointed, for the proceedings began with prayers offered by the ministers in turn, were followed by libations of corn and wine made by Lord Napier with classical elegance, two crystal bottles specially blown in the Glass House of Leith were interred with the stone, one filled with coin of the current year, the other with vellum scrolls inscribed with the history of the University, all with appropriate exhortation and benediction, which began at one o'clock and lasted most of the afternoon. Those who, like Walter, delighted in pageantry and symbolism and were strategically enough placed to see what was going on, enjoyed themselves much more than the majority of spectators who could hear little and see nothing at all.

"It's a fine thing the foundation stone's laid at last," said Will Clerk as Walter scrambled down to join him, "but at this rate I doubt it'll be my grandchildren, not me, that'll first set foot in their braw new hall."

"Havers, man," said Walter cheerfully, landing heavily on the cobbles and looking around for his stick. "After all yon carry-on the walls should fair fly together. If just one stone's laid for every word spoken this day the place should be roofed-in by the time you and I put on our advocates' gowns."

"Aye, mebbe," said John Irving sceptically, "provided there's as many guineas to bring Mr Robert Adam's airy-fine plan down to earth."

"Shame on you, John, for a croaking raven."

"And on you, Wattie, for attending this ceremony looking like a tattie-bogle," said Will Clerk, pulling a silk handkerchief from the tail pocket of his elegant blue coat and fastidiously dusting Walter down with it. "Man, you're a disgrace," he protested, as Walter only grinned and scrubbed some of the rubble off his breeches.

"Look at that coat of yours! It's shapeless as a sack, and your waistcoat's as drab as a wet morning. As for yon corduroys, bagged at the knees and rubbed as bare as – "

"Hout, never fash your thumb at my breeks, Will," said Walter indifferently. "They be good enough for drinking in." He twirled his stick airily and beamed at his critic. "Let's away to the Covenant Close for some oysters; I'm that parched after all yon shouting that I'll need a bumper of claret to wash them down."

Part Two

THE BLOSSOM SETS

Chapter 5

OYSTER taverns, such as Walter's favourite haunt in the Covenant Close, were a feature of student life in Edinburgh, for oysters were local and cheap, and the claret brought ashore at Leith not too hard on young men's pockets. Most of the students' clubs, in which Walter delighted, were nearby, like the Literary Society, which he joined at once, and its inner circle, The Club, to which he was soon elected.

Noise and nicknames were general at these gatherings on Friday evenings in Carrubber's Close. Walter was known as Duns Scotus before he had belonged to The Club a month, on account of his vast store of snippets of learning. Will Clerk, who had distinguished relatives, a witty tongue, and a tendency to give himself airs, was the Baronet, and John Irving, for some reason, Crab. A good deal of wine was drunk, and a great deal of nonsense talked, at their meetings, but the atmosphere was friendly and informal, and Walter soon began to try out his gifts as a public speaker, in spite of his shyness, and Will Clerk's sly teasing about his appearance, good-humouredly enduring the second nickname of "Colonel Grog", because he doggedly continued to appear in his old grogram coat and corduroy breeches.

It was possible, however, to goad even Walter too far, especially when the bottle had been passing round more rapidly than usual, and the violence of the explosion on such occasions was apt to take all those accustomed to his easy-going ways entirely by surprise.

Walter woke on the morning after one such episode with a drumming head, forced down his breakfast, and set off for the University with the impression that the grey buildings about him were wavering on their foundations. But the fresh air presently cleared his brain, and he gave a group of his friends in the quadrangle his usual cheerful greeting.

To his amazement, Will Clerk, standing directly opposite him, merely stared blankly, turned on his heel, and walked away. Walter was astounded. "What in all the world ails the Baronet?" he asked John Irving.

John Irving shook an admonitory finger. "Eh, Wattie, Wattie, when ye get your birse up ye're neither to haud nor bind! D'ye no' mind what ye told the Baronet he could do last night wi' himself and his damned Whig notions?"

"Never a word," said Walter in consternation.

"I'm not surprised," said John Irving frankly. "Ye were fou'."

"Man, was it all that bad?"

John Irving pursed his lips judicially. "It was – regrettable. I'll not deny it."

"I'm obliged to ye, John," said Walter contritely. "I'll have to see what I can dae."

That morning the discourse of the learned professor of Moral Philosophy went unheeded, as Walter, at the back of the lecture hall, pondered, chewed his quill, then briefly scribbled:

"Dear Baronet,

"I am sorry to find that our friend Colonel Grogg has behaved with a very undue degree of vehemence in a dispute with you last night, occasioned by what I am convinced was a gross misconception of your expressions. As the Colonel, though a military man, is not too haughty to acknowledge an error, he has commissioned me to make his apology as a mutual friend, which I am convinced you will accept from yours ever,

Duns Scotus.

Given at Castle Duns, Monday."

"Here, John," said Walter, thrusting the folded note into Irving's hands as the class broke up. "If this doesn't settle the Baronet, I doubt it'll be a question for the choice of weapons."

The shout of laughter with which the note was received brought the greatest relief, not only to Walter, but to all concerned.

One or two clubs, of course, were not enough for Walter. He

loved all gatherings of like-minded people, and his nostalgic memories of the Border country soon sent him round to the unimposing eating-house where the small company of students belonging to the Teviot Club met for supper once a month. Here he was presently accosted by a stout, dapper young man, with the sort of defiant diffidence of a provincial boy recently arrived in a capital city.

"Ye'll no' mind me, likely?" said James Ballantyne.

Walter stared at him blankly for only a moment. The Kelso schoolroom presided over by the incredible dominie, Mr Lancelot Whale, might almost have belonged to another life. But the stout young man who confronted him was not very different from the plump schoolboy who had always had something to eat in his pockets when he slid along the bench at the back of the noisy room to listen to another of Walter's stories. Walter slapped James Ballantyne resoundingly on the back.

"Jamie, ye auld tod, what's brought ye to Edinburgh?"

James Ballantyne spread out his hands in a deprecating gesture. "It's nae doing o' mine, Wattie. I'd have been well pleased to stay down yonder. But my feyther wants me to better myself."

"Fathers aye do that," said Walter, with sympathy.

"He's after turning me into an advocate," said James. "It seems one's needed in Kelso." He looked up at Walter anxiously. "I don't fancy the Law, Wattie. Can ye see me holding forth in Court?"

"Mebbe not," said Walter candidly. "But there's many other ways of making a living besides the Law, Jamie. Ye'll find one soon enough."

"Ye think sae?" said James, helplessly.

"I'm sure on't," said Walter, with rather more conviction than he felt. And James's troubled eyes brightened in grateful appreciation.

The two young men met frequently at the Club for a time. It was a light-hearted, recreational affair, with strong undertones of local associations which kept alive Walter's love of the Border. But their courses at the University did not synchronise, and when James returned to Kelso with only a smattering of legal knowledge, their association lapsed. Walter was rather more than fully occupied, for he had also joined the Speculative Society, a graver and more ambitious organisation than the light-hearted dining and wining student bodies, which appealed to his inquiring, eager spirit, but left such close friends as Will Clerk cold.

"I'm surprised at ye, Willie. You're the very man we need," Walter urged in his first flush of enthusiasm. "The Speculative Society's a serious debating body. Just listen to the topics listed for next session. 'Ought there to be an established religion?' 'Was the putting of Charles the First to death justifiable?' I'll have to say a word on that. 'Should the Slave Trade be abolished?' 'Has the belief in a future state been of advantage to mankind?' Man, ye'd argue the hind leg off Balaam's ass. Why will ye not join us?"

But Will Clerk, engaged with a plateful of oysters, shook his head vehemently. "Wattie, my man, ye dinna ken when ye have a bellyful. My only speculation is on the results of yon examinations. That's work enough. For mercy's sake, man, don't seek to make a labour of our evening's recreation."

Walter sighed, and left it at that. "There's another matter, Willie," he began, rather uncertainly. "It was the Speculative Society that put me in mind of it. Ye were mebbe right to say I could do with a new coat and breeches. Could ye oblige me with the name of your tailor?"

Will Clerk surveyed his obviously embarrassed friend with a quizzical grin. "So the Speculative Society's the reason for this sudden interest in new braws? Never in this world. Who's the lassie?"

Walter drew himself up, considered evasive tactics, then capitulated. He could, after all, do with a friend's advice. "I am speaking, Will," he said, deliberately bombastic, "of no mere lassie, but of a lady, a Lady in a Green Mantle. I've but seen her the once, outside Greyfriars Kirk in the rain."

"It's to be hoped you're sufficiently up with the times to possess an umbrella."

Walter nodded. But he now seemed plunged in gloom.

"Then cheer up, man. And keep on with your kirk attendance."

"I've never seen her at Greyfriars since. She's away to the country with her parents."

"And just as well, maybe, with the Trials coming on. You'd best keep your mind on your books till they're over. By then, as like as not you'll have forgotten about her, Green Mantle and all."

"Never, Willie. Never!" said Walter vehemently.

But his first encounter with his new love had been brief, and the next session at the University was sufficiently exacting, with an examination on Civil Law at the end of the year, to prevent his emotions from being too deeply involved. He and Will Clerk had already entered into a working partnership, studying together at one or other of their homes when there were no lectures to attend.

Their contrasting methods of study were characteristic. Walter set himself, with dogged determination, to hack his way through the almost impenetrable jungle of legal technicology, and was well served by his fantastic memory. But Will Clerk would skim above it with apparently effortless ease, dipping down every now and then to select the necessary information with a precision which delighted Walter as much as Will's indolence exasperated him.

But Walter had his own gifts. Enthralled by the course in Scots Law given to third year students by David Hume, nephew of the great philosopher, he only took brief notes at the time, but afterwards transcribed the lectures in full, to Will's astonishment, and had the whole transcript bound up for presentation to his father.

"I thought you'd be interested to see I'd not been idle," he said, as he laid the handsome volumes on his father's desk.

Mr Scott received them with surprise and pleasure.

"Wattie, my lad," he said, as he leafed through the clearly written, arduous pages, "this is a bonny work. Verbatim, I'd say. Aye, aye, these lectures will make very pleasant reading for my leisure hours."

"I hoped mebbe they would," Walter said.

Mr Scott sat down at his desk, caressing the handsome binding of his son's gift with his gnarled, rheumatic hands, a thin smile just lifting the corners of his habitually stern mouth. "Aye, a most opportune exercise, lad. For time's getting on. It'll no' be many months now afore ye come up for the Trials. Ye'll be doing us credit, I'm hoping."

"Aye, Father."

"Ye'll be bearing in mind that there's a thesis ye'll be expected to present to their lordships of Council and Session and the Advocates Faculty."

"I've made a start already, sir."

"Fine, fine. And what's the subject, lad?"

"*De Cadaveribus Damnatorum*," Walter said boldly. "Concerning the Disposal of the Bodies of Criminals."

"I have not yet forgotten my Latin," said Mr Scott dryly. "Ihmhm, it's an awful queer-like topic for a lad to choose."

"There's some fine stuff in some of the ancient writers," said Walter eagerly. "I propose to call evidence from the elder Pliny, Macrobius, Marianus Capella . . ."

Mr Scott gave one of his rare chuckles. "Gang your ain gait, lad. Ye ken what ye're about, and I'll not be the one to keep ye from your work, with the ordeal that's shortly afore ye. Are ye well up in your texts, sound on the *Institutes* and *Decisions*?" The note of anxiety in his voice made Walter realise, for the first time, just how ardently his apparently unemotional father longed for his success.

"I'll have every book in the syllabus at my finger ends by the 6th of July," he promised gravely.

"Good lad, good lad. It'll be a mercy when it's safely past. Away wi' ye now," said Mr Scott, reaching for his reading glasses.

The final trials for admission to the Faculty of Advocates consisted only of those on Scots Law, for Walter and Will Clerk had put their Civil Law trials behind them with credit the summer before, and when the day of decision came, Walter's only anxiety was that Will Clerk might have overslept. But he presented himself at the last moment, casual and elegant as ever, brushing a speck of dust off his coat sleeve as they entered the Law Courts together, raising an eyebrow at Walter's rumpled hair and clumsily folded neckcloth, wishing him good fortune with a wink and a dig in the ribs as they parted to face their respective examiners.

They had not long to wait for their results. Both had passed with credit and were authorised to assume the gown on the day before the Courts rose for the summer vacation. Walter turned from the notice board with a profound sigh of relief that set the papers fluttering.

"Aye, Will, it'll be me for the Borders the next morning."

"Hout, man, take your time. We'll have to give a bit chack of dinner to all and sundry first. D'ye think your father would come?"

"Mebbe," said Walter cautiously, "since it's a kinda special occasion. Then there's the Professors . . ."

The momentous day of triumph had its lighter side, for when the two new advocates had strolled self-consciously about the Outer House among their fellow advocates for some time, Walter gathered the stiff bombazine folds of his new gown about him, and imitated the high giggle of one of the servant lasses waiting at the Mercat Cross to be hired for casual labour.

"We've stood here an hour by the Tron, hinny," he told Will Clerk in a high falsetto, "and de'il a ane has speired our price."

"Hout, lass, that'll never dae," said an amused solicitor who had been within hearing. "I've got a wee commission that'll be worth a guinea."

Walter was in a high state of jubilation as they set off down the High Street together when the Courts rose at last. For three years' hard work was behind him, his father was happy, and he was off to the Border in the morning. He kept Will Clerk laughing as he talked without stopping, any nonsense which came into his head.

"This is a sort of wedding-day, Willie," he proclaimed, stopping suddenly outside an outfitter's shop. "I must go and buy me a new nightcap."

At last they reached the tavern where the dinner-party was to take place. Outside it their friends were already gathering to greet them in the late afternoon sunshine, and in the distance Walter could see his father's trim, spare figure, upright as the gold-headed cane he carried, in his snuff brown coloured cloth suit, bob wig, cocked hat and silver-buckled shoes; arriving at the scene of the evening's entertainment as punctually as he arrived at Parliament House each morning.

It was a triumphant occasion, to which Mr Scott, winkled out of his habitual austerity, contributed a number of dry jokes which convulsed the younger members of the company and made his contemporaries raise their eyebrows and chuckle. Healths were drunk, songs sung, and the company dispersed at a decorously early hour in a roseate glow of nostalgic cordiality. But next morning Walter rose early enough to catch the coach for the Border country, as eagerly as a tethered hound who feels the chain snap behind him.

At Kelso he received congratulations from his kinsfolk, changed into old clothes, inquired anxiously after the welfare of the horses on which he and his Uncle Robert had already made so many successful excursions, and urgently planned others. Within hours of arrival, he was soaked to the skin as he fell in and out of the Tweed, fishing-rod in hand. Here he and Jessie had wandered, hand-in-hand, but that dream had died and Walter, the newly emancipated young advocate, rejoicing in robust health, was almost another person from the boy who had written his first love poems in the rapture of newly recovered hope. He and Jessie had in fact met again during the intervening years, quite unexpectedly as far as Walter was concerned, in Edinburgh, to their mutual disillusionment. The dream was dead, and Walter was unaware of its ghost as he rode into Northumberland with his uncle, stood sorrowfully on Flodden Field, got lost among the Cheviot Hills, and pondered the scene of the victory of the Yorkist faction over the forces of the Red Rose near Hexham.

Even his thoughts of Williamina, the Lady of the Green Mantle, could not come between him and the joys of liberation from years of concentrated mental effort. He wrote importantly to "William Clerk, Advocate", at the familiar Princes Street address, about the delights of duck shooting, fishing, long expeditions on horseback and on foot, adding philosophically, "I have no prospects of seeing my *chère adorable* till winter, if then." Meanwhile, it was obvious that he had no intention of sitting about and mourning. In Jedburgh, he had encountered a former acquaintance, Charles Kerr of Abbotrule, and after inquiries and congratulations on his appointment to the Bar, came the inevitable question as to what Walter meant to do next.

"See something of the countryside, afore I start trailing the skirts of my gown round the Outer House," said Walter. "I've a great wish to know more of Liddesdale. It's a wild and trackless place, even yet, they tell me, but I've read so much about its moss troopers and its ballads that I'd like fine to see the place for myself. Hermitage, now, yon ancient great castle o' the Douglas folk, is yonder some bit. But it's strange country to me. I've never an idea of how to set about finding it."

"Hout, man, that's easy work. I can present ye to the very man ye need. Robert Shortreed's a kinsman of mine, and Sheriff-substitute of Roxburghshire forby."

So Walter was presented to Mr Shortreed, a shrewd sturdy man, with a love of open-air exercise and a great knowledge of the Border countryside. He took a fancy to the broad-shouldered, thoughtful young man with the charmingly candid smile, and was glad to be able to help him.

"Mr Scott, it's high time I revisited Liddesdale. And the country-side looks its best in September. I suggest you find yourself a good sound nag and meet me at Abbotrule in a couple of days' time with what you need for a fortnight's hard riding in your knapsack. I'll show you the way about a valley that's seen more history made and better songs sung than any other I know."

"There's nothing I'd like better, sir," Walter said.

So at the time appointed they set forth, to ride between the rolling Border hills, honey-coloured in the crisp autumnal weather which turned the bracken to gold and flame on the high-shouldered, roadless passes, following the green tracks that meandered beside the peat-coloured burns, past remote farmsteads where the rowan trees planted against witchcraft were hung with brilliant berries and the shorn sheep cried forlornly on the out-by pastures. The sheriff knew every farm, shepherd's bothy and manse in the valley. There were no inns, no villages, but in every homestead they received as courteous a welcome as if they had been visiting royalty. Now and again Mr Shortreed, who enjoyed his joke, caused some alarm to one of his hosts, who might have been guilty of contravening the law over some trivial matter, by indicating the silent, observant Walter, and murmuring:

"Wheesht, man. Yonder's an advocate frae Edinburgh."

But the sight of Walter, leading his own horse to the stable amid the acclamation of the farm dogs, in the most informal manner imaginable, usually quieted the goodman's fears for the fate of the recently arrived keg of brandy, which had not paid the customary excise dues.

And Walter himself was so delighted with everybody, so comical in his appreciation of his own ignorance, so anxious to hear the stories they had to tell, the songs they had to sing, that every company of farmers and farm-workers, spinsters and dairy-maids, shepherds, hinds, and even the ganging-about bodies with their packs, accepted him as one of themselves. He sat in a corner of many farm-kitchens, listening, scribbling, learning. He laughed at the jokes and joined tunelessly in the songs. He drank, too much occasionally, but always with the air of a gentleman, those about him said. And he enjoyed himself, perhaps, more than he had ever done in his life.

From his early childhood he had responded instinctively to every song and story which illuminated his country's heroic past. Now he was able to feel the very texture of that past, as it were between finger and thumb, since it was preserved in that remote valley from the contamination of a rapidly changing world. It was an unforgettable, intoxicating experience, which he was to repeat during the next seven years again and again, till the impact of the Border country became indelible, outwearing vigour and reason, to comfort him at the darkly shadowed end of his days.

His kindly mentor approvingly watched the young man shed his recently gained Edinburgh sophistication to become the lighthearted companion of every farmer and shepherd, personally caring for his horse as they cared for theirs, adored by every hound and terrier, mothered by the sturdy farmers' wives, shyly admired by barefoot bairns and sunburned dairy-maids. He was lame, admittedly, but that was of no consequence in a young man who rode the hills and forded the burns as fearlessly as they did themselves. They knew the legend of his heroic ancestor, Willie wi' the Bolt-Foot, as well as he did.

So the travellers went about Liddesdale, from one kindly homestead to another, guided here and there by reports of ballads to be heard at some remote fireside. At Milburnholm Willie Elliot and his horde of short-legged, long-bodied terriers of the Pepper, Salt and Mustard tribe made them most welcome, at the remote hill farm of Twislehope, Auld Thomas o' Twislehope played the melody of *Dick o' the Cow*, on his Border pipe. They drank smuggled brandy from the Solway, picked up precious trophies such as the ancient Border war horn discovered at Hermitage Castle, visited the historic homesteads of Eliots and Armstrongs at Larriston and Whithaugh, Shaws and Redheuch.

At last, when the October gales were whipping the vivid leaves from rowan and birch and the dusty tracks had turned heavy with the autumn rains, Walter reluctantly agreed to turn homewards. So they rode out of Liddesdale, past the grey cottages with their thatch renewed against the winter, the peat stacks built high against the lee wall. In Kelso, Walter saw his horse into winter quarters, said goodbye to his relations, and climbed to an outside seat on the Edinburgh coach with the words of a score of ballads jostling in his brain, the sound of the soft Border voices singing in his ears.

And in November, as the autumn session at the Law Courts began, he accompanied his father from George's Square to Parliament House, where the Writer to the Signet bade his son a formal farewell as he set off in the direction of his office, and Walter joined the light-hearted company of young advocates gathered round the great iron stove in the Outer House, amusing themselves as best they might in the long intervals between picking up a few small fees.

From the first, Walter's flair for storytelling, with his droll use of the lowland Scots which even Judges still used on occasion, and from the Bench, tickled his audience. And his unerring knack of dramatising brought the young men crowding round him to listen to the anecdotes which he seemed to collect as haphazardly as a squirrel to store, unlabelled, in his fantastic memory. Sometimes other storytellers protested.

"Hey, Duns Scotus," Will Clerk objected one morning, "that's my story you're telling. You only had it from me last night and you've turned it inside out this morning."

Walter did not attempt to deny it. Instead, he put an arm round his friend's shoulders with his most engaging smile, nodding to his audience, as he mildly parried the accusation.

"That's aye the way with the Baronet, gentlemen. He says I turn his stories inside out, but all I do is to put a cocked hat on their heads and a cane in their hands, to make them fit for company."

"Wattie, my lad, ye should go far in your career of prevarication," Will Clerk said wryly.

Someone had nicknamed the company of impecunious young advocates, with their high ideals and distaste for authority, the Montagnards, after the ardent young Left-wingers of the first hopeful years of the French Revolution, and the epithet had stuck, even after that "glorious dawn" which had so inspired Wordsworth had darkened to a scene of blood and violence before which even the romantic poets fell silent. For King Louis's desperate attempt to escape from France during the summer of 1791 had put an end to all hope of success for moderate reforms and finally discredited the monarchy. After his recapture the anarchists took over, and the storming of the Tuileries Palace in August was followed by the horrifying September massacres and the establishment of a French Republic.

The headlong progress of events was now the chief topic in all the European capitals, for France's new leaders had declared themselves ready to help any nation which rose against its oppressors. The significance of this was obvious to every monarch, and even the young Montagnards of the Outer House in Edinburgh gave the probable consequences some share of their attention.

"The contagion will spread, I doubt," said William Erskine, an erudite, sensitive young man who was to become Walter's closest friend. Their attraction was one of opposites, for though Will Erskine shared all Walter's passion for literature, he recoiled in horror from all violence, and shuddered even at the idea of sharing Walter's wilder athletic exploits.

"Why should the French contagion spread? Surely our folk have mair sense," said Walter stoutly.

"There have already been riots in Dundee. And elsewhere. In Sheffield, I believe," Will Erskine pointed out.

"Hout, never fash yourself for that," said Walter disdainfully. "Just a few idle loons that need a lesson."

"So do some of their masters," broke in Will Clerk, who was already as convinced a Whig as Walter was a Tory.

"Ye've only to look at the course of history, Baronet – "

"That may be so, Duns Scotus, but the course of history can change as well as that of a river. The folk that won't admit that will drown."

"In their own blood," said William Erskine fearfully.

"I'll admit," Walter said, "I'd never have believed France could go to such extremes. But maybe the pace will slow down now they can compel all the reforms they've been after."

"Why should it slow down?" asked Will Clerk dramatically. "They've been banging away at the dam till it's burst. Now who's to say who can control the waters?"

"What's that got to do with us?" someone retorted.

"Gentlemen, gentleman," bleated the elderly official who had been vainly trying to make himself heard for some time, "will Messrs Erskine, Clerk and Scott kindly present themselves in the High Court."

"Guid cess to the lot o' ye," shouted the rest of the company. "If the fees come to mair than five guineas, spare a thought for your lesser brethren."

"That puts me in mind of a story . . ." someone began. And as Walter and his friends strode importantly across the stone-flagged expanse, gathering their gowns about them against the December chill, the irrepressible laughter of their fellow aspirants defied the portents of the darkening year, with the confident conviction of the young that the next must surely bring better things.

But in January, 1793, Louis XVI was guillotined, and in February

Pitt could hold the nation's indignation back no longer. In February Great Britain declared war on France.

Montagnards of the Parliament House perversely flung themselves with enthusiasm into the study of German literature. For during the year in which France became an enemy, and Prussia an ally in the war against her, a German doctor named Willich, practising medicine in Edinburgh, began to hold classes on his own language and literature. Montagnards joined in a body, anxious to learn enough of the language to be able to appreciate the works of such men of genius as Goethe and Schiller, distracting their teacher by their impatient mirth at the pious mediocrity of the easier texts he prescribed. Walter, in particular, with his inspired guesses and headlong blunders, reduced the painstaking Teutonic doctor to despair.

"Ach, Mr Scott," he burst out, "never will you succeed, while you seek to build ze top storey without laying a foundation. Grammar, alas, you despise."

"Doctor, if I were to read no German literature till I'd mastered the grammar, I'd be spending my life in the basement," Walter protested. "I'm no' that gleg with our ain," he admitted, in a gale of laughter.

Eventually the class was allowed to divide into groups to study the branch of German literature which appealed to them most, after undertaking to submit to enough grammatical instruction to equip themselves for it. Characteristically, Walter chose the German Romantic tradition. So did Will Clerk and William Erskine, who laughed at some of Walter's blunders, but admitted that he had the knack of catching the violence and passion of the greatest German romantic verse.

"Aweel, ye see, the lad's in love himsel'," Will Clerk whispered slyly. And Walter made no attempt to deny it. His first encounter with the Lady in the Green Mantle in the doorway of Old Greyfriars Kirk had led to further meetings on her family's return to Edinburgh. Mrs Scott was a distant connection of the girl's mother, Lady Jane Belsches, and the families were on calling terms. Williamina Belsches was, at fifteen, just back from finishing school pretty, and pleased by the obvious admiration of the big, good-looking young man, who was such an attentive escort. She smiled decorously, as she had been taught to smile at all eligible young men of good family, and Lady Jane received him graciously, reassured by the knowledge that his father was a Writer to the Signet, his mother the descendant of the Rutherfords and Swintons of that ilk, and he himself already an advocate and entitled on that account to call himself a gentleman, as were the officers of his Majesty's forces. Had he been a mere medical student or his family contaminated by any association with trade, it would have been a very different matter. She could rest assured that there was no such contamination, since no young man with commercial associations would ever have been called to the Bar.

Walter was, of course, marginally aware of these niceties. But they mattered nothing by comparison with Williamina's Dresden-china prettiness, the flicker of long-lashed eyelids that revealed such a flash of blue, brown ringlets bobbing forward as she bent her head to hide a flush of pleasure at his compliments. It was a matter of some surprise to him that so lovely a young lady would some-times actually prefer to sit out a dance with him than take the floor with his surer-footed rivals. And Williamina, much flattered by the verses he composed in her honour, ventured to show him her own, not entirely unsuccessful attempts. Walter, enchanted to discover that this lovely creature seemed also a citizen of his own inner world, praised them with the bemused enthusiasm of a young man who has fallen headlong in love. Among the Montagnards his romance was now an open secret, and when Walter joined his friends of an evening at such favourite haunts as Fortune's or Walker's, his first toast was always to the Lady of the Green Mantle.

By now, however, his father had become aware that his sons were not devoting all their attention to legal matters. He had been much exasperated by young Tom's enthusiasm for the Edinburgh Volunteers, a company just formed to be used against invasion from France or riots at home. As a tall and athletic young man of twenty, Tom was determined to join the Grenadiers, an exclusive company consisting only of men over six feet, with an elegant uniform and high standards of performance.

"And how's your work in the office to be done, may I ask, when you're drilling all day?" his father demanded, as Tom let his dinner get cold while he talked of his new plans.

Tom ran his fingers through his fair hair and hastened to reassure him. "I'll be at the office as usual, Father. We're all professional men in the Grenadiers. We'll hae to drill in the evenings."

"And where will your mind be, I'd like to ken?"

"On my work, sir, as ever," Tom promised, with his most disarming grin.

"Ihmhm. Mebbe aye and mebbe heuch aye," said Mr Scott unbelievingly. "It's a mercy Walter's no' likely to take up yon caper, at least," he added. But Walter, who had already found the role of spectator more than he could bear, broke in disconcertingly.

"I ken Tom's Grenadiers have nae use for lamiters, Father. But what's to hinder us from forming a regiment of volunteer cavalry? Such a mobile force will surely be needed in emergency. I've spoken to a couple of dozen active fellows already, and they're all of my mind."

"Well done you," said young Tom admiringly. "But you'll need horses, surely?"

"There's a letter in the post to Uncle Robert," Walter said, "asking him to look out for a strong gelding, such as would suit a stalwart dragoon . . ."

"And who's to pay for the beast, may I ask?" said his father dryly.

"I'll sell my collection of Scottish coins to buy him," said Walter stoutly. Across the table Anne dropped her spoon to clap her hands, while Mrs Scott smiled proudly at her warlike sons.

"Eh, bairns, bairns," she chuckled, "we'll sleep sounder in our beds for knowing we've got such defenders."

But Mr Scott took his head in his hands and groaned. "What between grenadiers and cavalrymen, wha's like to be left to carry out the laws of the land?"

The infantry branch of the Edinburgh Volunteer movement prospered, and, in spite of his promises, Tom took more time off work, as enthusiasm mounted, than he had intended. He meant to do his best for the family firm, for he had sense enough to know that it offered him the best chance of earning a living he was likely to get. But he was neither brilliant nor hard-working, and his father, uneasily aware that his own health was beginning to fail, was often at his wits' end as he tried to drum into him at least the rudiments of his profession.

Fortunately, perhaps, the cavalry project lapsed for a time, though Walter continued to raise supporters for it. But he had, just then, too much on his mind. For his personal affairs were now teetering between hope and despair. His friends did all they could to help him, advising first one course of action and then another, as Walter seesawed between his anxiety to put matters to the test by making Williamina a definite proposal of marriage, and his longing to enjoy his dream world in which all things seemed possible.

But he still had no notion of sitting idle at his lady's feet. More work was coming his way at the Law Courts, and he bought his mother a silver taper-stand with his first sizeable fee. As usual, whenever the Courts rose, he made for the country, eagerly repeating his raids on Liddesdale; listening, scribbling and learning more about the songs and ballads of the Scottish Border. He went north, too, visiting the homes of his colleagues of the Mountain in Perthshire, Stirlingshire and elsewhere with Adam Ferguson or Will Clerk, spending an eerie night alone in a remote bedchamber in legend-haunted Glamis.

His enthusiasm for German romantic literature, deepened by his own romance, had been given a new turn that summer by the flamboyant success of the German readings given in Edinburgh by Mrs Barbauld from the ballads of the poet Bürger. Walter was able to get a copy of the original of *Lenore* from the German-born wife newly married by his kinsman, Hugh Scott of Harden, who was amused and delighted by Walter's enthusiasm for her native language. And Walter, who revered Scott of Harden as the immediate head of the family, meekly accepted his charming young wife's corrections of his spelling and grammar as well as his German, and was much elated by her praise.

But it was Jane Cranstoun, sister of his friend George, another Montagnard, who suggested the next step. Like Mary Erskine, Will's sister, she knew all about Williamina, and was determined that Walter should be properly appreciated.

"Walter," she said unexpectedly, during a supper party with the Erskines, "what about that German ballad you've been so taken with? *Lenore*, I mean. Why don't you translate it for Williamina? I'm sure you'd do it beautifully. It'd surely catch her fancy."

Walter looked at her in surprise. "Mebbe . . . mebbe I could," he said.

Jane Cranstoun clapped her hands. "Away home with you, then, and start."

The idea caught Walter's fancy. Once started, he could not rest. He worked all night and brought the completed translation to Jane Cranstoun next morning. She was amazed by its felicity.

"Why, Walter, you're going to be a poet!"

"Tuts, havers!" said Walter, highly delighted.

"Something between Burns and Gray, I'd think. Don't shake your head at me. You've always been too modest. Hark to me, we'll have this printed. Can you do any more? It's a wee bit on the thin side on its own."

So Walter translated another of Bürger's eerie ballads which specially appealed to him, with its shuddering sense of the supernatural, which had always meant so much more to him than the utilitarian righteousness of his father's dreary creed. And both *Lenore* and *The Wild Huntsman* went off to be printed. A specially bound, de luxe version was commissioned for Williamina, with others distributed among his friends. But by now Walter had worked himself up into such a state of anxiety that he could endure the uncertainty of his position no longer. Before the book was ready, he wrote to Williamina, making her a proposal of marriage.

Williamina replied, from the family's country house at Fettercairn in Kincardineshire. But her answer got him very little further, for she wrote so sweetly and yet so indefinitely that he could make what he liked of her ambiguities. She wished him to know how deeply she had been touched by his feeling for her, recalled with pleasure all their meetings and the understanding he had shown of her attempts to express so much that she scarcely knew how to put into words. But she implored him to be prudent and consider their youth and inexperience, begged him to believe her his true friend, urged him to do nothing hasty, but to wait for better times.

No one in his senses could suppose that she had accepted his proposal. But she could not be said to have refused it, either. Walter, who had been obsessed by the idea of his unworthiness, read the letter a second time, broke down and wept with relief.

Later, reading the letter for about the tenth time, he was assailed by doubts. Was he being vainglorious, reading into it reasons for hope which did not exist? He sent the letter off to Will Clerk, who had been the first to guess his secret, begging him to say what he thought Williamina really meant. And Will Clerk, who was too fond of Walter to bear to daunt him, and was quite uncertain himself of what the letter meant, could only write back to say that the general trend of the letter was both flattering and favourable, and he suggested that Walter should do just as she suggested, and wait for better times.

Walter waited. And remained none the wiser. But in the spring, when he set off for Aberdeen to attend the circuit courts there, the specially bound volume was in his saddle-bag. For, by a slight stretch of the imagination, Fettercairn could be said to be not too far out of his way, and he planned to present himself there on his way back, having shaken off his exuberant friends.

His letter requesting permission to call at Fettercairn on his return journey produced an invitation at least, and Walter rode south in a very different frame of mind.

Lady Jane greeted him with what seemed all her usual friendly courtesy, but her first words sounded a warning note.

"Williamina will be pleased to see you, Mr Scott, I am sure. But I must ask you not to fatigue her with too much of your most interesting conversation. She has not been well – "

"I am distressed to hear it. Would it be better if I did not trouble her at present?" Walter hesitated, then forced himself to add: "Perhaps I should go away."

"Not at all, not at all, Mr Scott," said Lady Jane calmly. "It will do her good to meet an old friend again. But broach no troublesome topics, I beg, such as the distressing state of affairs in Europe – or nearer home, indeed. Try and persuade her to walk about the grounds and show you the improvements we are making. She needs fresh air and gentle exercise."

"It will be a pleasure to escort her," Walter earnestly declared.

So the few days he spent at Fettercairn produced no revelations of Williamina's inner state of mind, though she certainly seemed glad to see him, to be able to read him her latest verses and take him to see the topiary work with which the gardeners had been diversifying the yew hedges, the new sundial, and the extension of the stableyard. Walter began to feel that he had some reason for hope. Surely she was enjoying the pleasant walks about the policies as much as he was? Admittedly, she was apt to excuse herself more often than he remembered, on account of fatigue, and retire to her room to rest. And Lady Jane seemed to guess intuitively the moment when an ardent inquiry was about to burst from him, in spite of all good resolutions, and pleasantly intervene to suggest some little task for Williamina while she entertained Walter herself.

But to have seen Williamina, to have been able to present his tastefully bound volume, to hear her exclamations of pleasure and admiration, made up for everything else. When he reluctantly made his farewells, and rode south to attend the opening of the summer session of the Edinburgh Law Courts, he was full of hope again, though had he analysed his reasons for his change of mood, he might have admitted that they did not amount to very much.

However, Walter was not given to self-analysis. And he cherished happy memories as he rejoined the Montagnards in the Outer House, capping their stories, as usual, with better ones, sending them into gales of laughter with his caricatures of legal dignitaries at Aberdeen. But there was something about him in spite of his gaiety, which the old folk of the north would uneasily have called "fey".

Among the older men, the mood in the city was generally troubled. The war in Europe was going very badly indeed. Revolutionary France had overrun the Netherlands and captured the Dutch fleet. The First Coalition of European Powers had disintegrated. Prussia had retired from it and Spain actually allied herself with France, where the name of Napoleon had recently been heard. That very year, 1796, he had been made Commander-in-Chief of the French army in Italy at only twenty-six, and in a whirlwind campaign he invaded Piedmont, defeated the King of Sardinia and drove the Austrians out of Italy in a brilliant series of victories before advancing towards Vienna itself.

Great Britain now stood alone, with a half-trained, incompetent army, appallingly inadequate artillery and wretchedly insufficient hospitals and medical supplies. Talk began to be heard, not only of defeat, but of invasion, mutiny and rioting at home. In Edinburgh the Volunteers were being joined by numbers of young men who gave all their free time to drill and musketry practice. Tom, of course, gave more time than his father's legal practice could spare, leaving the old clerk to supervise the work while he drilled new recruits. Mr Scott was in no position to protest, for his wife's fears for his state of health had proved only too well justified, and his first paralytic stroke had left him bedridden, irritable and incoherent.

John was overseas with his regiment, and Walter was prepared to do everything which the eldest son at home could do for his mother. But Mrs Scott, serene and steadfast as ever, insisted that his first consideration remained his work at the Bar.

"That would be what your father would wish," she assured him. And, as the old man's illness dragged on, his family came to take his wasted form, his incoherent speech and random gestures as part of the background of their lives, which their mother decreed should go on as usual.

Walter worried uneasily about his father's legal practice, now under Tom's haphazard control. But Tom made light of his anxiety.

"My dear fellow, leave it all to old Thomas Grierson. He knows more about our business than you or I could learn in a lifetime, ye can depend upon it. And I make sure of cheering the old boy on with my praise and admiration between the demands of his

Majesty's Volunteer Dragoons. How's yon business of the cavalry force that ye were so set on going these days?"

"Well, I believe," Walter said. "I'm hoping to offer our services to his Grace of Buccleuch as soon as I have sufficient stout fellows prepared to provide their horses and uniforms in the service of their country in any emergency."

"We may well need them, if this country's affairs go on from bad to worse overseas," Tom said solemnly.

Walter let himself hope throughout the summer. But his friends were uneasily aware of treacherous undercurrents. By September, one of the Montagnards was writing to another: "William Forbes marries Miss Belsches. This is not good news. I always dreaded there was some self-deception on the part of our romantic friend and I shudder at the violence of his irritable and most ungovernable mind . . ."

The news appalled his friends. There was anxious talk of duels, even of possible suicide, when the truth was out. They should have known him better, with his sudden firework rages over superficial matters, and the fundamental fortitude with which he received near-mortal wounds.

The news reached Walter, as such news often reaches the person liable to be most stricken by it, only after it had become an item of gossip among those less concerned. One evening in October, as he sat in a favourite tavern, eating oysters and drinking claret with half a dozen friends, the voice of a stranger at a nearby table happened to dominate a pause in the general hubbub.

"So the Belsches lassie is to marry young William Forbes, I hear? He's dune well for himself, I'd say. But by all accounts she might have done better."

The empty glass in Walter's hands crushed into fragments in his sudden, convulsive grip, and he sat staring stupidly at the slash of crimson seeping between his fingers. Then he fumbled for a handkerchief and twisted it round the wound, unaware of the stunned silence about him, the murmurs of compunction from his friends. In his frozen wilderness no living thing moved, no sound broke the hollow silence.

Someone put another glass before him. Automatically, he nodded his thanks, moved his roughly bandaged fingers towards it, the familiar toast almost on his lips. Then, very quietly, he set it down again, reached for his stick, and limped through the smoky haze of the low-ceilinged parlour towards the door and the tonic chill of the autumnal darkness beyond.

Chapter 6

THE former harness room overlooking the mews, rented from a well-known livery stables to the recently formed volunteer corps of Royal Edinburgh Light Dragoons, was in a state of considerable confusion. Blue uniform coats and white buckskin breeches lay about in heaps, sabres were stacked in corners, helmets rolled on the wooden floor with bundles of bedding and assorted pairs of riding boots.

At the trestle table in front of the small cobwebbed window Walter sat in his shirt-sleeves, his short hair on end, struggling with the lists of equipment which each man must take to camp. Dismissing, as ever, the problems of doing at least three things at once, he had accepted the posts of Paymaster, Secretary and Quartermaster to the regiment now being recruited, against the threat of French invasion, from the ranks of young professional men like himself under the active patronage of the Duke of Buccleuch, head of the great Border family to which he belonged.

The project had come at a time when Walter needed it most. For in January Williamina had married her young banker, William Forbes, and he had wakened from his dream to the iron-grey reality of an Edinburgh winter's morning. Characteristically, he wasted no time on self-pity, but added the new enterprise to his attendance at the Law Courts, his translation of German poems, and his interest in the Club and the Speculative Society. His enthusiasm for the Volunteers infected some of his more athletic friends such as James Skene and Adam Ferguson. But Will Clerk, indolent as ever, would have none of it. William Erskine, who never mounted a horse if he could possibly avoid it, shuddered at Walter's accounts of drills and cavalry charges on Portobello sands, and both of them did everything they could to distract him from his duties on such fine Saturday mornings as the present. Walter marked the place on his list with a heavy ruler and toiled on, ignoring the sound of voices below the window from the cobbled mews outside.

"Where the deuce has the fellow got to?" Will Clerk demanded loudly. "There's never a soul about. The very horses scarcely take the trouble to turn aside from their hay-racks. Fine looking animals, I must admit. Eh, Erskine?"

"No doubt, no doubt," said Will Erskine uneasily. "I trust the stable-doors are well secured. That big black has a most uneasily roving eye."

Will Clerk laughed, then read the name painted over the loose-box door. " 'Lenore'. By Gad, that's Walter's very charger, named for the German lass in Bürger's poem."

William Erskine turned his back on the big black horse. "I came to seek Walter, not his monstrous beast. Hah! I see him up yonder at the window . . ."

Walter scribbled doggedly on, muttering the items aloud to exclude the mocking voices. "The portmanteau is to contain the following articles: 2 shirts, 1 black handkerchief, 1 nightcap, woollen, 1 pair pantaloons, blue, 1 flannel shirt with sleeves, 1 pair flannel drawers, 1 waistcoat, 1 pair worsted stockings or socks . . ."

"Come away, man," shouted Will Erskine. "We know what you're about. Leave that monstrous drudgery and come for a walk on the Pentlands . . ."

"In the slip," murmured Walter, "in cover of portmanteau, a case with shaving things, combs and a knife, fork and spoon . . ."

"I might perhaps throw a stone at the window," said Will Clerk from below.

Walter raised his voice slightly. ". . . curry-comb, brush and mane-comb, with sponge. Over the portmanteau, the blue overalls and a spare jacket for stable; a small horse-sheet to cover the horse's back with, and a spare girth or two . . ."

"Walter, I found the finest collection of German ballads you could wish to see in that bookshop in the High Street you know of . . ."

"The horse-sheet may be conveniently folded below the saddle, and will save the back on a large march or bad weather."

"Walter," said Will Clerk dramatically, "never would I have believed you'd give your old friends the go-by to list hoof-picks and horse-sheets for a few old nags."

Walter sighed, swore, and gave up the struggle. He limped round the table and threw up the window to shake a fist at the laughing figures below.

"I give nobody the go-by as you very well ken. But we go into camp in a fortnight, and unless my lists are complete . . ."

"I suppose the world will come to an end?"

Will Erskine grinned impishly and struck a heroic attitude. "Draw your swords – by single files to the right of front – to the left – wheel!" he improvised. "Charge! I wager ye ken little more of wheels and charges, Wattie man, than I ken of the wheels of Ezekiel!"

But Will Clerk, who had not studied for three years with Walter for nothing, snapped his fingers at him and turned away. "You might as well save your breath to cool your porridge, Erskine. Once Wattie's set on a task, neither hell nor high water's like to stop him till it's done. Ye'll be at the Club tonight, though, Wattie?"

"I will that," Walter promised and slammed the rickety window.

In spite of the scepticism of young intellectuals such as Will Clerk, and the inclination to leave wars to the regular army, the country's position in 1797 was serious enough to justify such patriotically minded noblemen as the Duke of Buccleuch in the formation of volunteer forces for use in the event of invasion.

Even the British Navy was in a perilous state, and the climax came with a mutiny at Spithead, which might have ended disastrously but for the intervention of "Black Dick," as Lord Howe, the commander-in-chief, had been nicknamed by his men. The men's claims were heard, reforms promised, and the red flag of revolution hauled down, just as another name began to be heard after the victories of St Vincent and Camperdown. Nelson, still only a Rear-Admiral, was already preparing to challenge Napoleon, and the check to revolutionary principles achieved by the settlement of the Spithead mutiny meant at least that he would have a navy to command. Even so, the future still hung ominously in the balance, and the gravity of the situation was increased by the inevitable crop of rumours.

But recruiting for the Light Dragoons went well, and Walter was busier than he had ever been in his life. The regiment went into camp at Musselburgh during the spring recess, and Walter, with his great black charger, Lenore, won the astonished admiration of those who had only seen him limping awkwardly along the cobbled streets on his way to the stables.

Throughout the summer term the horsemen drilled, rising in the small hours to muster on Portobello sands at five in the morning when the tide was right, then hurrying back to eat an enormous meal, change into wig and gown, and decorously pace the Outer Court among the less energetic Montagnards.

As the Corps settled down to its duties, and the new recruits came in, there was soon no need for Walter to double the office of paymaster and quartermaster, and John Adams, an instructor at the Riding School, was appointed Adjutant. In what spare time remained, Walter was scribbling in his notebooks, consulting James Skene on his translation of the German ballads which still fascinated him, and attending the meetings of as many clubs as ever.

At home in George's Square his father's illness dragged on, engrossing most of his mother's attention. His elder brother, John, who had been granted extended leave from his regiment after long and frustrating service at Gibraltar, did his best to relieve the tedium of his father's bedridden existence, and find employment for young Daniel, who had so far shown no inclination for any sort of work whatever, while Anne, shadowier than ever, flitted about distractedly on the little errands her mother found for her.

When the Courts rose for the summer recess, Mrs Scott waylaid Walter on his return to George's Square from the mews where Lenore was stabled. Her plain, kind face was serene as ever, but there were lines of weariness about her shadowed eyes, and Walter noticed for the first time how grey her hair had become.

"Wattie, my lamb, I'm glad to have the chance of a word with ye." She paused to smile, her head tilted appraisingly as she looked up at her tall, broad-shouldered son. "Eh, but ye suit the uniform brawly, my man. I'm a proud woman, with my three sons serving their country." The smile faded, as she remembered Robert, who was gone, and Daniel, who was already an anxiety. But she went briskly on.

"It was about John I wanted to talk to you, Wattie. He's had a sore ordeal at Gibraltar, and now he's spending his leave in his father's sick-room. It's no diversion for the lad. Is there no jaunt ye've got in mind for your holiday that he could join?"

"Surely," said Walter at once. "Kerr of Abbotrule has been fair deaving me with the beauties of the English Lakes, and I was talking to Adam Ferguson this very day about a ploy I've had in mind of visiting them this summer. Mebbe John would join us."

"That's the very thing. I'll see he does," said Mrs Scott with satisfaction. "He's been a good lad to his father, and it's time he had a change. I'll not take no for an answer."

Nor did she. John, a reserved, unambitious young man, with little of his brother's gaiety, submitted to his mother's command that he and Wattie were to be off and play themselves, since she couldn't be doing with them cluttering up the house throughout the vacation. Walter summoned Adam Ferguson to his den in the basement, where their plans were worked out with the precision of a military operation. "We'll only need one more nag," said Walter, scribbling already at his desk, "for John, since we've got ours already."

Adam Ferguson, one elbow on the mantelpiece, cocked a whimsical eyebrow. "Ye're never taking yon great black beast that bolts from one end of Portobello sands to the other?"

"Steady exercise, at a reasonable pace, will do her a world of good," said Walter severely.

"You'll have to find me something steady, mind," said John, who was a very moderate horseman.

"I'll see to that," promised Adam Ferguson.

"We'll trot along as meek as ministers on their way to the Presbytery," Walter assured them gravely. Adam Ferguson shook a finger at him.

"I don't trust you an inch, my lad, with that look in your eye."

"Never fash yourself for that," said Walter, "but let's get the luggage settled. Since we're all pledged to serve in any emergency, wherever it may occur, we'll have to find room for our uniforms in our saddle-bags."

"Tuts, havers," said Adam Ferguson.

"It's our solemn obligation," said Walter. "We'll need little else save a change of linen and shaving kit. Now there's the route to be planned . . ."

"Let's not plan overmuch," said Adam Ferguson, who was a lighthearted young man with a fancy for taking life as it came. "Take my advice, Wattie, and set out with an open mind. Toss rules and regulations into the cupboard with your gown. Let the moths have them! We're for the road."

"Ye're mebbe right, Adam," Walter agreed. Then he screwed his careful notes into a ball and threw it at Adam Ferguson's mocking face. Adam ducked, snapped his fingers, and raised his eyes heavenwards.

"We'll ride out like knights errant, taking what the fates send us."

"That suits me brawly," Walter grinned.

John looked from one to the other and sighed. "But ye're still minded to take yon uniforms?"

"I am that," Walter said.

In due course the travellers set out on their haphazard journey. Walter kept his promise and saw that Lenore paced demurely beside the stout geldings ridden by his companions, by way of Tweeddale, Carlisle and Penrith to Ullswater and Windermere. Then they struck eastward, since Walter was attracted by the prospect of examining the ancient Roman Wall, and decided to spend a night or two at the little local spa at Gilsland, within riding distance of it.

Here they found, at the local inn, an artificial society entirely different from anything they had so far encountered, though to Walter it was not altogether strange.

"When I was a bairn," he said, looking round the company assembled at the miniature watering-place, "I mind seeing the very same sort of folk at Bath."

Adam Ferguson was amused. "I'm told," he said, as their horses were led off to the stables, "that there's to be a ball here at this wee hotel this evening. Mebbe ye were not so daft to see we stuffed yon uniforms into our saddle-bags, Wattie, after all."

"I wonder," said Walter dreamily, "if she'll be there?"

"The lassie we saw out riding this morning? I should hope so," said Adam Ferguson cheerfully.

It was mere idle talk, between young men who had all admired a pretty figure and the surreptitious glance from speculative dark eyes when they overtook a young lady who handled her horse with casual skill as she negotiated the same path across the Northumbrian hills. But Walter was in a more vulnerable state than he knew, and a more striking figure than he realised, as he reined back his powerful black charger to let the dark-haired lady and her escorting groom pass by. Adam Ferguson was always ready for amusement, and John had noticed nothing at all, except that the path the strangers had taken seemed to lead towards a hamlet where he might have a chance of getting off his raw-boned horse, whose awkward paces had been galling him nearly raw for days. But Walter turned Lenore off the path to follow the track which led to it like a man in a dream.

The little hotel, they found, was already in a state of extreme activity in preparation for the evening's entertainment. But the arrival of three military gentlemen from Edinburgh was most welcome. Rooms were found, their horses comfortably stabled, and the proprietor, when pursued into his office, was able to give Walter some of the information he required.

"Oh, aye, Captain, the dark-haired young leddy must be Miss Carpenter. French, she is, and taking refuge from yon monsters across the Channel, I'm told. She's here with her companion, Miss Nicolson, as the guests of the Reverend and Mrs Bird, from St Mary's Church in Carlisle. Ye'll be at the ball this evening, likely, sir?"

"We will," Walter assured him, adding, in an off-hand tone, "in full regimentals."

The innkeeper beamed. "That'll be the verra thing."

Walter paused in the doorway. "I would be glad to pay my respects to the Reverend and Mrs Bird . . . and party."

"I'll see to that, sir," the innkeeper assured him.

Walter, who innocently fancied himself, not without reason, in the blue and scarlet of the Light Dragoons, fussed over sartorial details for the next few hours. An obliging chambermaid pressed his uniform, bore off his hessian boots, and put a brilliant sheen on buttons and buckles. John, who had spent too many years in uniform to take much interest in it, yawned and grumbled, and lanky Adam Ferguson complained that his pantaloons had shrunk in the washing. But they entered the ballroom with a swagger as the fiddles struck up, well aware of the interest they aroused.

As Master of Ceremonies, the innkeeper bustled about, greeting the guests, making introductions, calling for more candles, placating dowagers, whispering compliments to pretty giggling girls, presenting newcomers. Walter lost sight of John and Adam as he followed the Master of Ceremonies to the corner where Mr and Mrs Bird had established themselves with their guests. He bowed, smiled, murmured appropriate inanities. And he found Miss Carpenter, demure in white, with white roses in her dark hair, even more devastating than she had seemed in her riding habit. Without a second's hesitation he asked if he might have the honour of escorting her to supper.

"I do not dance," he explained frankly. "An injury . . ." He tapped the leg, shrugged, and smiled. "But at least I shall have the pleasure of watching you, and the patience, I hope, to wait till my turn comes."

"I am so sorree because of your injuree." Her voice was charming, her accent obviously French, and her dark eyes full of concern. "You shall tell me more at supper. I shall keep that for you, Mistaire Scott, I think?"

"Scott. Walter Scott," he mumbled, blissfully watching her scribble his name on her pretty pink programme. "We shall not hurry over supper, I hope." Bemused, he saw her write his name against the succeeding dances. "I am vairy greedy, you see," she said, with a little girl's giggle. "But also, I like to talk."

Then her first partner claimed her, and Walter remained to make conversation to her companions in the alcove, as seemed both prudent and the best way of traversing the wilderness of time until the supper dance.

He found the clergyman and his lady both pleasant and informative, Miss Nicolson somewhat acidulated. But at least they were all agreed on Charlotte's hard lot, her parents dead, and her only brother far away in India, where an appointment had been obtained for him by their guardian, the Marquis of Downshire.

Walter was appalled to think of Miss Carpenter's forlorn state. He knew all about the wave of indignation against the France led by Napoleon, and his generous imagination could guess at the difficulties of a French girl in a country with which France was at war. At least Charlotte should find that some people in Scotland were unprejudiced, ready to fight the brutal forces in France who had butchered their ruler, on behalf of those who, like Miss Carpenter, were unable to fight for themselves.

When the supper dance was at last announced, Walter was ready to champion Charlotte against the world. He had taken the precaution of reserving a table for two, and as she returned from the dance floor, flushed and laughing, her gaiety seemed to his romantic mind as gallant as that of a survivor from a stricken field. At first he could find no words. He rose, bowed, and reverentially offered her his arm.

"Ah, ze suppaire." She consulted her programme. "And Mr Scott. I am starrr-ving. We go now, yes?"

"Mademoiselle," said Walter, as they crossed the floor together, "I fear I do not speak your language very well – "

"Sir, that matters not. I speak yours vorse. So we are quits. This is our table? By the window. Good." She fanned herself, watching him, as he took his place opposite her, her dark eyes unfathomable by contrast with his candid blue ones which could not hide his admiration.

"We shall watch the moon rise behind the far-off mountains as we eat," said Walter.

"You are a poet, sir?"

H.B.

Walter flushed with pleasure. "Yes. Well, not yet. I have made only a few translations from the German, recently published. By profession I am an advocate, recently called to the Scottish Bar – "

"Indeed? How learned that sounds! Already you – how you say – take ze cases?"

"Not many yet," said Walter honestly. "But more each year."

"You end up as a Judge, I think."

"Perhaps," said Walter doubtfully. Then as Miss Carpenter's eyes shifted, he became aware of the hovering waiter. "A thousand apologies, mademoiselle! Even the most exquisite cannot live on air. Till you have made your choice I will not say another word."

They ate. He talked, she listened. And before they parted they made an assignation to ride together next morning. It was the first of many meetings, and Charlotte's admiration of Walter's horsemanship, his fine black charger, his patriotic association with the Light Dragoons, comforted him more than he could have believed possible. And the sight of her own skill delighted him almost as much.

"Mademoiselle, you have the grace of Diana," he blurted out as they drew rein after a wild gallop.

She laughed. "We always have many horses at home. And – my name is Charlotte."

Before Mr and Mrs Bird announced their intention of returning to Carlisle, Walter had asked Charlotte to be his wife.

She held out her hands in an impulsive little gesture. "Zat is so like you. Warm and kind and good. You make me want to cry."

"I want to make you happy," Walter said.

"I know it. And perhaps you could."

"Then – "

She held up a gloved hand. "Wait. I must explain. For myself – perhaps – yes – "

"Charlotte!" He could not believe it.

"But it is not just me. I must consult my guardian. Without ze approval of Lord Downshire I can say – nothing."

"You will ask him?"

"I will write."

"Tonight?"

"From Carlisle. We return there tomorrow."

So Walter, left behind at Gilsland, shut himself away and wrote to his mother, while Adam Ferguson joked, and his brother John grumbled at his desertion.

"My dear Mother," Walter scribbled anxiously,

"I should very ill deserve the care and affection with which you have ever regarded me, were I to neglect my duty so far as to omit consulting my father and you in the most important step I can possibly take in life . . . You will probably guess from this preamble that I am engaged in a matrimonial plan . . .

"My dear mother, I cannot express to you the anxiety I have that you will not think me flighty nor inconsiderate in this business . . . I am also most anxious that you should be prepared to show her kindness, which I know the goodness of your heart will prompt, more especially when I tell you that she is an orphan, without relations, and almost without friends. Her guardian is – I should say *was*, for she is of age, Lord Downshire, to whom I must write . . ."

From her lodgings in Castle Street, Carlisle, Charlotte was also writing to her guardian.

"My Lord,

"We have latterly been such ramblers, and so uncertain as to our plans & place of residence, that I postponed the honor of inquiring after your health until we were settled. We went with Mr and Mrs Bird to Guilsland, we stayed there three Weeks, which time we passed very agreeable, they returned with us to Carlisle to introduce us to all their friends, who are the first people of this County but our stay here is only temporary, has neither the place, nor expenses can suit us, we are making every possible inquiries. I fear that the situation we want will be very difficult to meet with it, we have not yet found any single thing cheaper than in the west of England. I am always troubling you with my little concerns," wrote Charlotte anxiously. She nibbled the tip of her quill and pondered. Then, with a sigh which set the flame of the candle on her little table wavering, she dipped her quill and hurried on.

"I wish you would not write so fiercely, Charlotte," said Miss Nicolson from her place by the fireside. "The sound sets my teeth on edge."

Charlotte only paused for long enough to put her tongue out at her friend's primly shawled back, then drove her quill across the page faster than ever.

"I shall then begin my Lord with informing you that during my stay at Guilsland I got acquainted with Mr Scott, a Gentleman of Edinburgh, he paid his addresses to me, which I have accepted only as far as it should be by your consent and full approbation, he is of very good family, his profession is that of Advocate, & with his connections, & abilities he must rise, his fortune at present is moderate, but he has some great expectations, if you will permit my Lord, Mr Scott to address himself to you he could more fully explain his Situation, & refer you to some person who could give you every information concerning his family connections . . ."

"I trust you will shortly make an end of this writing, Charlotte," said Miss Nicolson presently. "It is already long past the hour at which we are accustomed to retire."

"One moment, and I shall have done," said Charlotte, murmuring her final phrase aloud. "May I hope my Lord, for the happiness of hearing from you soon . . . with every wish for health and happiness to attend.

I remain My Lord
Your much obliged
C. Carpenter.

Miss Nicolson presents her best compliments.
Palmers Lodgings
 Castle Street
  Carlisle."

The Marquis of Downshire lost no time in advising his ward to authorise Mr Scott to address his request for her hand in marriage to him at his London address. It was a very long time since, as young

Lord Fairford, he had received much kindness from M. Charpentier, head of a Riding Academy in Lyons, and his young wife, in consequence of which he had accepted the guardianship of Charlotte and her brother Charles, on M. Charpentier's death. Their mother brought them to London, where they made their home with the kindly family of M. Dumergue, a Frenchman with a successful dental practice in Piccadilly. Charlotte, who was a Huguenot, was baptised and confirmed, like her brother, as a member of the Church of England, and Charles was prepared for a post with the East India Company which completed Lord Fairford's obligation as far as he was concerned. His prospects were good, and he undertook to provide his sister with an allowance of £200 a year.

Now it seemed possible that Charlotte, too, would soon be off his hands. Walter's letter, which promptly arrived, seemed encouraging, provided his financial situation was sound. Lord Downshire replied accordingly.

"Sir,

"I received your letter with pleasure, instead of thinking it an intrusion. One thing more being full stated, would have made it perfectly satisfactory, namely, the sort of income you immediately possess, and the sort of maintenance Miss Carpenter, in case of your demise, might reasonably expect . . ."

Walter broke his return journey to Edinburgh at Jedburgh, to attend the assizes. There he confided his new happiness to Robert Shortreed, his travelling companion of the Liddesdale raids, in a torrent of words which made his pawky friend chuckle.

"Why, man, you're fair beside yourself!"

Walter rolled his gown into a bundle and tucked it under his arm as they turned to leave the robing room.

"Come away, Bob, and drink a toast to the loveliest, sweetest, truest lass that ever man set eyes on. I am the happiest man in the world – "

"Whiles, I think ye're the daftest – "

"You wait till I tell you – "

So they talked of Charlotte, and toasted Charlotte, and planned for Charlotte, in Mr Shortreed's comfortable quarters for most of the night, and next day Walter hurried to Edinburgh, where he hoped for letters, both from Charlotte and her guardian.

At George's Square, however, his exuberance was checked. Lord Downshire's inquiry into his financial position was reasonable enough. Walter had anticipated it, and was already considering what he could do to augment his earnings at the Bar. His fee-book showed a slow, but steady rise. In his first year at the Bar he had earned £24 : 3 : 0, in his second, £57 : 15 : 0, in his third, £84 : 4 : 0, in his fourth, £90, and in his fifth he had reached three figures with £144 : 10 : 0. But even this was obviously inadequate. Walter remembered something Bob Shortreed had said in Jedburgh, while they had touched briefly on the economics of marriage. It was possible that the Sheriffdom of Selkirk might shortly fall vacant. This, if obtained, would add £300 to his annual budget, and his association with the Edinburgh Light Dragoons would give him a chance of requesting the interest of the Duke of Buccleuch in his cause. Charlotte had £200 from her brother, but never would he so demean himself as to live on his wife. More funds would still be needed. Was there any appointment at the Bar for which he could apply? Would his father, for a time at least, help?

But he found his mother less reassuring than usual, when he brought his problems to her on the evening of his return. The October dusk had fallen, and a thrifty fire glimmered in the grate. Walter limped to and fro, while his mother busied herself as usual with the family mending.

"Well, Mother," he said at last. "Never a word have I had from you on the topic that's nearest to my heart. What's on your mind?"

Mrs Scott let her hands fall on her plump lap. Her broad, plain face was creased with anxiety. "Wattie, my lamb, I've had a sore work with your father. He's near beside himself with anxiety and Dr Daniel, your uncle, says he won't be responsible for his condition if he's crossed. Wattie, he's not satisfied."

"Why not?" said Walter hotly.

"Wattie, ye must try and understand. We ken nothing of the lady you propose to marry except that she is French, which is scarcely the best recommendation at present. No – don't interrupt me, lad. He wants to ken something of her family, her position, her prospects."

"The only prospect that matters, Mother, is that she'll do me the honour of becoming my wife – "

"Wheesht, lad, wheesht. Your father's a sick man."

"And I'm a determined one. I mean to marry Miss Charlotte Carpenter, Mother, with his consent or not. If he does not agree, we will emigrate. Her brother has a fine position in India – "

"No, Wattie – "

"Bide a wee, Mother," said Walter more calmly. "I will do what my father asks. I will write to Charlotte and explain what he wants to know – and to Lord Downshire, her guardian, with details of my own position. But I warn you, my mind is made up."

"Then away and write your letters," said Mrs Scott quietly.

Walter wrote hopefully to Lord Downshire. His earnings at the Bar were not spectacular, but on the increase. His father, he thought, would make him an allowance on his marriage, and he had hopes of being appointed Sheriff of one of the Border counties through the influence of the Duke of Buccleuch, head of the Scott connection and patron of the Edinburgh Light Dragoons.

But it was quite another matter to convey his family's anxieties to Charlotte, and Walter wrote and re-wrote the letter a dozen times before he finally consigned the final version to the post with misgivings which were not unjustified. Charlotte's prompt reply appalled him.

"Indeed, Mr Scott," she wrote, "I am by no means pleased with all this writing. I have told you how much I dislike it, and yet you still persist in asking me to write, and that by return of post. O, you really are out of your senses . . . I have no reason that can detain me in acquainting you that my father and mother were French, of the name of Charpentier; he had a place under government; their residence was at Lyons, where you would find on enquiry that they lived in good repute and in *very good style*. I had the misfortune of losing my father before I could know the value of such a parent. At his death we were left to the care of Lord D. who was his very great friend, and very soon after I had the affliction of losing my mother. Our taking the name of Carpenter was on my brother's going to India, to prevent any little difficulties that might have occurred. I hope now you are pleased," wrote Miss Carpenter indignantly. "Before I conclude this famous epistle," she added, "I will give you a little hint – that is, not to put so many *must* in your letters – it is beginning *rather too soon* – "

Walter's consternation on receiving this rebuke was mercifully relieved by Charlotte's second letter, written the next day, in which she graciously acknowledged the arrival of the miniature which Walter had had painted at her request. "I have only a minute before the post goes, to assure you, my dear sir, of the welcome reception of the stranger. The very great likeness to a friend of mine will endear him to me, he shall be my constant companion, but I wish he could give me an answer to a thousand questions I have to make – one in particular, what reason have you for so many fears you express? Have your friends changed? Pray let me know the truth – they perhaps don't like me *being French*. Do write immediately – let it be in better spirits. *Et croyez-moi toujours votre sincère,*

C.C."

A few days later the letter from Lord Downshire for which Walter had been anxiously waiting was forwarded by Charlotte. "Last night I received the enclosed for you from Lord Downshire. If it has your approbation, I shall be very glad to see you as soon as will be convenient. I have a thousand things to tell you . . ."

"Sir," wrote Lord Downshire,

"I received the favour of your letter. It was so manly, honourable, candid, and so full of good sense, that I think Miss Carpenter's friends cannot in any way object to the union you propose. Its taking place, when or where, will depend upon herself, as I shall write to her by this night's post. Any provision that may be given to her by her brother, you will have settled upon her and her children; and I hope, with all my heart, that every earthly happiness may attend you both. I shall always be happy to hear it, and to subscribe myself your faithful friend and obedient humble servant,

Downshire."

In a state of wild elation, Walter crammed a few belongings into a portmanteau, and set off to spend the remaining ten days of the vacation in lodgings as near to Miss Carpenter's as possible in Carlisle.

When he returned reluctantly to Edinburgh, Charlotte had agreed that she might be ready for their marriage before the end of the year, and the particulars of her parentage which Walter had been able to supply had enabled his mother to quieten his father's incoherent protests. Charlotte's letters were less formal now, but she made it clear that she did not intend to re-model her character for Walter's sake.

"... I don't think that very thoughtful people can be happy. As this is my maxim, adieu to all thoughts. I have made a determination of being pleased with everything, and with everybody in Edinburgh; a wise system for happiness, is it not? ... I am happy to hear of your father's being better pleased as to money matters, it will come at last, don't let that trifle disturb you. *Adieu, Monsieur. J'ai l'honneur d'être votre très humble et très obéissante*

C.C."

By the end of November, Walter's plans were maturing. On the 22nd, he wrote earnestly to Lord Downshire:

"My Lord Marquis,

"I have the honour to transmit to your Lordship for your inspection and approbation a Scroll of a Contract of Marriage settling upon Miss Carpenter & her heirs whatever fortune she is presently possessed of and whatever provision her Brother may be pleased to settle upon her ...

"My father's state of health has of late been very precarious, having been slightly affected by some paralytic disorder – In this situation I cannot immediately press him to make me any specific settlement – Whatever sum I receive from that quarter will I think most likely be nearly equal to purchasing a comfortable House . . ."

During the next few weeks while the business of the Law Courts kept Walter in bonds, letters between Charlotte and himself shuttled to and fro with increasing urgency.

But Charlotte's coquetry was like that of a bather who advances a tentative foot into deep water and then withdraws into the shallows which she instinctively prefers.

"I have taken Mrs Macleod's house at 10 Guineas for six months," wrote Walter, "that is till the next term when we will have had time to look about us . . . My Mother is very busy seeking us a Cook . . ."

"Pray never more complain of being poor," Charlotte wrote gaily. "Are you not ten times richer than I am? Depend on yourself and your profession. I have no doubt you will rise very high and be a great rich man . . . I am very sorry to hear you have such a bad head. I hope I shall nurse away all your aches. I think you write too much. When I am *mistress* I shall not allow it. How very angry I should be with you if you were to part with Lenore . . . I am very glad you don't give up the cavalry, as I love anything that is stylish . . ."

"Upon my word," Walter wrote exuberantly, "I wish you could look in and see me as I sit at present in the midst of the most glorious confusion you can conceive . . . A lawyer's gown and coif elegantly contrasted with a Light Dragoon's helmet and sabre – and to complete the whole, a set of bedding and linens blocking me out from my own fireside . . . In a word, I have this evening taken possession of *our* house – O, Charlotte, how I love that little word *Our* . . ."

As December began, Walter's anxiety for Charlotte to fix a definite date became acute. Charlotte wrote soothingly.

". . . You may depend on me, my dearest friend, for fixing as *early* a day as I possibly can, and if it happens not to be quite as soon as you wish, you must not be too angry with me. It is very unlucky you are such a bad housekeeper – as I am no better. I shall try. I hope to have very soon the pleasure of seeing you, and to tell you how much I love you, but I wish the first fortnight was over. With all my love – " She paused, giggled, and added: "and those sort of pretty things – adieu.

Charlotte."

Walter was now making eager plans. "To avoid increasing our baggage," he wrote, "I shall bring almost nothing to Carlisle, so you must not expect me to be a beau . . . I hope the ring is wide enough. I am very awkward upon some occasions. I dare say I shall blunder in putting it on . . . Take the utmost care, my best beloved friend . . . Do not go out but in the middle of the day & take great care of damp feet . . ."

By the middle of the month the formalities of the marriage settlement seemed far enough advanced for Charlotte to name a date. "I heard last night from my friends in London," she wrote, "and I shall certainly have the deed this week. I will send it to you directly, but not to lose so much time as you have been reckoning, I will prevent any little delay that might happen by the post, by fixing already next Wednesday for your coming here, and on Thursday the 21st, Oh my dear Scott – on that day I shall be yours *for ever*." She underlined the words heavily, gave her little giggle, and added: "Does not that sound very awful? . . .

C.C.

P.S. Arrange it so that we shall see none of your family the night of our arrival. I shall be so tired, and such a fright, I should not be seen to advantage."

Chapter 7

JUST over ten years ago, Walter had stood on Castle Hill, stricken and bewildered, on his return from Kelso, by his parting from his first love. On the far side of the vanished Nor' Loch, he had seen the first relentless thrust of the new roads, the felled trees, the razed homesteads, the devouring bonfires, that heralded the progress of Mr Craig's New Town of Edinburgh.

Now, all was changed, for the tide of building surged far westward from St Andrew's Square, and the carriages of the first occupants of the elegant dwelling houses now bowled along the wide cobbled thoroughfares of Princes Street and George Street, linked by Hanover and Frederick Street, while the builders were still noisily busy with Castle Street beyond, in which he had arranged to purchase the first home of his married life.

"But we must be patient for a little while," he told Charlotte, who had sagged against him as the post-chaise rocked northwards over the frost-bound winter roads, her head resting on his shoulder as she snuggled closer within the curve of his protective arm, limp as a tired kitten. "Builders seem always to take twice as long as they say, so we shall have to put up with my lodgings over the winter."

"I do . . . not care . . ." said Charlotte faintly. "I long only for ze chance of sleep . . ."

"And I," said Walter, "am as anxious for something to eat. Roast beef and apple pie, washed down with a good claret. By Gad, I feel as hollow as the Town Drum."

"How much farther must . . . we go tonight?" murmured Charlotte.

Walter peered through the grimy window, but could only see a vague perspective of winter-sere hedgerow, dimly illuminated by the stumpy candles of the carriage-lamps. He turned to kiss

Charlotte's nose, which projected, cold as marble, from the furred margin of her velvet bonnet. "Indeed, I am sure we must be presently at the inn," he reassured her, drawing the rug more closely round her slight figure with his free hand.

"Oh, Scott . . . do you think . . . zey will like me . . . at all?" she whispered forlornly.

"My little heart, I am quite sure of it. As sure as that I love you more than anyone was ever loved before."

"Dearest Scott . . ." He guessed at her smile in the darkness, felt her draw closer, till the awed awareness of her utter dependence on him brought sudden tears to his eyes.

As she slept, he tried to picture them all, his family, waiting to greet him as he brought his bride to George's Square after she had had the night's rest for which she had implored. She would be quite comforted once she had met his mother. He was sure of that. Tom would be gallant, and she had met John already. She would be kind to Anne, and Daniel always pleased ladies. She would have to see his father, of course. Walter wished he could have spared her that. His father, propped up on his pillows, gesticulating desperately with his emaciated hands, his pale eyes wide with anxiety as he tried in vain to make himself understood . . .

The housekeeper, Mrs Macleod, was on the doorstep to greet them when their chaise drew up at long last outside her house in George Street. A tall, angular woman with thin sandy hair and arms folded primly on her apron, who turned down the corners of her mouth and dropped a formal curtsy as Walter presented her to his wife.

"I trust ye'll have had a quiet journey, Ma'am? There's been sair talk of robberies on the road lately."

Charlotte smiled kindly, tucking her small gloved hand under Walter's arm. "I had no fear, not at all. My husband, he would defence me from all. And now, you will be good enough to show us where we shall go, yes?"

Mrs Macleod, bridling a little at the hint of patronage, primming up her lips at the foreign accent, stood aside and beckoned them in. "I'll show you all there is to see," she said. "It's to be hoped it's to your liking," she added, with a sidelong glance at the little foreign lady, whom she already suspected of outlandish ways.

"I'm sure it will be, Mrs Macleod," said Walter as he limped after Charlotte across the hall.

The dining parlour, with a round table neatly laid with plates and glasses on a clean white cloth, was mellow with candles, and a small fire burned in the grate. Charlotte was pleased, clapping her hands as gaily as a child.

"My books are already in the closet yonder," Walter said. "But there will be room for anything you please."

"You'd best see the kitchen," said Mrs Macleod. "The lassie has a meal prepared, and she can be dishing up while ye see the rest of the hoose."

The shy, barefoot Highland girl dropped a curtsy to her new master and mistress, upsetting a bowl of milk all over the floor in her agitation.

"Tch, tch," said Mrs Macleod. "Mop it up, Morag, and get the supper on the table as soon as ye can."

"Yes, m'm," said Morag, a little comforted by Walter's understanding smile.

"The principal bedroom opens out of the dining parlour," said Mrs Macleod, waiting for Charlotte's disapproval. But Charlotte nodded resignation.

"So it was at Carlisle. May I see the drawing-room?"

Mrs Macleod led the way to the first floor, and flung open a door with a flourish to reveal the room which was her most jealously guarded pride. It was typical of many such rooms in Mr Craig's New Town; large and pleasant with a gently bowed window fronting the street, across which curtains were now drawn, some good old chairs and tables, a fire too small to do more than take the edge off the December chill, and an acrid smell of candles which had been lit at the expected hour of arrival, then extinguished for economy's sake and re-lit as the chaise rattled to a halt outside the front door.

Charlotte pirouetted delightedly round the room, unable to conceal her pleasure at having a drawing-room, for the time being, of her own. "How pleasant this will be," she said. "It overlooks the street, yes?"

Mrs Macleod admitted it, somewhat suspiciously.

"I shall enjoy sitting here so much, watching ze world go by while you are being ze grave advocate at the Law Courts," she told Walter gaily.

Mrs Macleod frowned. "It's to be hoped ye'll no' be letting the light fade the best upholstery every day of the week," she said severely. "It's different on the Sabbath."

Charlotte drew herself up. "I sink, Madame, that my husband pay for ze use of the house?"

"Aye, mebbe. But I'd have ye ken – "

"I believe, my love, that our supper is on the table," said Walter hastily. "You'll understand, Mrs Macleod, that we are both tired and hungry after our journey," he added, mentally making a note that the sooner their permanent quarters in Castle Street were ready, the better it would be for all concerned.

Next day, as had been arranged, they paid their state visit to 25 George's Square in time for dinner at noon. Charlotte seemed entirely to have recovered from the fatigue of the journey, and her encounter with Mrs Macleod, by the time the post chaise arrived to convey them to the all-important meeting with Walter's family, and she had enchanted Walter with her married-lady airs as she sent Morag scurrying to and fro on little errands from the parlour where they breakfasted, to the kitchen below. For the departure of Mrs Macleod to stay with relations now that her tenants had settled in seemed to have lifted a shadow from the house, and Walter rocked with laughter at Charlotte's lifelike rendering of Mrs Macleod's condemnation of ladies who thought it proper to sit in a drawing-room every morning of the week.

At George's Square, Charlotte faced the family inspection with nervous gaiety, and her mother-in-law received her with disarming kindness which did not altogether conceal surprise that Walter's wife was so different from all the Scottish girls he had ever known. But since Wattie so obviously adored her, his mother did her best, and the younger members of the family were delighted by her chatter, her French accent, and her pretty efforts to make friends. Anne, in particular, found her arrival as exciting a novelty as the descent of a bright tropical bird upon a rookery, and followed her about from room to room with eyes as round as marbles. The visit to Walter's father in his sick-room was an ordeal which his mother made as brief as possible, since distress and embarrassment struck even Charlotte dumb. But when she followed her mother-in-law into the pleasant, spacious drawing-room, her clasped hands and exclamations of admiration made Mrs Scott smile.

"Ah, madame, but this is beautiful! Its outlook is so distinguished – ze furnishings so elegant. Tell me, madame – " She turned impulsively to her mother-in-law – "you sit here, often, yes?"

"Whenever I have the mind," agreed Mrs Scott, puzzled.

"Even in ze mornings? Not only on ze Sabbath?"

"I haven't mebbe all that time for sitting, first thing in the morning. But – "

"But zat Mrs Mac – Mac – how you call her, Scott?"

"Mrs Macleod, our good housekeeper, has shocked Charlotte sorely, Mother," explained Walter, smiling, "by hoping she will not fade the furnishings by using the drawing-room every day."

His mother chuckled. "There's mebbe something in what she says, my dear. We Scots have thrifty ways which whiles seem queer to other folk."

"But if I may not sit in my drawing-room, where shall I go?" cried Charlotte in dismay.

"When you have your own drawing-room, my dear, you'll be able to sit there as long as you like," said Mrs Scott pacifically. "You must go round to Castle Street, Walter, and see what progress has been made."

At last, they were able to move into their first real home. It was the climax of months of anxious conference between Walter and Charlotte, and between Charlotte and her mother-in-law, whose wisdom kept her from offering advice till it was wanted. In consequence, Charlotte made fewer mistakes than she might have done, and once they were settled, their pleasure in the Castle Street house was shared by Walter's brother officers of the Light Dragoons, who enjoyed Charlotte's informal supper parties as much as did Will Clerk, William Erskine, John Irving and Adam Ferguson of the Montagnards.

Walter himself was getting a number of briefs now, so that his attendance at the Law Courts was less nominal than it had been. He was still busy with his translations from the German, and faithful in his volunteer duties, to which the serious threat of a Napoleonic invasion via Ireland during the summer of 1798 gave an additional urgency.

Charlotte, meanwhile, was gaily settling into her lesser world. She had shrewdly established excellent relations with her domestic staff. The solid, kindly body whom Mrs Scott had engaged as cook soon fell victim to the young bride's pretty air of helplessness and her willingness to accept advice. Morag, who shared the gloomy servants' bedroom off the basement kitchen, was enchanted by a gift of ribbons and her new mistress's infectious giggle, while young Rob, who slept in a sort of cock loft reached by a ladder, blacked the boots and cleaned the knives, fetched his master's horse round from the stable and called a chaise when Charlotte wanted to go visiting, was her bondslave.

Scott beamed on his household with incredulous wonder at his own good fortune, and gave Charlotte more money than he could afford because she apologised so touchingly for being such a bad manager. If he was not earning enough, then he must find a way of earning more, that was all. For he and Charlotte could expect an addition to their family, during October, Dr Daniel Rutherford thought, and she and the child must lack for nothing, whether he could afford it or not.

But during the summer he brought home an unexpected retainer, whose welcome was less certain. Charlotte was in her drawing-room, enjoying the evening sunshine and matching patterns for a new dress which, in the circumstances, could not be considered an extravagance, when her husband limped in, the coat of his cavalry uniform bulging most oddly.

"Dearest Scott! You arrive just at the best moment! Come and look what I choose that I may do you credit at ze Assembly."

"My love, you always do me credit," said Scott tenderly. "But I have something to show you, too. I have brought you a camp follower of the cavalry. Look!"

As he unbuttoned his coat a blunt, brindle head, with small cropped ears and bright dark eyes of extreme intelligence appeared. Two sturdy white forepaws pushed strongly against Scott's chest as the puppy imperiously demanded to be released. Scott stooped and set him down.

Charlotte sent patterns flying as she flung up her hands and shrieked. "Scott! My new carpet. At once he will – "

"He has done everything he should, my dearest, in the back garden," Scott assured her. "What d'you think of him?"

Charlotte, hands to her mouth, surveyed the little dog uncertainly, while Scott surveyed them both with a broad smile of the deepest affection, and the little dog, quite unabashed by his new surroundings and his definitely doubtful reception, sat down on his solid brindle and black rump and scratched himself vigorously.

"Fleas, without doubt, he has . . ." Charlotte wailed.

Scott shook his head. "I gave orders for him to be bathed this morning."

"Oh . . ." Charlotte and the little dog surveyed each other uncertainly. Then, aware that the proceedings needed livening, the newcomer yawned, stood up on his squat legs, and made a dive at the vivid scraps of material scattered about the floor. As Charlotte shrieked and plunged to rescue them, he grabbed one and set off at full gallop, round and round the room, dodging spindle-legged tables, colliding with chair-legs, the scrap of bright colour streaming like a pennant. Scott roared with laughter, but Charlotte, her hands full of snippets of silk and satin, gave a cry of despair.

"It is ze one I choose. He will tear it to little bits!"

Still laughing, Scott plunged after the puppy, who, breathless now, took refuge among Charlotte's skirts, dropping the pattern at her feet as he gasped for breath.

"Ah, he has good taste at least," said Charlotte, snatching it. Then, as relief changed her mood, she too began to laugh, to the great concern of the little dog, who sat looking from one human being to the other in ludicrous bewilderment. Still laughing, Charlotte stooped to pick him up, hugging the sturdy little creature who presently reached up and licked the tears of laughter from her cheeks with a warm, rough tongue.

"Ah, what a clown thou art, my little one, my camp follaire. It is too long, that name, Scott. Camp is enough."

"Camp he shall be, my dearest," Scott agreed, wiping his own eyes.

"But what sort of dog can he be?" said Charlotte. "Never have I seen such a one."

"The breed is not well known," Scott admitted. "But I can assure you of his parentage. His sire is a black-and-tan English terrier, the property of Storie, the farrier in Rose Street yonder. His dam is a brindle bull bitch owned by Mr John Adams of the Riding School, our Adjutant."

"My mind is at rest," Charlotte giggled delightedly. "Camp is legitimate."

"And we have our watchdog." Scott stooped to kiss her. "Now, what is this new gown that he has chosen for you?"

"Now let me show you all ze patterns. You shall then see if you agree with us. It is, perhaps, ze most expensive, so if you prefer another, we must think again."

Camp fell off her knee with a resounding thud as she gathered the patterns together. Charlotte gasped. "He is dead, no?"

"No," Scott agreed, as Camp rolled over and stood up. "It takes more than that to kill a bull terrier, my dearest. Now, let us consider this most important matter. You must, above all, have the best . . ."

Camp, for the moment forgotten, cocked a speculative eye at his new owners, trotted across the room to make a small pool unobtrusively in a corner, then returned to sit, with an air of the greatest satisfaction, at Scott's feet.

His reception between stairs was, on the whole, favourable, and he received most of his education from Cook, who fed him, spanked him and put him out into the back garden till he realised its important amenities. Rob exercised him in the mews and the neighbouring streets while Scott was at the Law Courts, Morag cuddled and adored him, and he spent a good deal of time with Charlotte, standing on his hind-legs as he grew large enough to look out of the window when she told him that Scott might soon be expected home.

For though he was warmly affectionate to all accredited members of the household and very soon learned to challenge all unwelcome intruders, Scott was the king-pin of his universe, and though there might be a better fire and a softer hearthrug in the drawing-room, it was with Scott in his study that Camp spent the evenings when his master was not required to escort Charlotte to the theatre or help her to entertain their widening circle of friends.

Scott was now working on the translation of one of Goethe's tragedies, and Camp, busy demolishing a slipper or a shank bone on the hearth, heard thunderous phrases roll and mutter above his head with apparent interest, as Scott tried them out aloud, joyfully or despairingly according to the way the work was progressing. Every now and then, too, he spoke to the dog, as he always spoke to his animals, thoughtfully, and as to a friend.

"Camp, my man, I've made as sorry a job of these stanzas as you've made of that old boot of mine. I doubt I can do no more. Come away down the street for a breath of air. My head aches, but we'll say nothing to the missus."

So with Camp wobbling importantly at his heels, Scott went to cool his head in the gossamer summer darkness of the New Town, where adequate street lighting had not yet been installed, and wondered what it would be like in Liddesdale or by Tweedside. He always found himself longing for the country at this sweet season of the year. What would Charlotte say, he wondered, to having the cheapest little place it was possible to rent, so that they could spend the vacations among green fields, with a river to fish in and hills to ride across. They would soon have the child to consider, too. If he himself had not been brought up in the Border country, he had often heard his mother say, he would have died. Thoughtfully, he turned homewards, handed Camp over to Rob to be consigned to his box in the kitchen, and went to join Charlotte in the light collation which was served at ten o'clock. The faint birling of the Town Drum could sometimes be heard from the Old Town when the wind was from that direction, authorising householders in the towering tenements to tip the day's slops into the gutters below, as they had done for centuries.

Scott could hear it that evening, as he limped into Charlotte's drawing-room, and Charlotte was already dramatically holding her nose. He crossed the room to close the window. Smells, as well as sounds, were reaching them on the snell breeze.

"Thank you, Scott," said Charlotte fervently. "I am quite faint, sometimes, when zat wind blows. I wish zey would pull down zat Old Town, now we have ze New instead."

Scott flinched at the thought, as he drew a second chair to the supper-table, kissed his wife, and sat down. "My love, how would you like to have a country cottage outside Edinburgh? Then we could drive there for a few days whenever you wished, as well as during the vacations."

"Scott, I should like it extremely," Charlotte said. "Such a place would have a garden. We grow flowers and vegetables, yes? Perhaps we have a cow."

"Perhaps," Scott agreed, laughing at her excitement. "I will look into it," he promised, "and see what I can find."

He found, quite soon, a pretty thatched cottage at Lasswade, six miles from Edinburgh, with a couple of paddocks, an overgrown garden, and the Esk nearby, to which, as soon as the Courts rose, he transferred his household in the ancient family carriage, drawn by hired post horses and driven by the firm's coachman. The maid-servants were crowded on the rumble seat, with Charlotte, Camp and a vast quantity of luggage stowed around them within, while he and Rob accompanied them on horseback.

They spent the first of several blissful summers there, for though the purchase of a cow was agreed to be likely to produce too many complications, Scott's beautiful Lenore grazed happily in her new pasture, Charlotte enjoyed herself in running up new curtains and covers for the sitting-room, and Scott took over the garden after his fashion. With Rob's help, he cut away the profusion of creepers and felled saplings for a rustic archway at the entrance gate. Camp, now growing into a formidable young bull terrier, rabbited crazily in the undergrowth, and was ready to go shooting with his master whenever Scott picked up his gun.

The neighbours within driving range were friendly. Will Clerk's kinsfolk were at Penicuik, Professor Fraser Tytler at Woodhouse-lee, and the Duke of Buccleuch, to whom Scott had been presented with his brother officers of the Light Dragoons by Lord Dalkeith, was often to be found at his residence in the same valley. The country life cured Scott's headaches, and the round of visits on which he dutifully escorted Charlotte gave her fresh confidence in their future. But he was conscious, most of all of his desire, not to perch, as it were, on the margin of country life, but to belong there, as of right. The first hint of the possibility was given by the Duke of Buccleuch himself, when at his son's invitation Scott rode over to pay his respects, for the Duke, as the greatest landed proprietor of the Border counties, took his responsibilities very seriously, and had heard good reports of the young advocate whose hobby was the history and literature of the Border from the Sheriff depute of Selkirkshire, Andrew Plummer of Middlestead, himself an enthusiastic antiquary, whom Scott had often consulted.

The Duke greeted his son's brother officer kindly, hoped that his patriotic duties with the Light Dragoons had not interfered too much with his career at the Bar, and questioned him on his associations with the Border.

"I believe, your Grace, that the happiest years of my life have been spent there. I leave it only to return."

"Would you consider, as an advocate, undertaking legal responsibility for a Border county, should the office of Sheriff fall vacant? I have reason to fear that the health of a very good friend of mine is failing, and he has spoken to me in connection with his office in Selkirkshire."

"I would most gladly serve, your Grace, should I be needed. But I hope – "

"So do I, Mr Scott, so do I," said the Duke warmly. "But I shall be glad to bear you in mind."

Scott rode exuberantly home to Charlotte with the news that his name had been suggested in connection with the Sheriffdom of Selkirkshire, an appointment which might add another £300 a year to their budget in due course. So it was with the highest hopes that they returned to Edinburgh as summer faded, having made many new friends, and innocently enjoyed the country's pleasures. Charlotte was sure that Lasswade would give her baby a delightful background.

"Scott, I do believe you think already of his first pony."

"Well, my love, I'll admit I made a few inquiries . . ."

By the first week of October, everything was in readiness. Dr Daniel Rutherford called daily. Mrs Scott came from George's Square. The baby was born on the 14th. Next day it died.

Charlotte bore the loss with the unexpected stoicism which contrasted with her husband's distracted grief. "If it must go," she said tonelessly, "better at once, before I had come to love it."

The forlorn little household was surrounded by the anxious kindness of relations and friends. Charlotte found her mother-in-law's understanding, derived as it was from her own bitter experience, specially comforting, and as her health improved, she began to take up her small amusements. Scott solicitously escorted her to the theatre and the Assemblies, playing host at the informal supper parties for his fellow advocates and brother officers of the Light Dragoons. But he himself took refuge in his study whenever possible, scribbling his translations from the German with the boisterous Camp for distraction and company.

During the winter, however, William Erskine, back from London, introduced him to a fantastic little man whose gruesome novel, *The Monk*, had chilled the spines of fashionable London, and who was now on a visit to Edinburgh. Matthew Lewis was little more than a dwarf, with a round, childish face, protruding greenish eyes, and an enthusiasm for the weird and supernatural which matched Scott's own. Erskine had shown Lewis the translation of *Lenore* and *The Wild Huntsman*, which were just what the author of *The Monk* wanted for his forthcoming collection of *Tales of Wonder*. He invited Scott to dine with him at his hotel, declaimed his own verses, patronised Scott's first efforts and urged him to write more.

Scott, who had no opinion of himself as a poet, was delighted by the macabre little man, with his bloodcurdling imagination and candid delight in his soap bubble success, which brought him contacts with the aristocracy, about which he boasted unceasingly. Matthew Lewis was impressed by the efficiency of the Light Dragoons, when Scott took him to Musselburgh to dine at their quarters, heard James Skene recite a German soldier's farewell, and inspired Scott to compose a troop-song for his own regiment in the same rhythm. He left Edinburgh full of promises for the inclusion of Scott's ballad translations, and was able to find a bookseller willing to bring out his version of Goethe's tragedy with his name as translator on the title-page. And much more significantly, he had given him the idea of versifying on his own account instead of translating other people's work.

But the winter during which the first spark of Scott's poetic ambition kindled had been a hard one for Charlotte, in spite of all her gallant little gaieties. One evening towards the end of March, when uncleared snow had made the streets hazardous and isolated her more than she could endure, Scott came home from the Law Courts, joyously escorted upstairs by Camp, and found her in tears, alone by the fireside of her pretty drawing-room.

"My dearest girl . . . You are not ill?"

She shook her head against his shoulder. Dismayed, he took her into his arms.

"But you have been gone all day and Camp have upset my work-basket –" in the background, Camp wagged his stumpy tail uneasily, as Scott shook his head at him. "And I, oh my dearest Scott, shall I ever see my friends in London again?"

"Indeed you shall," Scott said warmly. "When the Courts rise next month, we shall set off together for London. It will do us both the world of good – "

"Oh, Scott, you cannot mean it?" She was already laughing with excitement through her tears. "We shall stay with my good friends, the Dumergues, and Lord Downshire shall be invited to call. Above all things, I long for you to meet."

He patted her shoulder reassuringly, rather as if he were gentling a favourite horse. "So we shall, my love, so we shall. And now, tell Kiki you have forgiven him. See how he sits there in disgrace, poor fellow."

"There, then, we are friends once more, yes?" said Charlotte, as she gaily beckoned the bull terrier to put his head on her knee and accept a still damp kiss. "It is well you understand not all your master say, for we are soon to leave you for a time. But Cook will feed you much, and Rob take you for walks. So all shall be well for the three of us. Oh, Scott, how happy I am. But, alas, what shall I wear?"

"That problem shall also be dealt with," said Scott cheerfully. And Camp, well aware that something was afoot, but thankful that it seemed to please the humans, unobtrusively abstracted a ball of wool from the overturned work-basket and proceeded methodically to demolish it.

Chapter 8

THE eagerly anticipated visit to London offered Charlotte all she had hoped for in the way of diversion, but the end of their stay with the Dumergues was saddened by the letter expressed by Tom from Edinburgh to inform Scott of his father's death. His first thought was of his mother, and his instinct to hasten north to be with her at the earliest possible moment. But the news that Charlotte was expecting another child made him reluctant either to hurry north without her, leaving her with the Dumergues, or to subject her to the stresses of too prolonged days of travelling. Instead, he wrote at once to his mother with warmth and common sense, to explain the reason for their delay, and Charlotte, who had been deeply touched by her mother-in-law's kindness after her first child's death, added her impulsive comment.

"P.S. Permit me, my dear Madam, to add a line to Scott's letter, to express to you how sincerely I feel for your loss, and how much I regret that I am not near you to try by the most tender care to soften the pain that so great a misfortune must inflict on you and all those who had the happiness of being connected with him. I hope soon to have the pleasure of returning to you, and to convince you of the sincere affection of your daughter,

M.C.S."

They then set off for the north at leisure, reluctantly cutting out the last few days of their visit. It had been a pleasantly frivolous interlude for Charlotte, full of French chatter and rather too expensive shopping expeditions, while Scott spent his time studying medieval armour and weapons in the Tower of London and the oldest manuscripts in the British Museum. That goblin-like personality, Mat Lewis, had enjoyed introducing his new Scottish discovery to his fashionable and literary friends, and Scott had been duly presented to Lord Downshire, whom he found very pleasant, at the Dumergues' Piccadilly residence.

On their return, they found Mrs Scott utterly exhausted and Anne in a state of nervous prostration after the long strain of caring for an invalid who had become terrifyingly irascible and difficult in the last stages of his illness. During the next few weeks of dreary formalities, family and business correspondence, and the clearing-up of the inevitable accumulation of possessions, Mrs Scott refused to consider leaving home, but when the Courts rose in July, she accepted Charlotte's urgent invitation to bring Anne with her to Lasswade for the summer. Here she was pleasantly occupied in making small garments for the expected grandchild, while Anne followed Charlotte about like an adoring shadow.

Once he had seen his family well established, Scott took the chance of getting back to the Border and the ballads. He spent a week with Shortreed in Liddesdale, heard with mixed feelings of the serious illness of his old friend, the antiquarian Sheriff of Selkirkshire, and responded with new awareness to the compulsive rhythms of the Border's living past. He returned to Lasswade with a newly stirring ambition, not merely to translate weird poems for Mat Lewis to include in his *Tales of Wonder*, but to write verses on his own account. He had visited his kinsfolk at Harden, too, that summer, and *The Eve of St John* was written of Smailholm Tower, which was their property and had been his childhood's delight. He was feeling his way, all the time, through a thicket of conflicting interests and obligations, breaking off his work to drive out with his women folk to visit a neighbour, to rescue Camp from a swarm of bees which he had inadvertently disturbed, or to make a rustic arch over the gateway to the cottage at Charlotte's request.

But always the tide of his imagination flowed underneath every enterprise, the rhythms repeated by the horses' hooves, the words he wanted flitting in and out of his mind, elusive as the swifts screaming overhead, or the butterflies that flitted among the roses of their trim front garden as Charlotte went to and fro with her flower-basket, talking and laughing with Anne, or sat demurely on the white garden seat beside her mother-in-law.

The Grey Brother, Thomas the Rhymour, Glenfinlas . . . were only echoes of all the ballads in which he had been revelling for most of his life. But they were also milestones in the development of a gift he had known he possessed, which was to grow like the Biblical mustard seed into the great tree which was to overshadow all his days.

"How nice it would be, Scott, to have a little light phaeton in which we could drive about the countryside instead of a heavy carriage for which we must hire post-horses," said Charlotte, pausing beside the desk in the corner of the sitting-room where he had taken refuge.

"Yes, my love," he said absently. "I will see what can be done."

"Scott, I do not think Anne looks well, in spite of all the good food and country air. What shall we do?"

He scribbled desperately for a moment, then gave it up, tossing down his quill. "What was that you said? Anne? I will send for the doctor."

"And Scott, I think your mother has done enough sewing for today. Shall we take a picnic to the riverside?"

"Yes, indeed, my precious girl, if it would not weary you too much."

So it went on, throughout the long, lovely summer days. But before returning to Edinburgh, Scott paid a visit to his kinsfolk in Kelso. He found his Aunt Janet at the garden, as keenly interested as ever in all his doings, but his Uncle Robert sadly failed. In the interval since their last meeting, he seemed to have become an old man. His nephew's presence evidently comforted him, and Scott stayed on, talking gently of the old days.

The arrival of James Ballantyne on the doorstep, with his brisk talk of the progress of *The Kelso Mail*, and his request for an article on a legal subject, was something of a relief. He scribbled a few hundred words, made the excuse of taking it round to the editor in order to see James's office, and was impressed by his former school-friend's artistic achievements in the setting up of type. As they

talked, he spoke of Mat Lewis, and his weird gift, recited some of
Lewis's ballads, said with pride that Lewis was willing to include
some of his own work.

"Let's hear what ye've been writing," James demanded.

"Man, it's never worth listening to after his."

"Let's hear it, just the same."

Scott read. James listened. Finally he slapped his plump knees. "I
ken fine which I prefer, Wattie. And it's yours, my man."

Scott was frankly incredulous. But admittedly the long delay in
the publication of the *Tales of Wonder* was tiresome to a man who
naturally wanted to see his work in print. He suggested that James
Ballantyne should print a dozen copies of his most recent poems,
calling it *An Apology for Tales of Terror*. Scott said with a smile that
he might well send a few copies to Mat Lewis in the hope of
accelerating the original publication.

James Ballantyne promised to put the work in hand at once, and
when Scott revisited the printing-shed, hung about with back
numbers of *The Kelso Mail*, he was delighted with the way it had
been done.

"I wonder, Jamie," he said enthusiastically, "why you do not take
on some booksellers' work, to keep those types of yours in play.
The Kelso Mail, after all, comes out only once a week."

James Ballantyne, wiping his plump hands absently on an
extremely dirty rag, surveyed his beloved printing-presses thoughtfully, as his natural indolence struggled with pride in his work.

"I've never given the notion a thought, Wattie. I've no acquaintance with the Edinburgh trade, ye ken. But I must admit my types
are good, and I could mebbe do the work more cheaply than a town
printer."

Scott sat down astride a rickety kitchen chair with half the back
gone, tilted it perilously on to its back legs, and considered the
situation. "I've been collecting old Border ballads for years," he
said thoughtfully. "And I believe I could put together, with little
trouble, enough for a neat little volume, which might sell for four
or five shillings. That's it, man," he said, slapping his knees as his
enthusiasm kindled. "I will talk to some of the booksellers when

I get back to Edinburgh, and if the thing goes on, you shall be the printer. How'd that suit you?"

"It would suit me fine, Wattie," said James Ballantyne. But his wry smile was somewhat sceptical. With a dozen projects on hand and his head in the clouds as usual, it seemed more than possible that his old friend might fail to give this daydream another thought.

But the salvage of the great oral tradition of Border ballads, increasingly threatened with oblivion as the last generation who remembered them grew old, had long been one of Scott's cherished ambitions, and such a collection as Mat Lewis was haphazardly assembling had given him an idea of how it might be done. So, as the Lasswade household began packing for their return to Edinburgh, he laid it aside to be dealt with as opportunity offered.

For the present, Charlotte must be his first care, since the birth of her second child was expected in November, and he was thankful that his mother and Anne were nearby. The whole household was in such a state of tension as November began that it communicated itself even to Camp.

"Oh, sir!" cried Morag, bursting unceremoniously into the parlour, where Scott and Charlotte sat at breakfast by candlelight one dark morning. "Camp's bit the baker. What'll we do?"

"Leave it to me, lass," said Scott, as he felt in his pocket for a suitable coin. "Stay with your mistress."

They could hear him chuckling to himself as he limped downstairs, though when he returned a few minutes later with the culprit at his heels, he was as grave as if he were in Court. Everyone was silent as he took his place, then turned to look for the offender. "Where's the dog got to?"

Charlotte giggled, pointing. "See, poor fellow, where he sits in the darkest corner. That dog, he has a conscience. Do not be too hard on him, Scott."

"Camp," said Scott solemnly. "Who bit the baker?"

The bull terrier, flattening his ears, rolled his eyes away from his master till the whites showed like crescent moons. Lifting one paw, he seemed to be trying to obliterate himself against the wall.

"It was bad, very bad," Scott repeated sternly. "But I see you know it. That is enough." He changed his voice. "The baker has been well paid. You are forgiven."

At once, Camp knew it. He rose, shook himself, and trotted across the room to his master's chair, his stumpy tail flailing the furniture triumphantly, in passing. Smiling across the room at his wife's evident enjoyment of the little drama, Scott put down a hand to fondle the dog's cropped ears, and received a rasping caress from a warm, wet tongue.

"Mother is to spend the day with you, my love?"

"So I hope," said Charlotte casually. For now, as the centre of everyone's concern, she had become the queen of her small domain, enjoying the fuss and petting, able to avert her thoughts from the ordeal ahead.

"And Uncle Daniel is to call?"

She nodded, sipping her chocolate.

"I will be back as early as I can."

She laughed at his anxious face. "Do not distress yourself, my dear Scott. I shall do very well, and Camp will be waiting for his walk all day long."

For since Camp, now a fully grown gladiator, had wrenched his lead out of Morag's hand and demolished a mongrel nearly twice his own size (who had made an unfavourable comment from the far side of the street), it had been thought better that Scott should supervise his excursions.

Later in November, news of birth and death came, as before, close on each other's heels. Charlotte's child, a girl, lived, and was christened Charlotte Sophia in the Castle Street drawing-room, sponsored by Lord Downshire, her paternal grandmother and her mother's kind friend, Madame Sophia Dumergue.

And at Middlestead in Selkirkshire the death of Andrew Plummer, the scholar and antiquarian, set in motion the influence of Scott's brother officers of the Buccleuch family with the Duke, and that of his earliest High School companion, Robert Dundas, with his father, Lord Melville, to appoint Scott as his successor to the post of Sheriff. By mid-December his appointment had come through.

So the year ended happily for the Castle Street household.

Charlotte was delighted with her baby and Scott enchanted with them both. Relief from anxiety set him free to attend his favourite Clubs, and continue his plans for the collection of Border ballads, in the evenings. He was making, too, many new contacts as his literary and historic interests became more widely known.

When the vastly learned medieval scholar and Member of Parliament for Oxford University, Richard Heber, visited Edinburgh that winter, Scott was one of those presented to him, and his candid delight in the older man's scholarship laid the foundations of a lifelong friendship. Heber's habit of browsing about in all sorts of unlikely places for early texts took him, one day, to a dusty little bookshop in the High Street, of which Scott was only vaguely aware.

"You might do worse than take a look round," said Heber, next time he met Scott. "I found two or three very interesting things on the shelves, and the bookseller struck me as an astute, obliging sort of fellow. Constable's the name, I believe, Archibald Constable, who plays host to a few young students who look too threadbare to have the price of many books in their pockets."

"As many a bookseller did to me, not long since," Scott agreed.

"But there was one hungry-looking lad I took a fancy to," said Heber, thoughtfully sipping his wine. "Perched at the top of a ladder like a stork on a roof-top, too engrossed in his book to notice when I happened to kick the ladder askew and he nearly came down on top of me. We got talking afterwards – I felt I owed him an apology. He comes from near the part of the world you talk so much about – Liddesdale. And it seems he's some sort of a poet."

"And I've never heard of him? That must be put right. What's his name?"

"Ah, that I cannot tell you," said the scholar from Oxford. "We were talking of medieval verse."

"I'll go to the shop tomorrow."

"You can't fail to see him. A great gaunt fellow, awkward as a spider and almost in rags, with eyes that go through you like a gimlet."

When Scott took Heber's description to the bookseller, Archibald

Constable laughed and pointed out a young man perched, once more, on the top of a ladder, with a battered volume open on his knees. So, in due course, Scott encountered John Leyden, the shepherd's son from Denholm, a natural genius who absorbed learning as blotting paper soaks up ink, yet had the creative passion of a poet and a disdain for creature comforts which made him ready to live on bread and water so that the rest of his pittance might be spent on the subtler nourishment to be found in books.

Here was an ally in a million, a Borderer by birth, a poet of genius, loving and knowing more of his native lore than Scott had ever hoped to discover. He practically shook the gaunt and shaggy student off his ladder, took him home and fed him, sat up half the night listening and talking, talking and listening, while he and Leyden worked through the mass of material already assembled for the book of Border Minstrelsy, now to be enriched by Leyden's contributions. For Scott, the friendship was an inspiration, since he was always generous in his appreciation of other men's gifts. For Leyden it was an opportunity of making contact with men of culture on Scott's enthusiastic introduction which he was not too proud to take.

Scott himself worked on, in every spare minute, to make the material he had already collected ready for printing. It was no easy task, for he had taken notes when and as he could, scribbling down the words in a corner of a farmhouse kitchen, often in a sort of smoke-hazed twilight, sometimes unable to hear the words as a dozen singers roared them out all round him. Often he had written in haste, so that he was later unable to read his own writing. So, inevitably, he filled in the gaps with words of his own choosing. And occasionally, the function of editor and author tended to fuse. As he had admitted to Will Clerk, he liked to add a cocked hat and cane, now and then, before presenting another man's story to society. Now, he could not always resist the temptation to cap a half-seen fancy or smooth a jolting rhythm as his own ear dictated.

> "*My hounds may a' rin masterless,*
> *My hawks may fly frae tree to tree,*

My lord may grip my vassal lands,
For there again maun I never be . . ."

he wrote for *Jamie Telfer of the Fair Dodhead.*

In between whiles, with the poems ringing in his ears, he kept up his dutiful attendance at the Law Courts, where more briefs were now coming his way, drilled with the Light Dragoons, played with his baby and played host at Charlotte's little parties. Camp, to everyone's surprise, was delighted with the tiny girl, who learned to crawl, as the months passed, by supporting herself on his broad back, while Camp looked from one parent to the other with an expression of idiotic beatitude.

Scott had not forgotten James Ballantyne and his flair for printing since his last visit to Kelso. But he had constantly regretted, during the winter, that Kelso was not more accessible in term time. By the spring, he had evolved a way of getting over this problem, to their mutual benefit. In a gravely formal letter which stressed the careful consideration he had given to every aspect of the problem, "with a view as well to the public advantage as to your individual interest. It is nothing short of a migration from Kelso to this place . . ."

He was writing, deliberately, as if he were preparing a brief rather than suggesting opportunities for a friend. For the removal he advocated must stake James Ballantyne's livelihood upon his technical ability.

"Three branches of printing are quite open in Edinburgh, all of which I am well convinced you have both the ability and inclination to unite in your person. The first is that of an editor of a newspaper which shall contain something of a uniform historical deduction of events distinct from the farrago of detached and unconnected plagiarisms from the London paragraphs of *The Sun* . . . The next object would naturally be the execution of Session papers, the best paid work a printer undertakes, and of which, I dare say, you would soon have a considerable share . . . The publication of works, either ancient or modern, opens a third fair field for ambition. The only gentleman who attempts anything in that way is in very bad health; nor can I, at any rate compliment either the accuracy or the execution of his press."

His characteristic enthusiasm began to oust his legal detachment, however, in his last paragraph. It was such a beautiful plan. If James Ballantyne brought his printing presses and his artistic skill to Edinburgh, what might they not achieve together? He went on to underline the advantages.

"It appears to me that such a plan, judiciously adopted and diligently pursued, opens a fair road to an ample fortune. In the meanwhile, the *Kelso Mail* might be so arranged as to be still a source of some advantage to you; and I dare say, if wanted, pecuniary assistance might be procured to assist you at the outset, either upon terms of a share or otherwise. . . ."

He read through what he had written. Surely no man of business could fail to take advantage of such an opportunity? With a final formal flourish he ended the letter.

"I hope, at all events, you will impute my interference to anything rather than an impertinent intermeddling with your concerns on the part of, Dear Sir, your obedient servant,

Walter Scott."

James Ballantyne read the letter with very mixed feelings. The idea of the sort of move that Wattie proposed frankly appalled his comfortable indolence. But he knew his work was good, and the prospect of finding greater scope for it was tempting. Finally, he put the letter aside and did nothing about it. Other papers drifted, thick as autumn leaves, above it. And there, for the time being, the matter remained.

Meanwhile, summer was approaching, and the Castle Street household was preparing to migrate to Lasswade for the vacation, and Charlotte had not forgotten her fancy for a phaeton, in which she and Scott could drive out to visit their neighbours.

But such a vehicle, it seemed, was not to be found in Edinburgh, and Scott wrote, as a last resort, to Richard Heber, now back in London for the summer session of Parliament that "Mrs Scott has set her heart on a phaeton, at once strong and low and handsome and not to cost more than thirty guineas." Should Heber be able to procure such a thing in the metropolis, Scott added, he would be infinitely obliged.

With Charlotte appeased by the news that the matter was in hand, they set off for the country as soon as the Court rose. But this year Scott was not able to spend the vacation beautifying the cottage garden, while Charlotte planned alterations for the pleasant drawing-room, and Camp rabbited joyously in the surrounding fields. As Sheriff of Selkirkshire, it was necessary that he should visit the area for which he was responsible, and the little inn at Cloven-fords, between Edinburgh and Selkirk, was suggested to him as a useful halfway-house by friends who went there to fish.

So the new Sheriff left Camp to police his little household, and rode on to Clovenfords. Here he was within easy riding distance of Selkirk, where he put in an appearance as required, and also within reach of the lovely valleys of Yarrow and Ettrick, at the heart of the ballad country. Inevitably, he spent all his free time riding about the district, receiving a kindly Border welcome wherever he went, talking of the ballads to the old people who remembered, aware that the young were beginning to forget. If that unique literature was to be preserved, something more solid than oral tradition was needed. The plan for a carefully edited collection of the *Minstrelsy of the Scottish Border* began to take shape at the back of his mind.

Chapter 9

WHEN Scott rode back to his family at Lasswade, Camp was always the first to greet him, bursting through the garden hedge while Scott was still some distance away, informed by some strange sense that the horse being ridden so eagerly homewards could be bearing only one person in the world. And Scott, dismounting at the little garden gate with the rustic arch he himself had laboriously made, spoke to the dog as to a personal friend, the soft Border burr in his deep voice stressed by his recent contacts with so many Borderers.

"Camp, my man, it's to be hoped you've kept all in order while I've been away. How's the wee girl that ye've had the care of?" He fondled the dog with his big, kind hands, stooping so that Camp could lick his cheek and gently nip his ear, as Charlotte, attracted by the commotion, came running to the gate.

"Scott! At last! Oh, Scott, forget the dog for but one moment to kiss your wife. Then I must tell you the news – "

"Good news, I hope, dearest girl?" said Scott as he slipped the mare's reins over her head and held out his arms.

"Indeed, yes. And the best of all is that you are home again," she said, lifting her face for his kiss. "Sophia? Yes, she is more beautiful than ever. But there is more yet!"

"What better news than that?" Scott teased her.

"The phaeton! It is here since yesterday!"

Scott shouted with laughter. "Sweetheart! We must go for a drive at once."

"You laugh at me, Scott!" She put her head on one side and smiled up at him. "But I have looked forward so much to have a truly stylish carriage. Come and look."

The phaeton, which would probably turn out to have cost more in post-horses to drive it from London, than its value, as Scott ruefully realised, was certainly an elegant affair, the light body slung between the four wheels, with a hood which could be raised or lowered according to the weather, to be drawn by a strong horse controlled by one of the occupants of the handsomely upholstered interior, instead of by a coachman perched high on a box. Camp evidently approved of it. He sprang inside, clearly indicating his intention of making one of any party.

Charlotte was enchanted to be driven to visit her neighbours in the new conveyance, but Scott soon came to consider a round of afternoon visits too tame, and planned more daring excursions. The light vehicle was pleasant to handle, and he was delighted by the opportunity of including Charlotte in his dearest projects.

"Now you too shall see Liddesdale, my dearest girl. We shall also make a tour of my Sheriffdom," he promised gaily, as he flicked the sturdy cob with his driving whip and took a corner at a spanking pace, "and end up at Hermitage Castle."

Scott did not forget the projected tour. August, 1800, promised well for his ultimate project, to drive their new equipage to the very walls of Hermitage Castle, where no wheeled vehicle had ever been seen before. The idea caught the fancy of his adventurous brother-officer, Lord Dalkeith, who promised to organise an escort over the hills and a picnic on arrival.

This prospect, with its attractive blend of adventure and distinguished company, delighted Charlotte, and Scott wisely minimised the outrageous nature of his final project, during the early stages of their progress. Charlotte was delighted by the warmth of their reception at Clovenfords, and friendly deference shown to their Sheriff by the townsfolk of Selkirk, and Camp alternately sat between Scott and Charlotte on the rug laid on the floor of the phaeton for his convenience or galloped by the roadside, intent on keeping up with the fast-trotting cob.

They stayed overnight at Hawick, resting the horse for longer than Charlotte, still unaware of the ordeal before them, could understand. And then, on a blissful summer's morning, they began the long pull up to the Limekilnedge. The road was perfunctory now, a track sketched out by the quarrymen's wagons. On the summit it faded out altogether. Scott checked the horse, let Camp jump out, and sat looking round him with the mischievous grin which his rivals on the Kittle Nine Stanes of the Castle rock would have recognised.

"Scott, there is no more a road!" cried Charlotte in dismay.

"Hout, never fash your head for that," said Scott, taking off his hat to mop his forehead. "There's drove roads, and sheep tracks. And folk that ken the way to guide us," he added, as a shout from a couple of riders in the distance made the cob prick up his ears.

The Liddesdale farmers who had been assigned the task of guiding Scott to Hermitage knew him well from his raiding expeditions and were greatly amused by the enterprise. Their laughter did more than their casually shouted instructions to reassure Charlotte, though she kept her eyes shut most of the time as they teetered among sheep-tracks by the side of the Whitterope Burn towards the comparatively level ground through which the Hermitage Water ran. The cob behaved well, and one of the farmers dismounted to lead him down the trickiest part of the descent, while Scott, blissfully happy and streaming with sweat, declaimed snatches from *Kinmont Willie* on which he had recently been working, and Camp bounced in and out of the heather, in frequent danger from the horses' feet.

"Ze Channel was nothing, but nothing to compare," said Charlotte through clenched teeth as they lurched on. "Soon I shall be sick . . ."

But Scott patted her knee with a large, hot hand, then pointed into the distance. "Courage, my love. We are almost there. See where the grey walls rise above the trees."

The group assembled by the castle had seen them now, and came crowding to the burnside as Scott guided the cob to the ford and sent him churning through it.

> *"He is either himsel' a de'il frae hell,"*

he shouted as they neared the far bank,

> *"Or else his mither a witch maun be;*
> *I wadna hae ridden yon wan water*
> *For a' the gowd in Christentie!"*

They crowded round, clapping and laughing. Lord Dalkeith helped Charlotte down, and his wife hurried forward with her vinaigrette at the sight of her pale face. Someone made her sit down on the smooth, sheep-cropped turf, someone else fanned her distractedly, Lord Dalkeith himself brought a glass of wine.

"I shall scold Scott for this," said young Lady Dalkeith. "It must have been a dreadful experience."

But Charlotte had begun to enjoy herself, and Scott, mopping his face and laughing at the comments of those helping him to unharness the cob, was obviously unrepentant. "I hope your ladyship will not be hard on him," said Charlotte. "It has given him so much pleasure."

"But you might have been thrown out! The phaeton must nearly have overturned many times!" they protested.

"But it did not," said Charlotte bravely.

"It shall be as you wish, Mrs Scott," said Lady Dalkeith. "And now, you must be famished. All is prepared. Let us eat."

So Scott escaped a scolding, but Lady Dalkeith found a few moments to ask him about the progress of his collection of Border ballads. "So many people are eagerly awaiting it," she said.

"The project is well forward, your ladyship. My friend Heber believes that he has interested a firm of London publishers in it, and I have a good friend, a printer in Kelso, who will bring out a very pretty version of it as soon as it is required."

"I am delighted to know it," said Lady Dalkeith. "But you know well, Mr Scott, that I am waiting for something from your own pen, which will be of even greater interest than your collection of the works of other men."

Scott smiled. "There may well be more of my own work than some will like in this collection," he admitted. "Where lines were missing, or a tale unfinished I – "

"No doubt you did. But I await such a ballad from your own hand, to which you can put your own name," said the young Countess, looking away from the ruins of Hermitage towards the honey-coloured surrounding hills. "Something . . ." She paused, picking a few florets of wild thyme and sniffing them as she pondered, "something like the adventures of one of the ancient minstrels

you are for ever quoting, as he wanders the Borders with his page."
She wrinkled her pretty nose and smiled at him. "But I don't mean
a romantic minstrel and a pretty page from one of the old tales.
He should be more . . . more gnarled and weatherbeaten, like the
Liddesdale folk, with a goblin-like creature in attendance and the
east wind keening round him." She tossed away the scented florets
and laughed at her own fancy.

But Scott was interested. He sat for a few moments, thinking.
Then he gave her a formal, but smiling little bow.

"Your ladyship's instructions, I promise, shall be obeyed."

"Now, Mr Scott, you are making fun of me because I venture to
teach a poet what poems to write," she said, blushing.

"I was never more serious in my life," said Scott. "I believe such
a thing might be well done. Let us suppose – "

But the general bustle of preparations for departure had now been
initiated by Lord Dalkeith, in view of the arduous manœuvre of
getting the Scotts in their phaeton on to more suitable terrain by
daylight. Surprisingly, this proved less alarming, if more arduous,
than the outward journey, and the presence of a dozen sturdy
farmers, who dismounted to steady the phaeton while others guided
the cob, gave Charlotte confidence enough to enjoy it. Scott urged
everybody on with snatches of heroic ballads, while Camp, who
had run himself to a standstill, snored at his feet.

The plans for the *Minstrelsy* continued to take shape in Scott's
mind throughout the rest of the vacation. The ancient ballads were
to be enriched by editorial notes of great historical interest, with
which he was now very well supplied. But he was always looking
for more. And so was Leyden, that most whole-hearted enthusiast,
who came and went with new discoveries which delighted them
both. Chief of these was the ballad of *Sir Tristrem*, preserved in the
Auchinleck MS. No sooner had Scott's household returned to
Edinburgh for the winter when Leyden burst in, dripping like a
dog just out of the river from the sharp shower which he had
never noticed, a bulky wad of manuscript bulging his threadbare
coat.

"Where's the master?" he demanded of Morag and Rob, who

were still clearing trunks, hampers and bundles from the entrance hall.

"In his study, maist likely," said Morag, who knew the wild-looking gentleman well, but regretted the puddles his wet clothes were leaving on her once-spotless floor. "But – "

"I ken my way," said Leyden, blundering on among the obstacles, to stride into the study, where Scott was already at his desk. Camp's warning bark was checked by Leyden's harsh, exultant voice.

"See here, my man, there's never a doubt in my mind that *Sir Tristrem* was the work of Thomas the Rhymer himself. See here – " He scattered half a dozen scrawled sheets about him, plunged after them just ahead of Camp. "I'll be obliged if ye'll let them be," he advised the bull terrier, who courteously withdrew, "Thomas Learmont, we believe was laird of Erceldoune at the hinder end of the thirteenth century. Now, from internal evidence of the manuscript itself and the strong support of local tradition which I've assembled here – "

Equally excited, Scott was thumbing his way through the closely scrawled pages. "Ye have a case, man. I believe ye have a case. If we can prove it, *Sir Tristrem* deserves not only a place, but a place of of honour in the *Minstrelsy*."

"Aye, that's just what I thought. Now, look ye here – "

Charlotte's amused but anxious voice from the doorway jerked the two men unwillingly back to the present and its lesser problems. "Mr Leyden, indeed if you do not take off zat wet coat, you shall catch your death. Scott, lend him something."

"Hout, Mrs Scott, never heed – "

"Also," said Charlotte firmly, "you drip on everything."

Scott rootled hastily through a pile of his country clothes, just brought in from the carriage. "So," said Charlotte, "that is better. Morag shall take yours to the kitchen, and you shall stay to dinner."

So the winter session began, with daily attendance in the Outer Courts for Scott, drill whenever possible with the Volunteer Light Horse contingent, besides his regular duties as Quartermaster and at the stables. In the evenings he found time to attend the meetings

of the Speculative Society and his less serious Clubs, to take Charlotte to the theatre, to play host to the little supper parties at Castle
Street attended by his friends among the Montagnards: Will Clerk,
Adam Ferguson, William Erskine, James Skene, John Irving and
their prettiest female relations. Yet somehow or other, he contrived
to keep up his work with Leyden on the *Minstrelsy*. Thanks to
Heber's recommendation the firm of Longman in London were
interested in its publication, and had agreed, after seeing samples of
the work done at Kelso, that James Ballantyne should be the
printer.

But 1801 began sadly, for Anne's health continued to deteriorate,
and Dr Daniel told the family frankly that he doubted whether she
would live more than a few months. Scott's only consolation was
that his mother's decision to give up the family house in George's
Square and take up residence in George Street, just round the
corner from his own house, meant that he and Charlotte were able
to be in and out, doing what they could to keep Anne company
and ease her mother's burden.

In March, Scott was introduced by Heber to another lifelong
friend, the erudite and witty George Ellis, who was at that time
preparing his collection of *Ancient English Poetry* and *Ancient English
Romance*, so that the news of Scott's work on the *Minstrelsy* was
of great interest to a scholar generous enough to welcome, rather
than suspect, another man's work in an adjacent field. He delighted
Scott by writing to express interest, and Scott at once replied.

"Sir,
    "As I feel myself highly flattered by your enquiries, I lose no time
in answering them to the best of my ability. Your eminence in
the literary world, and the warm praises of our mutual friend
Heber, had made me long for an opportunity of being known
to you. I enclose the first sheet of Sir Tristrem ... These pages are
transcribed by Leyden, an excellent young man of uncommon
talents ..."

George Ellis was sceptical of the two young men's enthusiasm for

Thomas the Rhymer's authorship of the medieval ballad, and said so, but so courteously that they were inspired to further efforts to convince him. The correspondence flourished, and ranged far beyond the original point of contact. In April, Scott, who was always more anxious about his friends than about himself, wrote to ask Ellis to intercede with Heber about Leyden, who was becoming restless, and had taken up "a most absurd resolution to go to Africa on a voyage of discovery. Will you have the goodness to beg Heber to write to him seriously on so ridiculous a plan, which can promise nothing either pleasant or profitable," Scott wrote unhappily. "It gives me great pain to see a valuable young man of uncommon genius and acquirements fairly throw himself away . . ."

Ellis agreed, after reading Leyden's work, and after consultation with Heber, made the alternative suggestion of finding Leyden a post in India, where he might use his extraordinary gifts to study Oriental languages. Leyden was interested, and not at all daunted when the only available vacancy for a post in the East India Company proved to be that of an assistant surgeon. To qualify for this Leyden would have to pass his examinations in medicine and surgery after six months, as opposed to nearly as many years of study, and be ready to sail for India by 1802. Leyden's opportunity was Scott's most grievous loss, for the work they had done together had been an inspiration to them both. But the help he had given him was as typical of his devotion to his friends as his desire to see James Ballantyne and his printing presses established in Edinburgh, though in Ballantyne's case their interests seemed to coincide.

His literary schemes made little headway that spring for James Ballantyne, uneasy about expense, was taking his time over his decision, Leyden was now immersed in the immense programme of medical studies which he had undertaken, and the family saddened by Anne's failing health. In June she died, and her mother stoically sought consolation in spending as much time as possible with Charlotte, who was now expecting another child.

Scott, as Sheriff of Selkirkshire, was in duty bound to leave his mother and his wife at Lasswade for the summer vacation while he himself went on to Clovenford to attend to the affairs of his sheriffdom. As always, he rode far and wide, revisiting old friends and making new ones.

It was at Blackhouse, on the Douglas burn, that another part of his life's pattern fell into place, when he was overtaken by darkness beyond St Mary's Loch, and turned towards the friendly lights of a farmhouse, the door of which was opened by the son of the house, a young man of about his own age, named William Laidlaw.

The farmer and his family made the Sheriff most welcome, and Willie, in particular, responded to his inquiries on local history with alert intelligence. He struck Scott as the type to be found at the University rather than on a small Border sheep farm, and since his interest in people was always practical, he said so, while they were riding to inspect the ruins of an ancient chapel nearby. Willie Laidlaw, smiling gently, said he had no ambition for a life of letters. The country suited him well enough. But Scott's enthusiasm for Border ballads interested him warmly.

"I'll have to take you to meet Jamie the Poeter," he said, with his shy, friendly grin. "I ken him weel. He's a fine hand with a ballad, and his auld mither kens mair about ancient poetry than ony ither leeving soul."

"I'll hold you to that," Scott said, "one of these days. But I must ride back to Lasswade tomorrow. Will you do me the kindness, meantime, to let me have news of any old ballads that you hear of between now and then?"

"I will that," said Willie Laidlaw enthusiastically.

"I'll be at Lasswade for the rest of the summer. And here's my Edinburgh address."

It was a casual beginning to an unspectacular friendship which was to be one of the most significant Scott ever made.

In October, their son was born, and, of course, christened Walter, to the delight of the entire family. Charlotte, proud and happy in the midst of the hubbub of congratulations, was briefly saddened by the news of Lord Downshire's death. But as she enjoyed her husband's anxious attention, smiled at her babies, and graciously received the congratulations of her friends the old unsettled days seemed very far away.

Painters and joiners were busy now at number 39 Castle Street, the elegant, bow-fronted house farther down the road, which Scott had recently bought, and where the family were to live for so many years. He complained lightheartedly to Ellis that the remaining painters and workmen seemed nowadays "not to proceed upon the plan of Solomon's architects, whose saws and hammers were not heard, but rather upon the more ancient system of the builders of Babel". But the move was a success, especially in the opinion of Camp, who imposed his seal of approbation on every available doorpost in a most Biblical way, till Cook banished him into the tiny, steeply sloping plot which his superiors considered more appropriate for such libations.

The new year of 1802 offered a brief interlude in the war with France, though the Peace of Amiens was in fact, no more than a year's truce in the Napoleonic struggle. For the little household in Castle Street it was a year of consolidation and progress.

During the spring vacation, Scott held Willie Laidlaw to his promise of taking him to see the Ettrick Shepherd, his friend "Jamie the Poeter". So one evening in the spring of 1802 Scott and Laidlaw rode to the farm in the Vale of Ettrick where James Hogg was now working as a shepherd, living with his mother in a ramshackle cottage, dreaming up his poems as he spent the long summer days out on the hills with his sheep. He greeted Scott with the half-humorous, half-wary defiance of the Borderer who suspects patronage, but Scott's candid interest in the ancient ballads disarmed him enough to agree to invite Scott indoors to hear his mother recite them, as few now living could.

So he led the way into the dim kitchen of the cottage by the burnside, with its twisted rowan trees to ward off witches by the doorway, and the stone-walled sheep-stall nearby.

The old woman surveyed them as warily as her son had done, and insisted that the visitors should first accept the hospitality of a meal of bannocks and ewes' milk. Then, as the light began to fail, she wrapped her plaid about her and took her usual place in the ingle-neuk beside the peat-fire which now began to glow like a jewel in the dusk. The young men, still at the table, watched her in awed silence as she began to declaim, swaying to and fro, one hand outstretched towards the smouldering peat, her features, gnarled and brown as an ancient oak-tree, shadowed by her plaid.

Scott fancied that she had some of the oracular quality of an ancient sibyl as her voice rose and fell in the simple rhythms which held so much of the sound of broken water in the moonlight, the clash of steel, the thunder of horses' hooves. He made what notes he unobtrusively could, but as the light failed, he could only sit and listen to the enchanted voice of another age. At last, when her voice died, and her son rose to kindle the thin glimmer of a rushlight, he found words with which to thank her.

The old woman accepted his tribute with an inclination of her head, then sat, staring into the glowing peats, without other recognition of his words of farewell.

"Mither," said James Hogg, as they girthed up their horses in the thin summer darkness through which came the cries of lambs, the deeper, reassuring murmur of the ewes, "Mither doesn't seem to spend much of her time on middle-earth these days."

His soft Border voice was sad but proud, as if he himself subscribed to another standard of values than those of worldly position and financial success which the new Sheriff might be thought to represent, and all Scott's candid enthusiasm did not disarm him at their first meeting. But as Scott and Laidlaw rode home, the younger man spoke with humour and affection of his friend.

"He's a grand lad, sir, forby his heid's fair stuffed wi' fancies. He can wrestle and fecht wi' the best, and he's a fine hand at the sheep-clipping for all yon talk o' fairies."

"Fairies?" Scott was startled. The brawny, off-hand young shepherd had not given him the impression of such ethereal interests.

"Aye. He claims to be the poet o' Fairyland. His grandfather on his mither's side, auld Will o' Phawhope, he'll tell ye, was the last man on the Border to have seen the wee folk. Whit's mair, he'll tell ye there were witches among his father's kin."

"Does he so? I'll have to see more of Jamie the Poeter," said Scott.

"Mind ye, he'll no' be laughed at," said Willie Laidlaw earnestly.

Scott was shocked. "Man, what made ye think I'd want to laugh?"

The first two volumes of *Minstrelsy of the Scottish Border* had come out by January 1802, and the beauty of its production attracted as much attention from publishers and booksellers as its contents pleased discerning readers. James Ballantyne was now printing the third volume which Scott had now completed. It was to consist of modern work in the ballad style by various authors, including his hobgoblin patron, "Monk" Lewis, Leyden, and himself, among others. *Sir Tristrem*, about the authorship of which George Ellis was still gently teasing him, was, after all, to make a separate volume. During the spring vacation, Scott enjoyed himself ordering copies of the earlier volumes to be sent to the people whose opinion he most valued, among them his mother in George Street, his uncle, Dr Daniel Rutherford, to whose care he owed so much, James Hogg, the Ettrick Shepherd, whose wayward genius had so much intrigued him at their recent meeting, and George Ellis in Sunninghill. The English man of letters wrote enthusiastically.

"The volumes are arrived, and I have been devouring them, not as a pig does a parcel of grains (by which simile you will judge that I must be brewing, as indeed I am) putting in its snout, shutting its eyes and swallowing as fast as it can without consideration – but as a schoolboy does a piece of gingerbread, nibbling a little bit here and a little bit there. . . ."

But the person on whom the enthusiastic reception of the Minstrelsy had the greatest effect was probably James Ballantyne, who wrote by the end of March from Kelso.

"Dear Sir,

By to-morrow's Fly I shall send the remaining Materials for the Minstrelsy, together with three sheets of *Sir Tristrem* . . . I shall ever think the printing of the *Scottish Minstrelsy* one of the most fortunate circumstances of my life. I have gained, not lost, by it, in a pecuniary light; and the prospects it has been the means of opening to me, may advantageously influence my future destiny. I can never be sufficiently grateful for the interest you unceasingly take in my welfare. Your query regarding *Edinburgh* I am *yet* at a loss to answer. To say truth, the expenses I have incurred in my resolution to acquire a character for elegant printing, whatever might be the result, cramp considerably my present exertions. A short time, I trust, will make me easier, and I shall then contemplate the road before me with a steady eye . . ."

Scott laid the letter aside with a smile. How like James that was, with his warm heart and careful craftsmanship and muddling anxieties. He must be left in peace to make up his mind. Meanwhile, as the Castle Street household left Edinburgh to spend the spring vacation as usual at Lasswade, he remembered his promise to the young Countess of Dalkeith. Snatches of a ballad about the Goblin Page had been keeping time with his charger's hoof-beats as his squadron of Light Dragoons wheeled and charged across Portobello sands in recent weeks. Soon after their arrival at the cottage, he tried them out on William Erskine and George Cranstoun when they paid them a visit and rain kept everybody indoors, so that he was obliged to read in the still disordered sitting-room, against a background of stentorian yells from young Walter, in the arms of his nurse, and a steady babble from Sophia, now nearly three, who was rolling about on the carpet, telling an unintelligible story to Camp.

Amid these distractions, gentle Erskine and matter-of-fact George Cranstoun tried to appreciate the new rhythms without success. The change from the familiar simplicity of the ballads surprised them, and the accompanying hubbub made Scott's deep rumbling voice difficult to hear. He was soon aware of it, and broke off with a smile and a shrug.

"It does not please you?"

"Well," said honest Erskine, "I must admit – "

George Cranstoun cleared his throat. "Well, since you ask me – "

Scott shouted with laughter. "I shall do nothing of the sort. You have given your answer. Come, the rain is over, and we should be out of doors." He snatched up his sturdy daughter and hoisted her to his shoulders, reaching for his stick as he limped towards the door. "Come, let us see if Camp can put up that hare he has been telling me about this long while."

They followed him with relief. But before he left to return to Edinburgh, Erskine found a chance to have a few words with Scott. "It may be, Wattie, that we were mistaken about this new poem of yours. I was somewhat distracted at the time – "

"No wonder," Scott agreed, with a reminiscent grin.

"But I must admit I cannot get the lilt of it out of my mind."

Scott clapped him on the shoulder. "Why, bless you, Will: no more can I."

But he laid the new venture aside for the rest of the vacation, which he devoted to his duties as Sheriff, the assembly of material for the third volume of the *Minstrelsy*, and the quest for further proofs of the identity of the author of *Sir Tristrem*. Then his duties as an advocate claimed his attention as the summer session at the Law Courts began. Leyden was engrossed by the approaching examinations on which his future depended, and Charlotte busy with her matronly duties, delighted by the opportunity of playing hostess to Scott's friends. It seemed likely that the new poem would die a natural death.

But Scott was still Quartermaster of the Edinburgh Volunteer Light Dragoons, and went into camp as usual at the beginning of the summer vacation. During one of the routine exercises on Portobello sands, he received a kick from a brother officer's horse which laid him up in his quarters with a monstrously swollen leg for several days, with nothing to do, and, what was worse, nothing whatever to read except military manuals. Out of sheer boredom, he began to write, in the galloping rhythm which he had tried out without success on his friends, the first canto of the poem which had changed meanwhile from the ballad of Gilpin Horner to become *The Lay of the Last Minstrel*.

> "*The feast was over in Branksome tower,*
> *And the Ladye had gone to her secret bower;*

> *Her bower that was guarded by word and by spell,*
> *Deadly to hear, and deadly to tell –*
> *Jesu Maria, shield us well!*
> *No living wight, save the Ladye alone,*
> *Had dared to cross the threshold stone . . ."*

He wrote, propped up on his narrow, comfortless camp bed with his own saddle at his back, hearing the horses gallop, matching his measure to their thundering hooves.

> *"Nine-and-twenty knights of fame*
> *Hung their shields in Branksome hall;*
> *Nine-and-twenty squires of name*
> *Brought them their steeds to bower from stall;*
> *Nine-and-twenty yeomen tall*
> *Waited, duteous, on them all;*
> *They were all knights of mettle true,*
> *Kinsmen to the bold Buccleuch . . ."*

So James Skene found him, as he tethered his horse and took the wooden stairs two at a time to see how the stricken Quartermaster was faring. Far away from the makeshift quarters of the Edinburgh Light Dragoons, with hastily scrawled sheets scattered round him, his quill scattering ink in all directions, he wrote, as ardently as he had ever galloped, his first epic of the greatest house of the Borderland.

"*Ten of them were sheath'd in steel,*" Scott declaimed, daring Skene to interrupt with an imperious gesture,

> *"With belted sword, and spur on heel;*
> *They quitted not their harness bright,*
> *Neither by day nor yet by night:*
> *They lay down to rest,*
> *With corselet laced,*
> *Pillow'd on buckler cold and hard:*
> *They carved at the meal*
> *With gloves of steel,*
> *And they drank the red wine through the helmet barr'd . . ."*

Skene stood, unmoving, in the doorway, as the galloping rhythm transmuted the familiar excitement of a cavalry charge into the heroic terms of immortal chivalry. He had known Scott as "Earl Walter", the wildest horseman, the best storyteller, the deepest drinker of the Mess. He knew, vaguely, that his friend was a collector of old ballads. But this was different. The very pulse of the past throbbed in his ears as he listened, and he felt he could listen for ever.

Then Scott stabbed his quill at the inkwell, missed it, and sent a torrent of ink cascading over the drab army blankets. Skene came to life, ran forward to check it, scrabbling for the spattered sheets at Scott's imperious roar.

"Man alive," said Skene huskily, "I never knew ye could write like this."

Scott turned to look at him as if he had never seen him before. Then he smiled slowly, like someone waking from a blissful dream.

"I . . . never knew it myself . . ." he said.

Part Three

THE FRUIT RIPENS

Chapter 10

It was April once more, April, 1803, and the white dust of the Great North Road billowed up in clouds behind the wheels of the postchaise which was bearing Charlotte and Scott south again, with Camp, happily alert, at their feet. They were on their way to stay first with the Dumergues in Piccadilly, and then with the Ellises at Sunninghill, hoping to be in time to bid Leyden Godspeed before he set out for the East. Scott had written a letter introducing Leyden to George Ellis before he left Edinburgh the previous autumn, begging Ellis to advise and guide his most unworldly friend.

Leyden, in consequence, had not only been most generously entertained at Sunninghill during many weeks of delay and frustration, but guided through the many formalities with India House in which he would otherwise have become hopelessly involved. In fact, had Ellis not been dissatisfied with the arrangements first made for him, Leyden would have sailed on the *Hindustan*, which foundered in mid-winter, before leaving the Channel. Now there seemed a good chance that he might still be waiting for another passage when the Scotts reached London.

Scott had been anxious to drive Charlotte south in the phaeton, but after the wild journey into Liddesdale, she was thankful when George Ellis, who had heard much about Scott and his dog from Leyden, specifically included Camp in his invitation.

"That ends the phaeton," Charlotte said. "Never could you control horse, dog, and carriage at ze one time. We should not land in one ditch but in many. Dearest Scott, I do not wish to die yet. Let others drive for us."

Reluctantly, Scott agreed. Charlotte must be humoured, for she had been looking peaky since the birth of her third child, a daughter, in February. The baby had been christened Anne, to her grandmother's great pleasure, and the trip to London had been planned as much for Charlotte's sake as his own.

The change of scene, the bustle of the Great North Road, with its thundering stage-coaches, ponderous wagons, spanking turn-outs and stylish riders, did Charlotte a world of good. Scott, as usual, had a way of commanding cheerful service at every inn, and Charlotte was thankful that he had not the care of horse and phaeton on his mind, for his authority alone prevented Camp from doing battle with every yard dog on the route. But Scott contrived, with some difficulty, to keep the peace, and as they approached London at last, he spoke to Camp earnestly, scratching him behind his ears.

"Camp, my man, we are to pay a round of visits, and you will be expected to do us credit. We'll have none of that rough stuff with the lads in the mews, if you please. The good name of all at 39 Castle Street is in your hands. Is that clearly understood?"

Charlotte giggled. "Dear Scott, how foolish you are! How can a dog understand?"

But Camp laid his head on the plaid rug wrapped round her knees, sighed deeply, and looked up at her with an expressive gleam from the corners of his little black eyes.

"He understands very well," Scott said.

Whether he understood or not, Camp behaved beautifully, though during their short stay at the Dumergues' extremely urban and Gallic establishment in Piccadilly West he had to endure more incarceration than he had ever known. On their arrival, Scott found a message from the shipping company to say that Leyden had already sailed. He was deeply disappointed, but Charlotte sighed, shrugged, and prepared to enjoy herself notwithstanding. She presented her husband to her distinguished French emigrant friends, insisted on his escorting her round the shops, and talked of her children to the kindly Dumergue ladies for hours on end, while Scott escaped to join his scholarly friends, Heber and Douce, who were able to guide his researches among medieval manuscripts for further clues to the authorship of *Sir Tristrem*.

And then, to Charlotte's regret and Camp's infinite relief, it was time to drive off for their visit to the Ellises at Sunninghill, where Douce and Heber were to join them later.

Leyden had earlier described his host and hostess in a set of Chaucerian verses, so that Scott and Charlotte felt they had already met the lean, hatchet-faced scholar with the piercing wit and kind grey eyes, the odd little sniff which was an unconscious mannerism; and his tiny, exquisite little wife, whose kindness at once touched their hearts.

After the usual inquiries about the journey and arrangements for their comfort, the talk was all of Leyden, and George Ellis gave Scott the letter Leyden had written from the Isle of Wight on the 1st of April, the day before he sailed.

"I am deeply sorry, my dear Scott, that he has gone without the chance of bidding you farewell. But I hope we have done all that could be done for this remarkable young man. It would not have been your Leyden if he had arrived like a careful citizen, as I think I have said before, with all his packages carefully docketed in his portmanteau. Oh, dear me, no! He was leaving for many years the country and the friends of his youth. And of course he had deferred to the last and till it was too late, and that could easily be done, which stupid people find time to do. He arrived with all his ideas perfectly bewildered – and tired to death, and sick – "

"He would, he would," said Scott.

"And he assured us that he perfectly remembered the poem you had committed to his care for us, and that he knew he had left it somewhere, and was therefore most confident of recovering it. In short," said George Ellis, chuckling, "his whole air and countenance told us: 'I am come to be one of your friends.' And we immediately took him at his word."

"I am most infinitely obliged to you," Scott said.

"And we to you. He is a most rare person," said George Ellis. "Now read your letter."

Scott broke the seal with reluctance, troubled by the intuition that he would never again see the writer, touched by the typically scrupulous arrangements Leyden had made for the settlement of his small debt, his kindly message to Charlotte. He read the final phrases aloud.

" 'And now, my dear Scott, adieu. Think of me with indulgence, and be certain that wherever, and in whatever situation, John Leyden is, his heart is unchanged by place, and his soul by time.' "

Mrs Ellis shivered suddenly. "It has the ring of an epitaph."

"You are being fanciful, my love," said George Ellis abruptly. "Now, my dear sir, we must have the latest news of your work. This *Lay*, of yours, which, owing to Leyden's tendency to scatter his belongings, we have not yet seen: you have it with you?"

"The Introduction and the first two or three cantos only."

"We shall find the opportunity of hearing you read them," said George Ellis. Then, with a smile, and a change of mood, he added: "Will you look at that dog, Scott? I have not often been so favoured." He gave his typical sniff and chuckle, and stooped to pat Camp, who was sitting beside his chair, looking up at him with an expression of the most intelligent admiration. "What is the reason for this? I have no tit-bits in my pocket, no favours to bestow."

"As one connoisseur, he recognises another," Scott said gravely. "He is a remarkable fellow, who understands all and forgets nothing."

"Come, come. Surely you confuse the dog with the elephant?"

"Not this dog. Listen." Scott turned to Camp and said gravely: "Camp, my man, who bit the baker?"

At once Camp's head went down, his ears flattened, he crept, almost on his belly, to the farthest corner of the room, the picture of guilt and dejection. Then Scott slapped his knees. "Camp, my man, all is forgiven. The baker was well paid!"

The dog, alert once more, shook himself, barked loudly, and trotted back to his position beside his host's chair, obviously delighted by the laughter and applause of the company.

"Bless my soul," said George Ellis. "Well, well, well, my boy. I am more honoured than ever by your discernment. Now, as to the plans I have made for your entertainment . . ."

The fortnight which the visitors spent at Sunninghill was a very happy one for all concerned. Scott read the first cantos of the *Lay* to Mr and Mrs Ellis under a great oak in Windsor Forest, and was greatly cheered by their approval. Camp's devotion to George Ellis continued to be second only to that for his master, so when the Scotts left Sunninghill to spend a few days in Oxford before driving north, the Ellises had promised to make their headquarters at 39 Castle Street or Lasswade whenever they visited Scotland, and Scott had undertaken that when a suitable mate for Camp had been found, the pick of the litter should be reserved for the Ellis household.

Once back in Edinburgh, the summer session at the Law Courts claimed much of Scott's time, and what remained he had to devote to *Sir Tristrem* and *The Lay*, with occasional new ventures into reviewing for the recently founded *Edinburgh Review*, now edited by his friend and legal colleague, Jeffrey.

But Scott's literary plans were to some extent disrupted by the renewal of the French war and consequent threat of invasion. The news that Napoleon was assembling 100,000 men at Boulogne and building a fleet of flat-bottomed boats to carry them across the Channel turned the light-hearted manœuvring of the volunteer forces into deadly earnest. For the withdrawal of almost all regular forces for the defence of the south made it evident that the country must be prepared to defend itself, if Napoleon chose to switch his offensive from the more obvious key-points and strike at the unguarded north.

So while Charlotte, revived by the change of scene and up-to-date contacts with the latest London fashions, took up her social life again and proudly displayed her nursery to her friends, Scott got up early to join the cavalry on Portobello sands with the galloping rhythms of *The Lay* underlying every exciting manœuvre, and sat up late at night scribbling them down, to the satisfaction of Camp, who lifted his head to listen with apparent pleasure as Scott declaimed a few of the stanzas which had pleased Ellis, to settle his mood for new work.

> *" 'Arthur's slow wain his course doth roll*
> *In utter darkness round the pole;*
> *The Northern Bear lowes black and grim;*
> *Orion's studded belt is dim;*
> *Twinkling faint, and distant far,*
> *Shimmers through mist each planet star . . .'*

Aye, Camp, my man, so it does. Now, to work."

Camp sighed, keeled over sideways, and stretched himself out to sleep as the well-known sound of Scott's urgent quill deferred the pleasant prospect of his final stroll through the gossamer dimness of the summer night.

So, in spite of the demands of his profession, and the strenuous military preparations for a national emergency, Scott's epic poem progressed, and the controversial edition of *Sir Tristrem* approached completion. Both would in due course be printed by James Ballantyne, since Scott had made this a condition for the publication of his work since his friend set up business in Edinburgh. Longmans were already interested in *The Lay*, but *Sir Tristrem* was a more doubtful proposition, and the astutely ambitious young bookseller, Archibald Constable, stepped in with a bold offer to bring out a limited edition. The price suggested, two guineas, was high, but Constable expected more of the author than of the book, and backed his intuition of Scott's future success by offering to share the risk of publishing *The Lay* with Longmans, in due course. And Scott, always impatient of commercial haggling, was content to leave the publication of his work to be settled between those concerned, provided only that James Ballantyne had the printing of it.

Meanwhile, as the summer vacation approached, he prepared to go into training quarters with the Edinburgh Light Dragoons, with more enthusiasm than ever. His first charger, Lenore, had now been succeeded by the powerful gelding, Captain, for Scott was a heavy, strong man, and the work made great demands on his horses. Even during the vacation, which he normally spent at Lasswade, so as to be available for the duties of Sheriff of Selkirkshire, he now considered himself liable to recall for duty with the volunteer forces defending the capital, and in due course this brought a protest from the Lord Lieutenant of Selkirkshire, which he took very much amiss.

His mother was surprised, one summer evening, by his arrival, on horseback, outside her drawing-room window in George Street. He called a lad to hold his horse, clattered upstairs, and greeted her indignantly, almost before the startled maidservant had announced his arrival.

"Mother, when have I ever neglected my duties?"

Mrs Scott laid down the little coat she was knitting for her youngest grandchild, to greet him placidly. "Wattie, my lamb, whatever's the matter? Sit down and tell me what in the world this is all about."

Somewhat abashed, Walter ran his fingers through his sweat-damped hair, smiled, and stooped to kiss her. "I called in at Castle Street to make sure that all was well, with Charlotte and the bairns at Lasswade, and found this letter from his lordship, which I resent extremely."

"Let me see it," said his mother placidly.

Scott produced the letter, which Mrs Scott unfolded and read with maddening deliberation, while he paced to and fro. At last she looked up, smiling.

"Wattie, it is a most courteous reminder that the law requires a Sheriff to spend four months of the year in the area for which he is responsible, in order to attend to his duties. This he maintains you have not recently done."

"I defy Lord Napier to name any duty which I have neglected."

"And have ye given the time laid down by law for your residence in Selkirkshire?"

"Mebbe not. But he knows as well as I do that many other Sheriffs give less. I have neglected no attendance at court or meeting – this is just the sort of old-maidish fuss that I would expect from a former Commissioner to the Assembly of the Kirk."

"That is not the sort of comment I would have expected from a man brought up to reverence the Kirk," said Mrs Scott.

"I'm sorry, Mother."

"Sit down, Wattie, there's a good lad. It gives me a crick in my neck to follow ye here, there and everywhere. Lord Napier suggests ye should give up the Edinburgh Light Dragoons – "

"I will never give up service with my oldest friends – "

"Very well, then. You must give up Lasswade, and find somewhere in Selkirkshire for the vacation, so that you can help organise the yeomanry of Ettrick Forest besides. That should satisfy his lordship, and fulfil the conditions of your appointment, provided you can contrive to be in two places at once when Napoleon lands."

She had made him laugh, at last. Now he would be more reasonable, Mrs Scott thought with relief.

And indeed, his brief flare of resentment had spent itself like summer lightning, leaving him thoughtful but calm.

"I will look about during the vacation," he promised, "and see what I can find within the jurisdiction. But I fear Charlotte will be displeased, after all she has done to improve the little place."

"Charlotte," said Mrs Scott, "is not unaware of her duty as the Sheriff's lady."

Her smiling tribute pleased him. He rose and stooped to kiss her. "The Sheriff will do his best to fulfil his. Now I had best be off to begin my researches."

But the summer vacation, that year, provided less time than ever for this extra item. Scott sent his household to Lasswade while he went into camp as usual with the Edinburgh Light Dragoons at Musselburgh. The cavalry unit to which he belonged had been strengthened by four troops of yeomanry, recruited from Scottish farmers, all tough, well-mounted men who were prepared for any hardship. Near them drilled three regiments of militia, and a park of artillery was not far away. Even Will Clerk had abandoned his nonchalant attitude and joined the volunteers, though the pacific William Erskine, to Scott's amusement, had discovered that his presence was required elsewhere.

The exacting programme of cavalry exercises, the regular stable duties, and his personal responsibilities as Quartermaster, left little time for the gruelling research for the background detail of *Sir*

Tristrem, but the rhythms of *The Lay* shaped themselves subconsciously into words as he wheeled and galloped with the rest, slicing turnips set on posts for sabre practice with a ferocity he could never have felt against the human heads they represented. And he was pleased to hear his *War-Song of the Edinburgh Light Dragoons*, which he had composed the year before, set to music and sung in the Mess.

Unfortunately for Napoleon, the Gallic navy found itself unable to elude the watchdog patrols which guarded the Channel approaches, and even Napoleon hesitated to jeopardise his entire invasion army in a swarm of unarmed, flat-bottomed boats which would have been at the mercy of Nelson and the weather.

But the threat persisted, so when the manœuvres were over, and Scott joined his family at Lasswade, he wrote to the Lord Lieutenant assuring him that he was on the look-out for a cottage within his jurisdiction, and offering his services to raise a troop of Ettrick Forest yeomanry. He also rigged up a fire beacon on a tall pole outside the cottage, to be kindled immediately the first flare of an invasion warning from the battlements of Edinburgh Castle should be brought in by one of the willing watchers on the nearest high ground.

Meanwhile, he was delighted by the chance of playing with his children, for Sophia, now a serious-faced child of four, and Walter, a mercurial two-year-old, had both emerged from the anonymity of babyhood. So he lost no time in finding a quiet pony on which to begin their education, anxiously watched by Camp, who preferred them to be more readily accessible.

In due course Scott rode to Clovenfords, making it his headquarters as usual for his scheduled visit to his sheriffdom, taking the opportunity of visiting the Laidlaws at Blackhouse Farm. He found Willie enthusiastic about the *Minstrelsy*, and glad to ride over with him to see James Hogg in Ettrick valley. Here he found a more qualified approval, for Hogg's local reputation as a poet was high, and though he thanked Scott warmly for his copy, the author sensed certain reservations which implied that Hogg could have produced a better book himself. He was a strange man, Scott realised, unevenly gifted, a much more complex character than Leyden, his fellow Borderer. The poet who could write:

> "*Kilmeny had been she knew not where,*
> *And Kilmeny had seen what she could not declare . . .*"

might have a surer intuition of the world invisible than Leyden ever had, but he lacked the dedicated austerity which made Leyden independent of the distractions which were in the end to cost Hogg nearly as much as they had not long since cost Burns.

Back at Lasswade, Scott found a letter from George Ellis, all about *Sir Tristrem*, with a postscript. "Is Camp married yet?"

The summer was passing fast, and the urgency of completing *Sir Tristrem* for James Ballantyne's presses drove all lesser considerations out of Scott's mind. So, early in September, he and Charlotte were awakened one morning by the little maid's anxious pounding on their bedroom door.

"Oh, sir. Oh, ma'am, are ye awake?"

"What's that? Is the alarm ablaze? Have the French landed?" Scott shouted muzzily, as he roused himself from the depths of sleep.

"No, sir. It's no' the French. But there's a lady and gentleman at the door."

"What? At this hour?" Charlotte scrubbed her eyes open, and yawned.

"Aye, ma'am."

"Whoever can they be? Scott, you must dress at once. What name did they give, Mary?"

The little maid hastily set her cap straight and smoothed her apron at the sounds of urgent movement on the far side of the door.

"Wordsworth was the name, I think, Ma'am. Mr William Wordsworth and his sister, Miss Dorothy."

Chapter 11

It was hard, Scott thought wryly, that his first meeting with the fiery young poet of the Revolution, so long awaited, so carefully arranged by a mutual friend at last, must be so bedevilled with apologies because young Wordsworth arrived before seven o'clock when he had not been looked for until noon. However, agitation would serve no useful purpose, and merely make his razor more likely to gouge cheek or chin.

So he took his time over the essential operation, dressed as usual in his country clothes; green shooting jacket, black neckcloth, corduroy breeches, heavy stockings and shoes. Sounds from below drifted up to his dressing-room: Sophia and Walter were evidently welcoming the visitors with pleasure and surprise.

"At last you are ready, Scott," said Charlotte from the doorway. "Let us then descend, with our apologies."

But the Wordsworths rose to greet their hosts with complete simplicity. "It is we who must apologise," said Miss Dorothy. "We left our carriage at Roslyn and walked down the valley in the perfection of early morning."

"Forgetting," said Wordsworth, with his rare, enchanting smile, "that we rise earlier than most people."

"It is a habit much to be recommended," Scott agreed, as presentations were made, and they all shook hands. "I believe I shall take to it. I need scarcely say, sir, what a pleasure it is to be face to face with a man whose work I already revere – "

"I, sir, can say the same. And – "

"Breakfast," said Charlotte urgently, "is at last served. You will eat first, gentlemen, and talk afterwards, yes?"

"Yes, indeed," said Miss Dorothy.

So, throughout the pleasant, informal meal, with the children silent and busy over their porridge, and Charlotte anxiously occupied in discovering their guests' preferences for tea or chocolate, the two poets observed each other with all the interest that courtesy allowed. They were just of an age, their poetry had already been acclaimed, but their contrasting loyalties made its appeal dramatically opposed. Scott, in his country clothes, seemed so much more the sporting Border laird than the poet that Wordsworth surveyed the author of *The Lay of the Last Minstrel* in bewilderment.

And Scott, on the other hand, looked at the ardent young revolutionary with candid admiration. Wordsworth's shock of dark hair, hawk-like nose and jutting chin were entirely in keeping with his earlier sonnets, but there was also a quality of inner gentleness about his eyes which matched his loving talk of country things. So, when they began to talk at leisure, of the roots of those loyalties which had at first seemed so opposed, each recognised in the other an unexpected kinship. The next two days, during which Scott escorted his visitors about the Border country, matching every vista of hill and valley, ruined peel and brawling burn with its appropriate ballad or old tale, were warmed with an increasing understanding. The Wordsworths approved the first cantos of *The Lay*, which Scott read to them in the intervals of their wanderings, and it was with the greatest regret that Scott was obliged to confess that he was due in two days at Jedburgh, to preside over the Sheriff's Court. "So I shall be obliged to leave you for a while, to fulfil my legal obligations."

"But why? We shall be most interested to attend the Court," said Miss Dorothy.

Scott turned to her with an impulsive gesture of entreaty. "My dear lady, I have but one request to make. Do not, I beg you, enter the Court. I should not care for you to see," he said frankly, "the sort of figure I cut there."

"But of course," said Wordsworth at once. "We understand."

So they did not meet, after Scott had ridden off to Jedburgh, till he had got rid of his cocked hat and robes of office. But he brought with him William Laidlaw, who had been serving on the jury, and was most anxious to offer his homage to William Wordsworth. They rode together beside the Wordsworths' carriage as they left the Border country. A new friendship had begun which was to endure for the rest of the two poets' lives, however circumstances were to restrict their future meetings. Wordsworth wrote from Westmorland:

"My sister and I often talk of the happy days that we spent in your company. Such things do not occur often in life. If we live we shall meet again. . . . Farewell. God prosper you, and all that belongs to you. Your sincere friend, for such I will call myself, though slow to use a word of such solemn meaning to any one – W. Wordsworth."

With the letter he enclosed a copy of the sonnet he had composed on Neidpath Castle, with which Scott had been greatly impressed, perhaps because the disciplined brevity of the sonnet form was something he himself could appreciate but never achieve. Within hours of his guests' departure, he was back at work on the challenging intricacies of *Sir Tristrem*, from which he took refuge in the galloping drama of *The Lay* from time to time. But, as always, the country life provided distractions which he found it hard to resist. Sophia and Walter must be lifted in turn on to the stout little pony in the rough field round which Camp and the greyhounds, Douglas and Percy, coursed in search of hares; picked up after the tumbles which their father refused to take seriously, and hoisted back, while Charlotte hid her face in her hands, to try again, for only practice would achieve for them the supreme bliss of being allowed to ride down the lane with Papa on his big horse as soon as they could manage the little pony properly.

But as the days shortened, the return to Castle Street, welcomed only by Charlotte, approached once more, and as the first frosts whitened the meadows, and brought the vivid leaves down on the pretty garden, the household bowled sadly back to winter in Edinburgh, with its incarceration in nursery or Law Court.

During the winter, an unexpected result of the *Minstrelsy* cropped up. James Hogg had become dissatisfied with his position in Ettrick valley, and decided to better himself. The success of the *Minstrelsy* made him feel that he could do as well or better. If Scott could imitate the ancient ballads, so could he. And he thought well of his own work. The collection he assembled and sent to Scott actually contained some poems of great beauty, which Scott praised warmly, to offset others which made no appeal at all.

Characteristically, James Hogg accepted the praise and overlooked the reticence. Late in December, he happened to be passing through Edinburgh after delivering a flock of sheep to one of his employer's northern customers, and had arranged to meet Willie Laidlaw there on his return. So both of them appeared outside Scott's house in Castle Street and were hospitably invited to stay for dinner.

Charlotte, thankful only that none of her more conventional friends happened to be dining with them that evening, greeted the Borderers graciously from the chaise longue on which she was reclining.

"My wife has been slightly indisposed," Scott explained.

"You'll not want to be troubled with folk in and out, then," said Willie Laidlaw in concern. "Mebbe we shouldn't have come."

"Never fash yourself, man," Scott assured him. "She'll be the better for the company. Seat yourself, lads. Dinner will be served directly."

Anxious to conform, gentle Willie Laidlaw took a straight-backed chair in a corner. Equally anxious, but determined to conceal it, James Hogg glanced at Charlotte, then stretched himself full length on the matching chaise longue below the other window. Charlotte, stifling a small shriek at the sight of his country boots by turning it into a cough, shot an imploring glance at her husband.

"And now, Mr Hogg, what are ze prospects for the lambing season?" asked Charlotte politely.

"Middling, ma'am, middling, like the prospects for my verses unless I can find myself a patron. I've got your good man in mind for that, unless he'd rather see the honour go to her leddyship of Dalkeith. I've been a shepherd long enough and that's a fact. I'm seeking to better myself. I'd make a good enough manager, ye ken, to a laird wi' sheep-farming interests."

"None better. What about the introductions I gave you not long since?" asked Scott, anxious to keep the talk going to give Charlotte time to fight down the giggles which he could tell, from her bitten lip and watering eyes, were threatening to explode.

"Hout, the tight-fisted old tods didna want to part wi' their siller," said James Hogg scornfully.

"Where are the children, my love?" Scott asked desperately.

"Zey look through ze keyhole this minute, I believe."

Scott smiled, limped across to the door, and flung it suddenly open. Sophia, Walter and Camp cascaded across the threshold and the stilted conversation was extinguished in a cheerful uproar.

The visitors began to enjoy themselves. Dinner at five o'clock was a pleasant family meal, at which Charlotte's attention was almost entirely taken up with her children's table manners. Scott made everyone laugh with the latest anecdotes from the Law Courts, listened to James Hogg's tales from the farm suppers he had attended at clipping-time, with a few sly jokes from Willie Laidlaw thrown in. When Sophia and Walter were collected by their nurse, Scott sent the bottle hospitably round. And round again. The laughter grew louder, the stories broader. James Hogg, gay as a lark on a May morning, and innocently referring to "Charlotte and Wattie" as his dearest friends. Eventually, he was persuaded by an anxious Willie Laidlaw that if they wished to secure the beds they had bespoken at the drovers' lodgings, it was time they left the hilarious company to claim them.

Scott would have thought no more of the affair, if James Hogg had not written, soon afterwards, not only to apologise for anything he might have said amiss during his visit, but to reiterate his anxiety for the publication of his many manuscripts. "I have as many songs beside me, which are certainly the *worst* of my productions, as will make about one hundred close printed, and about two hundred, printed as the Minstrelsy is. Now, although I will not proceed without your consent and advice, yet I would have you understand that I expect it . . ."

This posed a problem, for Hogg demanded Scott's assistance, not in selecting the poems most suitable for publication, but in finding a publisher for those of Hogg's own choice, signing a Memoir written about the author by himself, and in finding a patron, such as Lady Dalkeith, for the enterprise, from which Hogg obviously hoped for sufficient success to be able to become, without capital or experience, a tenant farmer of the Duke of Buccleuch.

Scott read the letter with very mixed feelings. James Hogg, as the Ettrick Shepherd, who rhymed as instinctively as he breathed, whose poems varied in quality as the light changed on the Border hills, was a comrade whom he could both love and respect. But the resentful rival, who made it quite evident that he considered his own gifts at least equal to Scott's, was quite another person.

Ultimately, Scott let the question of publication lie for a while, and dealt with the more immediate problem of Hogg's financial future, should he decide to give up his present occupation. Since his earlier letters of introduction had produced no results, he now wrote to say that he hoped to have a farm himself before long in the Selkirk area, and would be glad of the services of such a man as Hogg to manage it. Unfortunately, Hogg did not receive this proposal kindly. In January, 1804, he made this very clear.

"I have no intention," he wrote, "of waiting for so distant a prospect as that of being manager of your farm, though I have no doubt of our joint endeavour proving successful, nor yet of your willingness to employ me in that capacity."

The prospect, however, was not as distant as Hogg supposed. Ashiestiel, a country estate on the Tweed, within seven miles of Selkirk, where Scott had spent so many happy days with his cousins, fell vacant early in the year on the death of his uncle by marriage, Colonel Russell. The Colonel's eldest son was now in India and wished to let the place until his return.

Ashiestiel fulfilled the requirements laid down by Lord Napier, since it was within seven miles of Selkirk. It also offered Scott something of his heart's desire, a home in the Border country, within sound of Tweed. The solid, lime-harled farmhouse, over-looking the valley, had good outbuildings, a well-tended garden, and a perspective of honey-coloured hills. He was intrigued by the idea of owning a flock of sheep, though the technicalities of Black-face or Cheviot, tups, gimmers, hoggs or dinmonts, endlessly discussed round the market pens, were at first as much beyond him as the rival merits of long sheep and short.

At the beginning of May, *Sir Tristrem* was published, though cautiously, by Constable, who looked for prestige rather than expected much demand for the handsome, two-guinea edition of only a hundred and fifty copies. It sold out within the year, and was many times reprinted, as the demand for Scott's work grew. But the author, who had never expected to do more than interest antiquarians, was much more preoccupied with plans for his new home than with its reception by the public. The otherwise happy summer of 1804 was saddened by the death of his much loved Uncle Robert in June, and by the end of the following year his faithful childhood companion, Aunt Janet, had also gone. Captain Scott left his home in Kelso, where Scott had spent so many happy holidays, to his favourite nephew. But this did not shake Scott from his decision to rent Ashiestiel.

"Rosebank," he wrote to George Ellis, "is situated so near the village of Kelso as hardly to be sufficiently a country residence; besides it is hemmed in by hedges and ditches, not to mention Dukes and Lady Dowagers, which are bad things for little people."

Charlotte, who would rather have enjoyed the Dukes and Duchesses, was perhaps the person least interested in Ashiestiel. At Lasswade she had many friendly neighbours. Ashiestiel, by comparison, was in the wilderness. When Scott drove her in the phaeton to admire the neighbourhood, she sighed.

"Ze nearest place of habitation, how far is it?"

"Selkirk? Seven miles, my love," said Scott gaily, touching the cob with his whip so that they took a corner on two wheels. "But I shall be quite the laird of cairn and scaur."

"Indeed? And zat will please you?"

"It will also please Lord Napier, which is much more to the point. Dearest Charlotte, I will show you something of the greatest importance." He reined in the cob, pointing with his whip at something that looked like a deep seam on the sunlit surface of the opposite hills. "Do you see that? It is the Catrail, the ancient Celtic line of defence that George Ellis wishes to see above all things when he comes to visit us."

Charlotte shaded her eyes with her hand. "So? Then I think that ditches must be scarcer in Windsor Forest than I had any idea of. Let us now drive on to Selkirk. I must see ze shops."

There was still a great deal to do, however, before the flitting to Ashiestiel, which they had taken unfurnished, so that everything they needed must be bought from sales and second-hand furniture stores. The cottage at Lasswade must be let, the sale of Rosebank arranged, and Scott was obliged to break off all other activities to go into quarters with the cavalry for a fortnight, in July.

At last, however, the flitting was accomplished, and the haphazard pieces of furniture, assembled from many sources, were so disposed, thanks to Charlotte's skill and the hard work of a dozen official and unofficial helpers, in the small low rooms that they looked as if they had always belonged there.

Scott was astounded as he looked round the parlour soon after their arrival.

"My dearest," he told Charlotte, "you are a hitherto unknown genius. If I did not know that that dining table came from a shoddy sales room in the Canongate, the chairs from a roup in Selkirk, the chaise longue from my mother's George Street drawing-room, and the easy chairs from an auctioneer's premises in George Street, I would have said that they were all cherished heirlooms which had been in the family for generations."

Charlotte gave her little trilling giggle. "Dear Scott, I cannot write poems, nor lead a cavalry charge, nor even keep Camp from devouring all other dogs by the mere look in my eye. But eyes can be useful, I think, in other ways. So I use mine to make a room pretty, yes?"

Scott smiled contentedly round the little room. "Yes, we shall all be happy here," he said. "Hark at the bairns!" For Sophia, squealing with delight, was running up and down the short, unexpected flights of stairs linking different levels of rooms haphazardly added during the changing centuries of family life, with

Walter shouting and scrambling after her. At last they came tumbling down the steepest flight, and a roar of anguish indicated that Walter had gone sprawling on the flags.

"Wheesht!" Sophia could be heard admonishing him.

"I've *hurt* – myself!" wailed Walter.

"Never mind. It'll be better as soon as you stop crying. You know that's what Papa always says."

Presently they burst into the parlour. Walter was laughing already, Scott noted approvingly, though a smudge of dirt indicated where he had rubbed tell-tale tears from his face.

"Papa! Mamma!" Sophia shouted eagerly, "we've been looking for you everywhere. Camp has caught a rat in the stable yard, and the greyhounds are chasing hares all over the fields!"

Scott stooped and swung his five-year-old daughter shoulder high, while Charlotte kissed Walter and scrubbed at his face with her handkerchief. "Are they, indeed, my pet? We must go and watch old Camp at work, and make sure Douglas and Percy do no harm to the sheep. You like your new country home, then?" he asked gaily, as he set her down and let her tow him excitedly towards the stable yard.

Morag fled shrieking into the kitchen as Camp triumphantly laid the limp corpse at his master's feet.

"Well done, my man," said Scott warmly, patting the dog's broad brindle back.

They found the greyhounds innocently coursing up and down the rough field beyond, entirely ignoring the small flock of sheep huddled apprehensively in the far corner on the edge of the woodland.

Scott put a couple of fingers to his mouth and gave the piercing whistle he had learned in his High School days. Astonished, the greyhounds checked, then came bounding towards him.

"Good lads, good lads. Ye've got mair sense than I looked for. Now let's all go and take a look at the river. You give Mamma a hand, Walter, just to make sure she doesn't tumble. This path's a wee bit rough."

Charlotte giggled. But she took Walter's hand. "My dear Scott, he is only three. Already you teach him ze manners of a gentleman."

"Hout, he'll never learn younger," said Scott gaily.

As they neared the birling shallows of the summer-shallow Tweed the children left their parents to race on ahead, with Douglas and Percy cutting capers round them, and Camp thundering along behind.

"Oh, Scott, zey fall in, I am sure!" cried Charlotte apprehensively.

"What of it? There's not enough water to drown in, and Camp will see they come to no harm."

As they strolled across the broad meadow where the recently cut hay stood in little, beehive-shaped, sweetly scented mounds, Charlotte turned impulsively to her husband.

"Oh, Scott, I regret Lasswade no longer."

"I'm glad of that, my love." Scott twirled his stick and smiled as he looked back at the house and the hillside behind. "I wonder if young Russell would sell? It's kittle work being tenant of another man's property at a time when I should be buying my own."

"You could afford to buy?" said Charlotte quickly. "We are better off now, yes?"

"Aye, quite a bit. Rosebank is not likely to sell for less than £5,000. I have my share of my father's estate, my Sheriff's salary of £300 a year, and the stock settled on you and the bairns brings in a couple of hundred more. I'd say we could reckon on an income of a thousand a year, perhaps, setting aside what fees I earn at the Bar, and anything that comes in from books."

"But, Scott, that is riches!" said Charlotte eagerly.

Scott chuckled. "Scarcely riches, my love. But enough to feed my family, keep a horse or two – "

"Then," said Charlotte triumphantly, "there is one other thing which I believe is due to your position. It is time, Scott, zat we keep our own carriage. Then at last we live in proper style."

"But we have the phaeton – " Scott protested.

Charlotte threw out her arms in a gesture of despair.

"Oh, my dear Scott, I endure such terror in zat phaeton which you drive, as you ride, like fury. So many times we are nearly in the ditch. Not only me, but ze children. I shall be ill with fright. Now we have our country home, our horses, our little farm. So far, good. But we need now a carriage, such as your grand friends have. And a coachman who will drive, so that you may be free to accompany us on horseback if you wish. Or go elsewhere, if you must. Then I shall be able to pay visits just the same. Oh, please! I shall be so happy!"

It was hard to refuse her, when she laid her hands on his arm, and looked up at him with such earnest pleading in her eyes. Besides, the idea rather attracted him. He much preferred the freedom of riding his own horse, instead of guiding a horse encumbered by a vehicle trailing behind him, so that he must keep to the roads instead of taking a short-cut across country, jumping every obstacle in his path.

"Well, I will think on it, my dear," he said.

"Dearest Scott, how good you are!" Charlotte cried.

During the rest of the summer, Sophia and Walter were as often in the water as out of it, and if their father was nowhere to be found, the chances were that he had made an excuse to join them. But he also spent a good deal of time surveying the property, and one early morning, strolling through the woodland with Camp at his heels, a sudden crashing in the undergrowth recalled him from a reverie just in time to thrust out his stick and bring down headlong a man who was about to make his escape.

"No, Camp," said Scott peremptorily as the dog was about to spring. "Stay where you are, my friend," he added to the man who lay gasping and winded before him. "I do not advise you to run. I may be lame, but my dog is not."

Slowly, the man scrambled to his feet. He was a short, thick-set Borderer in early middle-age, his black hair just grizzling, his eyes alert under heavy brows in a pugnacious, deeply tanned face. A couple of rabbits, on which Camp kept a watchful eye, lay limply beside him.

Scott folded his hands on the crook of his stick and surveyed him judicially. "D'ye ken me, my man?"

Half defiant, half appalled, his prisoner surveyed him. "Aye . . . It's the Shirra," he said.

"You were poaching. On private property."

It was obviously useless to deny it. But Scott liked the way the man looked him straight in the eye as he nodded.

"What's your name?"

"Purdie. Thomas Purdie, Shirra."

"You know the penalty for a poacher caught red-handed?"

"Aye." Purdie did not flinch. Nor did he beg for mercy.

"Why did you do it?"

"I'm out of work, Shirra. My wife and bairns need the food." He stated it as a fact, rather than an excuse. Then, unexpectedly, he grinned, adding candidly, "And I like a wee bit of an excitement, whiles."

"What can you do?"

Tom Purdie surveyed his powerful, calloused hands thoughtfully. "I can turn my hands to maist things, Shirra. I'm gude wi' timber." Looking round him, he added, "these young trees need thinning badly, ye ken."

Scott nodded thoughtfully. "Can you manage livestock?"

Tom Purdie's face brightened. "I can that. Mind, I havena' muckle experience wi' horses. Peter Mathieson, him that's the wife's brither, he's the man for them. But cattle, now – "

"What about sheep?"

"I was bred for a shepherd. And I like the work fine."

"It's a shepherd I need," said Scott. "And I've no objection to giving you a trial."

"Ye'll not regret it, Shirra," said Tom Purdie with dignity.

"Come up to Ashiestiel this evening and we'll settle your wages."

"Aye, Shirra. And – " Tom Purdie looked down at the rabbits. Scott chuckled. "Take them home for the bairns. *No*, Camp. Come away home."

Tom Purdie grinned happily, whipped up the rabbits, knuckled his forehead, and set off down the path at a very smart pace. And Scott, returning to the house for breakfast with a disgruntled Camp pacing reproachfully behind him, wondered if he would ever see the man again. But that evening, as he was carefully picking up the books which still stood in teetering piles on the floor of his little study and putting them into the empty shelves, he heard Morag's voice behind him:

"If you please, sir, there's a man called Purdie speiring for ye in the yard."

So Tom Purdie came to Ashiestiel, first as a shepherd, then as Scott's right-hand man in the management of the little estate. And with his coming life at Ashiestiel settled into a blissful, orderly pattern as he proved the truth of his own forthright statement that he could turn his hand to most things. He was sturdily independent, uncompromising in his view, and dourly humorous. Children and animals loved him, his fellow servants respected him, and Scott, who appreciated loyalty above most things, was not too proud to accept his advice on questions of husbandry about which Tom Purdie knew more than his master. And Charlotte was delighted when Peter Mathieson joined his brother-in-law at Ashiestiel, as coachman, and drove her about the countryside in proper style.

When winter came, and the household must return to Edinburgh for the autumn session, Ashiestiel was left in good hands, and as long as the weather permitted, Peter Mathieson had the carriage ready on Saturday morning to drive the family down for the week-end, while his wife fired and victualled Ashiestiel for their reception, with the help of Tom Purdie, who brought in logs, cared for the sheep and patrolled the woodlands with all a reformed poacher's proverbial zeal.

Early in 1805, *The Lay of the Last Minstrel*, appropriately dedicated to Scott's brother-officer, Lord Dalkeith, was published by Longmans of Paternoster Row in London, and Archibald Constable & Co. of Edinburgh. It was received with acclamation by the entire reading public, critical and otherwise, throughout the United Kingdom. Politicians such as Pitt and Fox, bibliophiles such as George Ellis, the noble, the cultured, the wealthy and the sophisticated acclaimed its urgent vitality. Within a few weeks of publication, Scott had become the most celebrated literary figure in Scotland, though financially the first and second editions brought him less than £1,000. And while the literary world adjusted itself to the new phenomenon, Scott and Tom Purdie were happily occupied in the woodland at Ashiestiel.

Scott's friends among the Montagnards did not grudge the longer journey from Edinburgh, and during the spring vacation the comings and goings of people who had known him at High School, University and in the Outer House maintained the usual pattern. Charlotte made them all welcome, Will Clerk, John Irving, James Skene and William Erskine, the Montagnards who had greeted her as a young bride, and they all delighted in the country sports which Ashiestiel offered, riding madly across country with Scott and his dogs.

But it was William Erskine, who seemed so oddly out of place in the adventurous country life, shuddering at the idea of taking his horse out of a walking pace, or the wild fishing expeditions during which Scott and the children constantly fell in and out of the Tweed, that Scott took into his confidence.

"Come into my study, Will," Scott said, one spring evening, "I've got something I'd like to read to you. Just a few chapters I've roughed out. Something different."

When they were settled, he leafed through a bundle of papers. "*Waverley, Or 'Tis Sixty Years Since*, I thought to call it."

"Another poem?"

Scott shook his head. "Poetry's a scourging crop, Will. The land's got to lie fallow after it. Mebbe this will serve between whiles."

He read well, but Will Erskine found it hard to accept the pedestrian setting of a scene in prose after the racing rhythms of an epic in verse which carried the reader along with the speed of the galloping horses he himself would never dare to ride. He listened patiently, but his face remained blank. After a while, Scott looked at him over the sheaf of closely written pages. He opened a drawer of his writing-desk and tossed the pages into it. "My dear Will, don't try to soften the blow. You don't like it. Leave it at that."

"It seemed," said William Erskine bleakly, "somewhat slow, if you must have it, after *The Lay*."

"I have no doubt you're right, Will. Don't give it another thought." Scott shut the drawer, and turned back to his friend with a rueful smile.

"What I do not understand," said Will Erskine candidly, "is why you need write anything else at all, so soon after your success."

"That is something else about which I want your advice," said Scott. He pushed back his chair and limped towards the window, where he stood, looking out on the sunset beauty of the valley. "James Ballantyne needs more money."

"Again?" said Erskine. "Surely you established him with a handsome loan when he first came to Edinburgh."

"James," said Scott, "is an artist in his own way. His printing has attracted so much attention that he cannot maintain his output without new types, new presses, and dear knows what. He is not a business man – "

"Nor, my dear Walter, are you," said Erskine dryly.

"I am enough of a business man to realise that it would be a daft-like thing to cramp a growing enterprise like James's Border Press just when it is gaining recognition, for the lack of funds," said Scott, turning from the window and limping back to his desk. "But at the same time, Will, I am not in a position to stand such a drain on my own finances."

"What are the chances of such loans being sooner or later repaid?" asked Will Erskine shrewdly.

Scott sat heavily down again. "I do not know. He is my old friend, his work is excellent, but his business methods are haphazard, to put it mildly."

"If you do not help him now, what is the alternative?"

"He will be unable to fulfil his obligations. Consequently, people in need of a good printer will go elsewhere."

"Then you, weighing your own responsibilities, must choose, as I see it, whether you can afford to go on lending him money which you are, I gather, most unlikely to see again."

"There is another possibility," said Scott slowly. "I have put the money from the sale of my uncle's Kelso estate aside for the purchase of a suitable property. I would gladly buy Ashiestiel, but I fear the owner will not sell. Lord Dalkeith mentioned another, when I last visited him. He and his lady rode round it with me, and both considered that Broadmeadows would serve my turn well. But no doubt other opportunities will arise. And I cannot see James Ballantyne founder, nor afford to keep him afloat, without getting some return for my money."

"Quite so, quite so."

"And therefore, my dear Will, I am considering investing this money in the firm, provided that as a partner in the business, I receive a share of its profits. The firm's success should then be assured. Consider, Will, how much work I alone can put in James's way," he added urgently, as Erskine sat silent and grave.

"Consider also," said Erskine in dismay, "the consequences of any association with a commercial enterprise on the reputation of an advocate practising at the Bar."

"I have considered it," Scott said, "and already decided to withdraw from practice. No, wait. Hear me out before you talk of rashness," he went on with a smile. "Negotiations are on foot which may deviously obtain for me a seat at the August table of the Principal Clerks of Session, which, as you know, rates at £1300 per annum, and is quite compatible with the tenure of my Sheriffdom."

"I had not heard," said Erskine in surprise, "that any of the gentlemen at the Clerks' Table proposed to retire."

"That is quite correct. But one of them would dearly like to," said Scott. "George Home of Wedderburn recently confided to me that the work is getting too much for him. He is old and infirm, but he needs the money. I have offered to take his place gratuitously, so that he may continue to receive it, in lieu of pension, as long as he lives. It will give me the chance of complying with tradition, and doing something more useful than trailing my gown in the Outer House, at a time when abler men than I – such as yourself, my dear Will – are better supplied with briefs than I shall ever be."

Will Erskine smiled uneasily. "No one but you, Wattie, could ever have worked out a scheme so ingenious, not to say foolhardy."

Scott shook his head. "Consider, Will, that the poor old man cannot live much longer. His gratitude for the chance to end his days in reasonable comfort is in itself sufficient reward for assuming responsibilities which are well within the powers of an active man – "

"It will still require a commission from the crown – "

"Issued to us jointly. It has been done before," Scott said. "The matter is already in hand. A letter from Lord Dalkeith, who gives it his full approval, informed me some weeks since that his father has consulted Lord Melville, and considers that my business is in good train, though not yet certain."

"All this demands the greatest discretion," said Erskine in some anxiety.

"I have implicit confidence in yours. And I shall mention it to no one else," Scott assured him. "It will be the greatest relief to have it settled, as well as family troubles with which I will not weary you. My brother Tom has made a sorry hash of the family business, I fear. It is to be wound up and another appointment must be found for him. And poor foolish young Daniel has had to leave the country for Jamaica to sever a most unfortunate association. George Ellis wrote with the greatest kindness to his friend who is one of the most important men out there. We hear he has shown Daniel every assistance. So mebbe all will yet be well. Now, Will, enough of such serious topics. Camp here is wearying to get to the riverside, where he assures me the bairns have been enjoying themselves alone for long enough. Let us all join them."

The invasion scare reached its height that summer, and Scott returned for the opening of the session at the Law Courts to find Edinburgh converted into a city of volunteers, where professional men and commercial citizens did their day's work in uniform and kept their weapons handy by night. The sham battles and mock sieges which the new commander-in-chief, Lord Moira, continually organised as part of their training suited him admirably.

That autumn matters came to a head. For Nelson, who had hunted the French fleet so long, eventually encountered it off Cape St Vincent, early in November, and soon the stage coaches were thundering through England, with the guards blowing a fanfare as they passed through every village, tossing down the papers which carried the tremendous news of his victory at Trafalgar. But black ribbons were twisted among the garlands, for Nelson himself, hit by a bullet in the spine as he watched the battle from the quarter deck, died in the hour of victory.

Chapter 12

"ALMIGHTY and everlasting God, who art always more ready to hear than we to pray . . ."

Scott's deep, sonorous voice, softened by the trace of a Border burr acquired in childhood, filled the dining parlour at Ashiestiel as he read the Collect for the day. He had taken recently to assembling his household to hear morning service on Sundays while they were in the country seven miles from kirk and market. His family and retainers were grouped round the room as usual, heads bowed in the fashion of most Scots since the Reformation brought a reaction from the earlier practice of "kneeling meekly upon their knees".

It was the twelfth Sunday after Trinity, 1808, and as fine a summer morning as anyone just released from his professional labours at the Court of Session in Edinburgh could wish. Scott himself was seated in his wide-armed carving chair at the head of the table, with Charlotte on his right hand, his eldest daughter, Sophia, now a pleasant-faced, sturdy little girl of nine, on his left. Beside her sat young Walter, wriggling slightly at the constriction of the Sunday suit, to which, at six, he had now been reluctantly promoted. The two younger children, Anne, a dark-eyed, gay child of five, with a great look of her mother, and the baby, Charles, born the month after the victory of Trafalgar, sat one on either side of their governess, kind Miss Millar, who was inevitably more occupied in restraining their restless energy than in attending to the service.

Beyond them sat the Ashiestiel retainers, decorous but uncompromisingly Presbyterian, consoling their consciences for their attendance at the Shirra's Pisky goings-on with the knowledge that Peter Mathieson, upright as a ramrod in his hard-backed chair, would that evening hold a more seemly Psalm-singing in his cottage kitchen which they were all free to attend.

". . . and art wont to give more than either we desire or deserve . . ."

Tom Purdie was leaning forward, his hands clasped loosely between his knees as he studied the pattern of the carpet, and thought of the cottage on the estate which now housed him, with his wife and bairns, of the Shirra's seemly interest in timber and unexpected willingness to listen to men with greater experience. The lambs, he hoped, would do credit to his care. Cook, with her hands folded demurely in her lap, looking along the line of her assistants, and hoped they were taking the good words to heart, and not thinking of the herd laddies who came daffing to the back door.

"Pour down upon us the abundance of thy mercy; forgive us those things whereof our conscience is afraid . . ."

Sophia and Walter looked briefly at each other, remembering their anxious consultation on the matter of forgetting to feed the pony about which Papa would be undoubtedly angered.

". . . and giving us those good things which we are not worthy to ask . . ."

Charlotte suddenly remembered the bills which she had incurred with various Edinburgh tradesmen who were so ready to allow credit to Mrs Scott, whose husband had become so famous. Dear Scott! How good he was to her, how understanding of her need for pretty things. When she looked round the dining parlour, watched her children's faces, so sweet, so happy, in their country home, she felt herself glow with gratitude. If only things could go on for ever as they were now, she could ask no more of heaven. But sometimes she was afraid. Scott was so sought after, by such grand people, that sometimes she wondered if she could keep pace with all the complications that his success might bring.

". . . but through the merits and mediation of Jesus Christ, thy Son, our Lord . . ." Scott concluded earnestly. He paused for a moment, looking round the room, profoundly aware of the depth of his affection for all those in it, letting his hand rest for a moment on the head of his dog, who lay at his side. Camp was getting old now, too stiff to follow him over the hills with his lively grey-hounds, who were excluded from the service because they would have found it even harder than the children to keep still for even a few minutes. He glanced briefly at the upright figure of his neighbour, "Laird Nippy", of the Peel, who always surprised him by attending the brief morning services at Ashiestiel, because it would not be possible for them to attend the nearest kirk without interfering with the right of Peter Mathieson and his horses to the day of rest to which they too were entitled. Laird Nippy, also a Presbyterian, and as tetchy an individual as his nickname suggested, was also a most devoted supporter of the Sheriff, who had consulted him with due deference, on such matters as boundaries and the ailments to which Cheviot and Blackfaced sheep were subject. Why he should, consequently, attend the alien form of worship, was a question only he could answer. But the persuasive quality of Scott's personality was something which affected most of those he contacted throughout his life.

As he went on to read the Epistle, his hearers were dimly aware of its meaning, difficult though the words were – as if his deliberate phrasing and just emphasis were clearing a way for them through a thicket, Tom Purdie thought, though those sweeping strokes of his whiles laid good timber as low as the trash. He was better-handed with words.

". . . not that we are sufficient of ourselves to think of anything as of ourselves; but our sufficiency is of God: who also hath made us ministers of the new testament; not of the letter, but of the spirit: for the letter killeth . . ."

Sophia and Walter were looking anxiously at Camp, who had stretched himself out to sleep with his muzzle on his master's foot. It had been black when she first remembered him, Sophia thought. Now it was grey. It gave her a pain like toothache to think of him getting old. Walter noticed his legs twitching as if he were coursing a hare with the greyhounds again. He hadn't been able to do that for months. What a good thing he could still run as fast as ever in his sleep. I shan't be able to bear it if he dies, Sophia thought. Anne caught her mother's eye as Camp let out a series of excited squeaks, choking back a giggle as Charlotte put a finger to her lips.

". . . but the spirit giveth life."

Life, thought Laird Nippy, that was what the Sheriff seemed to have so much more of than other folk, whether he was cutting down a tree or louping a dyke on that great horse of his, or writing one of yon poems that he'd heard tell on, or telling a string of daft stories at the kirk supper that sent the men into roars of laughter. It did an auld ruckle of banes like himself as much good to be with him as to sit by a blazing fire.

The Gospel held the attention even of those whose thoughts had wandered a little during the Epistle's complexities, for the cure of the deaf and dumb man lost nothing of its drama in Scott's forthright rendering. He closed the book, all rose to repeat the blessing. Then Scott smiled, the Sabbath gravity of the company about him relaxed, as Camp rose, stretching himself with a prodigious yawn.

"Well, Mamma, would you say they've been good bairns?"

"Very good indeed, Papa."

"Good enough for us to carry our dinners to the riverside? We'll not go farther, or old Kiki will be shamed at lagging behind."

"What do you think, Miss Millar? Do they deserve to go?"

"I think so, certainly."

"Then away ye go, bairns, and let out the greyhounds."

As the servants followed the children, Scott paused for a word with his neighbour. "You and your wife won't join us?"

"We will not. I prefer to eat my dinner of a Sabbath at my own table instead of stravaiging across the countryside like gangingaboot bodies," said Laird Nippy briskly.

He retrieved his stick from behind his chair, and hobbled rheumatically off in search of his Sunday dinner, while Scott turned for a word to Camp.

"Can ye manage, my man? It's just to the riverside."

Camp rose at once, and followed his master laboriously from the room.

The years at Ashiestiel had certainly not been idle. Scott's mammoth editorial work on Dryden had been his constant preoccupation for the last four years. It had demanded less, in sheer creative expenditure, than the second great poetic epic, *Marmion*, the Tale of Flodden Field, which had been published in February.

But it had meant an immense amount of sheer hard, conscientious work on the historical, critical and explanatory notes which he had supplied, as well as a Life of the Author, for which the publisher, William Miller of Albemarle Street, London, had paid the editor £756. The new edition of Swift, on the same scale, had been bespoken by the astute Archibald Constable in Edinburgh, who had no wish to see himself outbid by Englishmen, and had offered £1,000 for the new poem *Marmion*, without reading a line of it, though he afterwards safeguarded himself by sharing the copyright with Mr Miller of Albemarle Street and Mr Murray, then of Fleet Street, who each jumped at the chance of a quarter share. Constable had not been nicknamed "the Crafty" for nothing.

Marmion's theme, the worst disaster that ever befell Scottish arms, was tragic, but the poem was written against the background of love and joy at Ashiestiel, in the prime of Scott's young manhood, when all things still seemed possible, so that his compassion for gallant death and unavailing heroism was kindled by his own happiness till it blazed like a torch held high against their darkness.

He composed the poem in snatches, up and down the estate, wandering towards Tweed in the twilight with old Camp trudging faithfully at his heels, to sit under an ancient oak and scribble till the midges drove him indoors, sometimes with tears streaming down his face for the Scottish King and the men who had died to save him.

> "*The stubborn spear-men still made good*
> *Their dark impenetrable wood,*
> *Each stepping where his comrade stood*
> *The instant that he fell . . .*"

The poem was received with acclamation by an even wider public than *The Lay*. But among the experts, occasional sour notes were heard. "Thank you," wrote Wordsworth, "for *Marmion*. I think your end has been attained. That it is not the end which I should wish you to propose to yourself, you will be well aware . . ."

George Ellis wrote at great length of his difficulties in deciding whether *The Lay* or *Marmion* should be reputed the most pleasing poem in our language, and decided against *Marmion*. But the most significant criticism was that of Scott's Whiggish friend, Jeffrey, who had formerly been able to discount politics in his appreciation, but now wrote warningly to Scott that he had written of *Marmion* in *The Edinburgh Review* exactly as he thought, but it would mortify him very severely to believe he had given Scott pain.

The review itself was very severe, commenting unsparingly on Scott's "ostentation of historical and antiquarian lore", complaining of "a broken narrative – a redundancy of minute description – bursts of unequal and energetic poetry – and a general tone of spirit and animation, unchecked by timidity or affectation, and unchastened by any great delicacy of taste or elegance of fancy".

Scott read the review when the family had returned to Edinburgh for the summer session, a few days before Jeffrey was due to dine at Castle Street. He answered the reviewer's letter gallantly, assuring him that the review had not disturbed his digestion, though he hoped neither his bookseller nor the public would agree with it. He hoped Mr Jeffrey would come to dinner as arranged.

Mr Jeffrey came, and was received by Scott with his usual friendliness. Charlotte, too, played the part of hostess, as she had promised to do, with care, and the occasion went off with somewhat uneasy brightness, so long as the children and their governess as usual were present. After they had withdrawn her restraint was more obvious and when Jeffrey, with some relief, had risen to make his farewells at a rather earlier hour than usual, she could contain her outraged loyalty no longer.

"Well, good night, Mr Jeffrey," she said, without offering her hand. "Zey tell me you have abused Scott in ze Review, and I hope Mr Constable has paid you *very* well for what you write."

"My dearest love – " Scott expostulated, as Jeffrey bowed in silence and turned to leave the room. He was deeply touched by the vehemence of her championship, yet appalled by its probable consequences for a long-standing friendship. He paused only to take her hand and raise it briefly to his lips. Then he shook his head, with a warning smile, and limped hurriedly after his outraged guest.

"The ladies," he observed soothingly, as he overtook him at the hall door, "do not look on these things, Jeffrey, as we old campaigners do."

"So, indeed, it would seem," said Jeffrey frostily. "I wish you, sir, a very good night."

The incident was to have, unfortunately, just the sort of repercussions which Scott had feared, though against the blissful background of summer at Ashiestiel the impact of political hostility, enhanced by not unjustifiably hurt feelings, was easily forgotten.

For the easy-going, out-of-doors life with his family, his horses and his dogs was sheer delight. He worked companionably with Tom Purdie among the trees, spent many hours on horseback daily, riding at breakneck speed over rough country with his greyhounds and his sporting neighbours, escorted by a vociferous tribe of hunting curs, all going pell mell after every hare they could put up, till even James Skene, bold rider though he was, expected his host to be brought home one day feet foremost on an improvised stretcher. But Scott laughed off all warnings.

It was the danger that appealed to him. He shared exuberantly in the wild excitement of "burning the water", when boats were rowed into mid-stream after dark and flares held high to illuminate the wavering, silvery bodies of the salmon attracted by the light. It deterred Scott not at all that the man with the spear was as likely to miss his quarry as not, deceived by the movement of the current, so that he followed his weapon into the dark water.

But even when he seemed to be resting on his many laurels after the completion of *Marmion*, several other projects had already been begun, of which the new edition of Swift was by far the most exacting. But he was also at work on a couple of Memoirs, and the London publisher, Murray, was anxious to interest the new celebrity, whom Constable was threatening to annex, in a *General Edition of British Novelists*, to be printed, of course, by Ballantyne, but published by himself.

It was immensely stimulating. Until quite recently, he had been a threadbare young advocate, anxiously totting up the totals in his fee-book and hoping for a few more briefs. Now, offers from publishers, proposals for books of all sorts, invitations to soirées, literary gatherings, and public occasions poured in by almost every post. He was frankly astonished, candidly gratified. But he kept his head. As one astute observer, Mrs Grant of Laggan, said: "Mr Scott always seems to be like a glass, through which the rays of admiration pass without sensibly affecting it; but the bit of paper that lies beside it will presently be in a blaze."

In order to find time for all his various commitments, however, Scott had realised for some time that he must adjust his time-table. If he worked late, he distressed Charlotte and gave himself head-aches. The main part of the day was bespoken, while he was in Edinburgh, for his duties as Clerk of Session, and when he was at Ashiestiel he considered it his duty as well as his pleasure to be out of doors, whether working on the estate, riding with his family or his neighbours, or entertaining the steadily increasing company of his guests.

There was, obviously, only one solution. He must get up early enough to break the back of the day's literary work before anybody else was about. Wryly he remembered how incredible it had seemed that Dr Adam, Rector of the High School, had been able to devote three hours to his classical studies before school began. But now, most methodically, he had come to do the same. He had the useful faculty of being able to wake precisely when he wished, whether in summer or winter. He lay for a while, assembling his ideas, then rose to shave and dress for the day – his military training had given him a distaste for bedgown and slipper students – answered the imperious scratching on the kitchen door by letting Camp out to join him, lit his study fire when the weather or the old dog required it, and sat down at his desk by six o'clock for three hours' work before breakfast.

Breakfast was always his best meal of the day. He needed it and ate prodigiously porridge, cold salmon, beef, ham, oatcake and cheese before calling for his horse, perhaps to ride to Selkirk to discharge his duties as Sheriff, to Blackhouse to set Willie Laidlaw down to further research, to a sheep sale with Tom Purdie, or to present himself at Bowhill at the summons of the Duke of Buccleuch.

For Camp, who had once attended him on so many of his journeys, the world darkened with his departure. With all the will in the world, the old dog's legs could no longer carry him far afield, and he retired stoically to Scott's study to await his return. Even the children, who adored him, could not console him for his inadequacy, though he responded courteously to their attentions. But somebody was always on the lookout for Scott's return, and hurried to give him the good news.

"Camp, my man," said Sophia, or Walter, or Tom Purdie, or Cook, "the Shirra's coming across the ford." Or sometimes; "the Shirra's coming down the hill." And Camp, perfectly understanding, rose laboriously, and heaved himself towards the stable yard or the front door, to await the greeting which he never failed to receive.

It was, as the pace quickened, an exhaustive, inspiring existence, as Scott himself admitted. "Aye, it was enough to tear me to pieces, but there was a wonderful exhilaration about it all: my blood was kept at fever-pitch – I felt as if I could have grappled with anything and everything . . ."

But George Ellis, that summer, wrote to protest at a conglomeration of activities which he deplored if they were likely to make Scott neglect his greatest gift, and write no more poems to equal *The Lay* and *Marmion*. "Seriously, I don't quite like your imposing on yourself such a series of tasks . . . surely the best poet of the age ought not to be incessantly employed in the drudgeries of literature."

Scott answered him very reasonably. "I have done with poetry for some time – it is a scourging crop, and ought not to be too hastily repeated. Editing, therefore, may be considered as a green crop of turnips or peas, extremely useful for those whose circumstances do not admit of giving their farm a summer fallow."

His problem was simple. At a time when his establishment was expanding, and his young family's needs on the increase, he had undertaken the responsibilities of a Clerk of Session, which took up a considerable amount of time without bringing in any extra money. The Court of Session sat in Edinburgh only six months of each year, in the summer from the 12th of May till the 12th of July, and in the winter from the 12th of November till the 12th of March, with a short break over Christmas. The hours were reasonable; since the Judges of the Inner Court did not take their places until ten o'clock, and rose not later than four o'clock in the afternoon. The Court did not sit on Mondays, and on every other Wednesday they were occupied with other business. The essential work of the Clerks was to record the verbal decisions of the Judges in technically accurate, written terms, which obviously demanded close attention and full understanding of the issues involved, often with further study of law papers and appropriate authorities at home in the evenings. All Scott's own literary work, therefore, must of necessity be done in the early morning, in Edinburgh as at Ashiestiel, and his enormously increasing correspondence fitted into the gaps between his prior obligations. While the Volunteer Light Dragoons still claimed some of his time, he at least got some exercise during the months in Edinburgh. But as the focus of the conflict with Napoleon shifted from the invasion to the blockade of Britain, even that active interlude ceased to enliven his sedentary existence, contrasting too violently with his programme during the vacations, when he drove himself to the point of exhaustion for the sheer love of country sports.

But during the summer of 1808 Napoleon, who had, as he thought, united most of Europe against Britain, decided to complete his conquest by attacking Spain and Portugal, only to be eventually frustrated there at a time when many people had begun to believe him invincible. As good news from the Peninsula began to alternate with the bad news to which they had become accustomed, the British people began to take heart again.

Scott wrote jubilantly to his brother Thomas, who had now taken himself and his family to the Isle of Man to escape from his creditors, "Excellent news today from Spain – yet I wish the patriots had a leader of genius . . . A Wallace, Dundee or Montrose would be the man for Spain at this moment . . ." The name of Sir Arthur Wellesley had as yet no particular significance, and Scott had as usual many other things on his mind. He was anxious to find a minor

Government post for Thomas, thankful that Constable had at last agreed to publish James Hogg's collection of poems, known as *The Mountain Bard*, on his recommendation, much interested in his meeting with the classical scholar and authority on Homer, J. B. S. Morritt, of Rokeby in Yorkshire, and his warm-hearted wife, who were to become two more of his closest friends.

But he was increasingly troubled by the trend of the *Edinburgh Review* as Jeffrey's Whiggish politics began to dominate the periodical's former literary detachment. Its clamour for peace at any price, even, by implication, that of surrender to Napoleon, and its consequent opposition to the war in the Peninsula, seemed dangerously defeatist. He decided he could no longer write for it, would not even have it in his house, a decision which annoyed its proprietor, Archibald Constable, very much.

It was at this point that young Mr Murray came north to meet his distinguished author and discuss plans for the future. One of these was the possibility of starting another periodical, very different in its politics, but equal in literary distinction, in London, to which Scott would be asked to contribute. And so *The Quarterly Review* began to take shape. George Ellis, when approached, was enthusiastic; the editor, William Gifford, chosen; contributions promised by a number of distinguished people, including Malthus, Richard Heber, William Erskine, J. B. S. Morritt, George Ellis, and Scott. Too late, Jeffrey got an inkling of the plans for the new periodical, and tried to appease Scott by promising that *The Edinburgh Review* would have no more to do with party politics.

For Scott had returned to Edinburgh after the summer vacation in a fighting mood, and his allies, the Ballantyne brothers, were both ready to support him to all lengths, from a variety of motives, of which genuine loyalty was one, ambition another, and in Johnny's case at least, a mischievious desire to upset the apple cart of so unreasonably successful a publishing bookseller as Archibald Constable.

The two Ballantyne brothers, so different in appearance, character and ability, were a constant source of amusement to Scott.

They both loved a good joke and a good meal at which the claret circulated briskly. Each, in his own way, could be extremely funny. James sang well in a fruity bass which matched his pompous manner and increasingly rotund figure; but John, though he liked his food and wine as much as his brother, never seemed to get any good out of it. He was thin as a lamp-post, agile as a frog, sang in a sort of cracked falsetto, and made fun of everybody, including himself. His faults, as Scott discovered too late, were a chronic dislike for anything like hard work and an inordinate desire to cut a dash in somewhat dubious society. He was a genuine humorist, and knew very well that he could escape the consequences of almost any escapade once he could make Scott laugh. And Scott, who revelled in absurdity and had given and received nicknames all his life, was now enjoying himself finding names for the gathering crowd of comic characters who came and went among the great folk of his novels with an almost Shakespearean breadth and vigour, found nicknames for the Ballantynes too. Johnny's fliberti-gibbet qualities were easily expressed in *Rigdumfunnidos*, but James's blend of longwindedness, pomposity and artistic perfection called for something more elaborate. Scott called him, among other things, *Aldi-boronti-phoscophornio*, rolling the syllables like an incantation, whenever he wished to make an important announcement.

He had long known James to be a muddler, a genuine and dedicated craftsman with a pedestrian soundness in criticism as far as his understanding went. So he had come to entrust him with routine correction of his proofs, but to rely for subtler judgment on Will Erskine, the other man who both knew the secret of his partnership in the printing firm and could be relied on to offer literary criticism without fear or favour, even to his dearest friend.

But James's hopeless inadequacy over money matters had been apparent from the first, and so, when he had assured Scott that his young brother John, whom Scott had only encountered as an impish, sharp-witted youngster at Dominie Lancelot Whale's school in Kelso, had been to London to learn accountancy, it seemed most opportune that he should be free of the family business in Kelso, and willing to join the partnership in Edinburgh as a clerk at £200 a year. What was not revealed was the extent of the mess John had made of the family business before it had been wound up, and the amount of work Scott was able to bring to the printing-house, both from his own immense enterprises and those of the less successful writers he constantly befriended, had so far concealed the fact that the company's profits were neither being as prudently handled nor as carefully recorded as they might have been. Scott's knowledge of mathematics was elementary. From boyhood it had bored him. Johnny had studied the subject. Scott accepted his confident assurance that he could deal with the firm's much neglected accounts.

So far, Scott's quarrel had been with *The Edinburgh Review* and its editor only. But that winter the trouble spread. A member of Constable's staff, named Hunter, was not only a supporter of the "peace at any price" attitude which had so angered Scott, but a quick-tempered man who disapproved of Scott's many editorial activities at a time when his firm had not only bespoken, but paid him for, his formidable work on Swift.

He not only hinted, but angrily told Scott that by undertaking to edit a number of other works for Mr Murray in London he was behaving dishonourably, since in his opinion all other activities ought to be set aside until his main task had been accomplished. Scott, who felt that he alone could be expected to assess his capacity, and had always maintained that the mammoth enterprise of editing the works of Swift must be his first concern, was not only wounded, but furious at the aspersion. He left Constable's office with dignity, but with new and revolutionary schemes already shaping in his mind.

On the 2nd of January, 1809, he wrote coldly to Constable, to say that if, on reflection, they felt they had too hastily committed themselves to the publication of his new edition of Swift, they were at liberty to cancel the agreement forthwith. Constable, in reply, regretted that Scott had not been "more willing to overlook the unguarded expression of our Mr Hunter . . . We are very much concerned that any circumstance should have occurred that should thus interrupt our friendly intercourse; but as we are not willing to believe that we have done anything which should prevent our being again friends, we may at least be permitted to express a hope that matters may hereafter be restored to their old footing. . . ."

But Scott was not to be so easily placated. He made it clear that no single unguarded expression would have influenced him to quarrel with any of his friends. But Mr Hunter's general opinion of his undertakings and ability to execute them had been expressed upon many occasions during the past five months, and his whole conduct over the bargain about Swift had been such that in Scott's opinion he ought to be the last to wish his interest compromised on that account. "I am only too happy the breach has taken place before there was any real loss to complain of." In conclusion, Scott offered to take his portrait by Raeburn, recently commissioned by Constable for the use of his house, off the publisher's hands. But to this Constable graciously refused to agree.

There, for the time, the matter rested. Scott considered the breach complete, but went steadily on with his work on Swift, though the destination of the nineteen volumes was now uncertain, his plans for contributing to *The Quarterly Review*, and for launching another and more speculative venture, to be known as *The Edinburgh Annual Register*, which would challenge Constable's offending periodical on its home ground. Lastly, but with discreet secrecy, he proceeded to draw up a deed which laid down the foundation of a new bookselling and publishing firm, that of "John Ballantyne & Co." which would confront Constable's monopoly from premises in Hanover Street. He was prepared to supply not only his own half-share of the capital, but the two quarter shares to be nominally owned by James and John, who, being without any capital, naturally looked to their patron. So, having drawn up the disposition of his forces for an unexpected reprisal with all the zest he had shown as the Quartermaster of the Edinburgh Light Dragoons on the eve of manœuvres, he was now ready, as he wrote to Mr Morritt in mid-January, "to turn the flank of Messrs Constable & Co." But as the new publishing house was not to begin operations till Whitsuntide, he then returned more calmly to the usual routine of a January in

Edinburgh; rising early to write, attending the Court of Session as required, and spending as much as possible of the remaining time with his family in 39 Castle Street.

One afternoon towards the end of January, he had left the Law Courts in good time and taken a chaise back to Castle Street. He and Charlotte had been invited to dine that evening by Mr Macdonald Buchanan, one of Scott's fellow Clerks of Session, who lived nearby, and he had brought home a sheaf of law papers to go through before he went out.

But as he crossed the hall, Charlotte ran to meet him in the greatest distress. "Oh, Scott, how glad I am you come – "

"My dearest love, you are all of a tremble. What is wrong? Is it one of the children?"

"No, no, no. But it is Camp – "

Scott dumped the papers on the nearest chair. "Where is he?"

"In your study. He has not been himself all day – "

Scott limped hurriedly across the hall. The study door was ajar, so that passers-by could look in to see if the old dog needed any attention. But all day long he had lain inert on the hearthrug, indicating appreciation when the children tiptoed in to stroke him, or Rob came to make up the fire, with only the slightest movement of his tail.

But at the sound of Scott's voice he had contrived to struggle to his feet, even to take a couple of paces. Then he stood, swaying, and Scott was just in time to catch him as he fell. As he knelt on the rug with the old dog in his arms, Charlotte and the children gathered fearfully in the doorway, and the servants tiptoed up the basement stairs.

"Kiki, my man, I'm here . . ."

Scott ran his hands over the old dog's body, heard the thready, broken patter of his failing heart, the faint thump of his tail. The little black eyes under the grizzled eyebrows opened for a moment, then closed again. The old warrior's body slowly went limp in his arms.

After several minutes, Scott laid the old dog's body down, put his arm round his daughter, and spoke huskily.

"Charlotte, my love, we are engaged to dine with the Buchanans this evening. But – "

"Oh, no, no. I could not bear it – "

Scott nodded agreement. "I will make our excuses. Take the children upstairs to Miss Millar, my dearest, while I write a note for Rob to take round."

As the sad little party drifted away, leaving only Rob, sniffing miserably in the doorway, Scott took off his coat and laid it over the dog's body. Then, in his shirt-sleeves, he moved over to his writing-desk, reaching for a sheet of paper as he sat heavily down.

"Rob, prepare a place for him. In the garden, outside my study window. We'll lay him in the shelter of the wall."

"Yes, sir," mumbled Rob, hunting desperately for his handkerchief.

"But first take this note round to Mr Buchanan." He scribbled briefly, asking his friends to accept his excuses. He and Mrs Scott greatly regretted that they would be unable to dine as arranged: "on account of the death of a dear old friend . . ."

Chapter 13

JANUARY, 1809, went darkly on at 39 Castle Street, for Camp had been a member of the household so long that his absence was unthinkable. The children were inconsolable, cross in consequence, and there were more quarrels and colds than usual in the nursery. In his study, of an evening, Scott's hand strayed absently to fondle the ears of his former companion, and Charlotte found that even the purchase of more materials than she needed for new gowns failed to cheer her as much as usual.

It was a dark time, too, at the flat in George Street, to which Mrs Scott had welcomed back her son John after his army service had left him with uncertain health, already a confirmed bachelor, seeking only a quiet life organised for him by his mother. Her youngest son, Daniel, who had been a problem before he left his teens, had soon afterwards drifted back from Jamaica, not only a diseased and hopeless drunkard but a man dishonoured by the stigma of cowardice in the face of a rebellion of coloured workers from whom he had ignobly fled.

His mother had received him with all her typical compassion, his elder brother, John, endured him, knowing that he had come home to his only remaining refuge. But Walter, who worshipped courage, had been shocked beyond endurance and felt he could never bear to set eyes on his brother again. By the end of the year Daniel was dead.

It was a time of crisis, too, for the whole country. Napoleon, outraged by the Spanish rebellion against the King he had imposed on them, and Britain's temerity in sending a contingent under Sir Arthur Wellesley to defend Portugal, assembled a formidable army to subdue the entire Peninsula. He was defied by Sir John Moore, the British commander in Spain, who fought a battle at Corunna, under cover of which the great bulk of the British forces were successfully embarked, though at the cost of the life of their commander.

After the evacuation of the British forces from Spain, Wellesley was threatened in Portugal, where the French were preparing to "drive the English leopard into the sea". Wellesley was also under almost intolerable pressure from the Whig faction at home against which Scott had so energetically campaigned. His men were in arrears of pay, short of supplies. The whole future of the campaign was balanced on a knife-edge. If he had given way, Napoleon would have overrun the western world.

But Wellesley had no intention of yielding. He realised the importance of defending Lisbon, itself built on a lesser peninsula, and spent the rest of the year directing the work of a local army of resistance to use every natural feature of rock, escarpment and river to make a defensive area in depth, the famous *Lines of Torres Vedras*, against which, in the following year, the French attack was to break in vain.

Scott, whose hopes of seeing active service had dwindled since the threat of French invasion had been removed, was passionately interested in the war which he rightly realised to be a turning-point in British history, with Wellesley as the one general who could direct it.

Since his wild scheme of offering his services was obviously out of the question, he contented himself by furthering his own lesser campaign by planning a visit to London as soon as the spring vacation liberated him from his still unpaid duties at the Court of Session. The younger children were delighted at the prospect of spending the vacation, under the care of Miss Millar, at Ashiestiel, but he decided that Sophia, who had felt the death of Camp more deeply than anyone except himself, should go with her parents. But he and Charlotte both considered it wise to accept the pressing invitation of Joanna Baillie, the Scottish poet and playwright, to look after the little girl in her pleasant family home in still countrified Hampstead, rather than bewilder her by the social activities of the Dumergue household in Piccadilly.

"We shall go by sea," Scott said. "It will be much less tedious, and far better for our health."

"Oh, Scott, will it be safe?"

"Thanks to Lord Nelson, it may well be safer than by land, where highwaymen still lurk and pickpockets abound. What do you say, my love?" he asked, tweaking his daughter's ear. "Shall you like that?"

"I shall like it exceedingly," Sophia said, with the smile which was so like his own.

The visit to London was a great success, though Charlotte suffered from seasickness, and was thankful when the sea-voyage, which Scott and Sophia greatly enjoyed, was over. Sophia was happy in Hampstead, and Charlotte for the first time realised that she was the wife of a literary celebrity. For Mr and Mrs Morritt were at their London home in Portland Place, where they were delighted to give parties for the author of *Marmion*, and Charlotte basked blissfully in the rays of his reflected glory. Mr Morritt, who was a shrewd judge of character as well as a classical scholar, was impressed by Scott's reaction to the exaggerated expressions of homage which would, as he noted in his memoranda "have turned the head of any less-gifted man of eminence". The two men's friendship matured as they grew to know each other in circumstances which tested Scott's humour as much as his judgment.

"Well, do you want me to play lion today?" he murmured to his host, as he and Charlotte arrived to face a glittering assembly. "I will roar if you like, to your heart's content."

"Do so, my friend," said Morritt, smiling. "My lords, ladies and gentlemen, it is my pleasure to present Mr Walter Scott, the author of *Marmion* . . ."

And Scott, with Charlotte by his side, would smile, and joke, and quote and bow before the men and women who clamoured for an introduction, drenched him with adulation, quizzed him unmercifully, overwhelmed Charlotte with expressions of delight at her husband's achievement, jabbered and questioned, begged to know the title of his next work of genius, and how soon it might be expected.

But when the hubbub died down, and the bejewelled dowagers, smiling débutantes, with their formidable or willowy husbands, fathers and attendant beaux, had drifted, chattering, down the marble staircase, Mr and Mrs Morritt would detain Scott and Charlotte for a few quiet minutes' chat. Then, as often as not, Scott would pull out a handkerchief to mop his face, and gladly take the chair they offered; commenting with his gentle smile on the recent lionising.

" 'Yet know that I, one Snug the joiner am – ' "

" 'A very gentle beast, and of good conscience,' " Morritt added, chuckling.

When the parties were over, and Scott had drawn up a plan of campaign with Mr Murray, conferring with George Ellis, Coleridge, and the publisher on the future of the *Quarterly Review*, the Scotts went north, by coach this time, breaking their journey at Rokeby, the Yorkshire home to which the Morritts had already returned. Scott was enchanted by the blend of glen and torrent with the gentler beauty of an English landscape that had seen history made for centuries by the family which owned it still.

That summer, in spite of what he had said to Ellis, another epic poem had begun to stir in Scott's mind, and as soon as the Court of Session rose in mid-July, he warned Charlotte to make preparations for another journey.

"We three are off again," he told the delighted Sophia.

"Oh, Papa, where shall we go now?"

"To the Highlands, my loves. Kind Mr Macdonald Buchanan has invited us to visit him, so that we may see Loch Lomond, and all the surrounding countryside."

And so, with the theme of *The Lady of the Lake* already working like yeast on his vivid imagination, they left Edinburgh for the Trossachs, Charlotte and Sophia driven in their carriage by Peter Mathieson, Scott riding alongside, and occasionally leaving them to set off on excursions of his own, checking time and distance for his chief character's headlong ride with the same meticulous care as he had once checked the equipment of the Light Dragoons.

It was when they were staying at Buchanan House that he was

first shown the satire in which a younger poet, Lord Byron, had amused himself at the expense of *English Bards and Scotch Reviewers*, among whom the author of *Marmion* was somewhat pungently included. Scott's quick temper flared at the allusion to the profits he had made out of the poem.

"It is funny enough," he wrote to Southey, "to see a whelp of a young Lord Byron abusing me, of whose circumstances he knows nothing, for endeavouring to scratch out a living by my pen. God help the bear, if, having little else to eat, he must not even suck his own paws. I can assure the noble imp of fame it is not my fault that I was not born to a park and £5,000 a year . . ."

Then, having blasted his way out of his angry mood, he set off serenely with his host and hostess to scramble with Sophia about the islands of Loch Lomond, while Charlotte discussed the latest London fashions with her hostess in the rowing-boat, and Mr Buchanan watched the exploration with an indulgent smile.

Back at Ashiestiel, Scott plunged headlong into the dramatic action of *The Lady of the Lake*, working as usual early in the morning, so as to be free to enjoy the rest of the day, relaxed by the comforting knowledge that he had accomplished the task he had set himself, and could then play with his children, ride with his friends, and discuss the affairs of the estate with Tom Purdie, as a free man.

The majority of the guests who came and went throughout the summer had not the slightest idea that Scott had been at his desk for at least three hours before he joined them, alert and ravenous at breakfast, though William Erskine, as his closest personal friend, knew, and James Skene soon found out the reason why Scott was able to edit so many volumes of literary and historical works, and yet share all the sport of his idler companions' days.

Scott intended *The Lady of the Lake* to be the first bright feather in John Ballantyne's impudently cocked bonnet, for the new publishing house in Hanover Street was to have it to bring out in the following year, together with the learned editions and collections on which he was also at work, the new *Edinburgh Annual Register* for which he had collected a distinguished company of contributors, and the works of a number of less successful friends. So James's printing presses would be kept busy, John's publishing house would thumb its nose at its rival, and the profits of each concern would enrich the other. What, as John Ballantyne said jauntily, could possibly go wrong with that?

Only John Ballantyne would have had the impudence to sustain a part for which he was not merely ill-qualified, but without any qualifications at all. But at first he succeeded in persuading most people to take him at his own valuation. He dressed the part of the prosperous head of a business concern, entertained elegantly, kept his horses and drove his own yellow-wheeled sporting gig, while James, with his genuine love of literature and fatal lack of grasp of financial problems, beamed at his success, and Scott laughed help-lessly at his irresistible jokes.

For Scott was happy at the progress of his campaign, so much so that he was ready to offer quarter to an enemy, whom like "sweet, meek Lord Manchester" in an earlier conflict, he "did not want to beat too much". He wrote to Constable, with the request that he, as an experienced publisher, would be so kind as to give Mr Ballan-tyne the benefit of his advice on certain questions regarding the setting up of *The Lady of the Lake*. This twig of olive was, rather surprisingly, accepted by Constable, who was perhaps wiser in his generation than any of his opponents realised.

Scott returned to Edinburgh earlier than usual that autumn, for the Laird of Gilnockie, as young Walter had been nicknamed by his father on account of his great admiration for Johnny Armstrong, and his ability to recite at least that ballad by heart, was to be entered at the High School, and his father wished to present him to the Rector in person. Young Walter was outwardly indifferent, but in fact greatly reassured by the knowledge that his family was back at 39 Castle Street during the first anxious days of his entry into that huge, noisy and alarming world. He was less appreciative of the quizzing of his father's friends, the learned gentlemen who sat with him at the Clerks' table at the Court of Session, whose conversation at the family dinner table often bewildered him.

"Gilnockie, my man," said Mr Macdonald Buchanan one

evening, when he and his wife were dining at 39 Castle Street, "you must have noticed that great people make much more work about your papa than they do about the rest of us. What do you suppose occasions this?"

Young Walter, who had not the slightest idea what he was talking about, since Scott never spoke of his poems in the family circle, pondered the question gravely, picturing his father, as he knew him best, escorting his children on their ponies, as they followed the greyhounds across the meadows surrounding Ashiestiel. He glanced anxiously over his shoulder. His father was fortunately not listening, but preoccupied with carving the joint at the head of the table. His mother, talking gaily to the guest at her right hand, was unlikely to come to his assistance. Sophia was making faces at him. The younger children looked blank.

"I suppose," he said desperately, "it's commonly him that first sees the hare sitting."

Mr Macdonald Buchanan chuckled, Sophia clapped her hands, and Walter took a long drink from his glass of water.

The Lady of the Lake came out, in fact, without the knowledge of any of the author's children, early in May, 1810. Scott had recently extended a further olive branch to his former publisher, Mr Constable, who had now taken into his office for training a young man named Cadell, who was to become a significant member of the firm and had already formed a very different opinion of Scott and his work from the choleric Mr Hunter's.

"Dear Sir," Scott wrote,

"I am sure that if Mr Hunter is really sorry for the occasion of my long absence from your shop, I shall be happy to forget all disagreeable circumstances, and visit it often as a customer and amateur. I think it necessary to add (before departing from this subject, and I hope for ever) that it is not in my power to restore our relative situation as author and publishers, because, upon the breach between us, a large capital was diverted by the Ballantynes from another object, and invested in their present bookselling concern, under an express assurance from me of such support as my future publications could give them; which is a pledge not to be withdrawn without grounds which I cannot anticipate. But this is not a consideration which need prevent our being friends and well-wishers . . ."

The new poem was received with greater public acclamation than ever, in which, for once, all the critics joined. George Ellis reviewed it handsomely, as might have been expected, in the *Quarterly*. But Jeffrey's wholehearted praise in the *Edinburgh Review* came as a complete surprise. It was Ellis who balanced his praise with a criticism of the eight-syllable stanza which Scott had used in all his epics, answering the letter in which Scott defended it with his usual candour: "I don't think, after all the eloquence with which you plead for your favourite metre, that you really like it from any other motive than that *sainte paresse*, – that delightful indolence – which induces one to delight in doing those things which one can do with the least fatigue."

Both the candour and the kindness of the criticism struck home. Scott might bluster, but occasionally he listened to his friends. Young Walter came off worse. He returned home to dinner from the High School one day during the summer term with a black eye and obvious traces of a nose-bleed, which he had not time to remove before the bell rang for dinner.

"Well, Gilnockie," Scott said sympathetically after grace, "you've been in a fight, it seems. What was it all about?"

Young Walter looked down at his plate and mumbled.

"Speak up, son. Papa cannot hear you," said Charlotte anxiously.

"They ca'ed me a *lassie*," Walter exploded furiously.

"A lassie?" Scott looked at his sturdy son in bewilderment. "But that's ridiculous. You must have misunderstood them. They could never have said such a thing."

"They did so," Walter persisted, sniffing.

Charlotte bit her lip, but a smile escaped her. "But indeed, my poor Gilnockie, that was a terrible slight."

"You can say what you like, Mamma," said Walter fiercely, "but I ken nothing worser in the world than to be a lassie that sits boring at a clout."

"No gentleman speaks to a lady in that tone, my boy," said Scott gravely.

"Sorry, Mamma."

"Now tell me," Scott cross-examined, "what did yon High School gytes exactly call you? Can you mind their very words?"

"Aye," said young Walter reluctantly. "They – they called me 'The Lady of the Lake'," he mumbled, crimson to the ears.

Scott and Charlotte exchanged anguished glances, but contrived to remain grave.

"The fault was mine, not yours, Gilnockie," said Scott cheerfully.

"How?" Young Walter stared, unbelieving.

"Not long since Mr Ballantyne published a poem of mine. It was called *The Lady of the Lake*."

"It's true, Wattie. Mr James asked me what I thought of it," said Sophia, anxious to help. "I told him I hadn't read it."

"Quite right, my love. There's nothing worse for young people than reading bad poetry," said Scott with a twinkle.

"That's what I told him, Papa," said Sophia, her twinkle answering his. Then the laughter which their parents had been suppressing for so long broke out at last, and even the little ones joined in loudly, though they had scant idea of what it was all about.

After the meal was over, Sophia lingered for a word with her father. Scott was devoted to all his "little people", but the bond between him and his elder daughter, whose sturdy courage and warm-hearted simplicity were so like his own, was a special one, while the laughing philosophy with which Charlotte habitually shrugged off unpleasant possibilities already appealed strongly to the light-hearted, less thoughtful young Walter.

"Papa," said Sophia, when the others had gone, "are we to set out on our travels again this summer?"

Scott folded his hands on the knob of his stick and smiled down at her. "How would you like to come with Mamma and me to the Hebrides?"

"I don't quite know where that is – "

"Tut, tut! I must have a word with Miss Millar."

"But I would like it extremely, just the same," said Sophia hastily.

"Then you shall come."

Sophia flung her arms round his waist. "Oh, thank you, Papa. What are the Hebrides?"

"They are islands, my love," said Scott, gently disentangling himself, and leading the way across the hall from the dining parlour to his study, in search of a map. "Kind Mr Macdonald Buchanan's brother is the Laird of Staffa – get me that atlas from the bottom shelf – aye, here it is – "

"Right in the midst of the sea," said Sophia excitedly. "Shall we go by ship, as we did to London?"

"We shall take the carriage as far north as Oban – here," said Scott. "Then we shall board the boats which the Laird has promised to send for us and cruise among the islands which are set like jewels in a sea which in summer-time can be blue as your eyes, to see all manner of strange sights – "

"I hope Mamma will not be sick again."

Scott, poring now over the map, paid no attention to such a trifling anxiety. "Let me see . . . Peter Mathieson had best put our own horses to the carriage, since there is no need for haste. So we shall be independent of posthouses, and I shall be able to leave you and Mamma in his care while I make my way on foot along whatever bridle path takes my fancy – there is much I must see by the way – "

"Oh, please let me come with you! I will not say one word!"

He tweaked her ear. "We shall have to see what Mamma has to say about that."

The expedition to the Hebrides was a more adventurous pilgrimage than anybody had expected, but an inspiring and invigorating success, in spite of a storm in which Charlotte lost her shoes, Scott his razors, and Sophia her collection of pebbles from Iona. Scott kept no journal, but made many notes, for the possibility of yet another poem was beginning to take shape in the back of his mind.

Back at Ashiestiel, in September, Scott's instinct for prose narrative was for the time being doused by a letter from James

Ballantyne, to whom he had shown the first chapters of *Waverley*, which William Erskine had already criticised unfavourably. James Ballantyne now agreed with him, which was not surprising, since Scott's poems were still selling so well that a change to prose seemed quite uncalled for. *The Lay* had just gone into its eleventh edition, *The Lady of the Lake* was already in its sixth. Why deprive the public of what they so obviously wanted?

His faint praise made his apprehension clear, and he underlined it with a warning that some of the weightier items on the first year's list which John Ballantyne & Co. were offering to the public were not proving as good sellers as Scott had hoped. Beaumont and Fletcher's plays, inexpertly edited by a struggling German whom Scott had hoped to help, still hung like lead on their hands. So did the History of the *Culdees*, since the dry record of the early Scoto-Celtic church, produced by Dr John Jamieson, who had been happier with his Dictionary, was unlikely to please either Episcopalian or Presbyterian supporters. Anna Seward's *Poetical Works*, too, were a dubious legacy, specifically bequeathed to Scott in the Swan of Lichfield's Will. Worse still, the demand for the twice-yearly volumes of the *Edinburgh Annual Register* was disappointing. That literary symposium which Scott had regarded as his heaviest gun for the bombardment of Constable's fortress, was proving too heavy for the public to endure. Honest James Ballantyne was anxious, and said so. But John, more of a gambler and a racing man than he was ever to be a publisher, continued to lay his bets, give his parties and cut his usual capers, confident that with such a winner as *The Lady of the Lake* on their books, they could carry any odds and still win at a canter.

Scott wanted to believe him. But there were times when the complexity of bookselling, the weary grind of the Court of Session, the worry over Tom's debts, weighed heavily enough on his spirits for him to contemplate cutting loose from the lot. It seemed possible that his first friend at the High School, Robert Dundas, the future Lord Melville, was about to go out East, and Scott wrote to his brother in the Isle of Man that November:

"I have no objection to tell you in confidence, that, were Dundas to go out as Governor-General to India, and were he willing to take me with him in a good situation, I would not hesitate to pitch the Court of Session and the booksellers to the devil and try my fortune in another climate."

But the sour mood did not last long. He was able to find Tom another job, as Paymaster to the 70th Regiment, which made it possible for him to pay his debts, leave the Isle of Man, and take his wife and family to Canada with the regiment.

The news of Leyden in India, which had given Scott the idea of following him to the East, continued to come erratically but in terms to kindle the imagination. For Leyden had become enthralled with the Orient: his uncanny gifts had enabled him to master half a dozen languages and put the ancient libraries of the fabled East at his disposal. His ability won the admiration of the colonial authorities, and he was actually made a Judge. This last piece of news was received by his friends in Edinburgh with as much incredulity as admiration. It gave Scott the passing fancy to emulate him, but though Charlotte was tempted by the prospect of seeing her brother again, the magnitude of the upheaval, and the possible effects of such an alien climate on the children, frightened her.

So Scott put it out of his mind, and worked on, during 1811, at the tremendous project on Swift, and a number of lesser editorial enterprises. His imagination had been so kindled by the progress of the war in the Peninsula that he even took time off to write a patriotic poem, *The Vision of Don Roderick*, as a tribute to the British commander whose success in holding the French advance at the lines of Torres Vedras had at last silenced his critics at home and was to bring him advancement, first as Marquis and then as Duke of Wellington. The proceeds of its sales Scott gave for the relief of Portuguese victims of war. It was a gesture which matched the great wave of joy and relief that swept Britain as the first crack appeared in the legend of Napoleonic invincibility.

First-hand news of the campaign came late in the summer from Adam Ferguson, on active service with the British forces behind the lines of Torres Vedras, who wrote to congratulate Scott on *The*

Lady of the Lake soon after Scott had posted him a copy of *The Vision*.

"My dear Walter," wrote Captain Ferguson of the 58th regiment, the famous "Black Cuffs".

"After such a length of silence between us, and, I grant, on my part so unwarrantable, I think I see your face of surprise on recognising this MS, and hear you exclaim – what strange wind has blown a letter from *Linton*? I must say that although both you and my good friend Mrs S. must long ago have set me down as a most indifferent, not to say ungrateful sort of gentleman, far otherwise has been the case, as in the course of my wanderings through this country, I have often beguiled a long march, or watchful night duty, by thinking of the merry fireside in North Castle Street . . .

"But now, quitting self, I need not tell you how greatly I was delighted at the success of *The Lady of the Lake* . . . Last spring I was so fortunate as to get a reading of it, when in the lines of Torres Vedras. . . . While the book was in my possession, I had nightly invitation to *evening parties* to read and illustrate passages of it. . . . At that time supplies of various kinds, especially anything in the way of delicacies, were very scanty; and in gratitude, I am bound to declare, that to the good offices of the *Lady* I owed many a nice slice of ham and rummer of hot punch, which I assure you, were amongst the most welcome favours that one officer could bestow on another, during the long rainy nights of last January and February . . ."

"The poor fellows, the poor fellows," Scott murmured, as he looked round the loaded breakfast table, at which his children were busily stuffing themselves, before rushing out to the riverside. "Mamma, you remember Linton?"

"How should I not?" said Charlotte. "He had ze best manners of any of your friends among – what did you call them – ze Montagnards."

"Charles, dear," said Miss Millar hastily, "how often must I tell you not to drink with your mouth full?"

"You must read this letter from him," said Scott, handing the first page across the table before reading on. "How I envy the old villain! He is serving, you know, under Wellington in the Peninsula."

"And you serve him just as well, I think, Scott, with your poem for ze wounded. Look at ze letters of thanks you have – from Lord Dalkeith, Mr Canning himself – "

But Scott sighed heavily, as he sketched the gesture of drawing an imaginary sword. Then he picked up the rest of the letter and read on.

"I had written all the foregoing botheration, intending to send it by a wounded friend going home to Scotland, when, to my no small joy, your parcel, enclosing Don Roderick, reached me. How kind I take it your remembering old Linton in this way. . . . You wish to know how I like the Vision; but as you can't look for any learned critique from me, I shall only say that I fully entered into the spirit and beauty of it . . ."

"Wily fellow," Scott murmured, chuckling.

". . . Of course, a present of this kind is not thrown away upon indifferent subjects, but it is read and repeated with all the enthusiasm your warmest wish could desire. Should it be my fate to survive . . ." Scott broke off to attract Charlotte's attention. "You must listen to this, Mamma." Then he read on aloud.

"Should it be my fate to survive, I am resolved to try my hand on a snug little farm either up or down the Tweed, somewhere in your neighbourhood; and on this dream many a delightful castle do I build."

"Why not, indeed?" said Charlotte cheerfully.

"I'll bear it in mind from now on," Scott said.

"But you must find a home for us first," Charlotte pointed out.

All round the breakfast table the children lifted their heads anxiously.

"But, Papa, our home is here, at Ashiestiel," said young Walter, indignantly.

Sophia spoke more slowly. "Must we leave Ashiestiel then, Papa?"

"I fear so, my love."

"Oh, Papa. *Why?*" Round-eyed, open-mouthed, they reminded Scott of a nestful of young birds in a hedgerow, clamouring at a parent bird who seemed to be failing in his task.

"Listen, my loves," he said. "Ashiestiel does not belong to us, but to our cousins, the Russells, who have been out in India, and now wish to return home. They let us rent Ashiestiel while they did not need it, and I tried to persuade them to sell it to us, so that it could be ours for always. But they would not agree. How could I blame them? If we love it, after only a few years, must they not love it more, since it has always been their home?"

The younger children sat silent, but Sophia said quickly: "Yes, of course, Papa. And – and I am sure you will buy us somewhere that we will love just as much, because it will be ours for always."

Scott turned to her, smiling. "Yes, my love, I will."

But it was not easy to find a property on Tweedside which had the homely, deep-rooted sturdiness of Ashiestiel, with its snug dwelling-house and convenient outbuildings, farmland and access to their beloved Tweed, yet was within their means.

That autumn Scott rode with Tom Purdie up and down the valley, consulted friends such as Willie Laidlaw at Blackhouse and the friendly innkeeper at Clovenfords, talked to farmers at market, local landowners at his Sheriff Court in Selkirk. At last they had news of a small property on Tweedside, between Selkirk and Melrose, owned by Dr Robert Douglas, minister of Galashiels, an old friend, but a shrewd bargainer. With the farm went a hundred acres of what he was warned by local farmers was indifferent land. But it ran down to the Tweed, just above its junction with Gala Water. And that clinched the matter for him.

"We'll have to take a look at it, though," Tom Purdie said.

"We will that," Scott agreed.

At first sight, the property was not attractive. Dr Douglas had never lived there, since his parochial duties had kept him in Gala-shiels, and the amount of work needed to make the place attractive had daunted him. Behind the broad haugh which bordered the river, the land undulated towards the hills, boggy and undrained, with a tumbledown farmhouse and kailyard, a muddy pond into which the springs from the hillside swampily drained, inadequate fences, and a few firs which the minister had planted as an inadequate screen on one side, with a gaunt barn on the other.

They halted their horses and surveyed it. Tom Purdie said tersely: "this'll never dae. It'd be a sair come-down after Ashiestiel."

Scott said nothing. They tied up their horses in the forlorn stable, loosened the girths, and went towards the house.

"The mistress wad never thole the want of a garden," said Tom Purdie.

"There's a kailyard yonder," Scott pointed out.

"Hout! It's never a fit place for a leddy's floors."

"We'd better take a look inside the house, though. I asked for the key."

Muttering to himself, Tom Purdie followed, as Scott limped up the cobbled pathway, rankly overgrown with weeds, to the front door, which was so swollen with damp that Tom had to use some force to shoulder it open. Inside, the paper was peeling from the walls, the boards creaked ominously, and birds had been nesting in the chimneys, so that straws and soot mounded the cold hearths. It looked, and smelt, utterly forlorn.

Tom Purdie sneezed explosively. "Let's get out o' here, Shirra," he said urgently. "I never want to set foot in sic a place again."

Scott flicked a cobweb from one of the filthy windows, slowly smiling. "I'm sorry to hear that, Tom. I bought it a week ago."

Tom stared at him in consternation. "Gude save us, Shirra," he burst out with all his usual candour, "what in a' this warld made ye do sic a daft-like thing?"

"Come outside and I'll show you."

He led the way up the rough hillside to where an upright stone rose higher than the waving grasses, overlooking the Tweed far below. "When I was a lad, driving with my father from Selkirk to Melrose," he said, "my father stopped the carriage, saying he had something to show me which was quite in my line. He brought me to see this stone, which marks the site of the battle between

Buccleuch and the Earls of Angus and Home, with the Kerrs at their back, for the custody of young King James V. The victory of Buccleuch changed the course of Scottish history, and this stone, ever since, has been called Turn Again. I was passing this place in the spring, without a second glance, when I remembered, and took another look at it. Man, where else could I want to live?"

Tom Purdie scratched his grizzled head. "There's everything to dae," he persisted, "afore it's like to make a home for gentlefolk."

"And if you and I cannot do it, Tom, I don't know who can."

Tom Purdie grinned. "Wha better?" he agreed more cheerfully. "But there's the name o' the place forby," he said indignantly.

"Cartney Hole?" said Scott, perplexed.

Tom guffawed. "Mebbe that's the name on the title deeds, but it's Clarty Hole folk call it. I canna think, Shirra, that a man in your high poseetion would thole hearing himself ca'ed 'Clarty Hole' up and down the Border."

Scott shouted with laughter. "You're right there, Tom. That's something we'll have to change."

He pondered, looking out over the neglected acres of his new property to where the Tweed birled over its pebbled shallows. Then slowly he raised his arm and pointed.

"This land once belonged to the monks of Melrose, Tom. There's a ford yonder that they must have crossed, winter and summer, to harvest their crops and tend their beasts, with the Abbot at the head of the profession, on his douce palfrey, to see how the work fared."

Tom nodded. "Aye, mebbe so. But – "

"We'll call it Abbotsford, man," said Scott triumphantly.

Chapter 14

SPRING came late to the Border country in 1812. The winter had been dour and hard, returning when the weary shepherds thought they had seen the last of it, with an April snowstorm that halted the mail coaches, buried the primroses, and played havoc with sheep and lambs. Then, at long last, the cruel wind dropped, the towering snowdrifts vanished, and the valley of the Tweed, which had lain so silent under its white shroud, quickened with the sound of rushing waters and the jubilation of a thousand birds. High above the hills, on which the snow still lingered, the spring call of the curlew tumbled earthwards like a cascade of jewels, and from the out-by pastures came the tremulous bleating of new-born lambs, the deep, reassuring murmur of the ewes as they nuzzled the little creatures on to their feet.

From the rough road that ran along the valley came less familiar sounds, the shouts of carters, the crack of whips, the excited voices of children and occasional bursts of laughter, as a procession of twenty-four farm carts, piled high with furniture and household goods of every sort, and clanking with Scott's collection of ancient armour and weapons made their way from the old home to the new. Charlotte, Miss Miller and the two younger children, sedately driven by Peter Mathieson in the family carriage, were almost eclipsed, as they brought up the rear, by a last-minute assortment of such things as hen-coops and chamber-pots, with old coats snatched from pegs in passing, doormats, sacks of pots and pans, Charlotte's gardening hat, flower basket and gloves. Charlotte herself was cherishing on her knee a long-dead Borderer's steel helmet, within which agitatedly clucked a recently hatched brood of young turkeys. Miss Miller was hidden by a tall laundry basket full of the children's clothes which nobody had had time to wash, Anne, wedged between a stack of lesson-books and a violin-case, cuddled a wide-eyed kitten, while Charles, clutching an ancient pair of pistols which his father had consigned to his special care, amused himself by making sick-noises as the carriage lurched over the ruts.

Scott, like a general commanding an expeditionary force in alien country, rode up and down the line, to hearten his followers, giving a few words of encouragement to the anxious dairy lasses in charge of recalcitrant cows, shouting a warning to a carter whose load seemed about to topple, exchanging a joke with Tom Purdie at the head of the procession, or the string of barefoot children from Ashiestiel cottages who straggled behind the carriage, leading an assortment of dogs and picking up odd items which had fallen unnoticed from the overloaded carts.

Sophia and Walter cantered ahead on their ponies, whooping with excitement as their journey's end approached, while Tom Purdie looked over his shoulder at the long line of carts, and shook his head at the possibility of finding space for half of their contents in the little farmhouse, now scrubbed, repaired and freshened with a new coat of whitewash to receive them.

"It's a mercy, Shirra, that the gude Doctor set up yon awful great ugly barn after a'," he said cheerfully, as Scott reined back his horse beside him. "Or maist o' oor plenishing would have had to bide on the cauld hillside."

"That's the very thing that crossed my mind when I first saw it," Scott agreed. "Now, you two," he told Sophia and Walter, "turn your ponies into the pasture at the back of the house. But pump some water for them first. There's a trough in the yard."

"Are the fences mended, Papa?" Sophia asked anxiously, remembering her first sad sight of the place the autumn before.

Scott tweaked her ear. "What do you take your Papa for? Then go and see if Mamma needs help to get out of the carriage with all that gear about her."

"Papa, may we go down to the river and see if we can guddle some trout for supper?" Walter asked. "We'll take the wee yins out of the way," he added diplomatically.

"Mind you have a care of them, then."

"We will, Papa," Sophia promised gaily.

Scott let them go, thankful to have them happily occupied and enjoying their first day in their new home. For there had been tears and grief at the idea of exchanging much-loved Ashiestiel, snug-set in its pleasant garden, for the derelict shell of a place on a wet hillside. When he had first taken them one sad day in autumn to see the new home that he had bought for them, they had stood in the cold kitchen and wept.

But now it was spring, and everything was different. As Sophia ran across the meadow to the river with the younger children at her heels, she remembered how Papa had comforted them, gathering them into his arms as he promised: "I will turn it into the loveliest home in the world." It had been hard to believe him then. But now, as they all sat down on the bank to tear off shoes and stockings to plunge into the same river that ran past Ashiestiel, she felt the promise already begin to come true.

The six months that followed Scott's impulsive purchase had been anxious and busy ones for him. Dr Douglas had asked a higher price for the derelict farmhouse and its hundred acres of neglected land than Scott had been able to find unaided. He had borrowed £2,000 from his brother John, and drawn as much from Messrs John Ballantyne & Co., on the security of the poem which was already planned, but as yet unwritten, the epic of *Rokeby*, home of his friend, J. B. S. Morritt. From the moment he first saw it, the Yorkshire manor house had made a tremendous appeal, and Mr Morritt had replied to the letter in which Scott first sketched out his project with enthusiasm, promising to make available all the information he possessed of the part played by his family in the Civil War. But he begged Scott to visit the place again, since first-hand observation would be far more useful than all the letters he could write and all the books he could recommend.

Scott cordially agreed, but it was obviously impossible for him to leave Scotland until he had surrendered Ashiestiel to its returning owners, and it would take at least six months' work to make Abbotsford fit to receive his family. So meanwhile, Mr Morritt wrote long informative letters, and Scott drew the money he required. Once the purchase was concluded, he set Tom Purdie at the head of a team of stout farm labourers to repair fences, and dig ditches, while carpenters and painters worked on the house itself. Young Daniel Terry, his fervent admirer, came north that autumn, anxious to put his skill as architect and draughtsman at Scott's disposal. They rode daily from Ashiestiel, ardently discussing plans for the conversion of the uninspiring place into the ornamental cottage, "something in the style of the old English vicarage house" which Terry suggested. An Edinburgh architect, Mr Stark, whom Terry warmly recommended, was commissioned to draw up plans, and the project began to take place.

Other things, as usual, had also claimed Scott's attention during his last winter at Ashiestiel. He had written to Leyden, in India, shortly after the purchase of Abbotsford, gently reproaching him for being such a bad correspondent, urged by an odd compulsion which he did not understand till his letter, written on 25th August, 1811, was returned to him unopened. For Leyden had died on the 28th, after three days' illness, from a tropical fever, against which, with typical lack of care for his own safety, he had taken no precautions. Scott, who cherished his friends, wherever they might be, received the news with real sorrow, and a sort of spine-chilling wonder that his thoughts should have been reaching out towards another poet of the Scottish Border on the very day that his last illness struck him.

The other Border poet, James Hogg, had now another collection of poems, *The Forest Minstrel*, in print, and Scott found time to send a copy, with an introductory letter, to Lady Dalkeith, who sent a gift of a hundred guineas to him for the author. Hogg received it with delight, as he had been for some time anxious to own a farm of his own, instead of being at another man's beck and call.

January, 1812, brought at least one favourable omen for the great new enterprise of Abbotsford. Thanks to a new superannuation act which provided a pension on retirement for certain office holders, Scott now began to draw the salary of £1,300 a year as Clerk of Session which he should have had five years before. But later in the month, he was saddened by the death of his first patron, the venerable Duke of Buccleuch, though as far as he was concerned, the Earl of Dalkeith's succession to the title was of great importance, since the new Duke was not only a man of Scott's own age but also a personal friend.

But perhaps the most significant event that winter was the publication of the first cantos of Lord Byron's *Childe Harold* by Mr Murray, of Fleet Street, who had already played a part in Scott's literary affairs. As Scott read the Romance, his remembered irritation at the author's satire was eclipsed by the chilling knowledge that he now had a most formidable rival in the field of epic poetry, for the poem and its author had been acclaimed by literary London, and was later to be greeted with respect even by the formidable Mr Jeffrey of the *Edinburgh Review*.

However, the strength of the forces arrayed against him had never daunted Scott in any field, and he set about the writing of *Rokeby* with all his usual enthusiasm, but under more than usual difficulties. For workmen were already busy expanding the little farmhouse, putting up a new range of buildings round the stable yard, which would provide Peter Mathieson and his family with adequate quarters, on a par with the cottage already allocated to Tom Purdie and his household, with rooms for bachelor visitors, and was collectively known as Peter's House by all concerned.

It was as well that Scott had taken to early rising, for only before sunrise was there any peace at Abbotsford that summer. Throughout the week, until the Courts rose on the 12th of July, he was, of course, in Edinburgh, but every week-end was spent on his new premises, where, by the long vacation, the parlour had been made habitable, but was also required as dining-room, drawing-room, schoolroom and study. Scott's table had been set in front of a window which looked out over the Tweed, and an old curtain nailed up behind it, to give an illusion of privacy. He wrote to the squire of Rokeby: "As for the house and the poem, there are twelve masons hammering at the one, and one poor noddle at the other – so they are both in progress – "

Apart from the rehabilitation of the farmhouse to Charlotte's satisfaction, one of the most urgent outdoor tasks was the plantation of trees which would transform the bleak slopes into a more varied and sheltered situation. Larches, in Tom Purdie's opinion, would be useful, quick-growing and decorative. So he and Scott laboured over the new plantations. But Scott longed for more varied and traditional woodlands, so acorns were planted, but with less success, for the field mice devoured them. An admirer sent Spanish chestnuts from Seville, but the supplier mistook the purpose for which they were intended, and had them boiled before dispatch.

At the beginning of July, less than a fortnight before his release from his duties at the Clerks' Table, Scott received a letter from Mr John Murray, in Fleet Street, who had heard from Lord Byron of the Prince Regent's interest in Scott's works, and hoped that it might provide an opportunity of introducing the poets to each other.

Scott considered the kindly offered mediation thoughtfully, then, with a smile and a shrug, wrote to Lord Byron with more candour than Mr Murray had perhaps reckoned on. He congratulated him on the first cantos of *Childe Harold*, thanked him for conveying the Prince Regent's kind remarks to Mr Murray, then, squaring his shoulders, went on to explain the circumstances, which Lord Byron had had the misfortune to misapprehend, in which *Marmion* had been written.

And he expected to hear no more. But at least he had put the record straight. Lord Byron, however, answered, both courteously and promptly.

"Sir,
"I have just been honoured with your letter. . . . The Satire was written when I was very young and very angry, and fully bent on displaying my wrath and my wit, and now I am haunted by the ghosts of my wholesale assertions. I cannot sufficiently thank you for your praise; and now, waiving myself, let me talk to you of the Prince Regent . . ."

Scott left Edinburgh for the long vacation with a considerably modified opinion of Lord Byron.

The children enjoyed the hurly-burly at Abbotsford all the more because they never knew when an avalanche of stones and rubble would effectively interrupt the girls' lessons with Miss Millar, or Scott's heroic attempt to hear young Walter the Latin he was missing on account of the family's migration to the Border before the end of the High School term. Walter was an even less enthusiastic Latin scholar than his father had been, and there were times when Scott feared that his yawns, courteously concealed though they were, would dislocate his son's lower jaw. The relief, when Scott at last tugged his ponderous gold watch from his breast pocket and declared that they had done enough, was mutual and unashamed.

Scott's own literary tasks could not be so happily laid aside. He was still working on the formidable edition of Swift, and steadily advancing through the epic on *Rokeby*, when he was taken with the idea of a slighter poem, *The Bridal of Triermain*. He and Erskine amused themselves with this in odd moments, for Scott had a fancy to avenge himself on the critics by publishing it anonymously, phrasing it in such a way that they would jump to the conclusion that Erskine had written it. It was no more than a summer holiday ploy for two friends who understood each other better than most. They got a good deal of fun out of it, but nobody was deceived.

Then, during the autumn, he received a letter from Mr Morritt which made him abruptly down tools, leaving Tom Purdie happily and importantly in charge of the work at Abbotsford for a couple of weeks, while he took the opportunity of giving his poem the first-hand observation of its setting on which the owner of Rokeby now insisted. Mr Morritt had written warningly and wisely.

"I hope . . . you will not be obliged to write in a hurry on account of the impatience of your booksellers . . . Do not be persuaded to risk your established fame on this hazardous experiment. If you want a few hundreds independent of these booksellers, your credit is so good . . . that it is no great merit to trust you, and I happen at this moment to have five or six for which I have no sort of demand

– so rather than be obliged to spur Pegasus beyond the power of pulling him up when he is going too fast, do consult your own judgment . . . above all be not offended at me for a proposition which is meant in the true spirit of friendship, I am more than ever anxious for your success . . .

Ever affectionately yours, J.B.S.M."

Scott was so deeply touched by the wisdom and kindness of the letter that he decided to make a family pilgrimage to Rokeby. Sophia and Walter were almost stupefied with delight at being told they and their father would accompany the carriage, in which their mother would be driven in state by Peter Mathieson with all the luggage, on horseback. They spent every available hour before their departure in grooming their ponies and checking the saddlery according to the high standard of efficiency insisted on by the former quartermaster of the Edinburgh Light Dragoons.

The expedition was a great success, as full of historical interest, unexpected adventures, and comical interludes, as Sophia and Walter could ever have hoped. On their return, their father reported, in a letter of thanks to his host, that "Sophia and Walter hold their heads very high among their untravelled companions, from the predominance acquired by their visit to England."

Towards the end of the year Scott was able to tell the squire of Rokeby that he hoped the whole poem would be printed by Christmas. In the same letter he exulted over Napoleon's second blunder, his attempt to call his defecting Russian allies to heel by invading them with an army of over six hundred thousand men, only to find Moscow a burned-out shell, and to be compelled to retreat through the murderous silent hostility of the Russian winter.

And the diversion of such a large army inevitably weakened his forces in the Peninsula so seriously that Wellington, attentively waiting in the background, was able to invade Spain and capture Madrid. By the end of the year the British Foreign Secretary was forming a Fourth Coalition against Napoleon, which included Russia, Prussia, Sweden and ultimately Austria. Slowly they gathered round France, as the wolves of the Steppes had gathered round the exhausted French soldiers whom their leader had abandoned in his anxiety to get back to Paris.

By 1813, as Scott had already expected, the writing was on the wall for Napoleon. But, in a lesser campaign, it was also written up in large capitals against the forces of John Ballantyne & Co. Publishers. Scott himself had been occupied with a multitude of things; the work of Abbotsford, which enthralled him, the completion of *Rokeby*, which engrossed him, the first letters from the poet Crabbe, Rector of Muston, near Grantham, who had been introduced to him by Mr Hatchard, and whose work was to delight him for the rest of his life. He had never been interested in financial diplomacy, and the implications of the bills of accommodation, by which John Ballantyne deferred his liabilities, were details which he too hastily set aside.

But as the year advanced, he began to realise that the campaign which he had initiated still showed few signs of "turning Constable's flank", and he was driven to issue a series of increasingly sharp reprimands to his lieutenants on the way they were deploying their forces and using the ammunition he provided. And these reprimands were not always well received.

One summer morning, John Ballantyne flung into the small, cluttered office in which his brother James corrected proof sheets, answered letters, and took refuge from the mechanical clatter of the printing-house.

"Jamie, the old warlock's been after me again."

James levered himself up from the swing-chair in which he had been reclining, and hastily shut the door. His brother's cracked falsetto, as he knew only too well, could be heard from one end of the printing-house to another.

"Tch, tch, Johnny, calm yourself and tell me what's the matter now," said stout James Ballantyne, belching unhappily. He had eaten something which disagreed with him the night before, and these scenes with his brother always made his indigestion worse.

"He scolds me roundly for not warning him in advance that I should need the money, but springing my demands – for a few paltry hundreds only, mark you – required for immediate settlement at a moment's notice – "

James Ballantyne sighed heavily. "Surely you know Mr Scott better by this time, Johnny. Why didn't you warn him in advance?"

John Ballantyne whipped his expensive beaver off and threw it violently into a far corner. His thin face was flushed, his usually merry eyes wild. "Warn him? And miss the chance of a gallant nag of my acquaintance coming in at such long odds that I'd have no need to warn him at all. Damn it, Jamie, whose fault is it that we're in such a pickle that I'm to go hat in hand to old Constable and offer him a share in Scott's copyrights if he'll help me to manage my publishing business? Who's to blame that I can't sell all the books on our list?"

James rooted in the drawer of his desk for a digestive tablet. "Mr Scott obviously thinks it's yours, Johnny."

John Ballantyne fastidiously parted the skirts of his elegant, pearl-grey driving coat, and sat down opposite his brother. "Just take a look," he said, wagging a forefinger, snugly encased in a fine chamois-leather driving glove, "at all yon tombstones that he expects us to lift! There's that half-daft German fellow's shocking job on Beaumont and Fletcher, the old professor's dreary tome on the Culdees – "

"Mr Scott's a warm-hearted man to his friends, I admit," said James unhappily. "Mind you, Johnny, if it hadn't been for him and the help he gave me I'd still be stuck in Kelso, using up my fine types on their once-a-week rag – "

"I wish to God I was back there, and that's the truth," John Ballantyne exploded, with sudden tears in his eyes. "I had good times in Kelso, Jamie. Fool that I was not to know it."

"You've had good times in Edinburgh too," his elder brother pointed out unhappily. "Too good, maybe, for the business."

"Always on at me for spending money," said John, pushing back his chair and rising to pace about the room. "You know very well I shan't make old bones. But you're as bad as he is, scolding me. How he dares? Look what he's spending on that Clarty Hole of his that he's calling Abbotsford . . ." He broke off in a sudden fit of coughing.

James covered his face with his plump hands. "After all, he earns the money he spends, every penny of it. And it's only his money that's keeping us afloat now."

"Well, we won't keep afloat much longer if I can't come to terms with that crafty chap Constable, and that's a fact," said John Ballantyne, retrieving his hat from the corner with a sudden cackle of laughter. "So you can spare me any more of your sanctimonious reflections on the character of Walter Scott, Esquire." He clapped his hat on his head, smoothed a few wrinkles from his gloves, picked up his cane, and gave his brother a mocking salute. "I'll do my best, Jamie. You know as well as I do that I'm devoted to him, in my fashion."

James groaned as the door slammed behind his younger brother, for he very much doubted whether his volatile personality would make much impression on that extremely shrewd man of business, Mr Archibald Constable. It was easy to write John off as a charlatan, an idler, a waster, who skated so gracefully on thin ice that he deceived most people until it cracked beneath him. He fancied he knew his brother better, if only because he loved him. But latterly, he had almost begun to lose hope of being able to grab him before the ice gave way. The youthful qualities of spontaneous gaiety and madcap, impulsive delight in riotous fun which had amused and delighted Scott, were in fact hardening into a reckless avidity for the good things of life at whatever cost to himself and others. "Eat, drink and be merry . . ." James sniffed unhappily, as the words floated through his mind. For he didn't know what to do, and he didn't want Johnny to die.

Scott's impulsive attempt to break Constable's monopoly in the publishing business could scarcely have been made at a worse time. With Wellington's success in the Peninsula, Napoleon's disastrous expedition against Russia, and the formation of the Fourth Coalition against him, victory was almost won. But the country as a whole was weary of the long-drawn-out war, the blockade, the shortages. Credit was hard to obtain, even for long-established and prosperous

firms. So the negotiations with Constable dragged on. John Ballantyne was unable to handle them, and Scott himself had eventually
to intervene.

Constable received his prodigal author with magnanimity, as a
victor who allowed the defeated general to retain his sword. His
outspoken colleague, Mr Hunter, who had triggered off the dispute,
was now dead, and the younger partner, Robert Cadell, very much
more diplomatic. Constable himself had changed considerably since
the early days when John Leyden had teetered on the top of a ladder
in the dingy High Street bookshop, and Scott had first found his way
upstairs to the obliging and alert young bookseller's sanctum in
which the same man, now portly and prosperous, in his forties, like
Scott himself, urbanely prepared to dictate terms.

It was a situation of the greatest delicacy. Constable was in an
extremely strong position, and both men knew it. The printing
firm had always done good work, and was likely to do more if it
could be disentangled from the misfortunes of the publishing house
which was so loaded with debt and unsaleable goods that it must
soon drag the original enterprise down with it to bankruptcy and
ruin unless some way of cutting its losses could be worked out.

But bankruptcy must at all costs be avoided, since the consequent
publicity would reveal Scott's connection with a shoddy commercial
concern with which no Sheriff and Clerk of Session should ever
have allowed himself to be associated. In this respect, Constable had
him at his mercy. But, on the other hand, Scott was a poet of
international status, the learned editor of many successful works,
who would soon complete the monumental work on Swift for
which Constable had contracted four years before. And Constable
was not fool enough to kill any goose who had already laid such
golden eggs, and might survive to lay many more. He agreed to
come to the rescue of the foundering publishing house, but on his
own terms. And these were rather different from those which John
Ballantyne had suggested. The most urgent, and quite the most
unwelcome of John Ballantyne's requests was that Constable should
take over the future of the moribund *Edinburgh Annual Register*, and
this Constable understandably declined to do, since, on examining

the trading record of the unfortunate periodical, he found it had been running at a loss of something like £1,000 per annum. But he was willing to take 300 sets of the stock in hand, and to consider the possibility of giving further help later. He was also willing to take over a substantial number of such deadweights as Weber's *Beaumont and Fletcher*, several hundred copies of *The Vision of Don Roderick* and a quarter of the copyright of *Rokeby*.

Scott left Constable's premises with the satisfaction of having at least gained a brief respite. He was well aware that it could be no more. As he wrote to John Ballantyne: "We have recovered our legs for a week or two." But he was optimistic enough to believe that his own earnings would soon swing the balance true. He had a new poem, with Robert the Bruce as the chief character, which he proposed to begin at once, and he was already negotiating for the purchase of more land for the Abbotsford estate, extending from the Turn-Again stone to Cauldshiels Loch, for which he would soon need money, so he offered the copyright to Constable for £5,000. Constable's acceptance elated him so much that he wrote authorising Daniel Terry in London to buy "that splendid suit of ancient armour" advertised by a London auctioneer. It would look well when a place large enough to hold his collection of such things was built at Abbotsford. But Constable was less willing to buy the copyright of *The Lord of the Isles* before a line had been written than he had once been to make sure of *Marmion* on the same terms. The summer vacation was ruined by a series of frantic demands for money from John Ballantyne, as bills of accommodation came in for settlement in shoals. By the middle of August, Constable, having completed his examination of the financial affairs of the Ballantyne printing and publishing companies, gave his considered opinion that one or both of them must be wound up unless Mr Scott could immediately raise £4,000. He also added dryly that if Mr John Ballantyne gave up bookselling and went into the auctioneering business, as he had already suggested, the situation would be greatly simplified.

Scott entirely agreed. "I am quite satisfied," he wrote to John, "that it is impossible for J.B. & Co. to continue business longer than is absolutely necessary for the sale of stock and settlement of their affairs." But even if a change of profession prevented John from incurring any more of the debts which had been jumping out at him like a crop of dragons' teeth all summer, he himself had still to find £4,000 prior to Constable's expected purchase. Anxiously he worked out his income from all sources. Including Charlotte's allowance from her brother, his own salaries as Clerk of Session and Sheriff of Selkirk, a generous but hypothetical sum for literary windfalls, it stood only at £2,100 p.a., out of which he and his family must eat and drink and his household be paid. And while he was in the midst of his uncomfortable calculations, he received a letter from the member of the royal household entrusted with such things, with the Prince Regent's offer of the post of Poet Laureate. It was an almost ridiculous complication, since the post had recently been held by the most unlikely people. To accept it was to risk becoming a figure of fun. To refuse it might cause dangerous offence.

Scott suddenly felt that the answer to both his problems might be obtained from his old friend the Duke of Buccleuch. He wrote carefully: "I am not asking nor desiring any loan from your Grace, but merely the honour of your sanction to my credit as a good man for £4,000 . . ." Then he went on to his second problem. "I have a very flattering offer from the Prince Regent, of his own free motion, to make me Poet-Laureate: I am very much embarrassed by it . . ."

The Duke answered promptly.

"I received yesterday your letter of the 24th. I shall with pleasure comply with your request of guaranteeing the £4,000.

"As regards the second problem," he went on, "I am never willing to offer advice, but when my opinion is asked by a friend I am ready to give it . . . Your muse has hitherto been independent – don't put her into harness. We know how lightly she trips along when left to her natural paces, but do not try driving. . . ."

Greatly relieved on both counts, Scott wrote to the appropriate member of the royal household, declining the honour so graciously that the Prince Regent himself was greatly impressed, and made a note that a man of such quality must certainly be presented to him on his next visit to London.

He was full of hope that autumn. For now, thanks to the Duke, the financial crisis seemed to have been averted, he had contrived to work doggedly through the summer, in spite of all distractions, completing his immense work on Swift for Constable, writing the first cantos of *The Lord of the Isles* so as to have enough to convince Constable of its merit when reopening negotiations. What was more, he had happened to find a bundle of papers in the drawer of an old bureau which had been consigned to an outhouse, while rummaging through its drawers in search of fishing tackle for a guest. The discovery made him forget everything but the first chapters of a narrative he had twice set aside. Now, at last, he saw what could be made of it. He dragged a packing-case forward, found a stub of pencil in a pocket of his shooting-jacket, and began for the third time to work on *Waverley*.

It had been a wonderful summer. The children were brown as gipsies and had been working in their gardens – the source of much friendly rivalry and occasional blows – helping in the hayfield or in and out of the river, all day long. Scott had found time to work with Tom Purdie in the new plantations, which were coming up well, and a source of considerable pride to his highly critical assistant. New stables and garden wall had been put up but plans for a new cottage were abandoned when Stark, the architect, died.

He also wrote warmly to Lord Byron about James Hogg in answer to Byron's request for information about the author of *The Queen's Wake*, which the Ettrick Shepherd had boldly submitted for his approval. But he viewed with less favour the suggestion which Hogg proceeded to make that he should compile a volume consisting of contributions from all the greatest contemporary poets, including Byron, Wordsworth, and Scott himself, which would be sold for his personal benefit. When the poets concerned declined to participate, and Scott added his remonstrances, Hogg took it very badly. The letter he wrote Scott began: "Damned Sir ..." and concluded "Yours in disgust." So Scott, who had, after all, many other matters on his mind, left him to cool off for a while.

The Town Council of Edinburgh decided to send a deputation to congratulate the Prince Regent on the successful outcome of the war, and Scott was requested to compose the address, which the Lord Provost duly presented. In due course Scott received from the Prince Regent a personal acknowledgement of "the most elegant congratulation a sovereign ever received or a subject offered".

In France, the exiled royal family returned from exile, and another Louis, brother of the murdered King, restored the Bourbon line as Louis XVIII. His welcome, however, was not without its discordant note. Adam Ferguson, who had been taken prisoner during the war in the Peninsula, was now released and enthusiastically welcomed by Scott and his family at 39 Castle Street. That evening he graphically described the refusal of the men of Napoleon's personal bodyguard to do homage to the French royal family, to the enthralled company round the dinner table. Scott and Charlotte urged food and wine on their old friend, who seemed leaner and lankier than ever after many months in a prisoner of war camp, and the children stared at him with worshipping eyes.

"There they were, those magnificent fellows of old Boney's Imperial Guard, looking as smart as pipeclay and brass polish could make them, in those blue uniforms, faced with red, that were the terror of Europe. When the procession passed, the crowd went wild – you know what Parisians are – but they stood like stone, glaring sheer hatred. You know, Scott, there's something no' canny in a fellow that can so enslave men's souls."

"I've heard it said," Scott observed thoughtfully, "that he is the incarnation of Satan himself. I wonder . . ."

"The Congress of Vienna has outlawed him, I understand. They're sending him to Elba."

Scott sighed. "So I believe. But I doubt there's likely to be no peace for ordinary folks till he sleeps with the tyrants of old. Now, Linton, let me fill up your glass."

"I cannot tell you, my dear Charlotte," said Adam Ferguson, turning to his hostess with a blissful smile, "just what it means to be here with you all again." He looked round him like a man waking from a long and troubled dream. The children's bright faces, well-brushed hair, the Sunday clothes worn in his honour, the untroubled candle flames, the firelight . . . Only another prisoner of war, reaching home at last, he thought, would understand the lump in his throat. But Charlotte impulsively laid her hand on his, clenched on the table for fear that emotion would overcome him.

"My dear friend, we also, we understand," she said.

As the year went on, Scott's literary horizon began to lighten. Will Erskine was enthusiastic about the final version of *Waverley*, and the first volume was submitted by the Ballantynes to Constable, who was not at first in the secret of its authorship, but agreed to publish it, dividing the profits equally with the unknown author, of whose identity he had the shrewdest suspicions. On 1st February an announcement appeared in *The Scots Magazine*: that "Waverley; or, 'tis Sixty Years Since, a novel in 3 vols. 12mo, will be published in March".

But meanwhile, Constable earnestly requested Scott to write the articles on Chivalry and the Drama for the supplement to the *Encyclopaedia Britannica*, the copyright of which he had recently acquired. Scott agreed, and the assignment inevitably delayed the publication of *Waverley*, though once he had completed it he wrote the final volumes with all the fanatical concentration of the Writer's apprentice, who had once transformed a hundred folio pages at a stretch without pause for rest or food.

The magnificent, nineteen volume edition of Swift was published by Constable in July, only a week before the mysterious *Waverley*, which Scott firmly refused to acknowledge, in spite of all the importunities of the Ballantynes, who were, of course, in the secret. So was Morritt of Rokeby, to whom Scott wrote, giving his reasons, soon after its appearance. "In truth, I am not sure it would be considered quite decorous for me, as a Clerk of Session, to write novels. Judges being monks, Clerks are a sort of lay brethren, from whom some solemnity of walk and conduct may be expected."

But there was more to it than that. Scott had always had a mischievous lad's love of a secret, from the days when he and Will

Clerk, as students, had amused themselves by contriving bogus antiques, hoping to mystify the experts.

So now, weary of haggling and recriminations, he amused himself by baiting another hook for the knowing ones, cast a new line over a familiar pool, and watched the first trout jump for it. Then, without waiting to gauge the response, he handed his rod to his not entirely mystified publisher, and left the river.

With Will Erskine, who was the other man in the secret, as he had been his partner in *The Bridal of Triermain*, he joined a few friends on a voyage to the isles which had been organised by the Commissioners for the Northern Lights, to inspect the far-flung beacons round Scotland's northern coasts. He could not have chosen a holiday which would take him more effectively out of touch with all sorts of news, whether good or bad. It proved to be one of the happiest holidays of his life.

The party went aboard a stout cutter, well victualled and equipped, which left on the 29th of July from Leith. This time Scott kept a Diary, which he headed: *"Vacation, 1814. Voyage in the Lighthouse Yacht to Nova Zembla, and the Lord knows where."*

Chapter 15

EARLY in 1815, the complacent deliberations round the Congress table at Vienna were rudely interrupted by the news of Napoleon's escape from Elba. He landed in France with eight hundred men and marched straight for Paris. By the end of March he had bounced Louis XVIII off his throne again, reassumed control, and declared his intention to live at peace with all other nations and establish a liberal government in France. The French people were stupefied, his loyal soldiers triumphant. But outside France nobody believed him for a moment. He was outlawed by the Congress of Vienna as a public enemy and disturber of the peace, against whom joint action must immediately be taken by the great powers.

Each undertook to raise an army of 150,000 men. But by mid-June only Wellington, with a combined force of British, German, and Dutch Belgians, and Blücher, with his Prussians, were ready to move on Paris. On the 12th Napoleon turned at bay, and led his army in a brilliant manœuvre designed to drive between Blücher's Prussians at Ligny and Wellington's forces at Quatre Bras, so as to demolish first one and then the other from the rear.

He very nearly succeeded. But though the Prussians were overrun, the immortal obstinacy of the British infantrymen held fast. The French withdrew, but only to re-form their forces. For the next twenty-four hours the future teetered. Then, on the 18th of June, Napoleon's empire, defended to the last by the heroism of his Imperial Guards, went down in the smoke and flame of the Wagnerian conflict near the village of Waterloo.

The previous autumn Scott had returned from his most successful and happy vacation expedition to inspect the Northern Lights, his diary crammed with notes and ideas for the completion of *The Lord of the Isles*, only to be stricken by the devastating news of the death of the gay and lovely Duchess of Buccleuch, to whose inspiration he owed *The Lay of the Last Minstrel* and many happy memories of hospitality at Dalkeith and Bowhill. His letter to the Duke was warm with the sorrow and sympathy of an old friend as well as the feudal follower of the great house of Buccleuch.

By contrast, the news that *Waverley* had achieved an astonishing success, which reached him when he and Erskine arrived in Edinburgh, scarcely seemed to matter. It had appeared on the 7th of July, and the first edition of 1,000 copies had been sold out in five weeks, in spite of having been anonymously published in the "dead season" for books. A second edition of 2,000 copies had gone during August, and Constable greeted Scott in September with plans for a third, with a fourth to follow in November. Constable was, naturally, highly delighted, and willing to finalise the terms for *The Lord of the Isles* at fifteen hundred guineas for half the copyright, the other to be retained by the author. The Ballantynes, of course, had been hopefully haggling with him during Scott's absence, in the hope of persuading him to take on more of their moribund "quire stock". But Constable was unwilling to add this concession to his terms for *The Lord of the Isles*. In his opinion, which he was too diplomatic to pass on to the author, Scott, as a poet, had shot his bolt. Had he ventured, he might have found Scott unexpectedly in agreement. He had written to Daniel Terry in London on the 10th of November: "I have fallen under the tyrannical dominion of a certain Lord of the Isles . . . The *peine forte et dure* is, you know, nothing in comparison to being obliged to grind verses; and so devilish repulsive is my disposition, that I can never put my wheel into constant and regular motion, till Ballantyne's devil claps in his proofs . . . O long life to the old hermit of Prague, who never saw pen and ink!"

But Scott had always been a story teller. And with *Waverley* he entered on his life's work. By the end of the year, he was planning the book's successor. *Guy Mannering* owed a great deal to a certain Mr Train, an Excise officer of Newton Stewart, whose little book of *Poems*, with notes illustrative of traditions in Galloway and Ayrshire, had interested Scott so much that he became one of the subscribers for its publication, and wrote to Mr Train to expres interest in any traditions and legends of the district which he might not need for his own use. Mr Train, greatly flattered, replied that he had indeed collected a great number of these, but forthwith renounced every idea of authorship for himself in order to put them at Scott's disposal.

Scott was most grateful, and took full advantage of Mr Train's offer. By the time *The Lord of the Isles* was published, in January, 1815, he had already completed two volumes of *Guy Mannering*, and the question of its publication arose. Constable was the publisher of *Waverley*, and he had just brought out *The Lord of the Isles*. But there was no obvious connection between the two, and no option for a second novel. Also, he had declared himself unable to take on any more moribund stock from the dusty Ballantyne basement. And, somehow or other, the stock must be disposed of, for the winding up of the publishing business had already taken too long, and the bills which John had sown broadcast were still bringing in their crop of tares.

Scott authorised the Ballantynes to offer a new novel by the author of *Waverley* to Longmans or Murray, provided they were willing to help them off with some of their stock, since, as they were no doubt aware, Messrs John Ballantyne & Co. were going out of publishing. He also insisted that Constable should share in the enterprise as far as the Scottish sales were concerned. When John Ballantyne, who had no objection to sharp practice, suggested that the London publishers should be offered, not only the new novel, but the next edition of the already successful *Waverley*, provided they were willing to take on enough of the moribund stock, Scott refused, on the grounds that he considered himself bound to Constable for *Waverley* so long as he continued to fulfil the conditions annexed.

The new novel alone was therefore offered to Messrs Longmans, who accepted it without demur on Scott's terms, and informed Constable of his share in the transaction, at the author's request. So *Guy Mannering* appeared, one month after *The Lord of the Isles*, in February, 1815, and had, as Scott did not fail to notice, a much better reception. He realised at once the implications of the public's choice. It came, on the whole, as a relief. Success had not turned his head, since he only valued it for its by-products, the contacts it brought him with all sorts of people, the opportunities of building up a background for his family. Now he had the opportunity both of furthering an enterprise which was already dear to him, and indulging in a mystification which amused him, by means of the storytelling gift he seemed to have been born with. So it was with the light heart of a man who has seen the answer to a crucial problem at last, that he embarked at Leith for another visit to London, accompanied by Charlotte and Sophia, just as the news of Napoleon's escape from Elba broke.

Everyone was happy, in spite of the immediate prospect of a buffeting from the March gales as the sturdy sailing vessel ploughed its way southwards from the Forth to the Thames. Sophia, already at sixteen an experienced traveller, was delighted to return to the Baillies' country home at Hampstead; Charlotte was gaily looking forward to exchanging the latest news with the Dumergues in their bustling house off Piccadilly. Scott himself had many plans. He had arranged to meet George Ellis and Heber again, been bidden by the Prince Regent, who had expressed pleasure at the author's gift of a copy of *The Lord of the Isles*, to one of his levees, and invited by John Murray to meet Lord Byron at his home in Albemarle Street.

The Prince Regent's *levee* was followed by a "snug little dinner at Carlton House", in Scott's honour, at which the Prince, always at his best on unofficial, friendly occasions, enjoyed himself by drawing out his guest, matching Scott's pawky legal stories with his own, addressing him as "Walter" throughout, and calling for a toast to "the Author of *Waverley*", which Scott gently parried, then unblinkingly drank with the rest.

The meeting with Byron was very different. Scott was hospitably welcomed by Mr Murray himself at the door of his house in Albemarle Street before he had had time to surrender his hat to the footman, and escorted upstairs to the beautiful drawing-room on the first floor. Byron was standing by the window, absorbed in his examination of a fine folio on which Mr Murray had requested his opinion. As he laid it down and came forward, Scott was aware that the irregular rhythm of Byron's footfalls on the polished floor most strangely matched his own, and all the innate warmth and candour of his nature was set free from the formality of the occasion to thaw the younger man's defiant resentment of an imperfection which had shadowed his life.

They spoke, inevitably, of each other's work. Byron knew very well that Scott, as a poet, had suffered by comparison with himself, and had refused to play the part of his successor. "If they want to depose Scott," he had said indignantly, "I only wish they would not set me up as a competitor. I like the man and admire his works ..."

Their mutual awareness of each other's vulnerability sparked off an attraction between natures so different that each offered the other a glimpse of an utterly unfamiliar aspect of life which both intrigued and mystified him. Scott, who had expected to find Byron, according to report, both strange and violent, was disarmed by his courtesy, and found his lost-soul beauty something to dream of. Byron, too, habitually revolted by the insincerity and self-seeking of his world, relaxed in spite of himself as he responded to a simpler set of values, listened to a countryman talking with enthusiasm of dogs and horses, coursing and duck-shooting, his plans for plantations and pasture land and cottages for his work people, with the zest of a modern patriarch. In his turn, he talked, brilliantly, bitterly, of experiences from which he had worked out a basic philosophy with which Scott often found himself in agreement.

When they parted, they agreed to meet again. Mr Murray gladly offered his house as a debating ground for two distinguished authors who had surprisingly taken such a liking for each other. They saw each other almost daily during Scott's visit to London, either at Albemarle Street or at the fashionable entertainments to which both were invited. Often they laughed together; sometimes, when the conversation turned on politics or religion, they differed. Occasionally Scott listened quietly while one of Byron's dark moods worked itself out, never exacerbating the crisis by argument, but awaiting the opportunity to divert the troubled current of his thoughts with a sly shaft of humour, in response to which Byron's mood would often change as dramatically as a thunder-shrouded landscape when the clouds roll away from the sun. Their parting gifts were typical: Scott gave Byron a splendidly gold-mounted dagger, once the property of an Eastern potentate, and Byron sent Scott a silver sepulchral urn containing bones which had been found in ancient tombs within the walls of Athens. At their last meeting they laughed together over their public's probable reaction to such sombre gifts.

"My friend, they will say that you wish to further some dreadful act of vengeance on my part, against I know not whom," said Byron, as he unsheathed the beautiful deadly weapon, watching the sunlight gleam on the blade's gold inlay as he turned it about with his long, slim fingers.

"And no doubt they will say also that your lordship is entrusting me with a receptacle within which the evidence of such a crime will lie forever concealed," Scott agreed cheerfully.

They parted with reluctance, exchanging promises to meet again whenever Scott was in London. But as they limped down the stairs of 50 Albemarle Street together, for the last time, Scott was troubled by an intuition of approaching crisis in the younger man's life which had underlain even Byron's most apparently untroubled laughter, and the memory persisted as he collected his family for their return to Scotland.

Napoleon's dramatic return to power, and the final campaign waged by Wellington and Blücher that summer, roused Scott's most passionate interest, and only his dogged sense of duty kept him from tearing off his gown and taking coach for the nearest sea port when the news of Waterloo reached Edinburgh. Charlotte hoped he would presently cool down, so she was appalled when Scott limped into her Castle Street drawing-room, waving a letter from Brussels which he had been given to read by a fellow advocate.

"This letter has set me on fire," he declared. "I must go to Brussels immediately the Courts rise – "

"Dearest Scott, why?" wailed Charlotte. "It will be all horror – "

"He writes of heroism," said Scott, limping urgently to and fro, "beyond comparison. Listen to this. He describes a Brunswicker of the Black Hussars: 'he was wounded and had had his arm amputated on the field. He was among the first that came in. He rode straight and stark upon his horse – the bloody clouts about his stump – pale as death, but upright, with a stern, fixed expression of feature, as if loth to lose his revenge.' "

Charlotte took her head in her hands and wept. "Oh, Scott, dear Scott – I beg you do not go," she faltered between sobs. "Who knows, such terrible men . . . they may seek their revenge . . . on . . . on those who had no part . . . on you, I mean . . ."

Scott at once stopped pacing about, came and sat down beside her, taking her hands from her tear-streaked face and kissing it.

"My dearest love, I shall not be in the slightest danger." He sighed. "The fighting is all over now, and I shall take two or three stout young fellows from the Border, who would give their ears for such a trip, as I well know. And I will write you such splendid letters as you ever had in your life – "

Charlotte dabbed at her eyes. "Often you will write?" she said unsteadily.

"Daily, my dearest," Scott promised. "But listen, we shall play a little game. I have a plan to make a book out of this journey. It shall be a book of letters, which will really be all for you. And they shall come to you at Abbotsford.

"I shall call it – let me think – *Paul's Letters to his Kinsfolk*, and though all the letters will be for you, my love, they will be addressed to a little make-believe company. I will give them different names which you will understand – it will be a little plot between us."

"Who, then, shall they be?" Charlotte began to be interested.

"First of all, Paul will write to a veteran officer, retired on half-pay – "

"Your brother, John," cried Charlotte triumphantly.

"Right again. Then some letters will be for a statistical laird – it does not matter much who that is – and others to a rural minister of the Presbyterian Kirk – "

Charlotte looked blank. "I know not much of Presbyterian ministers."

"The worthy Dr Douglas of Galashiels, who once owned

Abbotsford, will serve as a model," Scott decided. "And you shall be my commander-in-chief. Read all the letters to the children, not forgetting to invite Tom Purdie, Peter Mathieson and the rest to listen, as they arrive at Abbotsford. Then send them, if you will, to my mother in George Street. When she has read them to those concerned, request her to give them to Will Erskine, who will see James Ballantyne has them to print."

"So, we shall all be most busy indeed," said Charlotte, laughing at last.

"There's my dearest girl," said Scott with candid relief.

And so, in due course, Scott and three younger enthusiasts left Edinburgh by the stage-coach for the south at five o'clock on the 27th of July, while Peter Mathieson drove Charlotte and the children rather forlornly to Abbotsford, where Tom Purdie's welcome, the sight of their ponies, saddled and waiting, the hysterical delight of all the dogs, the sight of the haymakers busy on the broad meadow, and the siren song of the Tweed beyond, almost consoled them for the unusual absence of Papa.

Charlotte sighed, shrugged, then summoned up her light-hearted philosophy. "We, too, shall have our little enterprises, Miss Millar. We shall order the carriage tomorrow to drive us to Melrose. New chintzes we shall have for ze parlour. Curtains, chair-covers, all, as a surprise for Mr Scott on his return – "

The vacation passed uneventfully. Charlotte and Miss Millar enjoyed themselves among pins and paper patterns, piping cord and yards and yards of the most expensive floral chintz obtainable. Sophia, who would much rather have been out-of-doors, sewed diligently at a cushion because it was part of the exciting surprise for Papa, and dark-eyed, volatile Anne submitted to the drudgery of sewing on tapes because the enterprise gave such pleasure to Mamma. But the boys went duck-shooting with Tom Purdie on Cauldshiels Loch because men were not expected to concern themselves with such things.

In the evenings, whenever a bulky packet arrived from the Continent, the whole family assembled in the parlour, listening intently while Charlotte read Paul's latest letter, though occasionally

Walter, who at fourteen fancied he had the makings of a cavalry officer, ventured to correct him on military details.

Scott kept Charlotte meticulously posted on his movements, so that the date of his return, in the third week of September, was known far enough in advance for the final touches to be put to the furnishings of the parlour. James Ballantyne, anxious to check the details of some of *Paul's Letters*, duly delivered to him by Will Erskine, added himself to the reception committee, and James Skene, formerly of the Edinburgh Light Dragoons, established himself in the bachelors' quarters over the stable yard in time for the great occasion. Sophia and Walter drove to Kelso with Peter Mathieson to meet the stage-coach, and burst into the parlour while Scott was still disentangling himself from his luggage.

"Papa's here," cried Sophia. "And – "

"And he's brought all manner of things," shouted Walter. "French armour . . . swords . . . helmets . . ."

"He met the Czar of Russia – "

"And the Duke of Wellington – "

"And Blücher – " began Sophia. Then, as Scott appeared in the doorway, clankingly followed by Peter Mathieson, bearing the spoils of war, she was swept aside by the younger children, who rushed to their father, while Scott, smiling, held out his arms. "Mamma! My little ones! Ah, how splendid it is to see Abbotsford unshattered! Skene . . . James . . . I have seen so much desolation that I cannot forget. The battlefield is burned into my mind . . ."

He took Charlotte in his arms, allowed her to lead him to the waiting arm-chair, subsided gratefully on to the floral chintz, and took out a handkerchief. "My word, the heat of the journey was truly formidable, as they say on the far side of the Channel. Skene, you should have seen the Cossacks, as I did, cantering up the Rue de la Paix – ! Believe me, their commander reined his horse back on its hind legs at the sight of me, threw his reins to an orderly and ran to kiss me on both cheeks, fairly babbling of *Marmion* and *The Lay*. I was never so astonished in my life as when he begged me to join his staff at his next review, mounted on one of the fabled horses from the Ukraine!"

"But, of course, Papa," said young Walter stoutly. "Did you go?"

"I did, indeed, my lad. It was perhaps the second greatest occasion of my life."

"What was the greatest, Papa?" Sophia asked quickly.

"The day I met the Duke of Wellington," Scott said. "Ah, Skene, he is the greatest soldier of the world. In his presence I was abashed, as I have been before no other man."

"What had he to say of the battle?" James Skene demanded urgently.

Scott chuckled.

"He said it was the nearest run thing you ever saw in your life."

"Was the issue in doubt, then?"

"Aye, to the very end. If our fellows had broken under the last charge of the Imperial Guard, the story must have had a very different ending. But Wellington said he had never seen British infantry behave so well. When they flung back those fine fellows that Adam Ferguson saw pelted by the Paris mob for their loyalty, all was over, and Boney left the field even faster than Johnny Cope."

"If he had but died with the Guards – " said Skene sadly.

"He would have been among the immortals," Scott agreed.

But Charlotte could bear no more. "My dearest Scott," she exclaimed, "here, too, in Scotland, we have done our best, though not on ze field of battle, to welcome the conqueror home. Alas, he has noticed nothing!"

Scott looked anxiously round him.

"But you are sitting on it!" Charlotte cried. "And by ze windows, hangs our work!"

"Dearest Mamma," said Scott in consternation, "how could I have been so blind? It is all new! Chair covers, curtains – "

"Miss Millar, the girls and I," said Charlotte, "have made all new to welcome you!"

"My darlings!" Scott stood up to take in the splendour of his surroundings. "All is new! Curtains, chairs, cushions and – "

"I made the cushions, Papa!"

"I sewed the tapes on!"

"But we, Papa," said Charles promptly, "shot the wild duck which we shall eat for supper."

"Well done, lads," said Scott, who was now pacing about the room, blinking at the brilliance of cushions, chairs and curtains. And Walter shot his quicker-witted younger brother an appreciative glance.

"I cannot imagine, Mamma, how I could ever have missed such a transformation as you have produced," said Scott, tucking his arm through Charlotte's as he stooped to admire the elegantly flounced covering for a window-seat. "What else should I have seen?" he cautiously inquired.

"We planned, Papa," said Anne mischievously, "also to re-decorate your study – But – "

Scott stood appalled, picturing a reorganisation which would prevent him from ever finding anything again.

"But there was not time," said Anne, with her mother's little giggle.

"My dearest Scott, you know very well that we would never dare," Charlotte reassured him. "But tell me, did you see Lord Byron again?"

Scott nodded thoughtfully. "Yes, he dined with us at our hotel as we passed through London. He was in one of his gayest moods; almost fey, I thought. He had only mockery for my tales of the battlefield. Yet there was something wild and lost about him too. I hope we may meet again."

"Papa," said Sophia, who could never bear to see her father downcast, "you have not seen the ponies, and the children have been grooming them all the afternoon."

Scott was at once on his feet. "My love, I have been so dazzled with the beauty indoors that I can scarcely bear to leave it. But we must make a round of the stables at once. Is everything laid out, rugs, saddles, bridles, brush, comb and hoof pick as good troopers' kit should be, for the general's inspection?"

"Oh, yes, Papa."

"Be off, then. Stand by your horses. The inspecting general and his staff will follow immediately."

As the young people stampeded from the room, Scott turned to offer his arm to Charlotte, smiling blissfully. "How good, how very good it is to be back. Before the light fades, we must all walk down to the river."

The publication of *Paul's Letters to his Kinsfolk* had been arranged by John Ballantyne before Scott's departure. Constable, Longmans and Murray each accepted a third share of the first edition, and Scott now settled easily back into his usual routine, revising the proof sheets of the *Letters* with which James Ballantyne had greeted him, catching up with his correspondence, writing a poem on *The Field of Waterloo*, as he had done after the Peninsular War, to be sold for the benefit of the relief fund for the widows and children of the fallen. A new novel, *The Antiquary*, was also beginning to take shape in his mind, and the negotiations for the purchase of Kaeside were nearly completed. But the year ended sadly for Scott, with the news of the death of Mrs Morritt of Rokeby.

Paul's Letters were received, early in January, 1816, with interest and some speculation that their author might be the mysterious novelist whose popularity was growing with every book he produced. In the face of all inquiries, however, Scott maintained a bland and courteous blankness and changed the conversation.

Many dogs had come and gone in his household since the death of Camp, but none had ever been such a personal friend until, that April, Macdonell of Glengarry, who had been enthusiastic over *The Lord of the Isles*, presented him with a magnificent male staghound, named Maida, who made it clear from the first that he considered himself to be Scott's particular bodyguard. Scott was delighted with him, "the noblest dog ever seen on the Border since Johnnie Armstrong's time," he wrote to Daniel Terry in London. "He is between the wolf and the deer greyhound, about six feet long from the tip of the nose to the tail, and high and strong in proportion. He is quite gentle, and a great favourite: tell Will Erskine he will eat off his plate without being at the trouble to put a paw on the table or chair . . ."

The Antiquary got away to a somewhat shaky start at the beginning of May. As Scott himself wrote candidly to Morritt: "It is not so interesting as its predecessors – the period did not admit of so much romantic situation. But it has been more fortunate than any of them in the sale for 6000 went off in the first six days, and it is now at press again; which is very flattering to the unknown author."

And Morritt, who had been in the secret from the start, chuckled, as Scott had hoped he would.

It was a comfortless time of inappropriate cold, with the snow lying deep on the Pentlands and the Border hills, killing off the lambs and even the ewes, when Scott was summoned from Abbotsford by an express messenger with the news that his brother John's lingering illness had taken a graver turn and he was not expected to live more than a few hours. Peter Mathieson drove him through the night to Edinburgh, but he only arrived in time to undertake the desolate duties following his death, which included a letter to inform his brother Tom, in Canada, that they were now the sole survivors of Mrs Scott's large family.

Scott had broken new ground, in an unobtrusive way, with *The Antiquary*. Both his earlier novels had been carefully prefaced by quotations which set the tone of each chapter. But while correcting the new proofs, Scott rebelled against the additional drudgery of checking so many quotations. It was, after all, quicker to invent a few lines, in emergency, label them "Old Play" or "Old Ballad" than to spend hours checking up the source of a few appropriate lines, a sentiment with which John Ballantyne, who was habitually involved in such research, most heartily concurred.

For John, who was supposed to be winding up the affairs of his unfortunate publishing business, was anxious, just then, to find any excuse for not doing so. His brother James, newly married early in the year, was less attentive to business than usual. So, by making himself useful to Scott, John could hope to delay the moment when he must revert to being only the clerk of the surviving printing company, with no authority to draw money to bridge the gap between his earnings as an auctioneer and his expenses as a man about town. It was not in his scatterbrain nature to work out any such scheme in cold blood; but he acted instinctively, playing on Scott's optimistic estimate of his own health and capacity, guessing at his love of the Border country, which drove him to snatch eagerly at any chance of gathering more and more of it into the keeping of Abbotsford.

So, when Constable not only declined to take any more moribund stock from the Ballantyne publishing company, but also began to be reluctant to accept Scott's condition of having the printing of his novels done by James Ballantyne's firm, John encouraged Scott to offer the new series, to be called *Tales of my Landlord*, elsewhere. Mr Murray, of Albemarle Street, who had already shared in earlier publications, was the obvious choice, though Scott, with his sharp sense of honour, refused to allow the key-phrase "by the author of *Waverley*" to appear on the title page of the first Tales, those of *The Black Dwarf* and *Old Mortality*.

Mr Murray and his agent in Edinburgh, Mr Blackwood, were depressed by this refusal, but delighted to publish the Tales. They also agreed to take over a further block of moribund stock. Scott was greatly relieved, since it was obvious that the sooner he could get his feet free from his unfortunate attempt to rival Constable as a publisher the better. He urged John to further his efforts.

"Dear John," he wrote that August,

"I have the pleasure to enclose Murray's acceptances. I earnestly recommend you to push, realising as much as you can.

> " '*Consider weel, gude man,*
>   *We hae but borrowed gear;*
>   *The horse that I ride on,*
>   *It is John Murray's mear.*'

Yours truly,
W. Scott."

But the new enterprise was nearly wrecked, not by John Ballantyne, but by William Blackwood, who was then still an obscure antiquarian bookseller in the Old Town, though his ideas for the magazine which was to make his family name famous were already taking shape in his mind. Mr Blackwood read *The Black Dwarf*, which his principal in London had accepted, with increasing indignation. To his mind, it began well enough, but its conclusion was lame and inadequate. He was not, even then, a man to mince his words, even to "the Author of *Waverley*". He wrote to James Ballantyne, the representative of the author who preferred to remain anonymous, not only with his adverse opinion of the story's conclusion, but an alternative ending for the author's use.

The criticism alone might have been accepted. In theory, at least, Scott maintained that any informed comments on an author's work should be received with respect and attention. But the alternative ending which Blackwood had rashly written pricked sharply at the guileless vanity which success is apt to engender in most authors, however conscientiously they may seek to discount it. And Scott had recently been very successful indeed. His usually reliable sense of humour forsook him, and he blew up like an overcharged cannon. James Ballantyne received the full blast of his wrath.

"Dear James," he wrote,

"I have received Blackwood's impudent proposal. God damn his soul! Tell him and his coadjutor that I belong to the Black Hussars of Literature, who neither give nor receive criticism. I'll be cursed but this is the most impudent proposal that ever was made.

W.S."

James Ballantyne huffed and puffed over the furiously scrawled note in the greatest consternation. To transmit the message as it stood would be to risk a rupture of negotiations which they could ill afford. To suppress it might well produce a further explosion. In effect, the greatly watered down version he finally dispatched produced a surprisingly meek reply. And when he had cooled down sufficiently, Scott wrote a new ending to *The Black Dwarf* on the lines which Blackwood had ventured to indicate.

Meanwhile, he had been distracted from his work with Tom Purdie in the young plantations at Abbotsford, and his wish to discuss further building plans with the young architect, Blore, whom Terry had introduced, by a two-month visitation from the Dumergue sisters, who had shown the Scotts so much hospitality in London that both Scott and Charlotte were determined to make their first visit to Scotland a success. So it was, but not in the way they had hoped, since the rain never ceased from one end of it to the other, ruining the carefully planned tour to the Trossachs, and keeping them indoors at Abbotsford. Charlotte, who loved chatter, came off best, but every now and then, Scott, utterly exhausted by it, sneaked off to his study on pretence of work, where, one desolate morning, he took the chance of writing to Morritt at Rokeby.

"As to the important business with the which I have been occupied, I would have you to know we have had our kind hostesses of Piccadilly upon a two-months' visit to us. We owed them so much hospitality that we were particularly anxious to make Scotland agreeable to the good girls. But, alas! the wind has blown, and the rain has fallen, in a style which beats all that ever I remembered. . . . I have the gratification to think that I fully supported the hospitality of my country. I walked them to death. I talked them to death. I showed them landscapes which the driving rain hardly permitted them to see, and told them of feuds about which they cared as little as I do about their next-door mews in Piccadilly. Yes, I even played at cards, and as I had Charlotte for a partner, so ran no risk of being scolded, I got on pretty well. Still, the weather was so execrable that, as the old drunken landlord used to say at Arroquhar, 'I was perfectly ashamed of it;' and to this moment, I wonder how my two friends fought it out as patiently as they did. But the young people and the cottages formed considerable resources . . ."

The young Scotts were, in fact, growing up fast. Sophia, at seventeen, had always been closest to her father. Her sturdy, courageous nature had the candour and affection of his own, though he realised, with a mixture of relief and regret, that she had no literary gift whatever. Anne had always been her mother's girl, gay and mischievous, with the beginnings of her pleasure in style and social success. Walter, nearly as tall as his father now, delighted him by his love of good horsemanship and country sports. He had

Chapter 16

TIME telescoped for Scott as he groped his way back to consciousness through the weird images of drug-induced sleep. The doctors had bled and blistered him, poulticed his stomach with hot salt, and finally given him laudanum to ease the agonising pain of the jagged crystal of bile salts jammed in the bile duct as it forced its way towards liberation into the gut. As his eyelids flickered, his mother leant forward to mop the sweat from his grey face which days of agony had lined like that of an old man. Her soft, lavender-scented handkerchief rasped on the stubble of his unshaven chin.

"Well, Wattie, my lamb, what about a wee sip of barley-water?"

He ran his tongue along dry, cracked lips. His mouth was foul with the metallic taste of laudanum. The last wisps of illusion lingered as he opened his eyes, a boy of fifteen again, in his child-hood home in George's Square. Obediently he sipped, thanked her with the ghost of a smile. Then a crease of perplexity brought his heavy eyebrows together. His mother's hair was white, her homely, smiling face criss-crossed with the wrinkles of more than eighty years. Then he . . .

As memory flooded back, the panic caught him again. He fought it like a mortal enemy, while strange faces appeared at his bedside; bleeding, blistering, poulticing his stomach again till he roared aloud. Dr Daniel was only a shadowy figure in the background now that he had retired from practice, anxiously watching the younger men who seemed to have so little new to suggest, in spite of their airs of importance. Outside the door the great grey stag-hound lay watchful, making no attempt to hinder those who came to help his master, whimpering softly at every muffled groan.

Charlotte had been thankful when Miss Millar suggested that the children might occupy themselves in the parlour by writing a story for Papa. She settled them round the big table with paper and

pencils, while Charlotte occupied herself with her embroidery by
the fire, her spaniel, Finette, by her feet. Even she, who had once
set store by sitting in her drawing-room, even on weekdays, did not
wish to be alone there just then. At the table, Anne wrote diligently,
determined to do better than Charles, who kept leaning across to
compare progress. Walter wrote slowly, with laborious effort. But
Sophia suddenly dropped her pencil, buried her head on her crossed
arms, and wept.

Down in the tavern where the Teviot Club met, James Ballantyne
was surrounded on his arrival by members anxious for news of
Walter Scott. He stood in the doorway, a tubby, pompous figure,
puffing out his lips in an expression of the direst concern.

"Well, lads, I'm never the man that likes to be the bearer of ill
tidings, but I doot he's gotten his death-blow, ye ken. When I last
had a sight of him . . ."

They listened in solemn, respectful silence. But from the ingle-
neuk a wild, shock-headed figure which no one had noticed rose up
in wrath, crossed the room in three raking strides, and shook a fist
in his face.

"Say that again, Jamie Ballantyne, and I'll fell ye to the ground,"
roared the Ettrick Shepherd.

"Dear knows I hope I'm wrong," said James.

"Bah Goad, ye'd better be," said the Ettrick Shepherd fiercely.

Scott did not die. But it was a long time before life seemed worth
living again. He was dizzy from loss of blood: his ears dirled and his
eyes dazzled. The doctors told him that he had been suffering from
cramps in the stomach, which was at least part of the truth, and
assured him that it was not a killing complaint. Scott submitted
meekly to their ministrations and the dreary diet which cut out all
the food and drink he most enjoyed, but sometimes doubted
whether a man could survive many more prolonged bouts of
agony. And the laudanum which dulled them blurred his senses just
when he was most desperately anxious to get back to work, for even
the lethargy that plagued him could not check his eager plans for
Abbotsford's growing estate. He intended to offer Willie Laidlaw,
who had struck hard times, the tenancy of his recent purchase,

Kaeside, and the position of factor. But that was only the beginning of the master-scheme at the back of his mind. Once the negotiations for the adjacent estate called Toftfield were complete he would own the whole course of the burn beside which Thomas the Rhymer was alleged to have met the Queen of Elfland. The pleasant farmhouse, too, would be the very place for Adam Ferguson, who had dreamt, in the lines of Torres Vedras, of "a snug little farm, either up or down the Tweed, somewhere in your neighbourhood". And so the new, magnificent Abbotsford which his architect, Bullock Atkinson, was planning, should become the centre of a company of friends, with the estate craftsmen and labourers settled in their own new cottages in the hamlet of Abbotstown.

He had always been a feudalist who believed that his responsibilities towards those who worked for him equalled his privilege in having the work to give. The youngest herd laddie was as free to shoot and fish within his master's boundaries as Scott himself. The warmth of his affection, casual and undemonstrative though it was, could not be mistaken by anyone, from Tom Purdie, who had been his daylong companion in the young plantations from the beginning, to the newest apprentice carpenter or mason from Galashiels now at work on the new Abbotsford. Their answering love, the excitement with which his young family greeted every stage in the fulfilment of Papa's promise to build them "the loveliest home in the world", Charlotte's pride in her rising status, were his reward. But it was all costing money, much more money than he could have believed possible. For the lesser local lairds, always chronically in need of money themselves, had come to know that a word to Tom Purdie, when they met him, as if by chance, at sheep sale or market, might well bring the Shirra along to view any land which marched with Abbotsford that they had to sell. And the Shirra was less likely to argue about the price than most.

For the price had not mattered while he had his wits and his health and his supreme confidence that the unknown author of *Waverley* would continue to produce all the money that Walter Scott could possibly need. But during that dour spring his health had been so sorely shaken that only his indomitable will drove him on. Before the middle of March, he had heaved himself to his feet from the armchair in his bedroom into which he had sagged, exhausted, after the effort of dressing himself. Charlotte, who delighted to minister to minor ailments, had been frankly terrified by the recent ordeal, and begged him to be content, on the first day, with the brief progress to the drawing-room. Scott smiled at her.

"Havers! It's time I was back at my work. Call Walter, my love. I doubt I'll need a hand with the stairs."

Charlotte clasped her hands distractedly. "Oh, Scott, I beg you not to venture. Let me send for the doctor. It will be too much. I know it . . ."

"What is the matter, Mamma?" said Sophia from the doorway, breathless after running upstairs at the sound of her father's voice.

"Your Papa, he insist that he go downstairs to his study. He must work, he says. And he is scarcely out of death's door!"

"But, Mamma, if we keep him from working, he will fret," said Sophia earnestly. "And that will be much worse. The fire has been kindled in the study every morning . . ."

"To keep the books warm, I suppose," said Charlotte hysterically.

"Quite right, my dear," said Scott approvingly. "Now, if Walter can be found, I think I shall survive the journey. Believe me, dearest," he told Charlotte gently, "no medicine will do me more good than the sight of my study again."

So, with Sophia on one hand and tall young Walter on the other, Scott negotiated the stairs to the ground floor, with Maida at his heels, dignity so far relaxed as to beat the wall and the iron balustrade with his violently oscillating tail.

Once established, Scott looked about him with a smile of triumph. "There, my dears, you can forget me for an hour or two. I shall not overdo it. But there are letters I must write, papers I must consult."

"You are sure you have not overtired yourself, Papa?" Sophia asked anxiously.

"Quite sure, my love. Walter, if you would hand me over the file of notes for my next book, I should be obliged."

"Shall I stay with you, Papa?" Walter asked.

"No, son. I think better alone."

"I shall come back in an hour," said Sophia firmly. "And there is a bell on your desk if you want us to help you upstairs before that."

Very slowly, Scott's strength returned. His first gesture was to write to his friends who had been appalled by rumours of his critical illness. He admitted to Daniel Terry, in London, that he was "still weak as water from the operations of the medical faculty . . . After all, I believe it was touch and go; and considering how much I have to do for my own family and others, my elegy might have been that of the Auld Man's Mare:

> " *'The peats and turf are all to lead,*
> *What ailed the beast to die?'* "

To Morritt of Rokeby he admitted that he had had "a slight shake" in consequence of "a most violent attack, which broke up a small party at my house, and sent me to bed roaring like a bull calf".

By April he was writing to Willie Laidlaw about his proposal for Kaeside, which Willie accepted with delight, and during the month Peter Mathieson drove him with his family to Abbotsford, where the whole tribe of assorted terriers received him with delight, and the household, who had all run out to greet him, stood stricken as Walter and Peter Mathieson helped him from the carriage. For jaundice had muddied his usually clear complexion, bleeding and fasting had left him gaunt as a spectre, and he stooped over his stick like an old man.

But Tom Purdie, more distressed than anybody, gave the least sign of it. He strode sturdily forward, with his usual grin. "Welcome hame, Shirra. The caller air o' the Border will soon pit ye to rights."

Weary to death as he was, Scott's head jerked up, and he took an uncertain pace forward. "Aye, Tom, that it will, never fear."

"I'll saddle up Sybil Grey first thing the morn, Shirra, and we'll make a round o' the plantations. Ye're needing your dinner now, after yon long journey, though."

Scott smiled wryly. "My dinner's a poor thing these days, Tom. A piece of toast and a glass of water's all the doctors allow me."

"Hout, we'll soon have ye back to your usual, Shirra," said Tom

Purdie. "Rest your hand on my shoulder, now, and I'll settle ye by the fire. It's no summer yet, ye ken."

Scott moved like a man in a dream towards the entrance porch of the little farmhouse which he and Tom Purdie had visited that summer morning, only six years ago. Beside it now towered the new Abbotsford, spider-webbed with scaffolding, on which the contractor was discussing a problem with his foreman, Adam Paterson. In the background his masons were busy, the sound of their chisels clear as music in the clear air. Scott paused. "I'll have to take a look at the work."

"Aye, Shirra, so ye shall," said Tom Purdie. "But ye'll be the better o' bite and sup first."

"Ye're mebbe right, Tom," Scott agreed.

He dozed in his chair by the parlour fire while the family milled about him, with Maida at his feet, warning off the importunities of the lesser dogs with a slight curl of his upper lip, while Sophia stood, silent and watchful, behind him.

Scott suddenly chuckled. "If ye think I'm to be put off with a slice of toast when I can smell roast chicken, my love, ye're sorely mistaken."

For the old magic of the Border had begun to work again. And after a better night's sleep than he had had for many weeks, Scott woke determined on adventure. On that exquisite, rain-washed April morning the hills had the opalescent beauty only to be seen at that time of year, when the smoke from the last of the moor-burning still hazed the far distance, and the curlew's call came dirling down from the heights.

Tom Purdie brought round the stout, cobby mare, Sybil Grey, whose name came from *Marmion*. She had recently replaced Scott's splendid white charger, Daisy, who had always stood rock-still for him to mount till the day after his return from Waterloo. Then Daisy had reared up and thrown him, shuddering and wild-eyed, sensing perhaps the scenes of carnage which obsessed his mind. But kind Sybil Grey stood gently by the mounting block while Sophia and Tom Purdie helped Scott to crawl on to her back and sway there, fumbling for the reins.

Scott sagged forward, gripping the pommel of the saddle. His bony shanks flapped loosely as he tried to urge the pony forward. Wryly he glanced at his supporters. "I doubt I've lost the power of locomotion, this time."

"Never fear, Shirra," said Tom Purdie, urging Sybil Grey unobtrusively forward. "Ye were aye the man to set a stout hairt to a stey brae. We'll just daunder on and take a look at yon young larches."

Sophia stood and watched them go, instinctively aware that her father would be better in the company of men like Tom Purdie or Willie Laidlaw, now coming down the path to meet them, grinning with delight at the sight of his benefactor on horseback again.

"Eh, Willie, I'm pleased to see ye. Are ye settling in at Kaeside?"

"We are indeed. My wife and bairns are fair delighted."

"I'd like fine to ride by and bid them welcome . . ."

"What for no'?" said Willie Laidlaw cheerfully as he turned to walk on the other side of Sybil Grey.

Sophia returned to a frenzied scolding from her mother. "Your Papa, where has he gone?"

"To Kaeside, with Tom Purdie and Mr Laidlaw, I believe, Mamma."

Charlotte shrieked, covering her face with her hands. "So far? You let him go? You foolish, wicked girl. He was but to take a turn up and down before the house. He will kill himself. I shall send for the doctor to forbid it."

"Please, Mamma, do not. He is so happy."

"I wish we had never left Edinburgh," said Charlotte petulantly. "I am not needed here. Already Walter is off with his gun and his dog, Anne and Charles are saddling their ponies, and Miss Millar has a headache. So she must lie down. Nothing is there for me to do."

"Well, Mamma," said Sophia helpfully, "shall I tell Peter Mathieson to bring round the carriage? He might drive us to Melrose to look at the shops. I'm sure there are some things you need."

"Yes indeed." Charlotte's expression brightened. "Many things. During your Papa's illness I have bought nothing, but nothing for myself. Peter Mathieson shall bring round the carriage at once."

Scott returned from the morning's ride weary but triumphant, and slept soundly in his armchair all the afternoon. Next morning, he set off again with Tom Purdie, and this time he made Tom lead Sybil Grey round the new walls of Abbotsford so that he could have a word with Adam Paterson and his men. Little by little, his strength returned. He rode all over the estate, always escorted by Tom Purdie and the dogs, often accompanied by Willie Laidlaw, who greeted every suggestion of further adventure with the challenging question: "what for no'?"

Within a few weeks he was able to limp about Abbotsford almost as vigorously as ever. But the elasticity of youth had gone, and his hair was almost white, though he would not be forty-six till August. The attacks of pain recurred, from time to time, but less severely, and as the clouds lifted, he could see his promised land again. He tried his hand at a play, which he hoped Terry might be able to use, which was eventually called *The Doom of Devorgoil*. It was not good, but it got him into working trim again. And during May he had an idea for another novel, "by the author of *Waverley*." He invited Constable to drive down to Abbotsford to discuss it, and commanded lively John Ballantyne, in the capacity of negotiator, to attend him.

Archibald Constable was quite a commanding figure now, with his country house at Polton, his sedate dark green barouche drawn by two black horses, and a respectable coachman in dark blue livery on the box. Johnny Ballantyne, who preferred to drive his gaudy gig himself, made disrespectful fun of the somewhat pompous publisher in private, but was most artlessly respectful, even clownish as required, when in attendance at Abbotsford. Scott's appearance might still shock those who, like Constable, had not seen him since his illness, but he felt almost like himself again as he limped sturdily round the new building and explained his plans for a library, a drawing-room for Charlotte, and, above all, the armoury on which he had set his heart.

The new novel, he explained, dealt with the wild leader of the proscribed clan, MacGregor, with fastnesses in the remote glens and a refuge on the shores of Loch Lomond. But his story brought in all sorts of characters from the other side of the Highland Line. "There's a Glasgow weaver, now, that I'll ravel up with Rob," he said, smiling, as the outline of Bailie Nicol Jarvie came into his mind. "Young lovers, of course . . ." His eyes grew remote as he glimpsed in Diana Vernon the shadow of his unforgotten first love.

Constable was delighted. The new novel promised to have all the vigour of its predecessors, and after some demur Scott had allowed him to choose the title of *Rob Roy*. As to the terms, he left Johnny Ballantyne to discuss those with the publisher, as they journeyed comfortably back to Edinburgh in Constable's well-slung barouche.

The little auctioneer was on very sound ground, and well aware of it. If Constable did not see his way to accepting the new novel, as he gently pointed out, no doubt Messrs Murray and Blackwood would be happy to take it, as they had already taken the first series of *Tales of My Landlord*. But this Constable did not intend to allow, for he had not only regretted his failure to publish the *Tales*, but also been exceedingly annoyed by Blackwood's temerity in starting a rival magazine to his own cherished *Edinburgh Review*. "Ma Maaga", as Blackwood called it, in his deliberately uncouth way, was an impish, witty Tory periodical, which, in Constable's opinion, outraged every decent principle of literary journalism.

Rather than see the latest work by "the Author of *Waverley*" go to a firm which had any association with Blackwood, he was willing to agree to terms which in any other circumstances he would have indignantly repudiated. He offered an immediate advance of £1,700, and also took over a substantial quantity of the dead stock of the Ballantyne publishing concern. John Ballantyne was elated by his success as a negotiator, as well he might be, since Scott had always stipulated that he should have a third share in the bookseller's profits, while James must do the printing. So Constable could only sigh, and take the precaution of heavily insuring his author's life, which, considering the recent state of Scott's health, was not unreasonable.

Summer came late that year, and by the beginning of June, when

James Hogg was installed as tenant of Altrive, one of the farms on the Buccleuch estate, there was scarcely an ash tree in leaf, and since the Ettrick Shepherd had been as unlucky as ever in his transactions with livestock, his friends organised a subscription edition of *The Queen's Wake* at a guinea a copy to raise funds to stock it. The Duke's patronage, warmly endorsed by Scott, was a gesture to the memory of his lovely young Duchess, who had done so much for the improvident poet.

Scott was not only back at the Clerks' Table again, in spite of deathly weariness, and recurring attacks of pain, but also busy with several literary jobs. He had undertaken to write the History of 1815 for that limping periodical, *The Edinburgh Annual Register*, and the Introduction to a splendid quarto edition of *Border Antiquities*, in addition to Constable's new purchase, *Rob Roy*. But there were gaps in his knowledge of the book's background which fretted him, and so, when the Courts rose in July, he arranged a short trip to the west of Scotland with Adam Ferguson in order to check up on his facts. They visited Rob Roy's alleged retreat, a cave at the head of Loch Lomond, went on to Glasgow to study the cathedral, and were guided by a local bookseller about the city in search of a suitable birthplace for that sturdy weaver, Bailie Nicol Jarvie. When Scott's researches were complete, they drove on to Drumlanrig to stay with their brother officer, the Duke of Buccleuch. To Scott, who had seen much of him during his recent sorrowful years, the Duke seemed fairly well, as they laughed together over the old days in the Edinburgh Light Dragoons. But the change in him shocked the light-hearted Adam Ferguson.

Back at Abbotsford, *Rob Roy* began to move at last, though the usual impetuous flow of composition was periodically impeded by recurrent bouts of sickness and pain, and much of Scott's strength was needed to fight off the deadly lassitude which at times took all the colour out of life. One day James Ballantyne, coming to consult him on a batch of proof sheets, found him sitting at his desk with a blank page under his hand.

Scott smiled wryly at his obvious concern. "Aye, aye, Jemmy," he said, " 'tis easy for you to bid me get on, but how the deuce can

I make Rob Roy's wife speak with such a curmurring in my guts."

But there were better days, when the book went bravely and the new Abbotsford grew under the hands of the masons. Its walls were now higher than those of the little old farmhouse beside it, which Scott wished to keep as long as possible and only demolish when the new building was ready for use. His new study, of course, must look out on the Tweed, but he insisted that he must also have a window overlooking the yard so that when he wanted Tom Purdie, he had only to throw it up and shout. Beyond the study was the dining-room, splendidly spacious, with a wide bay window looking out across the meadow to the river. Behind the dining-room was the conservatory, and beyond both rooms the new armoury, extending from front to back of the house to give him a setting for his growing collection of historical relics which had been so long ignobly stacked in the good Doctor's unsightly barn. Overhead would be bedrooms for the family. And a beautiful drawing-room for Charlotte, a spacious library, and a really secluded study, to be reached by a private staircase from his bedroom above, were already planned, but could not be completed till the original farm-house had been pulled down.

Meanwhile, visitors came and went in shoals. Some, such as Washington Irving, over from America, the tragic, forsaken Lady Byron, the artist, David Wilkie, were most welcome. Others, who came uninvited to stare at the author of *The Lay* and *Marmion*, who was also suspected of being that "Great Unknown", the author of *Waverley*, took up a great deal too much time, and the most persistent had to be dismissed with Scott's occasional courteous firmness.

In spite of them all, Scott wrote on. And every now and then, when the pain from yet another impacted gallstone had eased, and the cloud of deadly nausea and lethargy lifted from his spirit, he assured everybody that he would soon have seen the last of his tiresome complaint.

With the end of *Rob Roy* in sight, Scott was already considering his next book. Well or ill, he must work on while his fabulous storytelling gift served him. For only the first stage in the building of Abbotsford had been completed. To the east of the new building which now ended with the armoury, the original farmhouse still stood, dwarfed and incongruous, its undistinguished outline blurred by trellises of honeysuckle and rambler roses. But the architects had doomed it. Only after its demolition could Abbotsford be worthily completed. Charlotte, poring eagerly over the new plans at a family conclave, warmly approved.

"Ah, my drawing-room! At last I shall have room for all my pretty zings! But I shall furnish it as I please, yes?"

"Of course, Mamma."

"All zis talk of oak panelling and carved bosses and stained glass and dead men's armour, it gives me ze creeps. I do not wish to live in ze Middle Ages, where tyrants were boiled in oil and heretics burnt at ze stake. My drawing-room, it shall be beautiful and new."

"Dearest Mamma," said Walter, putting an arm round her shoulders, "how truly right you are!"

"Of course Mamma is right," said Scott cheerfully. "She shall have the brightest and most beautiful furnishings that money can buy. And she need never see my jingling jackets, and auld nick-nackets in the armoury – "

"Except only when I pass through it to enter ze dining-room," Charlotte pointed out, looking down at the plan, "which I hope will be at least three times a day."

Everybody laughed. But Charlotte went on quickly: "Scott, that poky little study of yours, it will make a nice breakfast-room, when you have your fine new library and study beyond. That, too, I shall furnish as I please, yes?"

"Yes, indeed, my love," said Scott, rather sadly. He wished, as Washington Irving had done, that they could have kept the old farmhouse and its simplicities. But like Thomas the Rhymer, who had kissed the Queen of Elfland, he must now go where his fate led.

By November he had instructed Johnny Ballantyne to approach Constable again, with the offer of a second series of *Tales of my Landlord*, again featuring the whimsical Jedediah Cleishbotham, which he hoped to have ready for publication by the middle of

1818. Now that he was committed to the completion of Abbotsford, Scott knew that he would have to write hard to meet the final expenses, and he was anxious first to pay off his liability of £4,000 to the Duke of Buccleuch, which was his only outstanding debt.

John Ballantyne was delighted by the opportunity of twisting the Crafty's tail once more. The circumstances could scarcely have been more favourable. All he need do was to remind Constable that the first *Tales of my Landlord* had been brought out by Murray and Blackwood, but that Mr Scott was considering the possibility of offering him a half-share in the publication of the second, to make Constable ready to offer almost anything on earth for the chance of sole publication.

John Ballantyne, who had already been grievously humiliated by the "Lord High Constable", as Blackwood's young men called him, might perhaps be forgiven for enjoying himself as he gently tormented Constable with the possibility that the second series of *Tales of my Landlord* were more likely to be brought out, like the first, by Murray and Blackwood, unless, of course . . . He hesitated, as if he hardly cared to suggest the concession which might swing the decision the other way. Constable pressed him. Johnny still appeared to hesitate. Then, with the greatest apparent reluctance, he admitted that if Mr Constable could see his way to taking over all the remaining dead stock from the Ballantyne premises in Hanover Street, they might be able to come to terms.

Constable agreed. With the Duke's repayment in mind, Scott had stipulated that £5,000 should be made immediately available to him. So, since the dead stock in the basement of the Hanover Street premises amounted to no less than another £5,270, the agreement for the sale of 10,000 copies of the as yet unwritten novel, which was signed by the end of November, 1817, imposed a very heavy burden on his publisher.

But Scott had the greatest confidence in his ability to honour his bond. *Rob Roy* had scarcely been delivered before he was at work on its successor. *The Heart of Midlothian* was the story of Jeanie Deans, who walked from Edinburgh to London to obtain a reprieve for her sister, who was under sentence of death. It was to be one of the best loved of all the novels. And on the 7th of January, 1818, Scott had the pleasure of writing to the Duke of Buccleuch, who had proved himself so good a friend:

"My dear Lord Duke,
  "I have the great pleasure of enclosing the discharged bond which your Grace stood engaged in for me, and on my account. The accommodation was of the greatest consequence to me, as it enabled me to retain possession of some valuable literary property, which I must otherwise have suffered to be sold at a time when the book-sellers had no money to buy it . . ."

The other great event of the year was the search for the Scottish Regalia. Scott had contrived to interest the Prince Regent in its fate during his last visit to London. For rumour had long alleged that it had been secretly sent to London after the unpopular Union of the Parliaments in 1707. If this were true, then the great chest in the Crown Room of Edinburgh Castle must have been rifled of the Royal Crown, Sword of State and Sceptre of the Scottish Kings. A Commission, headed at Scott's insistence, by the Duke of Buccleuch, was now appointed to settle all doubts forever by opening the Chest on the 4th of February.

  But the Duke's health did not permit him to come to Edinburgh on the great occasion, and so, in the presence of the Provost of Edinburgh, the chief legal, military and financial representatives of Scotland, Scott watched the workmen advance across the dust of over a hundred years and break open the locks. Six inches of dust slid back as the lid creaked open. Those present scarcely breathed. Within lay the Honours of Scotland, in their careful wrappings, and with them, as they were unveiled, the centuries of which he had written came so vividly to life that the impact was almost more than he could bear.

  Sophia alone understood. On the following day, Scott took her to the Castle, with some of the other Commissioners who wished to show the Regalia to the ladies of their household. Someone, less aware of the historic significance of the occasion than the rest, lifted the crown and moved to place it on the head of one of the ladies present.

"By God, *no*!" Scott roared.

The company stood appalled. The insensitive Commissioner hastily restored the crown to its place, muttering an apology.

"Pray forgive me," Scott said, looking round for his daughter. He found Sophia, deathly white, leaning against the wall.

"Come home, my dear," he said gently.

So they set off together, in silence, walking down the Mound, along Princes Street, and up Castle Street, arm-in-arm, more keenly aware of the closeness of the understanding between them than they had ever been before.

Part Four

THE TREE FALLS

Chapter 17

Scott spent every spare minute on *The Heart of Midlothian* that spring. Both he and Constable had been well pleased by the reception of *Rob Roy*, which had appeared on the 31st of December. The first edition of 10,000 copies had been sold in a fortnight, and a second impression immediately printed. Constable strutted and complimented himself. Now that he had even given the author his title he might almost have written the book himself. But Scott was already absorbed in the heroic drama of Douce Davie Deans and his daughters, crazy Madge Wildfire, the Laird of Dumbiedikes and all the rest, set in the shadow of the ancient Tolbooth of Edinburgh, sardonically nicknamed the Heart of Midlothian. It was as well that the story ran straight and true, for he had promised it should be ready for publication by midsummer.

Yet somehow or other he found time to throw off a variety of articles. One on military bridges appeared in the *Quarterly Review*, another on Mrs Shelley's *Frankenstein* for Blackwood's celebrated Magazine. And since his writing and its purpose were now so closely entwined, he wrote many letters to Willie Laidlaw at Kaeside; about the new workers' hamlet of Abbotstown, the sawmill at Toftfield, the planting of more trees and hedgerows. And his letters to Daniel Terry were full of enthusiasm for the house itself.

"I am now anxious to complete Abbotsford . . . I am quite feverish about the armoury. I have two pretty complete suits of armour, one Indian one, and a cuirassier's, with boots, casque, etc; many helmets, corslets, and steel caps, swords and poniards without end, and about a dozen of guns, ancient and modern. I have besides two or three battle-axes and maces, pikes and targets, a Highlander's accoutrement complete, great branches of horns, pikes, bows and arrows, and the clubs and creases of Indian tribes. Mr Bullock promised to give some hint about the fashion of disposing all these matters; and now our spring is approaching, and I want but my plans to get on . . ."

During the spring vacation he and Tom Purdie were out and about again, discussing the merits of birch hedges, intermixed with holly and thorn, and the number of Italian poplars needed for the boggier areas. *The Heart of Midlothian* was approaching completion when the family returned to Edinburgh for the summer session in May.

It was the great occasion of the year for the Scottish Kirk, when the General Assembly brought ministers to the capital from all over the country for earnest discussion and seemly entertainment. Scott's early rising prevented him from attending many of the later evening entertainments, but he occasionally dined out with old friends, and one evening he returned from a dinner with a legal colleague much interested in the ability of a young Oxford graduate, recently called to the Scottish Bar, whom he had met there for the first time.

"I believe, Mamma," he said at breakfast next morning, "that I have found someone to help me with the historical work for the *Annual Register*. I formed a very favourable opinion of him, and it would be appropriate if we were to show him some kindness."

"It will be easy for me to show kindness to anybody, but anybody, who will stop you working so hard, my dear Papa," said Charlotte, with a gesture of whimsical despair. "Shall I arrange a dinner-party?"

"No, no, nothing of that sort. Nothing formal. Let him join us one Sunday evening, when all the young people, and one or two of our best friends besides, are with us." Scott looked happily round the table at his family, catching sight first of Sophia, who preferred informality and looked so pleased that he continued with satisfaction, "I shall ask him to join us next Sunday evening. Will Erskine will come as usual, but I doubt if his wife will be well enough. Will Clerk, the wily old bachelor, has not far to come. James Skene will bring his wife – "

"Stop, Papa!" Charlotte commanded. "There will be room for no more round ze dinner-table – "

"True, true," Scott agreed with a smile. "I had forgotten we were not already in the new dining-room at Abbotsford. But one more, in addition to the usual company, should make very little difference, after all. He is slim as a willow."

"Papa," said Anne eagerly, "we do not yet know the name of the young man who will make so little difference."

"His name? Why, bless my heart, I cannot recall it. Ah, yes, it is Lockhart. John Gibson Lockhart, he told me. His father is a minister in Glasgow, I believe, up for the Assembly."

John Lockhart was considerably intrigued by the invitation. He had been back in Edinburgh long enough to have heard on all sides of his illustrious host's countrywide reputation as a poet and conversationalist. He knew that everybody in the literary world guessed him to be the author of *Waverley* and the succeeding novels which had achieved such fabulous success. And he had been immediately attracted by the warmth and humour of the man himself.

So he came to 39 Castle Street with the most lively curiosity, and was astonished by the simplicity of the entertainment. Before the evening meal, Scott took him into his study, to show him the back numbers of the *Edinburgh Annual Register*, and Lockhart stood looking round him with all his intellectual scepticism unexpectedly disarmed by the homeliness of the great man's background. Books were everywhere, which was only to be expected. But on the top step of the step-ladder which gave access to the upper shelves, a large tiger-striped cat lay purring.

"Hinse of Hinsefeldt," Scott explained. "As I grow older, I admit the cat to my circle of friends, to which only dogs and horses were formerly eligible. Maida, for instance, is a member of the ancient nobility."

Lockhart permitted himself to be inspected by the great grey staghound, who had heaved himself up from the rug before the fire.

"You are accepted," said Scott with a smile, as Maida superbly wagged his tail and turned to thump down again on the hearthrug.

"Now you must face the lesser ordeal of confronting my family and friends."

Lockhart spoke little at the dinner table. He was a young man of dark, almost Byronic beauty, just twenty-four, who gave an impression of intellectual disdain which was chilling except to those who knew that he was slightly deaf. On Sunday evenings, in Edinburgh at that time, the music which usually followed dinner was considered inappropriate.

Instead, the older people talked, and the young ones listened, and then, after tea had been served, Scott, urged by Will Erskine, read, in his deep, soft voice, from the poems of Crabbe, whom he revered, but had never met, following these with a couple of Wordsworth's sonnets and part of Byron's latest poem, of which the author had sent him a copy.

Lockhart found the gentle, friendly scene enchanting, and was surprised at himself for doing so. As an extremely intellectual young man, with a merciless wit and a keen edge even to the practical jokes with which he occasionally confounded those who took themselves too seriously, he was accustomed to analyse himself as well as his victims without pity. But he was uneasily aware of a quality in Scott against which he could put up no ironic defence.

Scott's silver hair and massive shoulders, the resolution of the mobile mouth with its long upper lip, the absent-minded little gesture with which he pushed his reading glasses back into position when they tended to wander down his nose, were matched by an indefinable youthfulness of expression which defied the deeply-etched lines of pain and stress, and there was something heroic about the angle of the jaw. Lockhart, not habitually fanciful, found himself imagining that massive head surrounded by a casque of steel.

Mrs Scott, chatting gaily to Mrs Skene in her broken English, was an unexpected wife for such a man. Did she realise in the least, he wondered, the extent of his astonishing celebrity, or did the suggestion of petulance about her mouth, the occasional sharpness in her voice, indicate resentment of the innumerable claims it made upon his time?

The young people were not yet clearly defined in his estimation, though he smiled at the cheerful arrogance with which young Walter spoke of his practice drills with the local Yeomanry, which Lockhart himself had joined in response to the threat of Radical unrest, as if he were already an officer of the 18th Hussars. Charles was a bright lad, though handicapped, perhaps, by the slight deafness which he, as a fellow sufferer, immediately recognised. What did they mean to make of him, he wondered? His eyes had lit up at the talk of Oxford. With good coaching, perhaps. . . .

How different the two girls were, Lockhart thought: both pretty as flowers in their high-waisted, bell-skirted white muslin gowns, their ringlets bobbing up and down as they argued gaily with their brothers. One – was it Anne – came to sit at her mother's feet at last. It must have been Sophia who eagerly fetched the books Scott wanted from his study.

Lockhart was in and out of 39 Castle Street a good deal that summer, now that he had undertaken to work for Scott on the *Annual Register*. He also came to know more of the Ballantyne brothers, and attended the splendid dinner at which the publication, at midsummer, of *The Heart of Midlothian* was celebrated at James Ballantyne's house in St John Street, off the Holyrood end of the Canongate.

James was fond of his food – too fond, and Scott often teased him about it – so the dinners he gave were solid and gorgeous, by comparison with John's Frenchified, more fanciful banquets at the villa near Newhaven which he called Harmony Hall. In John Street, the company bidden to celebrate the publication of yet another novel by The Great Unknown began dinner with turtle soup, proceeded to a baron of beef or a haunch of venison, with a brandy-soused plum pudding made by their kindly, sensible hostess, with iced punch, ale and Madeira. Scott, Lockhart realised, enjoyed himself enormously, though he had, of course, officially no connection with the great occasion. After the cloth was drawn, and the loyal toast drunk, however, James Ballantyne rose to toast his patron, as the climax of the evening approached.

"Gentlemen," he declaimed, "there is another toast which never has been nor shall ever be omitted in this house of mine – I give you the health of Mr Walter Scott with three times three!"

The company roared, Scott's health was drunk, and he returned thanks with sincere pleasure. Then the applause died away, and the company sat silent as James Ballantyne rose again. This time, his voice was conspiratorially hushed, the hand with which he held his glass high seemed to tremble with emotion, as he said:

"Gentlemen, a bumper to the Immortal Author of *Waverley*!"

The cheering, the pounding of feet, the wild handclapping, made the glasses dirl on the table. Scott himself, smiling blandly, with the slightest wink in the direction of Will Erskine, clapped gently, looked down his nose like a small boy who knows where the sweets are hidden, and drank the toast with the rest. Lockhart, who was supposed to be as ignorant as everybody else, enjoyed the joke almost as much as Scott.

The Heart of Midlothian had a greater success than any of the earlier novels, and before Scott left Edinburgh for Abbotsford as usual on the 12th of July, he had the satisfaction of instructing John Ballantyne to offer its successor to Constable on the same terms, the first edition to consist of 10,000 copies. But this time there was no need to tie the purchase of dead stock to the agreement, like a tin can to a dog's tail. The new novel which Scott was planning was very different from the heroic story of Jeanie Deans, for his sure instinct warned him to change the theme of his novels often enough to prevent his public from complaining that he could harp only on one string. *The Bride of Lammermoor*, which he was now planning, was the only unrelieved tragedy he had ever thought of writing, but for a variety of reasons he did not begin it at once.

The arrival at Abbotsford, as always, was a moment of sheer delight. But Scott's pleasure in greeting Adam Ferguson, who had come over from Toftfield (now renamed Huntly Burn), Willie Laidlaw, and Tom Purdie, even the excitement with which he saw how high his new walls had risen in his absence, were eclipsed by the news which Adam Ferguson had to give.

For the Duke of Buccleuch's health was failing fast. What had seemed only a temporary indisposition in February, when he was unable to come to Edinburgh for the discovery of the Regalia, was evidently something much more serious. He was sad and sick and disinclined to live.

"Tomorrow I will ride over to see his Grace," Scott said. "It may be that the sight of a devoted old friend will cheer him. If not, we must think of something else. Travel, perhaps ... It may occupy his mind, if it does not lighten his heart. Come with me, Adam. You have the sprightlier wit."

Certainly, Adam Ferguson seemed to be one of the few people who could rouse the Duke from the profound melancholy which was one of the most distressing features of his condition, and Scott, who had spent so many happy days at Bowhill before the Duchess's tragically early death, scarcely wondered at it. "Yet he has done so much for his people, in spite of his sorrow," Scott said as they rode home again, "and the family is so greatly loved. If we could but kindle a spark – "

"He spoke with real interest of Wellington's campaign in the Peninsula," Adam Ferguson said thoughtfully.

"Aye, Adam, and those are scenes you know well. I wonder now – we must not thrust the idea at him – but if he were willing to go to Spain or Portugal, would you go with him?"

"Most gladly," Adam Ferguson said.

Scott let the matter rest for a while. But he did not forget it in the constant hubbub of the summer vacation at Abbotsford. The mystery which still surrounded the authorship of the Waverley novels inevitably brought more people to see for themselves the man now widely considered the greatest storyteller of the age, and Scott, skilled as he had now become at making his escape from uninvited adulation, was often caught off-guard, when returning from work on his plantations with Tom Purdie, or discussing details of the new building with masons or carpenters. So was Charlotte, and one morning Scott found her in a state of high indignation, having only just contrived to get rid of a couple of transatlantic visitors, eager young men dressed from head to foot in what they believed to be tartan, who had cornered her in her own rose-garden.

"It is not to be borne!" she declared, sweeping into the little parlour of the old farmhouse, now deeply shadowed by the rising walls of the new building. "I shall return to Edinburgh."

"My dearest girl, what did the foolish young men do?"

"Zey persecuted me!" said Charlotte dramatically. "Did zey not?" she demanded, turning to Sophia and Anne, who now appeared, helpless with giggles, in the doorway.

"Yes, indeed, Mamma."

Scott looked very grave, pulled forward a chair, and prepared, in his capacity of Sheriff, to hear the evidence.

"Pray tell me exactly, my love, what they did to offend you."

Charlotte touched her eyes with a lace handkerchief. "Zey – zey – pull out ze little notebooks, and zey ask zis and zat. I move on. Zey follow. Believe me, Scott, zey will not be content till I tell zem, not only your age, but mine!"

Incautiously, Scott burst into a roar of laughter.

"It is not so funny!" Charlotte said. "I am no longer prepared to answer such a question. I tell zem to go, or I will tell ze police!"

"Quite right, my love," Scott agreed. "And did they go?"

"Zey went," said Charlotte.

"Fortunately," said Scott, "they could not know how long it would have taken to bring the honest fellows out from Melrose. But now, my dear, I have a little bit of news which I have been saving up to tell you – "

"Good news?" said Charlotte. "I can bear no more calamities."

"That is a matter of opinion. Where are the boys?"

"Out on the hills, I believe, Papa," Sophia said.

"Walter," said Anne naughtily, "is no doubt instructing Charles on the correct manner to behave as an aide-de-camp to the officer commanding the 18th Hussars."

Scott chuckled. "Then they will have to hear the news later. It concerns Mamma most closely, after all."

Charlotte put away her handkerchief and sat up.

"I have been privately informed, my dears, that his Royal Highness the Prince Regent wishes to confer the honour of a baronetcy upon me."

Charlotte gave a little shriek. "I shall be Lady Scott – "

"Of Abbotsford, my love," Scott agreed, smiling. "Shall you like that?"

"I shall like it extremely," Charlotte said, with the little giggle which Scott realised with compunction that he had not heard so often lately.

"What shall we be, Papa?" Anne demanded.

"Just your own sweet selves, my loves, if I accept the honour."

"There can be no doubt in your mind, Papa, surely?" Charlotte's voice was incredulous.

Scott sighed. "A little. 'I like not such grinning honours as Sir Walter hath'," he quoted wryly. "And yet, my forbears have borne the title honourably enough. I must see what Walter thinks."

"Walter?" said Charlotte in surprise.

"He will be the second baronet one day."

"Oh, *Walter*!" said the girls, in identical tones of disdain.

"I must take time to think," Scott said. But he smiled reassuringly at his wife.

Among the many visitors to Abbotsford that September was Robert Cadell, deputed by Constable to discuss with Scott his firm's desire to purchase the copyright of a number of his earlier works. He was greatly interested to see Scott's country home, but observed the innumerable calls on his time with considerable concern. On the morning after his arrival, Scott denied himself the pleasure of working with Tom Purdie among his young trees and took his visitor for a tour of the estate instead, eagerly pointing out all the improvements which he was making on the formerly bare hillside.

Cadell, who was not a countryman, surveyed the new plantations, the extensive draining operations, the sheep and well-grown lambs, with some bewilderment. "I cannot understand, Mr Scott, how you ever find time to write any books in the country."

"Why not?" Scott said in surprise.

"Oh, I know," said Cadell, "that you contrive to get a few hours' work in your study early in the day. That may serve for the mere pen-work. But, tell me, when do you think?"

Scott strode on in silence for a minute or two, swinging his stick. He himself was not fully aware of the mysterious workings of his subconscious mind. The unceasing current of his imagination was like a river running strongly underground, unencumbered by all the superficial debris of daily life. When he sat down at his desk he became aware of it, as if the river had emerged to foam for a time through a resounding gorge or sweep idyllically between green pastures. Then, as he stopped listening, and laid his pen down, it disappeared again, but as his life resumed its easier jog, the echo of its tumultuous progress never entirely left him. He was laird, lawyer, courteous host, husband and father, as occasion required, and yet, far below the surface of his conscious mind, the unresting current swept on. How could he explain something he so imperfectly understood to Cadell?

"Oh, well," he said at last, "I lie simmering over things for an hour or so before I get up – and there's the time I am dressing to overhaul my half-sleeping, half-waking *projet de chapitre* – and when I get the paper before me it commonly runs off pretty easily."

"I see," said Cadell uncertainly.

"Besides, I often take a doze in the plantations, while Tom marks out a dyke or a drain as I've directed. Then one's fancy may be running its ain riggs in another world."

"And to very good purpose, it seems," Cadell agreed, obligingly.

It was on the 8th of October that Lockhart first saw Abbotsford. He arrived with an Oxford friend to find Scott about to set out for a stroll through the plantations with two former companions of his wild High School days, Lord Melville, the dignified First Lord of the Admiralty, who was now so different from the sturdy little boy who had been Scott's sworn ally in the madcap bickers in George's Square, and long, lean, witty Adam Ferguson, who had basically changed so little.

That evening there was a dinner party at Abbotsford, to which a number of the local lairds and their ladies were invited. It was a greater occasion than young Lockhart realised, as he made conversation to Sophia, whom he had taken in to dinner, and watched the proceedings with a less critical eye than usual.

"You must not suppose, Mr Lockhart," said Sophia earnestly, "that this is just an ordinary occasion."

"Why not, Miss Sophia?"

"Well, you see, this is the first time, I suppose, that Papa has had Lord Melville and Captain Ferguson to dine with him since they were naughty little boys together. It has made Papa very happy."

"Yes, I see it has," said Lockhart gently. He was unexpectedly touched to see the delight with which the girl beside him watched her father, laughing at stories which could have had little meaning for her, of the bickers between rival gangs of Edinburgh schoolboys, who must now be middle-aged men like themselves. Scott was gay as a lad again, and even Lord Melville's dignity relaxed as Adam Ferguson leant across the table, glass in hand.

"Remember the day we manned the Potterrow Port – "

"And held it against all the auld loons of the City Guard?"

"Remember the raid on the Cross Causeway?"

"And the ambush we led them into at George's Square?"

"Remember Greenbreeks?"

"Aye, Greenbreeks!" The distinguished, middle-aged men raised their glasses. "Here's to him."

"Where will he be now, I wonder?" Sophia whispered to Lockhart, between tears and laughter.

Her vivid, adoring face, as she shared her father's happiness with his boyhood friends, was the keenest memory that Lockhart took away from his first visit to Abbotsford.

"You must come again," Scott said, as the young man thanked his host and hostess. "Try to come down for the Abbotsford Hunt. We always arrange it for the end of the month, since the 28th of October is young Walter's birthday. Oh, it's a great occasion, a ramshackle affair that all the local farmers enjoy. They bring every sort of mongrel to make up the pack, and we have a supper afterwards from which few men go home sober."

"Yes, do try and come, Mr Lockhart," said tall young Walter, shaking hands with an air of magnificence which would have been intolerable if it had not also been so young. Behind Walter's back, however, Lockhart could see that Sophia and Anne were making faces at each other. "By this time next year, I hope to be serving with my regiment, the 18th Hussars, you know."

"So I had heard," Lockhart said gravely, trying not to catch Sophia's eye.

The expenses of equipping young Walter as a cavalry officer were going to be considerable, and there would be, too, the expenses of Scott's own baronetcy. So it was fortunate, perhaps, that Constable was anxious to buy the copyrights of a large number of the early works, including *Waverley* and the succeeding novels, and such remaining shares of the copyrights in his poems as Scott still retained.

But Scott was more gravely concerned, that autumn, with the further deterioration in the health of the Duke of Buccleuch, and on his return to Edinburgh in November wrote to the Duke's brother, Lord Montagu, at Windsor, "with feelings of the deepest anxiety . . ." Having sounded his urgent warning, and suggested that the Duke might perhaps now consider the change of climate which had at first been so unwelcome, Scott went on writing his usual affectionate, newsy letters to the Duke throughout the winter, saving up every anecdote or oddity which might be likely to amuse him, giving no hint of his own fears. But he was increasingly troubled for his friend of the gay young days with the Edinburgh Light Dragoons. December was a sad month at Castle Street, with news of the death of Charlotte's brother Charles, her only remaining relation, far away in India. They had not met since her marriage, her husband and children had been her life for over twenty years, but at his death she wept not only for the loss of a devoted brother, but also for herself, and for the far off days when growing old, and losing her looks and health and gaiety, could never really happen to her.

On New Year's Day it was the custom for the whole family at 39 Castle Street to troop round to Mrs Scott's George Street flat, to exchange the season's gifts. The old lady, alert and kindly as ever in her eighties, made her preparations for the ceremony weeks ahead, and the little pile of carefully chosen presents, personally wrapped and labelled, awaited their arrival on one table, with a tray of glasses, a decanter of Madeira, and a plate of shortbread biscuits on another.

It had always been a unique occasion, as far back as her grandchildren could remember, for their grandmother had not only the knack of choosing things which they really wanted, but the gracious art of receiving their own anxiously chosen tokens with real joy. On the 1st of January, 1819, everything began as usual, with "Happy New Years", excited hugs from Charles and the girls, and more decorous kisses from young Walter and his parents. But after all the lesser presents had been opened in a great crackling of paper and fumbling with knots of string, and a hubbub of eager thanks, Mrs Scott rose and crossed the room to a table on which her special treasures lay.

"Wattie, my lamb," she said, turning gravely to her son with her warm and candid smile, "you'll have noticed that there was nothing on yon table for you."

"Well, Mother . . ." Scott admitted. "I thought, maybe . . ."

"Well, I've got something special for you this year." She lifted two folio volumes. "It's your grandfather's Bible. I want you to have it now."

"Oh, Mother, no. I cannot take it. It is too precious to you . . ."

"That's why I want you to have it," said Mrs Scott calmly. "My dear lad, you're a great man now, and soon to be greater. I give you this, my most precious possession, to be your strength against all the troubles and temptations of greatness. And may it give you as much comfort as it has given me."

Scott bent down and kissed her. Then he took the books from her hands. On the flyleaf of the first volume he read the inscription in her still firm, spidery handwriting:

> *To my dear son, Walter Scott,*
> *from his affectionate mother, Anne Rutherford,*
> *1st January, 1819*

"I shall treasure this gift, Mother, to the end of my life," Scott said softly.

"I know you will, my lamb," said Mrs Scott. "And now, will you fill our glasses? We must drink to the New Year."

Scott began *The Bride of Lammermoor* cheered by the news that the Duke of Buccleuch had agreed to the suggested change of climate and was soon to leave Scotland for Portugal. Adam Ferguson was to go with him as confidential secretary, and they would stay in Lisbon, where the Duke of Wellington had offered his own house.

So the year promised well, with negotiations for the sale of copyrights complete, and the prospect of going to London in April to receive the insignia of his baronetcy from the Prince Regent. The Duke of Buccleuch wrote from Portsmouth, in much better spirits, reminding Scott of his promise to sit to Raeburn for his portrait.

"My prodigious undertaking of a west wing at Bowhill is begun," the Duke wrote. "A library of forty-one feet by twenty-one is to be added to the present drawing-room. A space for one picture is reserved over the fireplace, and in this warm situation I intend to place the Guardian of Literature. I should be happy to have my friend Maida appear. It is now almost proverbial, 'Walter Scott and his Dog'."

But in March Scott's agonising spasms began again. The doctors blistered and bled, according to tradition, but without relevance to his complaint. Hot baths alone brought any real relief, but after eight or ten hours of agony, only opiates such as laudanum could dull it, and Scott fought fiercely against any treatment which could only ease him by depriving him of his wits. All thought of going to London was obviously out of the question, but in the intervals of his attacks he worked doggedly on, wrote cheerfully to the Duke in Lisbon, and more candidly to Adam Ferguson, from Abbotsford in April.

"I think you would hardly know me. When I crawl out on Sybil Grey, I am the very image of Death on the pale horse, lanthorn-jawed, decayed in flesh, stooping as if meant to eat the pony's ears, and unable to go above a footpace. But though I have had, and must expect, frequent relapses, yet the attacks are more slight, and

I trust I shall mend with the good weather. Spring sets in very pleasantly . . ."

And the progress of Abbotsford still enthralled him. "I have got a beautiful scarlet paper inlaid with gold (rather crimson than scarlet)," he wrote to Daniel Terry, "in a present from India . . . James Ballantyne got me one very handsome bright steel cuirassier of Queen Elizabeth's time, and two less perfect for £20 – dog cheap; they make a great figure in the armoury . . . Sophia has been chiefly my nurse, as an indisposition of little Charles called Charlotte to town . . ."

Scott's recent attacks had left him so weak that he was glad to accept John Ballantyne's offer to take down *The Bride of Lammermoor* from his dictation. And when John returned to Edinburgh with the copy, Willie Laidlaw offered to take over, for Scott admitted that he would be thankful to be spared the fatigue of writing for a while. John Ballantyne, trained as a clerk, established himself at the table with a dozen quills cut ready, and a stack of paper to his hand, writing diligently while Scott lay on his sofa, writhing as the pain caught him. John Ballantyne had worked like an automaton. But Willie Laidlaw, enthralled by the story, could not help breaking in with muttered exclamations at the most dramatic points.

" '*Lucy Ashton loves you, Master of Ravenswood*,' " groaned Scott.

" '*It is impossible*,' said the Master."

"Gude keep us a'. Eh, sirs, eh sirs," murmured Willie Laidlaw.

Sometimes the dictation went well, for Willie's enthusiasm was heartwarming to a sick man. But sometimes, when the pain made him groan aloud, Willie could not endure it.

"Mr Scott, will ye not give over?"

"Nay, Willie," Scott said as soon as he could speak, "I will not. Only see that the doors are fast, for I would fain keep all the cry as well as all the wool to ourselves. But as for giving over work, that can only be when I am laid in woollen."

John Ballantyne had warned Lockhart to expect a sad change in Scott. But even so when he rode down to Abbotsford towards the end of the spring vacation, Lockhart was appalled. Scott was emaciated, yellow with jaundice, his hair almost white, and at dinner he ate only a little rice pudding. But Lockhart was amazed by the warmth of his welcome, the brilliance of his eyes, and his determination to reassure his anxious family. He noticed, too, that Sophia's eyes seemed never to leave her father's face.

Such a stricken home seemed no place for a stranger. In the morning he must leave. But next day, Scott himself tapped on his bedroom door before seven o'clock. "Don't think of going," he said. "I feel hearty this morning, and if my devil does come back, it won't be for three days at least. I want nothing to set me up but a good trot in the open air. You have never seen Yarrow. . . ."

So they rode out together, Lockhart bemused and Scott at the top of his bent as he pointed out landmarks and described the campaigns of Montrose. Lockhart returned to Edinburgh next day with all his intellectual arrogance knocked endwise by one man's courage, and the devotion of a girl he scarcely knew.

On the 5th of May Scott received an expressed dispatch from Lord Melville, reporting the death of the Duke of Buccleuch, in Lisbon. It came scarcely as a surprise. As he wrote to Lord Montagu, later in the day: "On Wednesday, when I had occasion to go to Yarrow, and my horse turned from habit to go up the avenue to Bowhill, I felt deeply impressed that it was a road I should seldom travel – To me the world is a sort of waste without him . . ."

Scott returned with Sophia to Edinburgh later in the month for the summer session at the Law Courts, leaving Charlotte and the three younger children at Abbotsford, because Walter wanted company while he prepared to join his regiment in July. So Sophia was alone with her father in Castle Street when the worst attack of all hit him. The symptoms were familiar, and she knew what to do. One servant was sent running for the doctor, others set to preparing a scalding bath, and Peter Mathieson summoned from the mews to help her father into it. But her father was by now the most famous man in Edinburgh. And within hours word spread through the city's clubs that he was dying. Crowds gathered outside the house. These she accepted. They were silent and respectful. But Lord

Buchan, an eccentric and opinionated nobleman, whose vanity was legendary, presently appeared on the doorstep and intimidated the servant who admitted him, with a demand to be shown up to Mr Scott's bedroom immediately.

Here he was checked by Sophia. "My Lord, I appreciate your kindness in calling, but my father can see no one."

"My dear young lady," said the Earl in his high, cracked voice, "you are doing your duty, I am sure, but my purpose in coming here is to relieve your father's mind."

"I will give him your kind wishes, my lord," said Sophia, grasping the door-handle firmly, as the old man showed every sign of wishing to push past her. "But, I must repeat, my father is too ill to see anybody."

"But that is precisely why I am here, my dear child," said the Earl, in his penetrating voice. "I have come to assure him that he have no anxiety about the details of the interment. I know very well that he has the right to be buried in Dryburgh. I will give the matter my personal attention. And – "

Among the servants clustered in the hall below, Sophia was thankful to see the stalwart figure of Peter Mathieson, just back from feeding the horses in the mews.

"Peter!" she cried desperately, "his lordship is about to leave. Kindly escort him down the stairs."

Peter Mathieson was beside her in a moment. "Your lordship, let me gie ye a hand. Yon stairs is kittle to them as disna ken them, and the licht's bad."

"My good man, you are mistaken. I have no intention – " But Lord Buchan teetered unexpectedly under the apparently accidental impact of Peter Mathieson's muscular shoulder, and would have gone headlong had the coachman not caught him on the top step.

"Have a care now, my lord. I kent how it would be. I'll just see ye safe doon . . ."

The moment of danger had somewhat obscured Lord Buchan's purpose. He felt shaky enough to accept assistance, found himself on the doorstep without quite knowing how he got there, heard the door close decisively behind him, and the key turn in the lock.

Sophia tiptoed back into her father's room. How much had he heard? What could she say? But the latest dose of laudanum had at last taken effect, and he lay relaxed in a profound, exhausted sleep. The relief overwhelmed her. She had endured the crisis, comforted the terrified servants, received the instructions of the doctors, all alone. Now, quite suddenly, she could bear no more. She fled from her father's room and across the landing, to throw herself down on the chaise longue in her mother's drawing-room and break into a storm of tears. It was not till she became calmer that she realised she was not alone in the room. She sat up, drew the back of her hand across her eyes, and turned to see John Lockhart, blankly dismayed, standing on the hearthrug.

"Oh . . ." She flushed furiously. "Pray forgive me . . . I . . . I did not know . . ." She rose, and was halfway to the door before Lockhart overtook her.

"My dear Miss Sophia," Lockhart said, more warmly than she had ever heard him speak before, "surely you have nothing whatever to cry about. I heard it all, for the front door stood wide. And I was on my way to your assistance, when I realised you needed none. You routed the bombastic old nobleman like an indignant guardian angel."

"Mr Lockhart," said Sophia unsteadily, "it is not kind of you to laugh at me – "

"My dearest Miss Sophia," said Lockhart in sincere distress, "nothing was further from my mind. I spoke in admiration – "

To her surprise, Sophia found that he was holding both her hands. She tried, but only half-heartedly, to withdraw them, looked uncertainly into his face.

"Dear Miss Sophia," said Lockhart with most unusual gentleness, "I have never known a girl quite like you."

"Then I think you cannot have encountered many girls. I am a most ordinary person – "

"Oh, no, Miss Sophia. There never has been, and there never will be, anyone quite like you again. Pray believe me, Miss Sophia, when I say that I – "

"Mr Lockhart," said Sophia in consternation, "I cannot listen to you any longer. It is very wrong to talk so, without Papa's knowledge. You must go at once."

"I agree. But I will write," said Lockhart, stooping suddenly to kiss the hands he held. "My dearest Miss Sophia, I regard your father as the most remarkable man I have ever known."

"And so do I," said Sophia earnestly.

"I called only because of the dreadful rumours I had heard."

"He will not die," Sophia said defiantly.

The house seemed strangely empty after Lockhart had gone.

Sophia blew her nose, mopped the traces of tears from her cheeks and tiptoed into her father's room again. He lay on his back among his tumbled pillows, utterly relaxed in the blessed relief from gruelling pain, his breathing stertorous but steady, his arms flung wide. With a sigh of relief, Sophia went, rather unsteadily, downstairs to reassure the distracted servants.

Next day Scott seemed almost himself again, but he was still so weak that he submitted without complaint to the doctor's instructions to stay where he was. His friends were not slow in coming. Will Clerk walked round from Rose Street, Will Erskine hurried over from the Law Courts, the knocker on the front door was constantly in use as friends and neighbours called to inquire, and Sophia, having given orders that only close personal friends were to be allowed to see her father, went round to George Street to give her grandmother the better news. Mrs Scott surveyed her granddaughter's paper-white face and dark-ringed eyes with concern. "Hout, lassie, ye look as if ye never slept last night."

"I didn't," Sophia admitted.

"This'll never do," said Mrs Scott briskly. "I'll not have ye wearing yourself out. Where's Mamma?"

"At Abbotsford, Grandmamma, with the others."

"Aye, of course. I was forgetting. Now just bide a wee, while I get on my cloak and bonnet and we'll walk round to Castle Street together. I'd like a word with your Papa."

They found Scott in earnest conversation with James Skene, his latest visitor, who had caught his attention with a story of a certain moneylender in York, a Jew with a daughter whom even the Christian knights admired.

"I can make something of that, I believe," Scott was saying as they came in. "I'll set the tale at the time of the Crusades, work on the ill feeling between Saxon and Norman, give them good measure of combats on the lists . . . Ah, Mother, how good to see you. Are you pretty well?"

"Well enough," said Mrs Scott, taking the chair James Skene placed for her, and thanking him with a smile. "But I wish I saw both you and Sophia looking better."

"Sophia has been a heroine, and I am on the mend."

"No doubt, but you would both be the better of a few days in the country. Peter Mathieson shall drive you down to Abbotsford."

"Very well, Mother," said Scott, absent-mindedly. For the high, sweet call of trumpets was already in his ears, and the neighing of war-horses, the dull shock of lance on shield, the rending clash of swords, seemed nearly as loud as the voices of those around him. Once he could get to his armoury, refresh his memory of the medieval chronicles, the story of *Ivanhoe*, he knew, would leap into life.

But before they left Edinburgh Dr William Dick, formerly of the East India Company, and now resident in Perthshire, called at Castle Street, in response to a letter he had received from Scott. "I happened to be about to visit Edinburgh," the little sun-dried man explained, "so I thought I might well see for myself how things were with you. My dear sir, I believe calomel will serve your turn well."

"It has been tried, I believe," said Scott wearily.

"Ah," said Dr Dick, "but not in the quantity I shall prescribe. Believe me, I have had more opportunity to study all disorders to which the liver is liable during my service with the East India Company than almost any other man in my profession. You will find the remedy both drastic and unpleasant. But I assure you it will work."

"I will endure no matter what," Scott assured him, "for the sake of a cure."

"In that case . . ." Dr Dick produced a jotting-pad and pencil, scribbled briefly, and handed Scott the prescription. "I shall give myself the pleasure of writing to my colleague in Melrose to report this consultation and request news of your progress," he added warningly, as he bowed himself out.

The long-awaited departure of young Walter to join his regiment was due before the end of July, and Scott was determined to be on his feet again before then. Dr Dick's prescription worked like a charm, which was fortunate, since the household was in such a turmoil about Walter's uniform, trunks, letters of introduction, and future prospects that only the utmost determination kept Scott at work with Willie Laidlaw in his study, dictating *Ivanhoe* against a background of assorted noises and conflicting conversations. For the workmen had at last set about the demolition of the old farmhouse at last, and half the neighbourhood, it seemed, called to wish Walter Godspeed.

Walter sunned himself in the excitement, Charlotte alternated between laughter and tears. Charles followed his brother reverently about, and Scott, tremendously proud of his son, advised on a score of problems and did what work he could. Charlotte could scarcely bear to let Walter out of her sight, but the girls found his airs of a cavalry officer almost more than they could bear. "The only thing to be feared," said Sophia with unusual vehemence, "is his dying of pride and conceit before he joins."

For Lockhart's letter had arrived and distracted her with anxiety, correct and controlled though it was. For he admitted that the uncertainty of her feelings had made him unhappier than he had ever been in his life. She wanted, above all things, to show his letter to Papa. But while Papa was trying to write his new book in the midst of such a commotion, she felt unable to do anything which would distract him further. She was further disturbed when Lockhart himself came down to Abbotsford to consult her father on various points connected with his work for *The Annual Register*, and though she had only a few moments alone with him, the brief contact made her realise that this apparently self-sufficient young man was, incredibly, at her mercy. As soon as Walter and Lockhart had gone she took Lockhart's letter to her father.

Scott had always put his children before his books. So now he laid down his quill, listened to Sophia's incoherent statement of her problem, and drew her close while he read the letter she had tremulously given him.

"My dearest child," he said as he laid it down, "you must know that your happiness is my heart's desire. What do you feel for this young man?"

"I – I do not know, Papa."

"Then wait until you do. The only way in which I can help you is to say that I have the highest opinion of him. I could wish for no better son-in-law. You have said nothing to Mamma?"

"Not yet, Papa," said Sophia anxiously.

"Nor will I, then, till he comes, as he knows he must, to ask her approval. Meanwhile, my love, consult your own heart – "

Sophia went to her room and began her letter to Lockhart, with anxious formality.

"Dear Sir,

"Although I fear I am doing very very wrong in writing to you without Papa's knowledge, yet after what passed to-day I cannot be happy till I do it. Believe me, we do not know each other sufficiently to have any reasonable prospect of happiness. Though my name is Sophia Scott I am not in the least clever, and fear, greatly fear that you give me credit for talent and information beyond what I possess. When I told Papa of your letter to me at Abbotsford, it went no further than himself, no neither Mamma, brothers or sisters know anything of it. That Papa had no serious objections I firmly believe, but only thought (and you must say with reason) that we were about to take a step, one of the most important of our lives, without considering sufficiently whether our different tempers and dispositions could make us happy through life. And now, Mr Lockhart, for God's sake if you love me do not be so unhappy; it makes me quite wretched to think that you are so, and to feel that I, who would do anything for your peace of mind, am the cause. Do not answer this, as I know that any further correspondence of this kind, unknown to Papa, would be very wrong, and believe me to remain,

Yours very sincerely,
Sophia Scott."

The letter left Lockhart in no doubt of what he should do next. He paid a formal visit to Abbotsford, requesting the permission of Sophia's parents to present his addresses to their daughter. Scott, who had already come to regard Lockhart as a future member of the family, and had found his presence in some sort an antidote to Walter's departure, gave his warm approval. Charlotte was gracious, but after Lockhart had gone, she turned to her husband with a Gallic shrug and a rueful smile.

"I suppose it is well enough, since you are confident that Sophia returns Mr Lockhart's affection. But I must admit, my dear Scott, that I would have been glad of – how shall I say – a little more style."

"My dearest girl – " said Scott, shocked.

"After all, you are about to bring a title into the family. It would be pleasant, yes, to have an Earl, or at least another baronet, as a son-in-law."

"Lockhart," said Scott, "is a young man of excellent family. He and Sophia may start from small beginnings. But so did we, my love."

"Yes, that also is true," she agreed, with a little sigh.

After the acceptance of his formal addresses to her parents, Lockhart was able to write to Sophia from Edinburgh, with rather less formality than she had written to him.

"My dear Sophia,

"Charles has just been dining with me, and as he says the packet I sent yesterday has not been sent, I cannot resist the temptation of talking with you one moment more. And yet I have nothing to say except how much I am obliged by your kind letter . . . I feel myself in a strange – a very strange state at present, and can scarcely pretend to be quite myself. When I look back a few months and compare what I am now with what I was then, how is it possible that my heart should not overflow with tenderness. My dearest Sophia, you have put great trust in me. God grant I may never cost you a minute's pain in return for all your kindness. If I can put any faith in my knowledge of myself, you are sure of always possessing whatever happiness my love can give you. I wish I had other things to lay at your feet – but I have no fear for my part – all will be very well, and we shall be very happy. Most affectionately yours, John Gibson Lockhart."

Charlotte, of course, felt that her daughter's wedding would gain style from being deferred till she could be given away by the new baronet. But once again, Scott's journey to London had to be postponed. On the 12th of December, Sophia and Anne returned from taking tea with their grandmother, who had never seemed more lively, quizzing Sophia about young Mr Lockhart, demanding the latest news of young Walter, sending them into gales of laughter with anecdotes of her own youth. But on Monday morning a scared servant came running round from George Street with the news that her mistress had suffered a paralytic stroke. Dr Daniel, immediately called out of his retirement, visited his sister that day and the next. But on Wednesday morning he rose from the breakfast table to stroke his favourite cat, and fell dead without the slightest warning. And two days later, Scott's favourite aunt, Miss Christian Rutherford, died equally suddenly, though she at least had been in poor health for some time.

The family at Castle Street were stunned by the triple blow. Scott stood by his mother's bedside, desperately trying to reconcile the motionless effigy, neatly disposed by her devoted servants among her spotless pillows, her sparse white hair concealed by a lace cap, her habitually serene face slightly distorted, her eyes vague, with the active old lady who had so forthrightly pointed out, not so long ago, all the respects in which his *Bride of Lammermoor* had departed from the tale she had herself first told him.

Behind him, the young doctor who had taken Dr Daniel's place coughed apologetically. Scott turned.

"It is all very distressing, Mr Scott," he said, "but it must be remembered that she is suffering no pain."

"Can you be sure of that?"

"I believe so. In such cases, the brain . . ."

Scott listened, desolately, to a string of technical phrases which he did not understand. But the horror continued to obsess him. In what strange borderland was his mother wandering, so far away that no word of his could recall her to awareness of those she so much loved?

He stooped over her, spoke almost in her ear.

"Mother . . ."

He wondered if he detected the slightest flicker of response.

Mrs Scott lingered for a week. She remained speechless, but on several occasions during the dreadful days when she seemed unable either to live or to die, her eyes had brightened, Scott fancied, at the sight of him, and of his children. Then, on 24th December, she died. The transition was so slight as to be almost unnoticeable, and when they summoned Scott later to her bedroom he had to steel himself against the prospect of seeing without flinching that unendurably distorted face. But he found himself confronted by the marble beauty of a stranger, from whose face death had not only taken the dreadful contractions of paralysis but every kind familiar line which love and humour and fortitude had deepened with the years. He turned and left the room, moving at random past her weeping servants without any clear idea of where he was going, only that he was groping instinctively for some sign, some reassurance, that would bridge the gulf between the smooth-faced stranger and the mother he had known.

He stood in the drawing-room which her absence had emptied of all personality. The cold grate, the carefully dusted, shining surfaces, reflected only the care of servants. The room was dim behind drawn blinds. He turned to leave. Then, in the shaft of light from the half-open door he saw the table beside her favourite chair, already piled high with the little parcels she had been collecting for them all, throughout the winter, ready for New Year's Day. As he touched them, his heart lightened. He gathered them into his arms, and went carefully out of the flat and down the echoing stairs.

Chapter 18

SIR WALTER SCOTT, BART., sat at the writing-desk in the fussily pretty drawing-room of the Dumergue mansion in Piccadilly, oblivious of the rattle of wheels and the clipper-clop of horses' hooves outside the window as he wrote to his eldest daughter.

"Dear Sophia,
"I have no letter from any one at home excepting Lockhart, and he only says you are all well, and I trust it is so. I have seen most of my old friends, who are a little the worse for the wear, like myself. A five years' march down the wrong side of the hill tells more than ten on the right side. Our good friends here are kind as kind can be, and no frumps. They lecture the Cornet a little, which he takes with becoming deference and good humour. There is a certain veil of Flanders lace floating in the wind for a certain occasion, from a certain godmother, but that is more than a dead secret . . ."

It was the 3rd of April, 1820, with the apple blossom bobbing in London gardens and excitement mounting at the prospect of the forthcoming Coronation. For George III had died at last, in February, and the new Baronet, complaining loudly of the awkwardness of Court dress, had returned from the new King's first levee the day before, attended by his tall son, resplendent in the uniform of a Cornet in the 18th Hussars, who had obtained leave for the great occasion. It had been a more triumphal visit than ever, for the popularity of *Ivanhoe* had beaten all records, and nobody was in much doubt as to the authorship, in spite of Sir Walter's innocence whenever the subject came up. His portrait had been painted by Sir Thomas Lawrence by express command of the King for the great gallery at Windsor Castle, and he had sat to Francis Chantrey, the sculptor, who at first intended to catch the poet's noblest expression, as Sir Lawrence had done, but fortunately changed his mind, and decided to show him in a conversational mood, "when about to break out into some sly funny old story".

"Aye, ye're mair like yoursel' now, my man," said Sir Walter, greatly relieved. "Why, Mr Chantrey, no witch of old ever performed such cantrips with clay as this!"

But he was glad to see the last of London. The hubbub of the General Election, the sordid commotion caused by the return of the King's estranged wife from abroad, and her determination to assert her rights as Queen Caroline, had wearied him, and he had written nostalgically to Willie Laidlaw of his longing to be back on his own braes. *The Monastery*, written more rapidly than ever after the completion of *Ivanhoe*, had been brought out by Longmans instead of Constable, which caused considerable offence to the lordly Scottish publisher, who took comfort from the news that it was not going well. Sir Walter took the unusual rebuff philosophically. "I agree with the public," he wrote to James Ballantyne, "that it is not very interesting; but it was written with the same care as the others – that is, with no care at all," he added, with his usual candour.

He left London for the north in the third week of April, accompanied by the Cornet, loaded with gifts for all his family and household, his head full of plans for the completion of Abbotsford, the purchase of more land and the building of a pretty cottage on it for Sophia and her husband. The wedding had been fixed for the 29th of April in view of the superstition which ruled out May as a wedding month.

So Sophia and Lockhart were married, according to Scottish custom at that time, in the evening, and in the drawing-room at 39 Castle Street, according to the rites of the Episcopalian Church in Scotland, into which Sophia and Anne had recently been confirmed. Lockhart was not a denominational man, and did not care to oppose his future mother-in-law on such a point, but he was very well aware why his parents had been "unavoidably prevented from attending the ceremony". For his father was a Presbyterian minister in Glasgow, and his mother a staunch supporter of his uncompromising creed, though they were too fond of the young people not to forgive them in the end. After the wedding, Sir Walter and Lady Scott entertained their guests to an informal supper, Sophia and Lockhart set off on their honeymoon, the Cornet returned to his regiment next day, and his parents drove off with Anne and Charles to Abbotsford.

On their arrival, most unusually, Tom Purdie was nowhere to be found. But Anne, in gales of laughter, later rushed into the parlour with the almost incoherent explanation.

"Papa, Mamma! you'll never believe what Tom and Robert have been doing? They – they've been out with the tar-brushes, painting an S before the W.S. on all the sheep!"

Robert Hogg, brother to the Ettrick Shepherd, was now in charge of the sheep at Abbotsford; Dalgleish, as sturdy a Presbyterian as Peter Mathieson, had recently been taken on as butler, and John Nicholson, an intelligent local lad whose reading and writing Sir Walter tutored in the evenings, was training under him to be a footman, to Charlotte's great satisfaction. At last, she and her husband were living in something like proper style.

The indifferent reception of *The Monastery* had piqued its author into following it with another novel on an associated theme. *The Abbot*, with its vivid portrait of Mary, Queen of Scots, came out in September, published by Longmans and Constable, and was much more popular. Over the summer the plans for Chiefswood matured, and Lockhart suggested that, with expert coaching, Charles might take a place at Oxford in a couple of years. So Charles joined the household of the Cardiganshire vicar, who specialised in coaching a few boys for his former university, and Sir Walter found another post for Dominie Thomson before returning to Edinburgh for the winter. Maida, who was getting old and stiff now, preferred his winter quarters in the big box filled with straw by the fireside of the kitchen at Abbotsford, but Charlotte was much affronted when her spaniel, Finette, chose to remain with Spice, and all the other Dandie Dinmont terriers, in the country.

Sir Walter worked diligently on *Kenilworth* throughout the

winter. He had no further attacks of devastating pain, and with his usual optimism he considered his health re-established for his lifetime, so life seemed good. Sophia was happily settled in Edinburgh, and Chiefswood, near enough to the big house for company, far enough away for independence, was an enchanting country home for the Lockharts and their baby, John Hugh, who was born in Edinburgh in February, 1821.

Kenilworth came out before the end of the year. It was the last of the novels, published by Constable, from which Johnny Ballantyne made his comfortable profit. His health had been causing anxiety for some time, but he was wilder than ever in his schemes. He knew he had not much time left when he built himself a villa in Kelso and returned in triumph to the native town which he had left under the cloud of failure. He was gay as ever, coughing continually, with his clothes flapping loosely about thinly covered bones, and he was delighted with Sir Walter's suggestion of editing the lives of various authors to be collected in a *Novelist's Library* for his sole benefit. The series was begun, and Constable agreed to publish it. But during the summer of 1821 John Ballantyne died, and Sir Walter had no heart to go on with it. John had got him into many scrapes, but he had also made him laugh more often than any other creature on earth. As he stood by his grave in the Canongate churchyard, he said sadly: "I feel as if there would be less sunshine for me from this day forth."

The Coronation of King George IV was due to take place in July, and though Sir Walter grumbled that the pace of life in London was getting too much for him, as the time approached for an occasion which must bring so much historic pageantry back to life he found himself unable to resist the chance of taking part in it, and wrote to the appropriate member of the Royal Household for two seats in the Abbey, since he felt sure that James Hogg would not only jump at the chance of witnessing the spectacle of a lifetime but of writing a poem about it afterwards. The Ettrick Shepherd, however, had his own scale of values. He thanked Sir Walter graciously, but pointed out that since the authorities had had the tactlessness to choose for the Coronation the same date as that of

St Boswells Fair, he, as a recently established farmer on the Borders, could scarcely afford to miss the local occasion.

So Sir Walter went without him, travelling by sea, on board one of the new steamships, called *The City of Edinburgh*, with which he was greatly delighted, though the volume of acrid smoke which rolled from its funnel was so great that he suggested it might well be re-named *The New Reekie*. He was delighted by the magnificent spectacle in the Abbey, distressed by Queen Caroline's desperate attempt to intrude upon it, and gratified at being recognised and rescued by a sergeant of the Scots Greys from the pressure of an over-excited crowd which was blocking the way back to his carriage.

But it was good to get back to Abbotsford, where his dream of a happy community of friends seemed to be coming true. With the Lockharts at Chiefswood, the Fergusons at Huntly Burn, his dearest friend, Will Erskine, on a long visit to Abbotsford with his daughters, good news of Walter in the army and Charles at his studies in Wales, Sir Walter was happier than he had ever been. The next few years were a sort of Indian summer, golden and benign, with as yet only a touch of frost in the air.

He was writing *The Pirate*, set in the wild Northern Isles which he and Will Erskine had visited together on the spectacularly successful cruise round the Northern Lighthouses. So Erskine's help and criticism were particularly valuable, and the pleasant work distracted him, as Sir Walter had hoped, from his personal grief. The families were in and out of each other's houses all the time. When there were fewer visitors than usual at Abbotsford, the Lockharts and the Fergusons strolled over to dine there, and when the great house was full of important people who required laborious entertainment, Sir Walter saddled up Sybil Grey at first light and escaped to Chiefswood for a few hours, escorted by Maida and a mob of noisy terriers, turning the mare loose to graze while he sat down under the great ash tree which overshadowed the cottage, making notes while he waited for the family to appear. After breakfast, he would resist the temptation to amuse his grandson, the frail, brilliant-eyed John Hugh, the "Hugh Littlejohn" for whom the

Tales of a Grandfather were so happily written, with just one more story. Instead he would retire upstairs to the room put at his disposal, and write the next chapter of *The Pirate*, which Will Erskine would later take the greatest pride in reading to the company assembled at Huntly Burn, Chiefswood, or Abbotsford itself, where work on the new drawing-room, library and study was moving magnificently towards completion indoors, and the court-yard, with its imposingly turreted wall and gateway, taking shape outside.

As usual, visitors came and went in an almost unending procession, and Sir Walter entertained them all, whether welcome or not, with regal generosity. There were plenty of young men from neighbouring families to escort Anne and the Erskine girls to picnics and dances, Peter Mathieson drove Charlotte about the countryside to call on her friends in state, and Sophia had a pretty little governess-cart affair drawn by two gentle donkeys whom Anne had gaily christened Hannah More and Lady Morton. In this she drove little John Hugh about in the arms of his nurse, with an alert lad in attendance, ready to run to the donkeys' heads, should the staid creatures show the slightest inclination to move out of a walk. It was a season of enchantment. And yet, there was just that touch of frost in the air.

For Sir Walter was spending too much, and at the back of his mind he was aware of it. But the restoration of much of his health and vigour had reinforced his confidence that he could earn all he needed, with Constable ready to pay generously for everything he wrote, and his sales, as far as he knew, continuing to break all records.

Cadell, coldly calculating by nature, admitted to his partner that the situation made him uneasy. "It would not surprise me," he said, "if Sir Walter had not passed the peak of his popularity. Since *Ivanhoe*, his sales have been dropping."

Constable shook his head. "I do not think so. There has perhaps been less hysteria in the first demand, but by and large, the sales have come in the end."

"He is writing too much," said Cadell. "Might a hint that he should keep the public waiting for his next book be well-timed?"

"It would not be well received," said Constable with a slight shudder. For the story of the Black Hussar of Literature, who neither gave nor accepted criticism, had not lost in Blackwood's telling. "Besides, I disagree with you. Popularity in the literary world is an ephemeral thing. He must write more, not less, while his books continue to sell, with a few fluctuations, I grant you, more than those of any other writer in the world today."

"You would not try to point out – "

"Certainly not. He needs the money. We need his books. He must be urged on, while the sun of his public's favour shines. You agree with me?"

"Not entirely," Cadell said. "But – "

"But we cannot afford to lose him, as we have done in the past, to Longmans and Murray," Constable thundered. He had not been named "The Emperor" for nothing, Cadell reflected ruefully.

"Then," he said, "we must offer him terms which will ensure that his books continue to be published by our firm."

"Certainly," Constable agreed. "What is more, I mean to secure our permanent interest in the books he has already written, by purchasing all his remaining copyrights. Surely you cannot deny the wisdom of this?"

"I do not," said Cadell. "Provided they retain their value."

Constable lost no time in opening negotiations on the lines he had indicated. Before Sir Walter reluctantly returned to Edinburgh with his family in November, he had agreed to part with the copyrights of *Ivanhoe*, *The Monastery*, *The Abbot*, and *Kenilworth*, for five thousand guineas. And now that they were his exclusive property, Constable brought them out collectively as "*Historical Romances* by the Author of Waverley".

He also demonstrated his confidence in his author's future, as well as his past, by an agreement to publish, on the usual terms, Sir Walter's next four works of fiction, unnamed and as yet unwritten, to be published in unbroken succession – which excluded the possibility that any of his rivals might break the sequence by grabbing a potential winner – each to fill at least three volumes, with proper adjustments in case any should run to four.

Sir Walter saw no objection. He certainly needed the money, and he had every intention of writing the books. As for the sale of copyrights, he looked on it with a countryman's eye, as money made by the sale of old, no longer profitable, cattle.

When *The Pirate* was published in mid-December, 1821, its reception delighted Constable and silenced Cadell's doubts. The wild, strange background of the Northern Isles, the Nordic vigour of the characters, the eerie personality of Norna of the Fitful Head, pleased both the critics and the public. *The Quarterly Review* praised it, and its readers loved it. The new agreement for the books to follow got off to a flying start.

The year ended with a most welcome letter from John Murray. Lord Byron, who had recently completed his great dramatic poem, *Cain*, had requested him to offer the dedication to Sir Walter, and enclosed a proof. Had he any objection? Sir Walter accepted the dedication "with feelings of great obligation", and wrote to John Murray at length on the "very grand and tremendous drama of *Cain*".

In January, 1822, William Erskine, already Sheriff of Orkney and Zetland, was raised to the Bench as Lord Kinedder. It was the fulfilment of a wistful, long-standing ambition, and there was great rejoicing among the former Montagnards of the Outer House. But Sir Walter, who knew his friend's constitution better than anybody, and had been troubled for some time about his nervous and physical state, feared that the longed-for honour had come almost too late.

It was to be a difficult, broken year for authorship. Constable had supposed that the completion of the four works of fiction for which he had contracted would take as many years, considering the author's other obligations, and the variety of lesser editorial assignments which he had, as usual, undertaken. But he had underrated the increasing urgency of Sir Walter's desire to clear his feet from the financial liabilities of which he was only too well aware. *The Fortunes of Nigel* appeared in May, and was so well received tha

Constable, jubilant at the vindication of his judgment, offered no less than £1,000 for a little sketch of a heroic episode at the battle of *Halidon Hill* which Sir Walter had written in two mornings, before beginning *Peveril of the Peak*.

Constable's own health had not been good lately. The doctors warned him that his complaint was "a threatening of water on the chest," prescribed digitalis, and a holiday in the south. From his south-coast resort he wrote almost deliriously of Sir Walter's current success and his own future hopes.

Meanwhile, Sir Walter found time to write anxiously to Lord Montagu – since the young Duke of Buccleuch was still a schoolboy at Eton – of the urgent need for repairs to Melrose Abbey, and accepted the heavy responsibility of making the arrangements for the visit to Scotland which King George IV had planned to make in August.

It was definitely a delicate assignment, and Sir Walter knew it. The last member of the Hanoverian royal family to enter Scotland was that "butcher Cumberland" who had extinguished the Jacobite hopes at Culloden. But that was more than half a century ago, the final Union of the countries was an accomplished fact, and the last representative of the Stewart line had lately died in Rome. Common sense looked forward. And Sir Walter knew the reigning King of Great Britain well enough to realise that he would be prepared to work hard to make his visit a real gesture of goodwill.

So he, too, set his own affairs aside and worked very hard indeed over all the intricate problems involved in persuading the leaders of the Highland clans to forget old wrongs as well as more ancient rivalries, and co-operate in the intricate programme of processions, receptions at Holyroodhouse, balls and levees with which the King's visit must be celebrated. But he worked with a sick heart, for Will Erskine, who had been for only a few brief months Lord Kinedder, was dying. He snatched every hour which could be spared from the endless meetings to arrange, pacify, adjudicate, and generally organise the forthcoming occasion, to sit at his friend's bedside and lighten his darkness with his own love and hope.

But on the very day the King's royal yacht and her attendant vessels anchored in the Firth of Forth, Will Erskine died. Sir Walter went through the next days in a dark dream. There were glimpses of splendour, as the procession was marshalled from Leith to Holyroodhouse, with pipers, heralds, horsemen, and carriages; moments of comedy, when the King, who had been meticulously arrayed in kilt and plaid of the royal Stewart tartan, with appropriate bonnet and skean-dhu, was confronted by a certain bailie of Aberdeen in precisely the same outfit. But there was also infinite exasperation in the discovery that the poet Crabbe, Rector of Muston, whom Sir Walter had so long venerated and longed to meet, had chosen this of all times to present himself at 39 Castle Street, decorous in dark coat and breeches, old-fashioned wig and buckle shoes, entirely bewildered by the commotion, and anxious only to talk of poetry to the author of *The Lay* and *Marmion*. And at the back of all the clashing colours, the pandemonium of pipes and shouting, the loyal speeches and the service in St Giles, was the quiet figure of Will Erskine, whose funeral, as well as everything else, it was his duty to arrange.

It was a relief to get back to the remoter problems of *Peveril of the Peak*. But it was scarcely surprising that this novel, published in January of 1823, was less warmly received than its predecessors. Sir Walter himself said wearily: "It smells of the apoplexy."

But he was already busy with its successor, *Quentin Durward*, the story of a Scottish mercenary at the court of Louis of France. James Skene had offered him the background, from his notes of a recent holiday abroad, and the novel had a marvellous vigour, as if it refreshed him even to write of the rough soldiering life he had been denied. He liked, too, to escape now and then from his exalted place at the Clerks' Table, and wander into the Outer Court to exchange gossip with the new generation of young advocates congregated round the stove at which his fellow Montagnards had listened to his stories, long ago. Their nonsense made him feel young again, though he sometimes wished they would not be so deucedly respectful.

One chilly morning, towards the end of the winter, he was limping through the throng of lounging advocates and scurrying clerks, his domed white head towering above those of lesser men, when a roar of sudden laughter rose from the group about the stove.

"What's the joke, lads? Come on, now, don't deny me. I could do with a laugh this morning."

But they all stood silent, shuffling their feet.

"Come away now, Lockhart." He took his son-in-law by the elbow. "You heard it." Lockhart saw he was not to be denied.

"Well, sir, it was Peter here," he poked a finger at a stout young advocate's ribs, "who said 'here comes old Peveril. I see the Peak.' "

Sir Walter stood for a moment expressionless. Old? He hadn't thought of that. He and his friends had been the same age as these lads only yesterday. Well, these young men belonged to tomorrow. He shouldn't have forgotten. But the joke was neat enough. Belatedly, he chuckled.

"Aye, aye, my man," he told the crimson-faced Peter broadly, "as weel be Peveril o' the Peak ony day, as Peter o' the Paunch."

The answering shout of laughter from Peter's companions comforted him a little because it was even louder than before.

The new novel, set as it was in France at the time of King Louis XI, was involving him in a good deal of research in the Advocates' Library, where maps and gazetteers helped him to work out the movements of his characters, and Histories of France filled in the gaps in his knowledge of the period. He read, as he wrote, with extreme rapidity, as if he had only to scan a mass of information to consign it to the great reservoir of subconscious knowledge from which the complete work of imagination would presently flow so fast that his pen could scarcely take it down.

He finished it within weeks, and sent it to James Ballantyne with a pang. How eagerly Will Erskine would have tried out his critical skill on its rich and complex setting. *Quentin Durward* came out to a slow start at the end of June, then gathered momentum as Paris acclaimed it. "It suffered a wee bit from frostbite," Sir Walter admitted. "But it'll do now," he added, as his thoughts began to turn towards the summer vacation and the completion of Abbotsford.

Now that the last section of the roof was on, the furnishing of the interior was his urgent concern. He had already written enthusiastically to Terry about the carved wainscot, pulpit, repentance stool and other lengths of beautiful dark oak sent to him by the magistrates of Dunfermline, to be used for the entrance hall, the twenty-four pieces of hand-painted Chinese wallpaper, given by his cousin, Hugh Scott, in the East India Company, which would be ideal for the drawing-room, the lengths of cedar wood he had obtained for drawing-room and library. Now he was fascinated by such innovations as air-bells, lighting by gas, and the heraldic enrichment of the entrance hall, with the arms of the chief representatives of the house of Scott: Buccleuch, Montagu, Harden and Thirlestane, now glowed in the stained glass of the Bellenden windows, the arms of the Border clans were emblazoned round the cornice with those of personal friends, such as Will Erskine, J. B. S. Morritt and Will Clerk, over the archway leading to the armoury, and those of his own ancestors, on escutcheons down the centre of the roof.

"Never heed that I've been able to let ye have only fourteen out of the sixteen coats that the best-bred folk should have," Sir Walter told the painter cheerfully. "Just sketch in a few clouds for the other two. I'll think up a motto. '*Alta nox premit*' might serve."

Constable now also aspired to be a landed proprietor. He had bought an estate at Balniel in Fife, his county of origin, and was determined to build himself such another mansion as Abbotsford, for which he had already sent gifts like the two elaborately carved boxwood armchairs, said to be from the Borghese Palace in Rome, and a great slab of antique mosaic in marble, which he had found in London. He now agreed to buy the copyrights of the latest novels, *The Pirate*, *The Fortunes of Nigel*, *Peveril of the Peak*, and *Quentin Durward*, which had been published on the usual half-profit terms between author and publisher, for a further five thousand guineas. But he also suggested, greatly to Cadell's relief, that it would seem wise, in view of the uncertainties of life and health, to enter into no further contracts till all the books already under contract should have been written.

Sir Walter, aware that he had now, with *Quentin Durward*, only one more book of the "four works of fiction" to write, agreed, suggesting that he might vary the series with a work, in dialogue form, on popular superstitions, for which he had ample material. But the delayed, though resounding, success of *Quentin Durward* on the Continent reassured Constable so much that he urged the Author of *Waverley* to produce another in the series forthwith.

"What shall it be?" Sir Walter wondered, as he rode with Willie Laidlaw towards Melrose across the Eildon hills. "I can't but think I could make better play still than Quentin in France with something German."

"Na, na, sir," said Willie Laidlaw urgently. "Take my word for it, you're aye best, like Helen MacGregor, when your foot's on your ain native heath. Look down yonder. What's going on in yon cottages? If ye knew, what a tale ye could tell."

"You're mebbe right, Willie," Sir Walter agreed. "Take a village like Melrose, tell the tale of the comedy and tragedy going on there in this month and year of 1823 – "

"What for no'?" said Willie Laidlaw enthusiastically.

Sir Walter's mind harked back to such another village, the village in which he had first met his wife, where the petty pace of country life had been accelerated by the arrival of irrelevant, incompatible strangers, drawn there by some social attraction, a spa, perhaps? Soon afterwards he began *St Ronan's Well*.

Throughout the summer visitors came and went at Abbotsford as usual, and Sir Walter continued to take refuge, when necessary, at Chiefswood, in order to get on with his work. But from one visitor, at least, he did not try to escape. Maria Edgeworth, over from Ireland, in August, paused in the gateway, where Sir Walter waited to receive a writer whose works he had so long admired. Flinging her arms wide, she cried impulsively, "Everything about you is exactly what one ought to have had wit enough to dream."

St Ronan's Well was published in December, and did not at first do very well. It lacked, perhaps, the wide appeal of earlier novels, though it gave the greatest pleasure to the inhabitants of the little Border town on which the story might have been based. Sir Walter did not allow himself to be influenced by adverse criticism. He began the new year of 1824 with a very different story, that of *Redgauntlet*. Here he was on sure ground, as he cast his mind back to the days when young men like himself and Will Clerk had passed their examinations and given just such "a chack of dinner" to their friends, to the great delight of the crusty old Writer to the Signet, whose portrait he drew from memories of his own father, before embarking on a fast-moving series of adventures on Solwayside, which involved a variety of striking characters, including Prince Charles Edward in his later years.

The book was, in many ways, among the best he had ever written, but its appeal was, inevitably, limited, so that it failed to reach the wider public which had responded to *The Fortunes of Nigel*, or *Quentin Durward*. It was the only novel he wrote during 1824. He had so much else on his mind.

For Abbotsford was finished at last. Gifts were arriving from all sorts of people, from the fifteen magnificent volumes of Mont-faucon's *Antiquities*, bound in scarlet with the royal cipher, from King George IV, the set of Variorum Classics, in a hundred and forty volumes, from Constable, to the chair, elaborately carved, made from wood rescued from the house at Robroyston in which William Wallace was betrayed, given by Joseph Train, who had done much to help Sir Walter with his first researches for *Guy Mannering*.

His family prospered. Young Walter was doing well in the army, Charles had got a place at Brasenose College, Oxford, and in October he himself had delivered an oration at the opening of the new foundation, The Edinburgh Academy, of which Charles's former tutor, Mr Williams, had been appointed Rector. Towards the end of the month, he had sadder news to report to Charles, at Oxford, for the magnificent old staghound, Maida, died in the warm straw bed which Sir Walter had ordered, and was buried beside his stone effigy, which the master mason had carved from life as a louping on stone the year before.

That autumn, Sir Walter planned a new series of *Tales of the Crusaders* with a medieval background, which would offer a useful contrast to his happiest Scottish settings. He was turning over such stories as *The Betrothed* and *The Talisman* in his mind.

But news of the death of Lord Byron at Missolonghi in Greece shocked Scott with real sorrow, though he knew very well that it was the sort of death the poet himself would have chosen, even if he had not imagined that Byron himself appeared, in his imagination at least, at Abbotsford to say so as he bade him farewell.

Hogmanay, the last day of the old year, had always been a special occasion on the Borders. In the morning the local children traditionally appeared at the back door of Abbotsford, and each received a penny and an oatcake. In the evening bands of boys fantastically dressed, the Guisards, came to act plays before their laird and lady. But this year a special occasion had been arranged on the 7th of January, in honour of young Walter, who had not only returned from Sandhurst with success in his military examinations for promotion, but had also announced his engagement to a young heiress, Miss Jane Jobson of Lochore.

It was an occasion for a great gathering of all those who bore the name of Scott and lived within driving distance. The Scotts of Harden had come over from Hawick, with a score of other local families. The Fergusons had come down from Huntly Burn, the Lockharts were staying at Abbotsford, Charles had come home from Oxford, Anne was enchanted to be no longer alone at home. They danced, under the new garish gas lights, till the young people could scarcely take the floor for another reel, even inspired by the unwearied piping of John of Skye.

Sir Walter and Lady Scott stood together, with young Walter and his heiress beside them, to accept the thanks and congratulations of their guests on the completion of Abbotsford, as they bade them good night. In the drive outside, the coachmen had returned with the carriages, footmen were ready at the doors for the lairds and ladies to emerge at last. The chilly horses stamped and fretted, and the frost, contrasting with the warm flicker from many carriage lamps, glittered mercilessly on the grass.

Chapter 19

YOUNG Walter married his heiress in Edinburgh on the 3rd of February, 1825. As Jane Jobson's trustees had stipulated, Sir Walter settled Abbotsford on his son, reserving, of course, his own liferent. He also bought him a Captain's commission in the Hussars for £3,500. Young Walter accepted it all with the easy grace and limited understanding which his privileged upbringing and chosen profession tended to induce. After all, why not? His father had been at great pains to assure him that parting with the ownership of Abbotsford, in the very year of its completion, was not such a sacrifice as it seemed, was in fact no sacrifice at all, Sir Walter had gallantly insisted. He had built the place for the love of it, and the knowledge that he had been able to present his son, on the day of his marriage, with a home worthy of the future second baronet and his sweet lady, gave him the greatest pride and joy. In the few years that remained to him –

"Oh, come, Papa," said young Walter, in real distress.

"Never heed, lad. My time will be long or short, as God wills. But I shall employ it to the best advantage, and hope to hand over a greater estate than you will own on your wedding day – "

"Really, Papa?"

"The Faldonside property is on the market again. You'll mind, I wrote to you about it quite a while since. But old Milne wants £40,000 for it, which would pare my nails pretty short, I admit – "

"Then never give it another thought, Papa."

"So that I might not be able to pay for your carriage, as I had intended – "

"Pray do not think of it, Papa. Abbotsford could scarcely be bettered – "

"It is a matter of pride to me that you should not bring less to the family coffers than your bride," said Sir Walter decisively. "Besides, with a little judicious planting, added to what is already there, the estate might be rendered one of the most beautiful in this part of Scotland. Well, we shall see, we shall see. I am enchanted by your little Jane, my dear boy, and wish her to lack nothing I can provide."

"Jane is already devoted to you, Papa. She hopes that you and Mamma will come to visit us in Ireland, when I have my troop, and can entertain you in proper fashion."

"So she has already told me," Sir Walter said. "We should like nothing better, I am sure. But first I must call a conference with my worthy friend Constable, who writes from the south of England in high spirits, and with all sorts of plans. When he returns to Scotland, I shall see what ideas he has for my next book."

The meeting with Constable took place at Abbotsford in May, with Lockhart and James Ballantyne also present. Constable had certainly returned from the south in a very different mood, and also, apparently, in better health. Sir Walter was astonished by the change in him. Not so very long ago the publisher had been reminding him gloomily that the amount of accommodation which his firm had granted to the Ballantyne partnership now exceeded £40,000, and he would be glad to have it reduced. He had also suggested the advisability of getting in an accountant to tease out the exact position of the Ballantyne finances.

Sir Walter had said cheerfully that this should not be necessary. He knew very well that most of the Ballantyne borrowings had been for his benefit, also that he himself had drawn further large sums on Constable direct. But against that, Constable, he fancied, must owe him nearly as much over the copyright transactions; Abbotsford was now completed, and Walter almost off his hands, and his own books (so far as he knew) as popular as ever. Why rake all the old scores together just at this point? In a year or two, with a few more books behind him, the balance would have swung level again.

His own optimism had so far been strong enough to offset Constable's gloom, and he knew very well that Constable disliked the dreary work of checking balance sheets as much as he did. But it was very pleasant to receive him at Abbotsford on that May morning, once more his expansive self, full of plans to persuade the nobility to pay as much for books as they expended in taxation.

"Take," he said, "this one absurd and contemptible item of the tax on hair-powder; the use of it is almost entirely gone out of fashion. Bating a few parsons' and lawyers' wigs, it may be said that hair-powder is confined to the flunkeys . . . Nevertheless, for each head that is thus vilified in Great Britain, a guinea is paid yearly to the Exchequer, and the taxes in that Schedule are an army, compared to the purchasers of even the best and most popular of books. Or take the taxes on armorial bearings, hunters, racers and four-wheeled carriages . . ."

"Aye," said Sir Walter, glancing out of the library window, "below me now lies a rich valley with many handsome houses. Yet I much doubt if any laird yonder spends ten pounds a year on books."

Constable agreed. "No, there's no market among them that's worth thinking about. They are content with a review or a magazine, or a paltry subscription to some circulating library forty miles off. But if I live half-a-dozen years . . ." His voice rose, his colour heightened, as he began to declaim in the old style, "I'll make it as impossible that there should not be a good library in every decent house in Britain as that the shepherd's ingle-neuk should want the saut poke. Aye, and what's that?" He was getting a little breathless now. "Why should the ingle-neuk itself want a shelf for the novels?"

It was a sort of euphoria, but there was sense in it, as his listeners realised when he went on to outline his scheme of the production of cheap editions, bound in cloth instead of boards, costing only half-a-crown or three shillings, "but selling not by thousands or tens of thousands, but by hundreds of thousands – nay, by millions!"

Sir Walter slapped his knees. "By God, man, you'll be the grand Napoleon of the realms of print."

"If you outlive me," said Constable with a chuckle, "I'll bespeak that line for my tombstone. Now, will you be my right-hand man when I open my campaign?"

"Surely," said Sir Walter, grave again. "I've often felt, of late," he added thoughtfully, "that the vein of fiction was nearly worked out. Often, as you know, I've seriously thought of turning my hand to history. What say you to my taking the field with a Life of the *other* Napoleon?"

"My good friend," said Constable, throwing out an arm in the gesture of a general ordering a charge, "start at once!"

Before the meeting broke up, it was decided that the great enterprise for bringing cheap books to the people should be launched under the title of *Constable's Miscellany*, which would bring out worth-while publications at popular prices at monthly intervals. Sir Walter began his research for the *Life of Napoleon* at once, for the project pleased him. He had been for many years almost as fascinated by Napoleon's character and career as by that of the Duke of Wellington, with whom he had often discussed him.

But he soon realised that for him, at least, it would be impossible to compress a Life of Napoleon into the strait-jacket limits of Constable's scheme. He must first give a brief outline of the French Revolution which had, as it were, conjured up such a leader, to be both the good and evil genius of his country. And behind the Revolution rose the people who had made it, suffered or prospered because of it. The subject grew under his hand, as Constable, at his request, sent him books by the score, on every aspect of his immense undertaking. A wagon-load of folios of *Le Moniteur* arrived from Paris. Authorities were consulted in London, Brussels, Amsterdam and Paris. Documents of all sorts were offered by people who had played a part in Napoleon's campaigns.

Sir Walter's study in Castle Street was soon so stacked with books and papers that the author could scarcely find space to sit down. Before Sir Walter had roughed out the Introduction, Constable realised that the work must be published as a separate book, in four volumes of the same size as *The Betrothed* and *The Talisman*, which were to be brought out together as *Tales of the Crusaders*. These, too, were the result of considerable research, since the author knew nothing of their background except what he could learn from books.

But *Napoleon* was different. Sir Walter had tramped over the

French countryside, talked to the people and seen the armies of occupation, studied at least one of the battlefields, questioned Wellington on his campaigns and been promised a chance to read his wildly scrawled dispatches. He became enthralled. He believed he could produce something of interest. But it would take time. And it would mean an immense amount of work.

When the Courts rose in July he decided to take a holiday in Ireland, first to visit young Walter and his wife, now installed in Dublin, taking it for granted that Charlotte would go with him, as usual. But she broke into his plans with a peevishness which startled him.

"No, Scott, I shall not go."

"My dearest girl, why not?"

"I do not feel I should enjoy all ze noise and commotion."

"But to see Walter and little Jane – "

"You shall leave me behind at Abbotsford, please."

"Don't you feel well, my love?"

"No, I do not. Let us say no more about it."

"You must see a doctor at once."

"I will do nothing of ze kind. But I prefer to be at Abbotsford."

"Very well, my dear."

Sir Walter, much troubled, had a word with the local doctor, who agreed that Lady Scott would have benefited from the change of scene, the chance of having her mind distracted from the minor ailments inevitable in later life. But, of course, it was not something to be insisted on against the wishes of, he suggested gently, a somewhat over-sensitive patient. So Sir Walter set out with only Anne and Lockhart, leaving Sophia behind at Chiefswood with little John Hugh, about whom his parents were increasingly anxious, to keep an eye on her mother at Abbotsford.

The holiday was outrageously successful. The newly gazetted Captain and his lady entertained them enchantingly, the society of Dublin acclaimed them, the common people mobbed them, as if Sir Walter had been a conqueror returning from the wars. He was candidly delighted, Lockhart was observant and gratified, and Anne had never enjoyed herself so much in all her life.

They set off for Abbotsford on the 18th of August, travelling by Holyhead and driving through North Wales, where Sir Walter was overwhelmed by the enthusiasm of the eccentric ladies of Llangollen, who appeared to have not only read all his works but also every press comment upon them, on through the Lake District to meet Wordsworth and his daughter, and so to Abbotsford by the end of the month.

When they reached home he embraced Charlotte and Sophia, hoisted John Hugh's light weight on his shoulder as he crossed the stableyard to greet Tom Purdie and the dogs, paused at the back door for a word with Cook and her lassies, returned to bolt the carefully chosen dinner which had been kept hot for hours in honour of the returning travellers, and then unexpectedly retired to his study, with an absent air and a few words of apology.

"Forgive me, my loves. I have neglected the Emperor too long. Anne and Lockhart will tell you how we fared."

"Well, indeed!" said Charlotte plaintively. "Not one word, no, not one, of inquiry for my health!"

"Are you not better, then, dearest Mamma?" Anne asked anxiously.

"No. I am worse," said Charlotte pettishly. "But he does not care."

"Oh, Mamma, I am sure he does," Sophia said quickly. "But he is so bad at noticing things. Do you remember the new chintzes we made for his return from Waterloo?"

"All evening he sit there, seeing nothing new, yes," Charlotte agreed. "But – "

"But when he found out he was most dreadfully distressed," Sophia interrupted.

"One day he finds out how ill I am. But it will be too late," said Charlotte dramatically. "Now, Anne, tell us about your travels. Lockhart must fill in ze gaps when you forget."

But Lockhart was not listening. Instead, he was watching his wife, who had sent four-year-old John Hugh back to bed at Chiefswood with his nurse, and was obviously making a great effort to keep her attention on what was going on round her. When the meal was over at last, and Charlotte settled on her chaise longue in the beautiful new Chinese drawing-room, with Anne on her favourite low chair beside her, Lockhart took Sophia by the arm.

"Let us ask to be excused, my love. Mamma and Anne will have much to laugh about together, and your Papa will not leave his books till bedtime."

"Oh, yes, please," said Sophia quickly.

As they walked together along the familiar path to Chiefswood through the still September evening, Lockhart said quietly:

"Something's wrong. What is it? Johnny?"

"Yes. Oh, Lockhart – I can scarcely bear to say it – he means so much to you, too – "

"He didn't look well. I saw that at once."

"He hasn't been well – Oh, it was nothing new – no need to call you back. But the doctor said he ought to see someone in Edinburgh who works specially with children. So he came down. And he said – he said – "

Lockhart pressed her arm closer to his side. They could feel each other tremble. "He said?" Lockhart said quietly.

"He said that Johnny could not stand another northern winter. In a gentler climate he might have a chance. But not – in Scotland."

"Then we must go south," said Lockhart. "It grieves me much, for I had hoped to be able to lighten your Papa's burden. *Napoleon* will be a heavy task – "

"Papa will understand," said Sophia confidently. "You must find other work in London. He has many friends there, and will send you to the right people, I know."

She was not mistaken. Her father's first thought was how he could help to avert the tragedy which threatened his beloved grandson, and he at once sat down to write out the names of people in the literary world who might be able to offer Lockhart a suitable position.

The Quarterly needed a new editor, he knew, and Mr Murray had Lockhart already in mind. Earlier in the year he had suggested a lesser literary post, which Lockhart had declined. He had at that time no wish to go south, nor any intention of being an editor. But things were different now, and Mr Murray's new offer was most welcome. So Lockhart set off for London to discuss the proposition, look about for rooms for his family, and settle other urgent business, while Sir Walter completed his Introduction and embarked on the first chapter of the *Life*, comforting himself with the conviction that Chiefswood's hearth would not be cold long. Scotland's winters might be hard, but her summers were beautiful. Johnny's parents would no doubt take him to the south coast, which he would find as recuperative as the Prince Regent and Archibald Constable had done. By May they would all be together again.

The Tales of the Crusaders was going well. As Constable had hoped, *The Talisman*'s romantic brilliance sustained the weakness of its companion, *The Betrothed*. And he shrewdly realised that if he left his author to write about Napoleon in his own way, he would presently have a new achievement to lay before a public who might have had almost enough of historical romances. And the second edition might be condensed sufficiently to take its place in his *Miscellany*. So he let the *Life of Napoleon* grow under Sir Walter's hand like the Biblical mustard seed, not displeased when the project of another novel, set in Cromwellian times, began to suggest itself as a corrective to too much arduous research. From the early days, Sir Walter had liked to have two contrasting themes on hand at once, turning from one to the other when he needed a change of occupation. So *Woodstock* was begun, as Lockhart left for London, and there was a brief pause in the stream of visitors to Abbotsford.

It was a relief to turn back to the familiar technique, a reassurance that things were really going on as usual. Sir Walter even gave himself a day off to take part in the Abbotsford Hunt, that gorgeous assembly of local friends and their assorted terriers, which had been an October fixture ever since he had been at Abbotsford. But this year, in a mood of defiance, he urged Sybil Grey to jump the Catrail. The trench was wide, and the mare faltered. She fell and threw him heavily. He was helped home, and took his place at the evening's celebrations, bruised and sore though he was. But his nerve for wild horsemanship was broken at last, and he returned sadly to his books again.

Lockhart, in London, had begun to hear disturbing news. There had lately been a wave of speculation in the City, which had even affected the book trade. Responsible publishers diverted their revenues into all sorts of soap-bubble concerns. Bankers were uneasy, and rumours of insolvency were in the air. Lockhart heard on good authority that even Hurst and Robinson, Constable's London agents, were threatened on account of having plunged wildly on hops. Current talk went so far as to hint that the house of Constable was in danger. Lockhart was disturbed by the news, and though he supposed that Constable's failure would mean only the loss of the proceeds of the latest of the Waverley novels, he wrote at once, reporting what he had heard.

Sir Walter replied by return of post, confidently repudiating the possibility. "Shake who will in London, my friend in Edinburgh is rooted, as well as branched, like the oak." So there Lockhart left it till he returned to Chiefswood at the end of October. But he could not forget the persistent rumours, though at first the sight of his wife, the agonising eagerness of Johnny Hugh's welcome, put all other considerations out of his mind.

Then, a few days later, he received a letter from a barrister friend in Lincoln's Inn, who told him categorically that Constable's London banker had "thrown up his book", or in plain English, closed his account.

"I shall have to tell Papa of this," he said to Sophia.

"Without delay, my dearest," she agreed.

So Lockhart rode across to Abbotsford. It was a crisp, autumnal evening, and Sir Walter was alone in his study, considering the day's work over the cigar and glass of whisky and water which he allowed himself when no visitors had to be entertained. He greeted his son-in-law with pleasure.

"Why, Lockhart, I had not expected to see you again today. Sit down, and help yourself."

"I think, sir, you should read this letter," Lockhart said abruptly. "I found its contents most disturbing."

Sir Walter, wreathed in cigar-smoke, held out his hand. He read the letter without any change of expression, and returned it with a smile. "I am much obliged to you for coming over, but you may rely upon it, your friend has been hoaxed. I promise you, were the Crafty's book thrown up, there would be a pretty decent scramble among the bankers for the keeping of it. Can you doubt," he added, as he lighted another cigar, "that if Constable had been informed of this yesterday, this day's post must have brought me intelligence direct from him?"

"Such news," said Lockhart uneasily, "is not the sort that he might wish to circulate."

Sir Walter chuckled. "Ah, but the Crafty and James Ballantyne have been so much connected in business that Jamie would be bound to hear of anything so important. D'you suppose he could keep it from me? He could as soon keep his eyebrows in place if there were a fire in his nursery."

"I had not thought of that," Lockhart admitted. "Well, I apologise for troubling you. Your confidence relieves my mind extremely."

"My dear boy," said Sir Walter, "you know how much I welcome such evidence of your support. How are things at Chiefswood, since I saw your wife and son this morning?"

"As to that," said Lockhart, "I scarcely know what to say."

"Nor I," Sir Walter agreed sadly. "I'll be over in the morning."

He arrived much earlier than he had been expected. For Lockhart had not finished dressing, when the unexpected sound of carriage wheels brought him to the window, with Sophia beside him.

"It's Papa!" she cried. "And Peter Mathieson is on the box. The horses are steaming as if they had been driven through the night!"

Lockhart hurried down to admit his father-in-law. Sir Walter was weary, but smiling. He had already climbed out of the carriage, and was helping the delighted Johnny Hugh to feed the ducks, who were circling the little pool outside the cottage.

"Ah, there you are, Lockhart," he said serenely. "I was more taken aback by what you said last evening than I let on. So, as soon as you had gone I ordered Peter Mathieson to get the horses out and drive me to Polton. I found Constable just putting on his nightcap, but I kept him up long enough to be sure there is not a word of truth in that story . . ."

"Look, look, Grandpapa," yelled Johnny Hugh, "that duck has taken all the bread from the little ones!"

"Then throw one piece to her, and all the rest to the others," advised Sir Walter gravely. "He is fast as Ben Lomond, I believe, Lockhart. And now, since Mamma and Anne did not know what my errand was, I thought it well to breakfast here, and set Sophia and you at your ease before I went home again."

Lockhart was relieved, yet troubled, by the visit. Though later reports contradicted the rumour that Constable's banker had "thrown up his book", yet the anxiety which the report had caused Sir Walter gave Lockhart the first inklings that such a disaster might involve him in more than the loss of the profits on a single novel.

S on afterwards, John Murray sent the Editor-elect of the *Quarterly Review* a transcript of Lord Byron's *Ravenna Diary*, with permission to show it to Sir Walter. The spontaneous entries made a great impression on him. Byron wrote as he might have talked to his most intimate friend, Sir Walter thought. As he himself might, in fact, have talked to Will Erskine. But now Will Erskine had gone, and there was nobody to whom he could talk in just that way. Like Byron, he would keep a *Journal*. With that intention, and the most dogged confidence in his publisher's stability, he drove up to Edinburgh with Charlotte and Anne, for the opening of the autumn session at the Law Courts, in November 1825.

And yet, at the same time, he was instinctively uneasy. He decided to look in on Constable at his elegant new premises in Princes Street, just to see how things were going, on his way to Parliament House. But he found Cadell, not Constable, behind the managerial desk. Cadell did the honours graciously. A chair? A cigar? What news of *Napoleon*?

"What news of Constable?" Sir Walter demanded bluntly.

"He did not come in from Polton this morning, Sir Walter. I. understand he has an attack of the gout."

"Gout?" Sir Walter spoke sharply. "He may well suffer from

worse than gout if he dallies at Polton with things so unsettled in London. What news have you of Hurst and Robinson?"

"None," Cadell admitted. "I must say, I myself have been uneasy."

"And with reason, I believe. My son-in-law brought most disturbing reports from London."

Cadell was alert at once. "Mr Constable is aware of this?"

"I tackled him with it at once. He denied roundly that anything was amiss. But that was three weeks ago, and I have heard worse since. If Hurst and Robinson go down – "

"The house of Constable must follow," Cadell agreed. "Sir Walter, I will have a letter sent out to Polton at once, requesting Mr Constable to acquaint me with the latest position of Hurst and Robinson's affairs. My messenger will wait for his answer."

"I am much obliged to you," said Sir Walter, as he rose to go.

That evening Cadell called at Castle Street with reassuring news. Constable had denied, with scourging quill-strokes, that Hurst and Robinson were in trouble. The London money market was certainly in poor shape, but his agents would undoubtedly weather the storm. Sir Walter let himself believe him, and slept better for it. But four days later he learned more of the true situation from Constable himself, who had joined his partner in Edinburgh, hobbling on sticks, in obvious agony, but apparently frank and courageous. He admitted that Hurst and Robinson had been in trouble – few London commercial concerns had not – but while their associates supported them they had every chance of winning through.

"As I see it, we have no choice in the matter. For our own sake, we must support them now."

"I agree," Sir Walter said.

Cadell nodded, silently.

They discussed ways and means of borrowing money for the London firm's benefit. Constable's hopes were high, and Sir Walter's rose with them. He even agreed, though reluctantly, to execute a £10,000 mortgage on Abbotsford, as Constable, prompted by Cadell, suggested. If it seemed necessary, Constable undertook to go to London, but he would naturally prefer to avoid such a journey, in mid-winter, while matters seemed likely to right themselves there without him.

Sir Walter went home with a somewhat easier mind. But he made out a list of drastic personal economies in his *Journal*. Sophia and Lockhart with little Johnny came to stay before setting off for London, where Lockhart had found furnished rooms in Pall Mall, and Lockhart learned enough of his father-in-law's position, as the only moneyed partner in James Ballantyne's printing firm, to realise just how serious the consequence of Constable's bankruptcy would be for him.

On the 5th of December, the Lockharts set out for London, very early in the morning, in order to avoid the anguish of saying goodbye. Sir Walter came downstairs about eight o'clock to find them gone. "This was very right," he entered in his *Journal*. "I hate red eyes and blowing of noses . . . Of all schools, commend me to the Stoics."

He sat down to work on *Napoleon*, sustained by the conviction that the financial crisis had blown over. But it had, in fact, only just begun. In the middle of December, one of London's great private banks closed its doors, and a new panic blew up in the City. On the 18th, James Ballantyne brought the news that Hurst and Robinson were bankrupt. This was the end. For the inevitable chain-reaction would drag Constable after them. And if Constable went, the Ballantyne firm must follow. There was nothing they could do to avert the landslide. After James had taken a sombre leave of his partner, Sir Walter sat for a while alone in his study while the full implications of the disaster overwhelmed him.

His wife and children would be safe. Charlotte had her own settlement. But Abbotsford . . . and all those who so confidently depended on him there . . . Tom Purdie, Willie Laidlaw . . . his dogs. Tears filled his eyes as he thought of their absolute trust. He must find them, at least, kind masters. But the news would make sad hearts at Darnick, and his little hamlet of Abbotstown. James Ballantyne, too. At last he braced himself to go upstairs and break the news to Charlotte.

He could hear Anne singing as he climbed the stairs. The sound heartened him, for *The Bonnie House o' Airlie* was one of his favourite Scottish songs, and he guessed that the good girl was practising for his sake, since her own taste ran to more highfalutin' Italian or German music. But now that Sophia had left for London, he missed his Border ballads. So Anne had noticed it? In spite of everything, he was smiling as he opened the door.

Charlotte, on the chaise longue which had been drawn into its winter position beside the fire, was inattentively sorting embroidery silks. The corners of her mouth were turned down, and she looked quite disagreeable.

"Ah, Sir Walter," she said, with a little bow, "so you are to honour us zis evening wis your company? Zat is a *great* surprise."

"I have something to tell you, my love," said her husband heavily.

Anne lifted her hands from the keys. "Shall I go, Papa?"

Sir Walter sat down in the armchair on the other side of the fire. "No, my dear. You must stay. This concerns us all."

"It is bad news," said Charlotte decisively, as Anne came to perch on the other end of the chaise longue. "I feel it – here." Her voice was breathless, her hand on her heart.

"I fear you are right," Sir Walter said flatly.

"Zen speak! I can endure anything – but anything – except suspense."

"I have just learned," said Sir Walter tonelessly, "that Constable's London agents have gone bankrupt. Their failure must drag down Constable. And if he goes, Ballantyne must go too. Since I am a partner in Ballantyne's firm – "

"You, too, are ruined," said Charlotte shrilly.

"I fear so," Sir Walter agreed.

The basket of vivid silks tumbled to the carpet as Charlotte flung up her hands in a gesture of despair. "I knew it! Always your grand plans, your wild extravagance! Why could we not remain in our little cottage where we were so happy? So we are to be beggared? I have only one thing to say. It is all your fault."

Her husband sat silent, his hands clasped loosely between his knees, his head bowed.

"Oh, Mamma," Anne cried anxiously, "do not blame Papa! It will be an adventure!"

"I do not feel well enough for adventures," said Charlotte forlornly. Her breath came in gasps, her colour was patchy. "Never did I suppose – " Her head fell back on her cushions.

"I will send a servant for the doctor," said Sir Walter, rising.

"No, Papa," said Anne quietly. "I have the doctor's draught. Stay with her while I mix it."

It was impossible to assess the gravity of the attack, which was soon over. But Sir Walter went to bed with the conviction that his misfortunes might well kill his wife.

Late that night he wrote in his *Journal* that the feast of fancy was over. "I can no longer have the delight of waking in the morning with bright ideas in my mind, hasten to commit them to paper, and count them monthly as the means of planting such groves and purchasing such wastes." Abbotsford, Abbotsford, Abbotsford! What was to become of his "romance in stone and lime?"

But before he went to bed Cadell came round with the news that Hurst and Robinson were not yet beaten after all. In the morning James Ballantyne arrived before breakfast to confirm this, and Constable himself drove up in style shortly afterwards with additional reassurance. It was all so different from the mood of the day before that Sir Walter felt almost crazy with happiness, as he wrote a few verses to the familiar tune of *Bonnie Dundee*. He was declaiming them as he limped upstairs to tell Charlotte, who was breakfasting in bed.

> "*Come fill up my cup, come fill up my can,*
>   *Come saddle your horses, and call up your men;*
>   *Come open the West Port and let me gang free,*
>   *And its room for the bonnets of Bonnie Dundee!*"

Charlotte put down her cup of chocolate and stared at him with frightened, dark-ringed eyes. Had her husband's misfortunes already unsettled his wits?

Laughing, Sir Walter guessed it. "No, no, I am still in my right mind, and happy to be bearer of better news. Lady Scott, I take pleasure to inform you that it seems we are not reduced to bread-and-water after all. Constable, Cadell and Ballantyne have all been here to say that Hurst and Robinson have weathered the storm."

"Well, indeed, Scott," Charlotte said tartly, "I sink you men should all show better sense. First you frighten me next to death, then you say dere is nossing to fear – "

"Forgive me, dearest. But I was frightened next to death, too," Sir Walter said, smiling. "Oh, I all but forgot – " He hunted through the pockets of the formal black suit which he wore as a Clerk of Session – "Lockhart writes that the journey went well. They are comfortably settled, he assures me, and will write of the state of the money market in his next."

"Never do I wish," said Charlotte, as she held out her hand for the letter, "to hear of money-markets again."

"Nor do I, my love," said Sir Walter. "Now I must be off to Parliament House." He stooped to kiss her, purloined a fragment of toast from her tray, and went out of the room, singing *Bonnie Dundee*.

He was coming home early, these days, as often as possible, to do a good evening's work on *Napoleon*. One never knew, after a scare such as they had all just had, how soon it would be wanted. And he was enjoying himself. "I think it comes off twangingly," he wrote in his *Journal*. "The story is so very interesting in itself, that there is no fear of the book answering. Superficial it must be . . ."

He even composed a few more verses of *Bonnie Dundee*, though later, surprised at himself, he wrote in his *Journal*, "can't say what made me take a frisk so uncommon of late years as to write verses of free-will. I suppose the same impulse which makes birds sing when the storm has blown over."

They all drove down to Abbotsford on Christmas Eve, to spend a much quieter vacation than the year before. But the contrast with the dreadful anxiety of the past weeks was so great that Sir Walter was lighthearted, as he greeted Willie Laidlaw and listened to Tom Purdie's trenchantly expressed opinions on what should be done in the plantations. On Christmas Day Sir Walter noted in his *Journal*

"On this day of general devotion I have a particular call for gratitude."

But as January, 1826, began, Lockhart's letters from London again sounded a note of warning, and the old cat-and-mouse game began once more. What was Constable doing? If he had gone to London as he had promised, there should have been news of his success by now. Yet Lockhart wrote that Hurst and Robinson were in worse trouble than ever. And Constable was still at Polton. He had already executed the mortgage on Abbotsford, which the terms of young Walter's marriage settlement allowed him to do, and put it at Constable's disposal. Now he was working steadily on *Napoleon* and *Woodstock*: when these were done another £12,000 should be forthcoming. Surely, in the end, all would be well?

The anxiety, however, had told on his health, and he had been obliged to resort to calomel again, which worked its usual disagreeable magic. The first days of the year were crisp and hard. James Skene brought his wife to stay, which took his mind off money troubles. But on the 5th of January he noted an ominous experience in his *Journal*:

"Much alarmed. I had walked till twelve with Skene and Russell, and then sat down to my work. To my horror and surprise I could neither write nor spell, but put down one word for another, and wrote nonsense. I was much overpowered at the same time, and could not conceive the reason. I fell asleep, however, in my chair, and slept for two hours."

Later, he comforted himself with the explanation that he had taken an opiate left by the doctor the night before, and not slept it off properly. True enough. And yet the memory lingered.

It was not till the middle of January that he heard from Constable, and then only to say that he was setting off in haste for London. Sir Walter was astounded. The man should have been there long ago. Now ten to one it was already too late. "It strikes me," he wrote in his *Journal* on the 14th of January, "to be that sort of letter which I have seen men write when they are desirous that their disagreeable intelligence should be rather apprehended than expressed."

The snow muffled all sound, almost all thought. The water in

Sir Walter's dressing-room was frozen to flint, but he trudged along the woodland paths, his hand heavy on Tom Purdie's shoulder as he listened to his shrewd humorous talk of sheep, and markets, and weather prospects, and felt reassured by the sheer sterling goodness of the man who was less a servant than a friend.

Next day, the 17th of January, Peter Mathieson drove the Scotts back to Edinburgh. Among the letters waiting at Castle Street was one which he had, oddly enough, known would be there. It was from Cadell. That night Sir Walter wrote in his *Journal*: "Came through cold roads to as cold news. Hurst and Robinson have suffered a bill to come back upon Constable, which, I suppose, infers the ruin of both houses. We shall soon see."

James Ballantyne was on the doorstep first thing next morning. In the midst of his own anxiety, Sir Walter was distressed for him. He was stoically prepared to accept the consequences of a disaster which he could not avert. It was hard, after having fought such a battle. But the question was now what to do next.

"Bear up, James, all is not lost yet."

"As near as may be, I doubt," said James sombrely.

"Havers, man. Mair were lost at Sheriffmuir. I must first see Cadell. What next? Take legal opinion, of course. I believe the best action would be to form a trust for the execution of my obligations."

"I'm with ye there," agreed James Ballantyne.

"Depend upon it, James, we'll warstle through. I'll never forsake you," said Sir Walter, as James Ballantyne turned sadly towards the door.

During the following days offers of help poured in, first from his friends, and then from his legal colleagues, as news of his association with Constable's bankruptcy spread. James Skene came next, summoned to Castle Street by an urgent request, delivered by a servant, to call on Sir Walter on his way to Court. Greatly surprised, since Sir Walter had been dining with him only the evening before, Skene found Sir Walter in his study, apparently already at work by candlelight.

His old friend rose to greet him. "Give me your hand, James," said Sir Walter, who saw no reason to deny himself the consolation of a dramatic flourish. "Mine is that of a beggar!"

"What in the world is this?" Skene demanded in bewilderment. As Sir Walter explained, his first thought was only of how much money he could raise. But Sir Walter waved his offer aside, as he was to wave all others.

"I just need to have warmhearted folk about me for a while," he said, with an apologetic little gesture. "We can leave money matters to those that understand money's ways."

Letters came next, from Constable, who sounded quite distracted, from Hurst and Robinson, who said they were determined to pay everybody, and added in a postscript that had Constable been in London ten days sooner, all would have been well, and from Lockhart, who had seen Constable on his belated arrival in London, and now reported with indignation the publisher's wild suggestions that Lockhart should drive with him to the Bank of England, and support his request, as a friend of the author of *Waverley*, for a loan of £100,000 or even £200,000, on the security of the author's copyrights which he held. Alternatively, he pressed Lockhart to ask Sir Walter to borrow £20,000 in Edinburgh and send it at once to him in London. It was scarcely necessary to add, Lockhart wrote, that he had refused anything of the sort without consulting his father-in-law, to Constable's rage and dismay.

The support of his friends during these desolate January days astounded him. And, as the dust began to settle after the fall of the three business houses which had dragged each other down in ruin, he needed all the comfort that their loyal support could give.

For it seemed at first as if everything must go. The Bank of Scotland, as Ballantyne's largest creditors, saw at first no way of getting any of their clients' money back except by taking everything Sir Walter had, including all proceeds of the books on which he was still working, *Napoleon* and *Woodstock*, and taking legal proceedings to set aside the marriage settlement made the year before, so that they could claim Abbotsford.

The prospect of this shook Sir Walter as nothing else had been able to do. It hardened his heart, once and for all, against Constable, who had refused to admit the danger until it was too late to mend it, urged him into a futile mortgage, remained inactive when he should have intervened, and made outrageous demands on him for saving a situation which was already lost. He had nothing but praise for the stoicism with which James Ballantyne had accepted the disaster, arranged to move to a smaller house and give up all his little indulgences. He was pleased to think that Cadell, who had consulted him and kept him constantly informed, still considered him an author to be reckoned with. That Cadell might regard him as a means to rebuild his own fortunes did not occur to him. But on the blustering, bombastic, sorely stricken Constable he had, for once, no mercy.

Constable, back from London, came to Castle Street towards the end of January, and tried to assume, in the face of Sir Walter's coldness, that they had weathered so many storms together in their time, that they would come through this one, too. He was shocked to hear that Sir Walter considered his unfinished books to be his own property, most anxious to be assured that he could count on Sir Walter's co-operation in the business he intended to rebuild, and appalled to realise that now he had broken with his partner, his most distinguished author intended to go with Cadell. He was weary, despondent, broken in health. But he made one more effort.

"Come, come, Sir Walter," he said, with a ghastly parody of his old jovial smile, "matters may come round, and I trust that you and I may yet crack a cheerful bottle of port together at Abbotsford."

The last word finished his hopes with the man who saw himself about to lose his dearest possession. "Mr Constable," said Sir Walter coldly, "whether we ever meet again in these conditions must depend on circumstances which yet remain to be cleared up." He rose, and limped across his study to open the door.

And yet, in the end, he was not to lose Abbotsford. His trustees – led by Sir William Forbes, head of one of the great private banking houses in Edinburgh, were deeply impressed by his determination to pay, given time, every penny of the Ballantyne debt, which he candidly recognised to be largely his own. The Bank of Scotland withdrew its claims on their recommendations, Sir Walter settled down doggedly to complete the *Life of Napoleon* and *Woodstock*, and came to an arrangement with Cadell for their publication. Willie Laidlaw was summoned from Kaeside to meet the trustees, drastic economies planned for Abbotsford, and the sale of 39 Castle Street agreed. Though it was a dark time, with Charlotte distracted when the prospect of leaving 39 Castle Street brought the disaster really home to her, yet there were compensations, too.

Sir Walter had dreaded his first day back at the Clerks' Table, imagining himself stared at with contempt, or dismissed with a few words of pity. Instead, he found himself surrounded by men who could find no words to express their sympathy, but paused in silence to shake his hand.

Offers of help continued to pour in. From Ireland, his daughter-in-law wrote to offer her fortune. Sophia and Anne's music instructor, Mr Pole, offered his life savings of £600. An anxious letter came from Lord Montagu and championship from J. B. S. Morritt in Yorkshire, who reported a friend's indignation at Sir Walter's predicament. "Good God, let every man to whom he has given months of delight give him a sixpence, and he will rise tomorrow morning richer than Rothschild." There was talk of a national subscription, an offer of £30,000 from a reader he had never met. He declined them all, graciously but unhesitantly.

"My own right hand shall pay my debt," he declared, like one of his swashbuckling Border heroes. And he had no intention of pulling a long face about it. Nor was he vindictive against Constable, though he had declared their association at an end. "While I live," he wrote to Lockhart, "I shall regret the downfall of Constable's house, for never did there exist so intelligent and liberal an establishment . . . My dear Lockhart, I am as calm and temperate as you ever saw me, and working on *Woodstock* like a very tiger."

To Laidlaw, he wrote requesting him to come to Edinburgh and discuss the necessary economies at Abbotsford, adding: "For myself, I feel like the Eildon hills – quite firm, though a little cloudy." Only to his *Journal*, with its neat lock and key to be carried on his watch-chain, did he ever admit that there were times when he was very near despair.

On the 14th of February, a FOR SALE notice appeared outside 39 Castle Street. House and furniture were to be sold by the trustees as soon as the family had gone to Abbotsford in March. Charlotte, who had at first wept and reproached him, scarcely seemed to notice it. He insisted that she should see the doctor again.

Meanwhile, he found a vent for all his pent-up exasperation by writing a series of *Letters of Malachi Malagrowther* for Blackwood, who was delighted to have anything as inflammable as nationalist propaganda against the decision of Parliament at Westminster to deprive private banks, including those north of the Border, of their cherished privilege of issuing their own notes. The *Letters* were nationalistic and pungent enough to cause great offence in Ministerial circles. But Sir Walter did not care. He felt that his creditors, the Scottish bankers, had been both patient and generous, and it gave him pleasure to strike a blow in their defence.

In Castle Street the dreary business of dismembering their home began. Books were crated, pictures taken from the walls, trunks packed. Charlotte was apparently indifferent, Anne inarticulate, Sir Walter distressed beyond bearing. The distance they had drifted insensibly apart was underlined by the entry in his *Journal*: "I am glad Lady S. does not mind it, and yet I wonder, too. She insists on my remaining till Wednesday, not knowing what I suffer."

The Courts rose on the 11th of March, and he would have liked to go at once. But she seemed determined to linger. There were things she wished to do, people she wanted to see, small treasures she must pack. Sir Walter made the excuse of going on ahead by coach to prepare the Abbotsford household for their arrival.

"*Ha til mi tulidh*," he quoted from the Gaelic lament as he closed the door behind him. "I return no more."

Chapter 20

SIR WALTER stood before the fly-blown mirror in the front bedroom of the furnished house in Walker Street which he had taken the previous autumn, adjusting the black cravat with unusual care. It was the evening of the 23rd of February, 1827, and he was going out to take the chair at the first public function he had attended since his troubles, the dinner organised by the Manager of the Edinburgh Theatre in aid of impoverished and aged actors. His affection for Daniel Terry, the Siddons, the Kembles and many other theatrical friends had made it hard to make excuses, but he still felt himself branded by the financial failures of the previous years, and he wished, as he dressed for the occasion, that he had refused.

This place he had rented, for instance, because he could not leave Anne alone with only the servants at Abbotsford during the legal terms, what a sad come-down it was from their home in Castle Street. It smelt of mice and damp, in spite of all the traps Dalgleish put down and the coal fire he had lighted in the rusty grate. But it was a deal better than Mrs Brown's wretched lodgings, where he had spent the first summer term after putting 39 Castle Street up for sale. He could scarcely have taken Anne there. But Dalgleish had begged, with tears in his eyes, to share his exile, insisting that the Shirra could not be left to fend for himself in sic a like spot. "It's not to be thought on," Dalgleish had insisted. "John Nicholson's trained up well, and can do all that's needed at Abbotsford nowadays, for Miss Anne and the ither Miss Scott that's keeping her company over the summer, now that . . ." He lowered his voice lugubriously, "now that her Leddyship's nae mair."

Sir Walter flinched at the mention of Charlotte's death. She had seemed to live so little, during the last desolate weeks in Castle Street, to be so indifferent to the sale of all the once-cherished pieces of furniture, the pictures, the pretty things which marked this anniversary or that throughout their married life, that he had come to take her complete inertia, even at Abbotsford, for granted. And so, when the spring term began, he had returned to his miserable lodgings in Edinburgh, without anticipation of any sudden change. Dalgleish had indomitably come with him to Mrs Brown's sordid premises, championed him against all adversaries, determined to serve Sir Walter's meals as if he had been sitting at the head of his beautiful dining-table, instead of in the dark and dingy parlour which smelt of damp and cats. He had cared for Sir Walter's clothes, brushed his shoes, kindled his fire and gone down to the basement in the evenings when his master was working late, to eat kippers and drink porter with Mrs Brown in her subterranean kitchen and talk of the glories of Abbotsford.

Then, four days after their arrival in Edinburgh, news came from Abbotsford that Charlotte had failed to recover from an attack of cardiac asthma. And Sir Walter's dogged stoicism went down before an obliterating wave of grief and memory. She was no longer the peevish "Lady S" whom it was almost impossible to please, but his Charlotte, the dearest girl who had exulted with him over his early triumphs so gallantly.

He sighed as he put on the black coat which Dalgleish had carefully laid out after Celia, Anne's maid, had pressed it, wondering whether the light waistcoat he was wearing, so as not to look too much of a crow at a theatrical dinner, was ill-chosen. After all, it was not yet a year since poor Charlotte's death.

But what a year it had been, he thought, as he stood with an elbow on the mantelpiece, looking down at the sinking flames. Anne, bless her heart, had been quite worn out with grief after nursing her mother, and he had been thankful that her cousin, the other Anne Scott, had been able to stay at Abbotsford till the Courts rose in July, and released him to return to the country. He thought it had comforted her a little to go with him to London before the winter term began, most economically, of course, but also urgently, since he must check all available records, verify a number of points with the Duke of Wellington, before going on to Paris for final researches on *Napoleon*.

It had certainly done them both good to stay with the Lockharts in their pleasant home in Sussex Place, overlooking Regent's Park, and admire the new baby, Walter Scott Lockhart, who had been born less than a month before poor Charlotte's death. But Johnny Hugh had been ill again, and Anne had gone with Sophia when she took him to Brighton for the sea air. Afterwards, he and Anne had gone on to Paris, where their reception had been almost as phenomenal as the Dublin triumph. All the excitement of celebrity had brought a little colour to the good girl's cheeks. She had enjoyed the visit to Oxford, too, on the way home. More, actually, than he had. It had been grand to be entertained so splendidly by Charles in his rooms at Brasenose, of course. But, somehow, he had not been able to recall the ardour of his earlier enthusiasm. The place was beautiful as ever, of course, but the urgent youth of young men who clattered up and down the hollowed stairs made him feel old, and he was reminded of poor Charlotte at every turn. Camp, too, of course, chasing the college cat across the lordly lawns of Trinity . . . He sighed.

Sir Walter had all the warm-hearted extrovert's aversion from the idea of death. Those whom it overtook were its victims. He thought and spoke of them invariably as such. "Poor Byron . . . poor Will Erskine, and poor, poor Charlotte . . ."

But such melancholy reflections, he told himself, as he turned from the mantelpiece and limped towards the door, would not do. He had a difficult evening before him, and the sooner old Dalgleish found him a sedan chair, which would save his white silk stockings from being splashed on the way to the Theatrical Club's dinner, the better it would be.

Anne, who was entertaining a girlhood friend for the evening, called gaily from the drawing-room as he passed. "You look most magnificent, Papa. I hope they give you a good dinner."

"So do I," said Sir Walter, rather gloomily.

On his arrival, he was surprised to be taken aside by Lord Meadowbank, one of his supporters at the high table, who had been deputed at short notice to propose his health. As an old friend at the Law Courts, he knew very well that this was the first time Sir

Walter had appeared in public since things had all gone wrong for him, and was determined to take the opportunity of convincing him of the universal admiration of his contemporaries.

"Look here, Sir Walter," he said earnestly, "you know I have the task of proposing your health. I trust you will not think me indelicate if I make a distinct reference to the parentage of the Waverley Novels? After all, considering what has passed, you must admit that the matter is scarcely any longer in doubt?"

Sir Walter smiled. He, too, felt that the mystification had more than run its course. "Do just as you like, my lord. But I beg you will not make too much about so old a story."

The dinner, at which about three hundred people were present, went well, for Sir Walter was an experienced chairman, and once he was launched on the duties he had carried out so many times, his nervousness left him. The entertainment was lavish, the guests mellow, when Lord Meadowbank rose benignly.

"Gentlemen," he said, almost confidentially, as he looked round the crowded hall with a little, secret smile, "I would beg leave to propose a toast – the health of one of our Patrons – a great and distinguished individual, whose name must always stand by itself, and which, in an assembly such as this, or in any other assembly of Scotsmen, must ever be received, I will not say with ordinary feelings of pleasure or delight but with those of rapture and enthusiasm . . ."

His audience was intrigued. Heads turned this way and that, as they speculated as to which of the distinguished figures confronting them best fitted this description. Lord Meadowbank went on to intrigue them further, by enlarging on the difficulties of speaking in this way without intruding on the modesty of the great individual to whom he referred. Light was breaking now. His audience, warming to the drama, exchanged smiles and glances, as Lord Meadowbank approached his peroration.

"The clouds have been dispelled," he declaimed, "*the darkness visible* has been cleared away – and the Great Unknown – the minstrel of our native land – the mighty magician who has rolled back the current of time . . ."

Men were getting up, waving their glasses, drumming their feet or pounding on the tables. Sir Walter sat very still, looking down at his plate, twirling the stem of his wine glass in a nervous hand.

"And conjured up before our living senses the men and the manners of days which have long passed away, stands revealed to the eyes and the hearts of his affectionate and admiring countrymen."

The rumble of applause prevented him from going on. Then a tense silence fell, as Lord Meadowbank glanced briefly at his neighbour, and continued:

"Knowing, as I well do, that this illustrious individual is not more distinguished for his towering talents, than for those feelings which render such allusions ungrateful to himself, however sparingly introduced, I would on that account still refrain – "

Cries of "No, no!" drowned his words, as enthusiasm mounted, so that for a time his voice went unheard, as his audience left their places, climbed on chairs, roared their delight.

"But this I hope I may be allowed to say," he went on when he could make himself heard, "we owe to him, as a people, a large and heavy debt of gratitude. He it is who has opened to foreigners the grand and characteristic beauties of our country."

His audience began to clap, to stamp, almost to mob the high table. Lord Meadowbank was aware that their enthusiasm could not be denied much longer. "He it is," he proclaimed, "who has conferred a new reputation on our national character, and bestowed on Scotland an imperishable name, were it only by her having given birth to himself. Gentlemen, I propose the health of Sir Walter Scott."

He had struck the very note for a generous-hearted, dramatically inclined audience. They drank the toast in a pandemonium of delight, shouting, clapping, and stamping their tribute to a man who had achieved so much, and was now engulfed in such a sea of troubles. It was several minutes before Sir Walter was able to rise and reply, in his deep, soft voice with the Border burr which was always most marked in moments of emotion.

"Gentlemen," he said, in a tone of mild surprise, "I certainly did not think, in coming here tonight, that I should have the task of acknowledging a secret which, considering that it was communicated to more than twenty people, has been remarkably well kept."

The friendly laughter that drowned his voice kept him standing for a couple of minutes. "I am now at the bar of my country," he went on at last, "and may be understood to be on trial before Lord Meadowbank as an offender . . ."

"No!" they roared.

"And so quietly did all those who were *airt and pairt* conduct themselves, that I am sure . . ." he paused to smile, "every impartial jury would bring in a verdict of *Not Proven*. I am willing, however, to plead *guilty* – nor shall I detain the Court by a long explanation why my confession has been so long deferred . . ."

Cheers and laughter drowned his voice. He was happy and at ease now, grasping the lapels of his coat as if it had been an advocate's gown, swinging a little from side to side as if he were addressing a jury, when they let him go on at last.

"Perhaps caprice might have a considerable share in the matter . . ."

"Aye, aye!" they roared.

"I mean, then, seriously to state that, when I say I am the author, I mean the total and undivided author. With the exception of quotations, there is not a single word that was not derived from myself, or suggested in the course of my reading. The wand is now broken, and the book buried . . ."

"Never! . . . We're just waiting on the next . . ."

Sir Walter held up his glass. "You will allow me further to say, with Prospero, it is your breath that has filled my sails, and to crave one single toast . . ."

So they drank the health of Bailie Nicol Jarvie, on the author of *Rob Roy*'s instructions, with such shouting and stamping and pounding of tables and clinking of glasses, that Sir Walter was able to sit unobtrusively down and accept hand-shakes and congratulations from Lord Meadowbank and the rest of the distinguished company at the high table, under cover of applause which, as Sir Walter remarked, Dominie Sampson would have called PRO – DI – GI – OUS!

The dramatic circumstances in which the Author of Waverley had revealed himself at last – though his identity had not really been in doubt for many years – caused a newspaper sensation on a national scale, at which Sir Walter merely chuckled. But the uproarious delight with which his confession had been received, the candid affection and confidence in his future achievements which his audience had shown, was the most reassuring thing that had happened since his troubles began. And, as Lord Meadowbank had intended, it gave him a glimpse of what he and his work could still mean to his shrewd, quick-tempered, sentimental countrymen.

And Sir Walter needed such reassurance. It was a long, dreary winter, with snow, rain and even fog on a London scale. He had a good deal of trouble with rheumatism, and found he could scarcely keep up with Will Clerk when they walked home from the Court together, chuckling over a further theatrical tribute extemporised the evening before in *High Life Below Stairs*.

" 'Who wrote Shakespeare?' one of the good ladies asked," Will Clerk quoted. "One said 'Ben Jonson' and another 'Finis'. 'You have it all wrong,' said another, quick as a flash, 'it is Sir Walter Scott; he confessed it at a public meeting the other night.' "

"They miss no tricks, those fellows," Sir Walter said. "I spent a very merry evening with them."

"You shall have another, if you will dine with me at Rose Court," Will Clerk promised. "We bachelors do ourselves well, you know. I shall choose pleasant company, if only I can wheedle you away from that vast work of yours. How is *Napoleon* faring these days?"

"Steadily, but not as fast as I could wish. Ballantyne now talks of nine volumes, when all I meant to produce was a mere pamphlet. But Cadell remains calm. And I shall soon have Boney tied up in St Helena."

"And we shall celebrate the event accordingly at Rose Court," Will Clerk said as they parted.

The dark tedium of the winter days was broken by a letter which arrived, entirely unexpectedly, from Goethe in Weimar, who had, perhaps, heard of Scott's misfortunes, and took the opportunity of a friend's return to Scotland to express his long-standing admiration for Sir Walter Scott's work, and his appreciation of what Sir Walter had done to bring his own writings to the attention of the Scottish nation.

The letter delighted Scott, when it had been deciphered. He answered it enthusiastically. And at the back of his mind he began to cherish the possibility that when he had completed the monumental task before him he might take a holiday, perhaps even pay homage to the greatest German literary figure of the age in person. But that could not be just yet, he told himself, as he settled down at his desk and hunted abstractedly among piles of books and sheaves of notes for his detested spectacles.

The Lockharts were constantly in his thoughts these days. The news of Johnny was sometimes better, sometimes worse. He missed the child extremely, and wished he could devise something likely to give him pleasure. But he must not let his mind wander till he had done his best with the Emperor. There seemed no end to it. He and Anne spent the spring vacation as usual at Abbotsford, and Tom Purdie was insistent that Sir Walter should have a pony to take the place of Sybil Grey. He knew of a quiet, steady beast, who would plod along even when his rider's attention was on other things. His chief recommendation had been, Tom admitted, his ability to take his rider home safely, even when dead drunk.

Much amused, Sir Walter agreed that such steadfastness was just what he required. The pony was a stout, undistinguished creature, dun-coloured, with black legs, mane and tail, no turn of speed, but a unique ability to anticipate every involuntary movement of his rider. He came to Abbotsford, was renamed Douce Davie, and carried Sir Walter wherever Tom Purdie thought he should go. The estate, these days, was sadly curtailed. The Fergusons were still at Huntly Burn, but Kaeside was in the hands of the trustees, and Willie Laidlaw living with relations in the Vale of Yarrow, though he rode over regularly to Abbotsford whenever Sir Walter was at home. Peter Mathieson, who now had fewer opportunities of taking the carriage out, filled in his time as ploughman on the in-by fields. Tom Purdie had no regrets for the departure of the livestock, since he much preferred to be Sir Walter's personal attendant, and in charge of the plantations. The kitchen staff had been reduced to a minimum, the farm had been given up and dairymaids were no longer needed, while John Nicholson was now the only manservant, apart from old Dalgleish, who still officiated in Edinburgh in term-time and pottered about Abbotsford in the vacations.

By mid-May, Scott and Anne were back in their Edinburgh lodgings with Dalgleish. Sir Walter was nearing the end of his gigantic Napoleonic labours at last, though the conclusion still eluded him, as the summit seems to retreat before the weary mountaineer. He wrote in his *Journal*:

June 3: Wrought hard. I thought I had but a trifle to do but new things cast up; we get beyond the Life however for I have killed him to-day . . ."

That week it was finished at last. He felt quite light-headed with relief. As he wrote in his *Journal*:

June 10: Rose with the odd consciousness of being free from my daily task. I have heard that the fish-women go to church of a Sunday with their creels new washed, and a few stones in them for ballast, just because they cannot walk steadily without their usual load. I feel something like them, and rather inclined to take up some light task, than to be altogether idle . . . A good thought came in my head to write Stories for little Johnny Lockhart from the History of Scotland, like those taken from the History of England. But I will not write mine quite so simply as Croker has done. I am persuaded both children and the lower class of readers hate books which are written *down* to their capacity . . ."

The same day that he finished *Napoleon* he began the first series of *Tales of a Grandfather*. He had chosen a good time for them. Johnny Lockhart was better, so much better that his mother ventured to bring her children north. They took lodgings at Portobello for the rest of the summer term, so that Johnny should enjoy the sea bathing, as another fragile child, his grandfather, had done half a century before. They spent the summer vacation at Chiefswood, and Johnny was well enough to sit on a quiet pony and pace with his grandfather along the lanes and through the now towering plantations, with the watchful Tom Purdie in attendance, as Sir Walter sketched out the stories he proposed to tell and noted the child's reaction. For Johnny was no yes-man, but a tragically intelligent child who lacked only the physical equipment to bear his ardent spirit. He disliked some of the instructive passages extremely, and said so in no uncertain terms. His grandfather chuckled, but adjusted the balance in accordance with his critic's wishes. And so much of the tenderness and joy with which he watched Johnny bob beside him on his docile little pony found its way into the book, that it went straight to the hearts of his readers, young or old. It was to be more successful than anything he had written since *Ivanhoe*.

Meanwhile, Cadell had brought out *Napoleon*, the printing of which was already well advanced by the time the last lines were written, in nine volumes, before the end of June. And half of the new series of *Chronicles of the Canongate*, a collection of short stories, had been already written by the time the vacation began. The success of *Napoleon* was startling. It pleased the general public so much, though critics, on the whole, ignored it, that it ultimately brought in £18,000 for Sir Walter's Trustees. And the relief from the unfamiliar work of biographical research was so great that he found time to throw off a paper on *The Planting of Waste Lands* for Lockhart, as editor of *The Quarterly Review*, which was inspired by love of another sort, for the woodlands of Abbotsford.

In July the news of the death of Archibald Constable offered Cadell another opportunity to repair the damage caused by the Hurst and Robinson disaster, and establish himself as the publisher of Sir Walter Scott. In the crisis he had thrown his lot in with Sir Walter for reasons of his own; now he showed himself to be a shrewd man of business, and so far Sir Walter's interests matched his. The copyrights of all Sir Walter's earlier works, which Constable held, were to be offered for sale that winter. If they could be secured, Cadell would be in a position to bring out a complete new edition of the Waverley Novels, with a general introduction and prefaces by the author, which he believed would do very well indeed. Sir Walter agreed, Cadell acted accordingly, and by the end of 1827 the copyrights were purchased at a cost of £8,500, borne equally by Sir Walter and Cadell.

Sir Walter had now had enough of the Walker Street lodgings, so next term he rented a furnished house in Shandwick Place, where he and Anne, attended by the faithful Dalgleish, Anne's maid, Celia, and the essential cook and kitchen maid, would be more comfortable, now that he had been encouraged by Cadell's assurance that he would have earned his Trustees something like £40,000 between January, 1826, and January, 1828, to feel that he could afford something better than comfortless lodgings. And since his Trustees had allowed him to retain his salaries as a Clerk of Session and Sheriff of Selkirkshire, he could afford to meet such expenses.

The new year, 1828, began well, with news of the birth of Sophia's third child, christened Charlotte Harriet Jane, in London; and an urgent call from the booksellers for second editions both of *Napoleon* and *Tales of a Grandfather*. So great was the clamour that the booksellers suggested that the printing should be shared by several firms in case Ballantyne could not meet their demands. James went anxiously to Sir Walter, who wrote at once from Abbotsford to Cadell.

"My dear Sir,

"I find our friend James Ballantyne is very anxious about printing the new edition of the *Tales*, which I hope you will allow him to do, unless extreme haste be an extreme object. I need not remind you that we three are like the shipwrecked crew of a vessel, cast upon a desolate island, and fitting up out of the remains of a gallant bark such a cock-boat as may transport us to some more hospitable shore . . ."

James Ballantyne did the printing as usual.

By the end of the spring term Sir Walter had finished *The Fair Maid of Perth*, the Second Series of *Chronicles of the Canongate*, and begun the Second Series of *Tales of a Grandfather*. It had meant steady concentration, writing early and late, but the weather had been dreary and his health indifferent, so he had been thankful to have something to take his mind off his rheumatism and occasional biliousness. Once the manuscript was safely in James Ballantyne's hands, he had promised Anne a treat. They would both spend the spring vacation in London, staying with the Lockharts, for young Walter's regiment had been recently posted to Hampton Court, and Charles, who had come down from Oxford the summer before, had recently taken his desk at the Foreign Office, and was living in Sussex Place with the Lockharts. It should have been a triumphant, happy time, but London's winter fogs had been too much for Johnny. To Sir Walter's grievous disappointment, Sophia had to take him to Brighton again, and Anne went with her, leaving Lockhart to entertain his father-in-law. It was not a heavy task, for Sir Walter was in greater demand than ever, breakfasting and dining with old friends and new, sitting for another portrait, visiting Chantrey the sculptor again, trying to advise Daniel Terry, whose speculation over the Adelphi Theatre was ending in disaster, making happy excursions to Hampton Court and seeing as much as possible of Charles.

Before the London visit ended, Sir Walter was commanded to a private dinner party by King George IV, and to Holland House by the Duchess of Kent, where he was warmly greeted by Prince Leopold, and presented to little Princess Victoria. "I hope they will change her name," he wrote in his *Journal*.

By the end of May, Sir Walter and Anne were on their way north again, breaking the journey with Mr Morritt at Rokeby, and spending a few days at Abbotsford before moving on to Edinburgh for the beginning of the summer term at the Law Courts.

At dinner, the first evening in Shandwick Place, Anne found her father surveying her somewhat ruefully across the table.

"I fear, my love," he said, catching her eye, "that there will be fewer junketings for us in the near future. It is sad work for you, after all our merry times, to be left with only an old curmudgeon like myself for company."

Anne's eyes filled with unexpected tears. "Dearest Papa, never say such a thing again," she said impulsively. "We have had so many wonderful times together, all of us. How shall I grudge you the time you must give to your writing now? After all, I have many friends in Edinburgh."

"Yes, I am glad of that," her father said. "For I have been very idle. Now I must make up for lost time."

"Yes, I know," Anne said. "And yet . . ."

"Yet what, my love?"

"Do not – do not drive yourself too hard," she said in a suddenly frightened voice.

Cadell had good news for Sir Walter next day. The Trustees had, after some deliberation, approved unconditionally the expenses associated with the publication of a new collected edition of the Waverley Novels, with notes and prefaces, besides all necessary embellishments and engravings. Sir Walter was able to report that his Majesty would be graciously pleased to accept the dedication.

"So the *Magnum Opus* goes forward," said Sir Walter with the greatest satisfaction. "Well, that should assist our affairs a little."

"I believe it will help them considerably," Cadell said, cheerfully.

"And I have the Second Series of the *Tales* to write, a new novel on my mind, and all the notes and prefaces to supply. It seems I shall not want for occupation."

"I have never known you to be in such a situation yet," Cadell said, smiling.

So Sir Walter began *Anne of Geierstein*, and with it a controversy with James Ballantyne which was to have far-reaching consequences for the two lifelong friends. James felt that Sir Walter was mistaken in his choice of a theme and said so from the first. He pointed out that Sir Walter's greatest successes in the Waverley Novels had been those set in the countryside he knew best. Sir Walter raised his bushy eyebrows. "What of *Ivanhoe*?"

"I grant you *Ivanhoe*. But this story will be set against a background of which you know nothing. It will be entirely derived from books – "

"So was *The Talisman*."

"But more of your readers know Switzerland in 1828 than could know Palestine in the time of the Crusades."

"Well, James," said Sir Walter, "you may be right. I know that you mean me well. I admit that I know nothing of Switzerland except what guide books can tell me. But I know mountains, and the people who live among them. And I believe I can tell a tale of star-crossed lovers as well as ever I did. Does that convince you?"

"It does not," said honest James Ballantyne.

There was no more to be said. James went to see Cadell, in a state of considerable anxiety. But Cadell was not to be stampeded into action.

"Let us see what he makes of it," he said.

The rest of the year passed quietly, with such an uneventful alternation of work, in Edinburgh and at Abbotsford, that Sir Walter had little or nothing to record in his *Journal*. He was delighted to hear from Sophia that Johnny was better, and the whole family hoped to spend the following summer at Chiefswood.

But the death of his chief trustee, Sir William Forbes, distressed him deeply, not only because of the generosity and kindness he had received in his recent financial troubles, but because of the many memories they shared, as young officers in the Edinburgh Light Dragoons, over a quarter of a century ago. How much did Sir William remember, he wondered, of their rivalry? Did he ever know how stricken Walter Scott had been when William Forbes married the lovely Williamina? Well, death settled all scores. And Sir William's brother, he understood, was to take on the office of Trustee.

He wrote to give Lockhart the news of Sir William's death in October, adding: "I am getting very unlocomotive – something like an old cabinet that looks well enough in its own corner, but will scarcely bear wheeling about, even to be dusted. But my work has been advancing gaily, or at least rapidly nevertheless, all this harvest . . ."

The letter made Sophia uneasy. London was very far away. Her father and Anne would be lonely when Christmas came round again. So Lockhart went north, making an excuse of the questions

Sir Walter had asked him about his affairs, and found his father-in-law well, except for his rheumatism, which he bitterly resented, but had undoubtedly brought on by falling in and out of the Tweed in his younger days, and never changing out of his wet clothes. Anne was delighted to see her brother-in-law, to whom she could talk freely about her hopes and fears for her father, and Lockhart was amused to find that Sir Walter had set his guests, Mr Morritt of Rokeby and Sir James Stuart of Allanbank, to read the proof sheets of *Anne of Geierstein* and tell him what they thought.

Fortunately, their verdict was favourable. Both Morritt and Stuart, who had travelled widely in Switzerland, found it hard to believe that his descriptions were the result of imagination, based on factual guide books, and their praise made the author, who had been more uneasy than he admitted after James Ballantyne's forthright criticism, feel very much better.

So when Sir James began to speak of the remarkable gifts of a young man called Greenshields, the son of a farmer on Lockhart's elder brother's estate in Lanarkshire, Sir Walter was ready to be interested.

John Greenshields had started as a stonemason, and accidentally discovered his gift of hewing out remarkable likenesses of people in stone. His work had already attracted the notice of Lord Elgin, who invited him to come and see him. But Greenshields abruptly broke of his examination of the marbles as soon as he heard that Sir Walter, who had gone with Lockhart to Lockhart's parental home in Lanarkshire, was not far away.

Sir Walter liked the shy boy who reminded him so much of Burns. But the voice was the voice of Tom Purdie. After their meeting he wrote to Lord Elgin, suggesting that the lad should be sent to study in London. But John Greenshields went away dreaming of the statue he wanted to make above all things, that of Sir Walter Scott.

That winter things were going wrong for honest James Ballantyne. His warm-hearted, sensible wife was taken ill in the middle of February, to poor James's utter distraction. On the 17th she died. James called to inform Sir Walter that he had named him, with

Cadell and two others, as his trustees, as if he hoped only to die too, and announced that he was taking his children into the country, somewhere near his native town of Kelso. Sir Walter was sincerely sympathetic but a trifle too bracing for the desolate husband. When he tried to recommend the Stoic philosophy which he himself had found invaluable, poor James, who was no Stoic, fled. And for some weeks he did not return to the printing house, in spite of Sir Walter's rousing letters. Rumour said that he had taken up with some extreme religious sect, become a rigid teetotaller and developed a morbid interest in all his minor ailments. Time, Sir Walter hoped, would mend that, as it mended most things. Meanwhile, the best thing he could do would be to finish *Anne of Geierstein*. It was exasperating to find writing made more difficult by chilblains – "a most babyish complaint!" as he wrote in his *Journal*.

Early in March Cadell brought excellent news of the *Magnum Opus*. The collected edition of the Waverley Novels was to appear at monthly intervals, a few volumes at a time, and a prospectus had just been issued to the trade which had already produced such a demand that the first edition would have to be increased from 7,000 to 12,000 copies. If this went on, and Cadell saw no reason why it should not, the end of their troubles – "this Pisgah prospect", as Sir Walter called it, rather wistfully – might be remotely in sight. So there was jubilation that evening, when Willie Laidlaw came to dine and make a report on the way things were going at Abbotsford.

"We'll have you back at Kaeside, Willie, before long," said Sir Walter cheerfully.

"What for no'?" Willie Laidlaw joyfully agreed.

A few days later, James Ballantyne broke silence with a letter expressing his utter disapproval of *Anne of Geierstein*. Sir Walter was appalled, since he had now nearly finished the third volume, and could not endure the prospect of having to do it all over again. But Cadell, when consulted, remained calm, and undertook to discuss the matter with James when he had had time to settle back to work. While he was still unable to face ordinary life again, it seemed likely that much of his criticism might be discounted.

Anne of Geierstein was finished before breakfast on the 29th of

April, and Sir Walter left the breakfast table to begin *The History of Scotland*, which he had promised to undertake for the proprietors of Dr Lardner's *Cyclopedia*. It would be pedestrian work, but at least it would bring £1,500 into the Trust. Cadell successfully overcame James Ballantyne's scruples about the novel's Swiss setting. The book was published later in the year and did as well as any of Sir Walter's later novels.

Now that the collected edition of the Waverley Novels was successfully launched, Cadell began to plan the parallel republication of an illustrated edition of the Poems. Sir Walter now held most of the necessary copyrights, and the few still held by Longmans Cadell was arranging to buy. But a quarter of the copyright of *Marmion* was still in the hands of John Murray, and in view of all that his publishing house had meant to Sir Walter in the early days, he felt that he should approach Murray personally now. He wrote to Lockhart, therefore, asking him to call at 50 Albemarle Street, and explain the situation.

The letter he received from John Murray was typical of the man he remembered.

"My dear Sir,
"Mr Lockhart has this moment communicated your letter respecting my fourth share of the copyright of *Marmion*. I have already been applied to by Messrs Constable and by Messrs Longmans, to know what sum I would sell this share for – but so highly do I estimate the honour of being, even in so small a degree, the publisher of the author of the poem – that no pecuniary consideration whatever can induce me to part with it.

"But there is a consideration of another kind, which until now I was not aware of, which could make it painful for me if I were to retain it a moment longer. I mean the knowledge of its being required by the author, into whose hands it was spontaneously resigned in the same instant that I read his request . . ."

Meanwhile, the sales of the *Magnum Opus* were soaring far beyond anything Sir Walter or Cadell could have hoped. During

1829, eight volumes were published, at monthly intervals, and monthly sales had climbed to 35,000 copies. There seemed no reason why the entire Ballantyne debt should not be extinguished, without much further effort on Sir Walter's part, in a very few years.

The summer vacation at Abbotsford glowed with returning hope. Sir Walter was busy with the notes and prefaces for later volumes, and the next in the series of *Tales of a Grandfather*. When autumn came, he felt free enough to jog out on Douce Davie and give Tom Purdie a hand, or at least his advice, on the necessary work on the plantations. October, even November, were months he specially enjoyed in the country, with the summer's brilliance mellowed, the hay and harvest safely carried, the trees still glorious in their metallic colouring of copper and bronze and gold.

He was tired in the evenings, but it mattered little. He always rose early, spent two or three hours at his desk, rode out among his splendid young trees with Tom Purdie at Douce Davie's side, and the young staghounds, Nimrod and Bran, pacing nobly ahead as old Maida had done, with a riot of terriers at their heels. As dusk came down they turned homewards, talking of the work done that day, arguing about the work to be done tomorrow.

Sometimes Sir Walter rode out earlier, and came home, invigorated by the exercise, to write letters during the afternoon. But always, the work and the companionship comforted him. And Tom had always got some story or other to make him laugh, so that he forgot the weariness that made him sag forward on Douce Davie's back like a forest tree which has endured a thousand storms but bows at last towards its fall.

One day in late October they came back early, well pleased with the morning's work. Tom went home for his dinner, and Sir Walter, after a brief respite, sat down at his desk for the afternoon. Several hours later he turned the dogs out of doors and strolled into the courtyard for a breath of fresh air before dinner.

"Shirra! Shirra!" The voice was familiar, the note strange. Sir Walter turned to see Mrs Purdie panting towards him, grey-streaked hair escaping from under her neatly goffered mutch, her apron trailing to the ground, one corner wet and muddy where she had trodden on it, her face patchily flushed.

"Oh, Shirra, it's Tom!" She broke off to get her breath.

"He left me in the highest spirits this morning," said Sir Walter anxiously. "He's not ill?"

"Na. He's – deid," said Mrs Purdie bleakly.

Chapter 21

FOR the first time since he and Tom Purdie had stood at the Turn Again stone, looking down on the Tweed and planning the conversion of the forlorn little farm which had not yet been called Abbotsford, Sir Walter was glad to return to Edinburgh in November. Abbotsford without Tom Purdie was like Olympus without Vulcan, the pawky, crooked smith of the gods. He heard the details later. Tom had come cheerfully home, eaten his dinner as usual, then laid his head down on his arms, just as he sat, for a nap. Some hours later his unnatural stillness had attracted the attention of his wife. He was only sixty-two years old.

Sir Walter had not recommended the Stoic philosophy to James Ballantyne without conviction. He returned to his work as Clerk of Session, reviewed Pitcairn's *Ancient Criminal Trials*, and wrote a number of *Essays on Ballad Poetry* for the collected edition of his poetical works, for which Mr Murray's generous letter had now left the way clear. But he was overtaxing his powers. One afternoon in February, 1830, he came back from the Parliament House, apparently in his usual state of uncertain, but determined, health. He spent half an hour with an old friend who had come from Hawick to show him some papers of great interest, then asked to be excused, tottered from his study to the drawing-room, and fell unconscious at Anne's feet.

It was a pattern which, during the next two years, was to be many times dreadfully repeated. On this first occasion, however, his speech and mobility returned within a few hours. The doctors reassured him. It was from the stomach. He agreed, but did not believe them. He had not forgotten his father's death. Nor the look in his mother's eyes, as she lay helpless in her George Street flat, with all her New Year gifts neatly parcelled in the drawing-room.

But as he recovered he worked on. He had promised a series of

Letters on Demonology and Witchcraft to John Murray, and planned a Fourth Series of *Tales of a Grandfather*, on French history, this time, for Johnny. He completed both, with the second volume of his *Scottish History* for Dr Lardner's *Cyclopedia*, and reviewed Southey's *Life of Bunyan* during the summer.

His work had once been a joy to him; sometimes latterly he had found it a burden. Now it had become a necessity. His passionate determination to clear off the Ballantyne debt was reinforced by the reassurance that the completion of each assignment brought him. While he could still knock off an essay, a review, or even a collection of stories for "Hugh Littlejohn", surely there could not be much wrong with his wits.

But the daily drudgery of the Clerks' Table had long taxed his patience, and he was not sorry when the question of reducing the numbers of Clerks from six to four, which had recently been brought up, gave him the opportunity of negotiating his retirement at the end of the summer term. True, his pension would only come to three-quarters of his salary, but he would be saved the expense of renting a house in Edinburgh. He would miss the old friends, and the old jokes, but the new men who were crowding in had no patience for either. He would not be so thrust aside by the country folk.

The Lockharts were at Chiefswood to welcome him home, Willie Laidlaw back at Kaeside, the Fergusons at Huntly Burn, and Swanson, the young forester whom Tom Purdie had trained, humbly doing all he could to render Sir Walter the same routine service, well aware that he could offer no more. So, after a fashion, life at Abbotsford followed the usual pattern of any summer vacation. The Lockhart children filled the great echoing rooms with noise again as they rolled about on the library carpet with Nimrod and Bran while their grandfather surveyed them benignly over the rims of his glasses as he sat at his desk. Anne arranged picnics, Sir Walter was hoisted on to Douce Davie in spite of his rheumatism to plod over to Chiefswood in the old way, to take Johnny out for a ride, and tell him the latest *Tale*. Little Walter was gay as a puppy, the baby, Charlotte, already enchanting. And Johnny –

"He's better. Don't you agree, Papa?" Sophia said, again and again.

"Yes, my love," her father said, with all the conviction he wanted to feel.

But as the summer passed, the undercurrent of anxiety disturbing Sir Walter's family grew stronger. For this time, the summer vacation, that blessed interlude between terms of routine work at Parliament House, would not end as the days darkened. Sir Walter's home would now be in the country all the year round. It was bitter to think that nothing would once have given him greater delight than to take part in the strenuous exhilarating occupations of the winter countryside, and now, when he was at last free to enjoy them, his disabilities totally prevented him from doing so.

"I am afraid for Papa," Anne admitted to Sophia and Lockhart one evening when Willie Laidlaw had dined at Abbotsford and was now writing to Sir Walter's dictation in the library. "When the weather is bad, and he cannot go out, what is he to do? You know very well that idleness drives him frantic."

"Surely," said Lockhart, "he has enough work to do for Mr Cadell on the prefaces for the *Magnum Opus* to keep him busy all winter."

"I hope so," said Anne uncertainly. "But you know his determination to pay off his debts. I believe he may be determined to write another book. And then he will get ill again. I know it. I know it . . ." She took her head in her hands.

"I will write to Cadell," said Lockhart, "and ask him to come down with the latest news of the sales of the *Magnum*. Surely that will show him there is no need for anxiety."

So Cadell came to Abbotsford, early in September, greatly troubled by Lockhart's report, and anxious to persuade Sir Walter that he had already done enough to ensure the ultimate repayment of his debt. The *Magnum Opus*, he assured him, was an outstanding success. By October the Ballantyne debt would have been reduced to a mere £60,000, less than half what it had once been. All Sir Walter need do now was to provide the *Prefaces* and notes, which no one else could write, and within a couple of years, he was confident, their present anxieties would be things of the past.

Unfortunately, his factual reassurance had the opposite effect from the one he had intended. What stuck in Sir Walter's mind was the formidable figure still outstanding, not the fact that it was less than half of the original liability. Too late, Cadell realised it.

"I must let you have something new," Sir Walter said.

"There is no great hurry for that," Cadell protested. "Meanwhile, I believe it would be useful if you could draw up a catalogue of all the most interesting and unusual objects which you have collected, over the years, at Abbotsford."

"I could do that," Sir Walter agreed. "Yes, I could well do that, with Willie Laidlaw's help. I will make a start tomorrow."

When they were told of the plan, Sophia and Anne were overjoyed. "*Dear* Mr Cadell, if it would not be unmaidenly, I should throw my arms round your neck and weep on your shoulder. You cannot know what a relief this promises," said Anne.

"My dear Miss Anne," said Cadell sadly, "I can well guess it. Believe me, I would not otherwise seek to humour so great a man."

Sir Walter began to dictate the record of his possessions next day. But the routine task did not hold his interest long. Within a week he had written to inform Cadell that he must work to better purpose. He had been turning over the story of *Count Robert of Paris* in his mind.

"What shall we do now?" Anne cried in despair.

"Wait and see how the book turns out," said Lockhart temperately.

So the first chapters of *Count Robert* were written and sent off, as usual, to James Ballantyne, who had now resumed control of the printing office, though sombrely different from his former self. He read through the manuscript pages, neatly inscribed by the uncritical Willie Laidlaw, with his bushy black eyebrows describing arcs of agitation. And since his recent emotional experiences had increased rather than diminished his acute sense of duty, he wrote to Sir Walter to protest that in his considered opinion, *Count Robert* was inferior to anything he had ever produced before.

The news came as a considerable shock. But James Ballantyne had been through an acute mental ordeal that year, Sir Walter remembered, and it was unlikely that he had altogether regained his critical faculties. Time would show, when he had more of the story before him. He wrote on, calling in Willie Laidlaw when his hands were too painful to take down scenes which he dictated, though not with the confidence of a man drawing on the unfailing stream of intuitive knowledge which flowed as surely as his beloved Tweed, far beneath his conscious understanding.

His dictation was erratic now, and he sometimes broke off in the middle of a sentence, looking round him in bewilderment for a phrase which his conscious mind could not provide. At the moment of his greatest need, though he did not yet know it, the river of his subconscious inspiration was running dry. Willie Laidlaw waited patiently, aware of a mortal weariness, not knowing what to do, distressed beyond bearing by a tragedy which he dimly realised. But the book grew, by fits and starts, urged into a shape which parodied the author's intention, by his heroic will. And every few days, chapters were dispatched to Edinburgh as usual, over which Cadell and James Ballantyne anxiously conferred.

"What I do not understand," Cadell said, "is why his letters are as alert, vigorous, even as amusing as ever. But this – " He let the latest sheets of *Count Robert* drift forlornly across his desk.

"I agree," said James Ballantyne, his eyebrows flickering up and down. "What shall I do?"

"Nothing, yet," said Cadell.

At Abbotsford, Sir Walter's family met in anxious conclave. Soon the Lockharts must go south, but the thought of leaving Sir Walter alone in the echoing halls of Abbotsford except for Anne, Willie Laidlaw and his devoted household servants appalled them. As his physical faculties failed, his nervous energy seemed to increase. He was unsatisfied by his usual routine of dictating his normal quota to Willie Laidlaw, answering his many letters. Politics, which had always been a background interest, began to impinge disastrously on his unquiet mind.

King George IV had died that summer, and the General Election which followed had brought the reforming party of Lord Grey to power, with plans for electoral reform which the new King, William IV, was thought to favour. At first the unrest which was to convulse the whole country was scarcely felt on the Border. In October Sir Walter went to Jedburgh, to second the nomination of his young kinsman, a Scott of Harden, as member for Roxburgh-shire, and his speech was received with acclamation. Young Scott of Harden was elected for the third time, unopposed. It was a gentle, neighbourly triumph. Sir Walter returned to Abbotsford with the feeling of a good job well done.

But early in November he had another slight stroke. With rest, he recovered, but his anxious family called in the local doctor, who summoned specialists from Edinburgh. They told Sir Walter frankly, as they had told him before, that he had driven his brain beyond the limit of endurance. If he did not rest, the earlier attacks would inevitably recur. He must give up his work.

Sir Walter looked at them with a gentle smile. "As for bidding me not work, Polly might as well put the kettle on and say 'don't you dare boil'."

When the doctors had gone, Lockhart tried to add more personal arguments. His health was too precious to those who loved him to be thrown away. Sir Walter did not again attempt to fend him off with a joke. Instead he said, with a hesitant but obvious anxiety to speak the absolute truth: "I understand you, and I thank you from my heart. But . . . I am not sure that I am myself in all things. Yet in one point there is no change. If I were to be idle, I should go mad. I would rather die."

So there was, it seemed, no more to be said. But this did not satisfy Sophia. "My dearest," she said to Lockhart, at Chiefswood that night, "no one can turn him from his purpose. That I realise. But for Johnny's sake, and your own work, we must soon go back to London. What if he should be taken ill, in the depths of winter, here at Abbotsford, with the doctor at the far side of the county, and snow deep on the ground?"

They consulted Dr Clarkson of Melrose, who suggested that Sir Walter might be willing to employ someone to list the books and papers in his library over the winter. If so, he could arrange for a medical student to take the term off. But Sir Walter, who had already been persuaded to spend more time than he considered he could well spare on that task, vetoed it absolutely.

"Then," said Dr Clarkson, "I must instruct a member of his household to use the lancet in emergency."

John Nicholson was the obvious choice. He had served Sir Walter since he was a lad, learning to read and write from his master. He was steady, intelligent and devoted. Now that old Dalgleish had retired, he was the most responsible man on the place.

"Summon him," said Dr Clarkson.

John Nicholson was duly instructed, Willie Laidlaw promised to go to Abbotsford daily, and the Lockharts left for London, feeling that they had done all they could. Whether *Count Robert of Paris* was good or bad, they fancied it would occupy the author for the winter. They had reckoned without James Ballantyne and his honest, but occasionally ill-timed, outspokenness. And they had not expected the rising tide of vicious controversy about the projected Reform Bill to reach Abbotsford. They knew the Tweed-side country folk were decent and loyal, and Sir Walter seldom opened the daily papers these days, but they forgot that the new weaving communities had brought many Radical elements to the Border, and that to a man who had lived through the ugly excesses of the French Revolution the word "Reform" might well seem a shorter word for the same thing. Sir Walter might not read the newspapers, but he still exchanged letters with many eminent men who were as troubled about the country's future as he was himself.

By December James had seen enough of *Count Robert* to feel that its publication would not only damage its author's reputation but also interfere with the success of the *Magnum Opus*, on which all their hopes hung. In great distress but with dogged determination to do his duty, he sent Sir Walter, still groggy from his slight but definite stroke, the strongest protest he had ever made. Sir Walter received James's anxious letter with bewildered indignation. But he controlled himself sufficiently to answer it, he hoped, magnanimously.

"My dear James," he wrote with painful effort, the words straggling up and down across the page,

"If I were like other authors, as I flatter myself I am not, I should 'send you an order on my treasurer for a hundred ducats, wishing you all prosperity and a little more taste'; but having never supposed that any abilities I ever had were of a perpetual texture, I am glad when friends tell me what I might be long in finding out myself. Mr Cadell will show you what I have written to him. My present idea is to go abroad for a few months, if I hold together so long. So ended the Fathers of the Novel – Fielding and Smollett – and it would be no unprofessional finish for yours,

Walter Scott."

To Cadell he wrote at greater length and with some moderation, agreeing that it would be disastrous if *Count Robert* really turned out to be bad enough to affect the sales of the *Magnum*, and repeating his newly formed plan of foreign travel.

"I may perhaps take a trip to the Continent for a year or two, if I find Othello's occupation gone. . . ."

But he added a reference to Malachi Malagrowther, whose sardonic *Letters* had been such a useful outlet for his pent-up exasperation at the time of his financial crisis, which had an ominous ring.

Cadell, greatly disturbed, decided to go down to Abbotsford, and insisted that James Ballantyne should go with him. But he waited for a few days, since Sir Walter's Trustees were due to meet in the third week of December, and he hoped to have better news to bring after the meeting. The delay gave Sir Walter time to look about him for other occupation. For, as he wrote to Cadell while waiting for his visit: "Being idle will never do, for a thousand reasons. All this I am thinking of till I am half sick. I wish James, who gives such stout advice when he thinks we are wrong, would tell us how to put things right . . . Perhaps it may be better to take no resolution till we all meet together . . ."

Meanwhile, he began to consider how his own fear and dislike of the projected Reform Bill might be expressed in another of the scathing *Letters* imputed to Malachi Malagrowther. As before, he found relief in the vehement expression of his uncompromising opposition to the new government's legislation, which seemed bound to wreck the country. He smiled as he laid the completed outburst aside to show to Cadell and Ballantyne. He believed it would shake them. And many others, too.

The Trustees duly met, were most deeply impressed by the rapidity with which the Ballantyne debt was being extinguished, and felt that another vote of thanks to Sir Walter for his efforts would be inadequate. Unanimously, the resolution was passed:

"That Sir Walter Scott be requested to accept of his furniture, plate, linens, paintings, library, and curiosities of every description, as the best means the creditors have of expressing their very high sense of his most honourable conduct, and in grateful acknowledgement for the unparalleled and most successful exertions he has made, and continues to make, for them."

Sir Walter received the Chairman's letter with pleasure and surprise, answering it the same day.

"My Dear Sir,

"I was greatly delighted with the contents of your letter, which not only enables me to eat with my own spoons, and study my own books, but gives me the still higher gratification of knowing that my conduct has been approved by those who were concerned.

"The best thanks which I can return is by continuing my earnest and unceasing attention . . ."

That evening Cadell and James Ballantyne arrived at Abbotsford. They found Sir Walter peaceful and happy. No controversial subjects were brought up that night. They talked only of the letter from the Trustees, and the heavy load it had taken off Sir Walter's mind. Sir Walter was assured once again that the astonishing and continued success of the *Magnum* should be enough to wipe off, in a year or two, the remaining debt, even if he never wrote another line. He spoke of his refusal to accept the post of Privy Councillor, which his late Majesty had offered, and the message from the new King, that his Majesty would bear in mind Sir Walter's request that instead of the honour which he considered himself too old and poor to accept, he would use his brother's good will for the advancement of Charles Scott in his career at the Foreign Office. Then he outlined the provisions of his last Will, which he had decided to execute as soon as possible. At last, on the best of terms, they all went to bed.

But it was very different next morning. Sir Walter had asked for a conference on his latest work, and he had no intention of evading it because he had so far satisfied the Trustees. But first he gave Ballantyne the latest Malachi Epistle to read. It was certainly vitriolic. But that mattered less than that it was ill-informed, so that it gave the impression of violent, unreasoning opposition to progress. The Epistle had grown beyond the limits of Ballantyne's Weekly Journal. Sir Walter wished it to appear as a separate publication. Cadell was obliged to speak out. Such a pamphlet, the authorship of which must be universally, if unofficially, known, could do Sir Walter and his associates inestimable harm at a time when the continued success of his collected works was vital. To be branded as a hopelessly prejudiced supporter of the forces of reaction must undermine Sir Walter's popularity by setting the mocking army of political journalists to make game of "a foolish, fond old man".

Incredulously, Sir Walter turned to Ballantyne. "You agree?"

Unhappily, James agreed.

After a long and difficult argument, Sir Walter was sufficiently convinced to consent to the Epistle's suppression, but also angry enough to limp across the room and toss the offending pages into the pleasantly burning fire. Then he slumped back into his chair, very red in the face, and breathing heavily.

Cadell recognised the emergency. "But, Sir Walter," he said, "I must urge you not to despair of *Count Robert*."

"Eh?" Sir Walter roused himself.

"I believe," Cadell improvised hastily, "that you may have

attached too much importance to what has been said about the early chapters. You agree with me, James?"

"Er – yes," said James Ballantyne, nonplussed by Cadell's sudden change of front.

"I suggest that such defects should best be considered in terms of the finished novel. I believe they will then seem slighter than was at first supposed. To oblige me, will you resume work on it?"

"Certainly," said Sir Walter, with the ghost of his old smile.

When they left Abbotsford, Cadell turned to the mutinous James Ballantyne, who felt he had been coerced into a departure from truth. "If we did wrong," said Cadell, as they settled themselves into the roomy, stale-smelling interior of the Blucher coach for Edinburgh, "we did it for the best. To have spoken out as fairly on *Count Robert* as we did on *Malachi* would have been to make ourselves the bearers of a death-warrant."

And Sir Walter, left behind, settled back to complete his novel. But he had not forgotten his intention to execute his last Will. At the end of January, 1831, he went by coach to Edinburgh, escorted by John Nicholson. Cadell invited him to his own house in Athol Crescent, and there he was stormbound by a snowstorm of such violence that he was unable to leave Edinburgh for ten days. Cadell and his wife made him most welcome, inviting such old friends as Will Clerk and James Skene to dinner, leaving him alone with his books and papers every morning. Their kindness comforted him. He began to believe that everything might turn out all right after all. Occasionally, in spite of the weather, he dined out, going and returning in a sedan chair.

Back at Abbotsford by mid-February, he did his best to conform to the routine advised by his doctors, recording his day's programme in his *Journal*. "Rose at seven, dressed before eight – wrote letters, or did any little business till a quarter past nine. Then breakfasted. Mr Laidlaw comes from ten till one. Then take the pony and ride – quantum mutatus – two or three miles, John Swanston walking by my bridle-rein lest I fall off. Come home about three or four. Then to dinner on a single plain dish and half a tumbler, or, by'r Lady, three-fourths of a tumbler of whisky and water. Then sit till six o'clock, when enter Mr Laidlaw again, who works commonly until eight. After this, work usually alone till half-past ten; sup on porridge and milk and so to bed."

But he was not to be left in peace for long. On 17th March he wrote in his *Journal*: "little of this day, but that it was so uncommon windy that I was almost blown off my pony, and was glad to grasp the mane to prevent it actually happening. I began the third volume of *Count Robert of Paris*, which has been on the anvil during all these vexatious circumstances of politics and health. But the blue heaven bends over all. It may be ended in a fortnight if I keep my scheme. But I *will* take time enough.

"I thought I was done with politics, but . . . I have a letter from Sheriff Oliver, desiring me to go to Jedburgh on Monday . . ."

For his landed neighbours, violently opposed to the Reform Bill and quite ignorant of his state of health, were most anxious for him to bring all the weight of his influence to bear against it. And Sir Walter did not feel that he could honourably refuse. He was still Sheriff, and though he had promised to write no more inflammatory pamphlets, he considered that other Border Sheriffs had a right to ask him to attend their meetings and speak in accordance with his convictions. So, on the 21st of March he agreed, in spite of Anne's entreaties, to go, as a neighbouring Sheriff, to a meeting of the freeholders of Roxburghshire, held at Jedburgh, and packed with representatives of the progressive party.

Nothing in his experience had prepared him for the pandemonium outside and even inside the Court-House. His speech, with its cautionary references to the French Revolution and its dire consequences, his admiration for Edmund Burke, its great opponent, infuriated the crowd. For the first time in his life, Sir Walter was shouted down. His supporters got him out of the Court-House, and to his carriage, which had been driven into a back street. But if it had not been for the sturdy workers from Abbotsford who accompanied it, he might not have got off with a pelting of stones and rotten potatoes, and the contemptuous shouts of "Burke Sir Walter!" which set the terrified horses off at a gallop for home.

Two days later, as Sir Walter noted in his *Journal*, the Bill was carried in the House of Commons, but only by a single vote. This comforted him a little. So he had not been the only one to speak out in support of the old ways. "It is vain to mourn what cannot be mended," he concluded the day's entry.

The incident had shocked him profoundly. But he made little of it, to reassure the anxious Anne. And he wrote less of it in his *Journal*, which dealt with homelier things.

April began hopefully, with another portrait painter to make a picture of him with his staghounds, Nimrod and Bran, and Jane Erskine, Will's daughter, to stay. They all breakfasted with the Fergusons at Huntly Burn, and afterwards the two girls walked up the Rhymer's Glen. "I could as easily have made a pilgrimage to Rome with peas in my shoes, unboiled," Sir Walter said ruefully.

But on the 16th, Lord Meadowbank, who was on the Jedburgh circuit, came to stay at Abbotsford, as usual, and Sir Walter made an effort to entertain him in the old lavish way, with a dinner party at which he overtired himself as host and drank two or three glasses of champagne to keep going, against his doctors' orders. That night he had another partial stroke, which kept him in bed for several days. The family was informed. Walter and Sophia arrived in haste, and Lockhart brought the children to Chiefswood later, for the summer, as usual. But Charles was not with them. He had recently been posted to the British Legation at Naples.

As time went on, Sir Walter rallied. But there was trouble again over the final chapters of *Count Robert*, which James Ballantyne considered worse than ever, and Sir Walter's intention to begin another book, called *Castle Dangerous*, about which only Cadell had been informed. James paid one last visit to Abbotsford, alone, but it was acrimonious, and he left early next morning, without saying goodbye. Sir Walter announced his intention of completing *Count Robert of Paris* as soon as possible, so that he could get on with *Castle Dangerous*, about which he had no intention of inviting James's opinion.

"Papa is writing as hard as ever," said Sophia in despair. "The doctors say it will kill him. What are we to do?"

"Shall we beg Mr Laidlaw to devise other business which will prevent him from working at Abbotsford with Papa?" Anne suggested. The girls were standing in the big bay window of the dining-room which overlooked the Tweed. It was far enough from the library to prevent any chance of being overheard.

"No, no," said Sophia quickly. "That would be too unkind."

"Perhaps Lockhart could persuade him to lay *Count Robert* aside for a while," Anne suggested hopefully. "Ask him at once, Sophia."

Sir Walter agreed quite gladly. He had worked on the thing so much that thinking of it any more made his head swim. But as he immediately took up the Fourth Series of *Tales of a Grandfather*, nothing was achieved.

"We must invite pleasant people to stay," said Anne. "Papa says that Miss Ferrier's conversation is less demanding than that of any author, female at least, that he has ever met."

"Full of humour, too, and not the least like a blue stocking," Sophia agreed. So Susan Ferrier, author of such successful novels as *Marriage* and *Inheritance*, came to stay, and her devotion and tact were invaluable. She noticed at once that though Sir Walter would start off to tell one of his celebrated anecdotes as gaily as ever, he now tended to falter and lose his way and sit staring round him in bewilderment. When one of his anxious listeners prompted him too obviously, he was distressed. But Miss Ferrier bridged the gap much less obviously.

"My dear Sir Walter, I seem to be getting as deaf as a post," she often said. "I haven't heard a word since you mentioned . . ."

"Ah, yes, my dear. Well, this is what comes next . . ." And the recapitulation carried him smoothly across the gap.

After she had gone, Lockhart drove with him about the country-side, to see the ruined fortress on which he had modelled *Castle Dangerous* and meet his own kinsfolk again, as well as the young sculptor, Greenshields, in the west. But, back at Abbotsford, Sir Walter merely said that he could now finish *Castle Dangerous* in a fortnight, and get *Count Robert* out of the way for good, besides.

"At least you kept him away from his work for quite a while," said Anne. "We shall do better still if we can persuade him to go abroad for the winter, I believe."

"After all, Charles is at Naples. I shall write at once and ask him to make arrangements first and inform Papa afterwards," Sophia said decisively.

"But Papa must promise not to write a line," Anne insisted.

"It will all be so interesting that he won't have a chance," Sophia said. "I wish I could come with you. But there is Lockhart's work . . ."

"And Johnny," his father said sombrely.

Sir Walter was quite pleased with the plan of spending a winter abroad. After all, the idea had been in his mind for some time. Ever since the letter from Goethe, he had hoped for a chance to present his homage in person. And with Charles writing so warmly from Naples and planning to have the whole family as his guests for as long as they cared to stay, his friend, Sir Frederick Adam, inviting him most urgently to visit the Ionian Isles, and all the treasures of Italy to be seen, on the homeward journey, by way of Weimar and the meeting with Goethe, they might spend the dark months very pleasantly elsewhere.

As to the question of money, Cadell had been most insistent that matters were going so well that he need not trouble himself about that. Anne had been a good, kind girl. He liked to think he could give her a little pleasure and variety. So it was settled. A naval friend, Captain Basil Hall, heard of their plans, and unobtrusively contrived to arrange that King William's Government should put a frigate at Sir Walter's disposal for his voyage to Naples. Cadell was delighted to hear of Sir Walter's plans when he came to Abbotsford with the artist, Turner, who had been contracted to do the illustrations for the collected edition of the Poems, and came now to make preliminary drawings.

"My dear Sir Walter," Cadell said warmly, "nothing could give me greater pleasure than to hear you are going to give yourself a holiday. No one in this world deserves it more."

"You do not think," said Sir Walter anxiously, "that I should remain at home and work?"

"Most certainly not," said Cadell, in consternation. Then he recovered himself as he received a very shrewd glance. "After all, we are making excellent progress. The debt is all but paid off – "

"All but paid off? Paid off? Indeed? This is excellent news," said Sir Walter, greatly gratified. But only the words he most needed to hear sank into his mind.

It was not true. But Cadell did not undelude him. After all, if things went forward as they were doing now, it would be true, next year. Or the year after. Meanwhile, it gave Sir Walter just the extra confidence he needed. He smiled and said no more.

Plans went rapidly forward. Young Walter, now a Major, with his regiment posted at Sheffield, turned up unexpectedly, and announced that he had got a bit of leave owing to him, and had arranged to go with his father as far as Naples, where Charles would be in charge. Anne was delighted. For, though she would not have admitted it for worlds, and John Nicholson and her own maid, Celia, were treasures, she had been just a little frightened of the responsibility. Sophia left on the 20th of September with the children, to make preparations for her family's arrival at Sussex Place, and Lockhart stayed behind to help Walter with the final arrangements. Sir Walter was happily occupied making a long list of things to be attended to during his absence by Willie Laidlaw. The last item, firmly underlined, was: "be very careful of the dogs".

Last of all, Wordsworth and his daughters came to say goodbye. The two writers had met at intervals, many times since the early morning when Wordsworth and his sister had surprised Sir Walter and Charlotte at Lasswade, so the changes of thirty years surprised neither. But both were old men now, not unaware that this meeting might well be their last. Scott, emaciated by illness, still had the same transfiguring smile, but the fire of the young revolutionary had been quenched by time. Wordsworth's shock of hair was white, his eyes were troubling him, and he wore a green shade to save them from the light. Sir Walter's arrangements were completed: he wished for one last glimpse of Newark. Next morning Peter Mathieson drove Wordsworth and Sir Walter through the Vale of Yarrow, and as they turned homewards Wordsworth began to shape the sonnet which was also a message of farewell:

"A trouble, not of clouds or weeping rain . . ."

On the 23rd of September, the party set out from Abbotsford for London. Sir Walter was in good spirits, alert and interested in everything he saw, stopping the carriage and insisting on clambering out to inspect anything of historic interest by the roadside. At Rokeby he said farewell to his good friend Morritt and requested him to make inquiries about a ring which he usually wore, but must have left behind at one of the inns they had stayed in. It had been dug out of the ruins of Hermitage Castle and when it was found Mr Morritt must wear it for his sake till he returned to claim it.

London, when the party arrived, was in a state of uproar at the rejection of the Reform Bill by the House of Lords. Broken glass lay all over the cobbles outside the town house of the Duke of Wellington. So he was not alone, Sir Walter reflected, in having been rejected by the people. In some ways it made him feel better; in others, worse.

Sophia, troubled by the responsibility of sending her father for so long a journey on which she could not accompany him, called in her doctor, on the excuse that Dr Robert Ferguson, like Sir Adam, was a member of a family Sir Walter had known all his life. Dr Ferguson, constantly in and out of the Sussex Place house, apparently took his summons for granted. But he called in two of his seniors for consultation. All agreed that there was evidence of incipient brain trouble. But they considered that if their patient would abstain entirely from mental work throughout his travels, the trouble might be arrested. Naturally, they did not put the situation as bluntly to Sir Walter, but only indicated that the rest and variety of scene would do him all the good in the world.

Sir Walter promised to follow the Spartan régime they prescribed, and to write nothing whatever. He was, in fact, greatly relieved. At the back of his mind he had feared he was going insane. Now all was changed. The doctors had assured him that with reasonable care and abstinence he would do well enough. Cadell, too, had reported that his monetary affairs were now in order. He could give his friends presents again. He began to talk of drawing money on Coutts. Cadell would accept the bills. After all, now that his debts were paid off . . .

Sophia, who knew from Lockhart that though less than half of her father's liability remained, £50,000 was still outstanding, went anxiously to her husband. "Will you not reason with Papa, Lockhart? He does not understand."

But Lockhart shook his head. "Let him enjoy the pleasure of being a little generous again. We can put things to rights later. Cadell is quite of the same mind. All will be paid off in the end."

In his *Journal*, Sir Walter wrote: "A total prostration of bodily strength is my chief complaint. I cannot walk half a mile. There is, besides, some mental confusion, with the extent of which I am not perhaps fully acquainted . . . I would compound for a little pain, instead of this heartless muddiness of mind."

On the 23rd of October they all arrived in Portsmouth, since Sophia was determined to see the party off, and Walter joined them there, to board HMS *Barham*. Contrary winds prevented them from sailing for a week, the Bay of Biscay behaved as usual, and everybody was seasick. But once they were in smooth water again, heading for Malta, Sir Walter was the first passenger on deck.

Malta enthralled him. The entries in his *Journal* were becoming almost illegible now, but he tried to record his delight in all the available records of the Knights of St John, in the ancient streets of Valetta, the Church of St John, where the knights were buried, the Strada Stretta, where they fought their duels. When they went on board the *Barham* again, to sail on for Naples in December, he looked intently at every medieval detail of the beautiful harbour, as if he were trying to fix them in his mind. Half to himself, he murmured: "It will be hard if I cannot make something of this."

Anne drew Walter aside. "Did you hear what he said?" she whispered anxiously.

"Yes," said young Walter, adding, with a despairing shrug, "but what is one to do?"

The *Barham* anchored off Naples on the 17th of December, 1831.

Charles was on the quay to greet his family, and escort them to the quarters he had bespoken for them in the Palazzo Caramanico. The King of Naples was delighted to honour Sir Walter, who appeared at Court in the green uniform of the ancient Bodyguard of Scottish Archers, modernised by George IV on his northern progress of 1822. But he had not come to Naples for official formalities: he was much more interested in collecting Neapolitan and Sicilian ballads and broadsheets.

On the 16th of January he received from London the news which, perhaps, shattered his contact with superficial things as dangerously as the hostility of his countrymen had shattered the Duke of Wellington's windows. His beloved grandson, Johnny Lockhart, was dead, at ten years old.

"Poor Johnny Lockhart!" Sir Walter wrote in his *Journal*. "This boy is gone, whom we have made so much of . . . I went to the Opera this evening . . ."

Soon afterwards, he began to spend several hours each morning on a new novel, *The Siege of Malta*. And Anne implored her brother to try and stop him from relaxing his obedience to the Spartan diet on which his doctors had insisted.

"What can I do?" said young Walter, in despair. "I have overstayed my leave already. I must rejoin my regiment. Charles must deal with this."

But Charles, too, was perplexed. Sir Frederick Adam had invited Sir Walter to visit the Ionian Isles, where he was stationed, and that was to have been the next phase of their travels. Sir Walter had not forgotten Byron's love of Greece, and was looking forward to the visit. Then Sir Frederick was unexpectedly recalled, and the invitation lapsed. But Sir Walter's desire to visit Goethe remained. Charles got leave from the Legation to escort his father to Weimar, since young Walter had now returned to his regiment. Sir Walter had planned to return home by way of the Tyrol, to some extent to see Innsbruck, and the castles of the Rhine, but above all to visit Goethe. But before they set out the news of Goethe's death, on 22nd March, reached them in Naples. It seemed to shatter Sir Walter's last bastion of normality.

"Alas for Goethe!" he said. "But at least he died at home. Let us return to Abbotsford."

His cry indicated his heart's desire. More prosaically, it was obviously useless to keep him wandering across Europe when he had already begun to write, which, as his doctors had told them, would be to sign his own death warrant. Charles agreed that they should leave Naples as soon as possible. They bought a roomy barouche, on the back seat of which, if necessary, Sir Walter could extend himself, and made arrangements for post horses. On the 16th of April they set out for home.

Sir Walter was hazily aware of the journey, as if they travelled among mountains, between clouds. At Rome he was only anxious to visit St Peter's in order to see the tomb of the last of the Stewarts. At Bracciano he was most interested in the steward's dog, which greeted him like one of his own. At Venice, he cared for nothing but the Bridge of Sighs. His impatience seemed to increase with every mile, as the carriage bore them through Munich and Heidelberg, to Frankfurt. Here Charles persuaded him to walk through the town, and hoped to interest him in the booksellers' shops. But the first thing he was shown, as the proprietor heard English spoken, was a lithograph of Abbotsford.

He stared at it, said abruptly, "I know that already," and demanded that they should drive on at once, by night as well as by day. His only thought was to return home, and the imminence of further trouble was so obvious that John Nicholson had to use his lancet more than once before they reached Mayence and the Rhine. Here they went on board a steamboat, and for a while he seemed content, as they drifted past the castles and the monasteries which he had first heard of in the German ballads of his youth, and later in the *Childe Harold* of his friend, Byron. But at Nijmegen, on the 9th of June, he collapsed. If it had not been for John Nicholson and his lancet he might have died there, still far from home. At last he was carried aboard an English steamboat at Rotterdam.

He knew little of the rest of the journey. For three weeks, after he reached London, he lay in a sort of stupor in St James's Hotel in Jermyn Street. Neither Sophia nor her husband had expected him home so soon, and to move him farther was out of the question. He recognised Cadell, who had come south from Edinburgh immediately, with pleasure, and the voices of his children could rouse him for a few moments from that strange dark land in which he was wandering, to smile and murmur a greeting. But beyond his bewilderment, one idea alone recurred all the time. He wanted to go home.

"Abbotsford . . . Abbotsford . . ." His lips formed the word soundlessly, again and again.

The doctors finally agreed that no purpose would be served by keeping him in London. On the 7th of July he was lifted into his carriage and carried to the docks to embark on a steamboat for Edinburgh. Sophia, Anne, Lockhart, Cadell and one of the London doctors went with him, since Charles had been obliged to return to his post at the Legation. He lay like a log throughout the journey, scarcely seemed to notice the arrival at Newhaven, his removal to an Edinburgh hotel, the departure in his carriage for Tweedside. But the air changed as they approached the Borders, and he seemed to revive, even to murmur, under his breath, the familiar names.

At last he saw the Eildon Hills. Then they could scarcely hold him in the caarrige, as he waited for the first sight of Abbotsford.

Willie Laidlaw was waiting in the doorway. He helped to carry Sir Walter into the dining-room.

"We've made up his bed yonder, in the bay window."

Sir Walter roused himself as they eased him into a chair. For a moment he stared about him, then his eyes focused. He held out his arms. "Ha! Willie Laidlaw! Eh, man, how often I've thought of you. You and the dogs . . ."

They were all round him at once; Nimrod and Bran, and all the lesser brood of terriers, only to be restrained by force, as they sought to overwhelm him, leaping up and licking his hands.

They put him to bed at last, exhausted but content.

But he had not yet reached the end of his journey. Next morning he wakened almost clear-headed. They wheeled him through his beautiful rooms in a Bath-chair, pushed him out into the garden.

"I have seen much," he said wonderingly, "but nothing like my ain house. Give me one turn more."

Then the shadows closed again. In this last ordeal, all lesser conflicts seemed blended, so that he sometimes fought astride a bench in the High School yard, sometimes against the lads of the Cross Causeway at the Potterrow Port or George's Square. At other times he seemed to hang by his finger-tips to the overhanging rocks as he worked his way across the Kittle Nine Stanes on the Castle Rock, thundered against Blackwood as one of the Black Hussars of Literature, defied bankruptcy for Ballantyne's printing-house, or endured derisive cries of "Burke Sir Walter!" in Jedburgh.

On the 15th of August Willie Laidlaw found time to answer James Skene's letter of anxious inquiry.

"Dear Sir,

". . . Your friend is helpless, and requires to be attended in every respect as an infant of six months old. Of his powerful mind, which, as it were, shone over the civilised world, there remains only a pale and uncertain glimmering. Sometimes, though but rarely, it blazes out for a brief moment, and this makes the melancholy sight more hard to bear.

"They tell me he is seldom conscious, and he complains greatly and speaks much, and he is generally extremely restless and impatient, and, they tell me, irritable. I have rarely seen him show such symptoms, for he always knows me, seems relieved to see me, holds out his hand and grasps mine, and looks into my face, and always attempts to speak. Often he seems anxious to inquire about or to tell me something, but he rarely makes out a sentence . . ."

The doors of Abbotsford, which had been so long open to all the world, were locked against all comers save Laidlaw and the doctor during the last weeks, as Sir Walter fought his way through the shadows. On the 21st of September a change came. His desperate fight was almost over. His friends seemed about him again. He saw them quite clearly . . . his allies in the High School Yards . . . the

Montagnards of the Outer House . . . He tried to raise a hand in greeting but it lay like lead.

And the dogs . . . they were all there, too. Camp, Maida, Nimrod, Bran, the wise little terrier, Spice, and all her Dandie Dinmont progeny, moving to and fro about their own affairs among the lengthening shadows in his mind.

The valiant defender of lost causes had been making his peace with life for six weary years. Now he had come to terms with death at last. His work was done. Walter's heritage awaited him, and his sons, and his sons' sons. Hidden below the horizon of the future was the strange twist of fate by which not only Walter and Charles, but both Lockhart's sons, were to die childless, so that it was not Walter's son, but Sophia's little daughter Charlotte, who would ultimately carry on the traditions of Abbotsford.

It was very quiet in the bay window of the dining-room. Sir Walter had been in a deep coma for many hours, utterly unaware, it seemed, of his four children who knelt round his bed. The windows had been flung wide to the early autumn sunshine, and a slight breeze drifted across the haugh from which the hay had long since been carried, bearing the murmur of Tweed, as it bickered over its pebbles, to the great house on the slope above. In the distance, hounds were out, and the watchers could hear the sweet note of the huntsman's horn sounding faintly, high above Sophia's sudden, desperate sobbing. Then, as the dying man's harsh breathing faltered into silence at last, it rang out clearly, far across his beloved river, a trumpet sounding for him on the other side.